Believing is Seeing

Believing is Seeing

A Guide for Responding to John's Gospel

Bruce McNab

RESOURCE *Publications* · Eugene, Oregon

BELIEVING IS SEEING
A Guide for Responding to John's Gospel

Resource Publications
An Imprint of Wipf and Stock Publishers
199 W. 8th Ave., Suite 3
Eugene, OR 97401

www.wipfandstock.com

PAPERBACK ISBN: 978-1-4982-9805-6
HARDCOVER ISBN: 978-1-4982-9807-0
EBOOK ISBN: 978-1-4982-9806-3

Manufactured in the U.S.A.   AUGUST 4, 2016

This book is dedicated to my friends and
fellow students of John's Gospel,
Neal Batson, Elliot Branson, Keith Gardner, and Joe Myers.

*"Did I not tell you that if you would believe
you would see the glory of God?"*

—JOHN 11:40

Contents

Contents

Contents

Maps and Illustrations

Acknowledgments

This book would never have been completed without the loving encouragement, patient assistance, and diligent editorial efforts of my theologically-educated and dearly beloved wife and ministry partner, Joan. She read and re-read every portion of the manuscript numerous times, offering helpful and objective advice at every stage of the two-and-a-half year writing process. After that, Joan copy-edited the final product and helped with the page proofs. Her name deserves to be on the cover along with mine because *Believing is Seeing* is truly "our book."

In addition to the constant help of my spouse, I am grateful for the expert theological and editorial counsel provided by my dear friend of more than half a century, John Wiederholt. A gentle Presbyterian pastor and wise brother, John knew when to say "Stop right there!" and when to say, "Why don't you have another go at that chapter? You're very close to getting it right." He conceived the book's apt subtitle, *A Guide for Responding to John's Gospel.* An expert Bible teacher himself, John has an intuitive sense of what might feel most useful to a general audience and what probably will not. I'm also indebted to my friend Darren Quintenz, a dedicated young lay minister and servant of the Word, who read and annotated every chapter. The "Doing Your Own Theology" sections of questions are based for the most part on Darren's comments and observations. In addition, my friends Dave Hatfield, Rob Johnson, Mark Ramseth, and Mike Stanberry each read parts of the manuscript at one stage or another and I profited from their advice and encouragement.

Finally, I acknowledge the great debt of gratitude I owe to the two most important people in my early spiritual formation—my mother, Audrey Brueggeman McNab (1915–1997) and her mother, Charlotte L. Brueggeman (1885–1982). These devout and caring women, dedicated Bible teachers, loved me unconditionally and taught me from my earliest years to expect to hear God speaking through the Scriptures. *"Rest eternal grant them, O Lord, and let light perpetual shine upon them."*

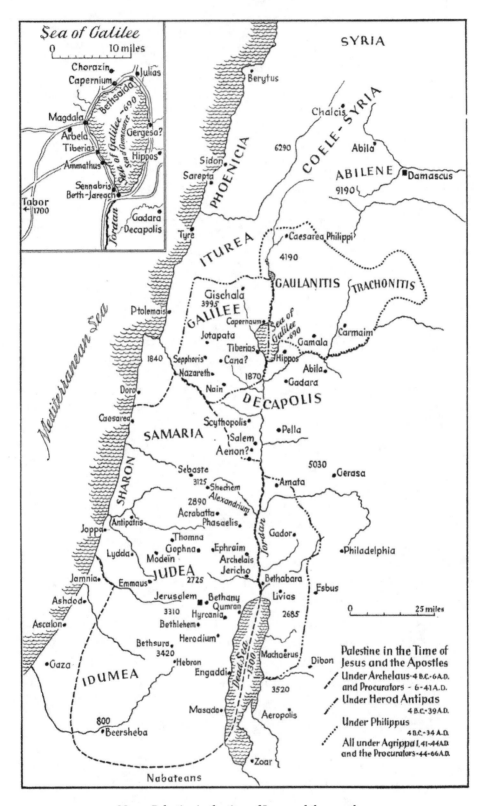

Map 1. Palestine in the time of Jesus and the apostles.

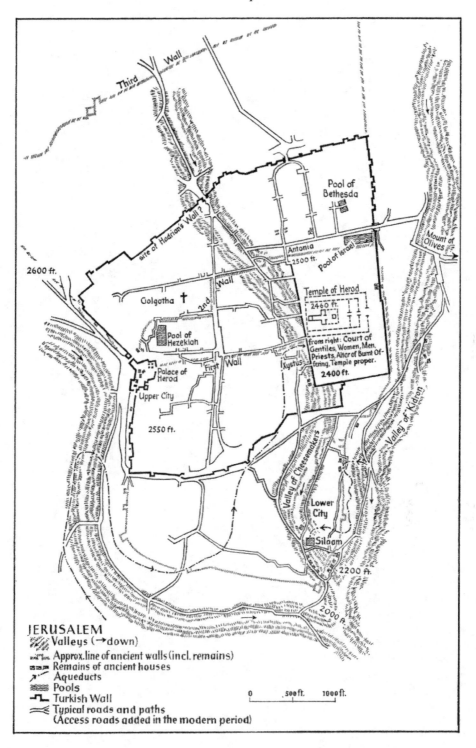

Map 2. Jerusalem in the time of Jesus and the apostles.

Preface

How shall we respond to
what we read in John's Gospel?

Of the Gospels found in our New Testament, only the fourth, the Gospel according to John, claims to be the testimony of an eyewitness.[1] The name of this eyewitness is never given; he is simply called "the disciple whom Jesus loved." That makes it exceptional, whether its claim of eyewitness authorship is credible or not and whether any of the other gospels might contain eyewitness material or not. Furthermore, John's Gospel alone unabashedly asserts that Jesus of Nazareth is not only a prophet greater than Moses, and not only the Messiah, but indeed God incarnate, worthy of worship. The other three gospels each imply Jesus's possible divinity in various ways. John unequivocally and from the very beginning of the book declares that Mary's Son is the unique human face of Deity, the enfleshment of the pre-existent *Logos*, the perfect revelation of the one true God. The Johannine portrayal of Christ ultimately shaped the creeds of the church. Most modern Christians' understanding of the person of Christ is dominated by the Johannine point of view.

The other three gospels portray Jesus as having relatively little to say about himself. In them, Jesus asks his disciples what other people are saying about him, and they tell him some think he is perhaps John the Baptist or one of the old prophets brought back to life. Then he asks the twelve who *they* say he is. Simon Peter alone offers an answer; he says, "You are the Christ, the Son of the living God" (Matt 16:13–16; cf. Mark 8:27–29; Luke 9:18–20). Jesus accepts this identification, and in Matthew's account even blesses Simon for his words and asserts that the insight was given him by God. Yet he charges his disciples "to tell no one that he was the Christ" (Matt 16:20; cf. Mark 8:30; Luke 9:21).

Jesus says little about himself in Matthew, Mark, or Luke. But in John he talks about himself all the time. In the Fourth Gospel Jesus's identity and relationship with

---

1. Bauckham, *Jesus and the Eyewitnesses*, 114–54, discusses the significance of eyewitness testimony in general, both in the gospel tradition and in ancient literature.

his heavenly Father are the primary subject matter of numerous lengthy monologues, called "discourses" by specialists. What the other three gospels regard as private or hidden is treated overtly in John. The Johannine Christ knows God intimately as his Father and tells his followers he is "one with the Father." Because of the unity they share, Jesus says he only does what he sees the Father doing and only says what the Father gives him to say. In the other gospels, Jesus occasionally engages in sharp controversy with the Pharisees, who find fault with him for failing to keep the Sabbath and neglecting to observe the traditions of the elders. He, in turn, criticizes them for spiritual pride and hypocrisy. John depicts Jesus's relationship with the Pharisees and chief priests in much more starkly oppositional terms than do the other gospels. The priests and prominent Pharisees become Jesus's implacable foes early in John's story, and they quickly begin to plot his death. Jesus calls them children of the devil (8:44).

John's Gospel is unique and, therefore, intriguing. In forty-plus years of ministry I have more often been asked to lead studies on John than on any of the other gospels. *Believing is Seeing* is written out of that experience. I wrote this book with lay people in mind, not clergy, although it could be of value to pastors preparing sermons on readings from John. This is not a traditional commentary, however, and not a fresh contribution to serious Johannine scholarship. I am an ordinary pastor with no better than an ordinary pastor's ability in Greek, a well-educated Bible student rather than a professional New Testament scholar. I've read a great deal, but my reading has only skimmed the surface of the ocean of literature dealing with the Fourth Gospel. I was formally trained as a historian, however, and history is a related discipline.

Having described what this book is not, I must explain what it is. *Believing is Seeing* is a book meant for people who read the Bible because they want to know God, discover spiritual insights, find inspiration, and get direction for their lives. It is for readers who respect the moral and spiritual authority of Scripture. Historical research is not their main reason for reading the Bible. These readers hope to find God's wisdom, nurture for their interior life, and guidance in prayer. They're not reading the Bible to prove or disprove something. They aren't searching for authoritative texts to sustain their position in a theological debate with friends who belong to a different church.

Believing is Seeing has the subtitle, *A Guide for Responding to John's Gospel.* Contemporary readers will respond differently to this gospel than its first audience did at the end of the first century of the Christian era. Specialists propose that it was addressed to a small sect of mostly Greek-speaking Jews—perhaps in Asia Minor, though this is by no means certain. These Jews had departed from the norms of their national religious tradition and begun worshiping Jesus of Nazareth as the pre-existent Son of God and Savior of the world. Their worship of Jesus led to their rejection by other Jews, who regarded such a practice as blasphemy—treating a mere man as "another God." Because of this unacceptable veneration of a mortal, many (but not all) of their co-religionists began to treat members of the little sect of "Jesus people" as outcasts. At the same time, however, worshipers of Jesus drew attention from non-Jews who were seeking the One God. Some of these Gentile seekers began to join their fellowship. For this reason, John's Gospel frequently offers an explanation of matters which Jews would automatically understand, but Gentiles would not.

John uses ideas and references which his original audience would easily grasp. But our historical, social, and cultural context is substantially different from that of John and his first readers. Our life circumstances are poles apart from those of the gospel's initial audience. That being the case, I developed two objectives for this book. The first is to help lay people recognize how those who read John at the end of the first Christian century might have understood it. The second is to relate this gospel to the daily life and faith of twenty-first century American readers in a way that will enable them to express a personal response to what they read. Furthermore, because we speak English rather than Greek or Aramaic and because Americans use an assortment of different English translations of the Bible, lay people sometimes need help in coming to a working understanding of certain texts.

American Christians' relationship to the world around us is very dissimilar to that of John's first readers. They were members of a tiny Jewish sect rejected by many other Jews. Most of them had grown up in a small province of the vast Roman Empire, and shortly before John's Gospel was published their nation had suffered a crushing defeat by the Romans. In our time, American Christians are members of the numerically dominant religious group in the most powerful nation on earth. We are among the most highly privileged people in the world. John mentions "the world" more frequently than the other three gospels put together—fifty-seven references in John, compared to a total of fifteen in Matthew, Mark, and Luke. However, we think about the world in dramatically different ways than the author of the Fourth Gospel did. *Believing is Seeing* attempts to re-contextualize John for contemporary Americans.

I read John as a book whose author sets out to proclaim God's truth—which for him is not in the form of intellectual propositions, but is rather embodied in the *person* of one particular man, Jesus his Lord. Jesus reveals God to human beings while also revealing to us our true identity, our relationship to God, and our role in the divine plan. John writes concerning the incarnate Word, "from his fullness have we all received, grace upon grace. For the Law was given through Moses; grace and truth came through Jesus Christ" (1:13*b*-14).

For John, *truth* is the gift of God's only-begotten Son. The first words Jesus speaks in the Fourth Gospel are to two disciples of John the Baptist who leave their teacher's company and begin to follow Jesus. He turns around, sees the two men, and asks, "What are you looking for?" (paraphrase of 1:38). I believe the first words of Jesus in this gospel are also addressed to everyone who reads it. *What are you looking for?* My answer is, "I'm looking for you, Jesus. I want to know you, and I want to know the truth you came to reveal." When I use the word "truth," I'm not referring to a dogmatic proposition, or a mathematical certainty, or a historically documented fact; I'm thinking of something for which all of us have an innate hunger, a hunger connected to our need for God.

It's tricky to nail down truth with a single definition. Christian theology traditionally groups goodness, truth and beauty together as the transcendental objects of human desire. Truth is that for which we would gladly pay any price, even our own life. I read John's Gospel looking for the truth of Christ that has power to form (and *re*form) me. When we read the testimony of the Beloved Disciple and spend time meditating on the picture of Jesus he paints, we are nourished with the truth for which human hearts hunger, "the bread which endures to eternal life" (6:23).

There is an approach to Scripture which is purely personal and spiritual—not an attempt to resolve academic historical or theological questions, but rather an effort to build a more intimate relationship with God. This is the approach I adopt in *Believing is Seeing*. As stated above, the book's subtitle is *A Guide for Responding to John's Gospel*. I choose to focus on the personal response that each passage from this gospel evokes in me. How do these verses connect with my life? What do they ask of me? Do they inspire me? Correct me? Challenge my value system? Move me emotionally? Do they remind me of something? Do they bring to mind particular images or stories or personal experiences? My approach is an inquiry after the spiritual truth expressed in a particular gospel text within the *context* of our own situation in history, living in the United States of America in the opening decades of the third Christian millennium.

Such an approach is inevitably a search for inspiration, because the conclusion to which a truly prayerful reader comes must be a gift of the Spirit. The practice of seeking inspiration should be a routine activity for serious Christians, keeping in mind that not every biblical text will have personal significance and relevance for every believer. Each of us reads the Bible through the unique lens provided by our personal context: culture and ethnicity, individual history, education, psychology, spiritual formation, private concerns and interests, and sense of how God communicates with his children.

It is not my purpose in *Believing is Seeing* to offer readers an education in church history, hermeneutics, or theology—though some of the observations I make in the book may fall into one of those categories. The Fourth Gospel is a work of ancient literature intended originally for a Greek-speaking, mostly Jewish audience residing in a province of the late first century Roman Empire, an audience whose personal and family roots are mostly in Galilee and Judea. If twenty-first century American readers are to derive the greatest possible enlightenment from reading John, it's necessary for us to be aware of at least a few key facts about the history, culture, and religious practices of the gospel's original audience—information the gospel writer took for granted his readers would possess. Therefore, in the objective, analytical introductions which precede each separate section of the gospel text, I include comments of a historical, literary, or sociological nature, meant to aid readers in grasping the significance and immediate context of the Beloved Disciple's words. Each of these introductions is a digest of various commentaries, published articles, and other resource material.

The much more individual and subjective responses that follow each section of the gospel text occasionally contain a bit of historically illuminative material, but they are not formal theological, literary, or historical investigations of the text. They are my personal musings *inspired* by the text—my own responses to John's Gospel, which I offer in hope that they might be a springboard to launch readers into their own ruminations on the testimony of the Beloved Disciple. To help facilitate this, some questions for readers' private reflection are found in a separate section labeled "Doing Your Own Theology" at the end of each chapter. I encourage readers to do theology on their own, not merely absorb my opinions. My goal is the same one expressed by John himself. I'm writing so that those who read this book "may believe that Jesus is the Christ, the Son of God, and that believing you may have life in his name" (20:31).

My prayer is that each reader of *Believing is Seeing* will discover enlightenment, inspiration, and deepened faith—using this book as a guide. To further this process, you who are reading might ask yourselves questions such as these: In what way does this passage open my eyes to see Jesus? How does it help me know God? Does the Lord stake a claim on my life through these words? Am I intellectually, spiritually, or morally challenged by what I'm reading? Does this particular passage invite me to do something differently or pray differently or simply think about God in a new way? Does it point to a truth about me or my spiritual journey that I have not considered before?

This book is at least as much a testimony of faith as it is an exercise in scholarship, which means some of my responses and reflections may seem more like what you hear in a sermon than what you read in a traditional commentary. If the Holy Spirit inspires in you quite different responses to John's stories than those to which I am led, ascribe the difference to the power of the living Word, who searches the depths of every heart and speaks to the circumstances of each human soul.

Believing is Seeing includes the complete Revised Standard Version (second edition, 1971) text of the gospel, thus permitting readers to manage a single book rather than juggle a Bible along with a second volume. Because this book is not a commentary, I do not try to offer an observation about every theological point or attempt to explain each interesting historical detail. Nor do I claim to provide an exhaustive survey of scholarly opinion regarding the Fourth Gospel. John's Gospel is brilliantly constructed, subtly nuanced, and abounding in symbolism. Readers interested in pursuing technical or specialized questions should consult some of the many commentaries and other books and articles available in print and on line.

The title *Believing is Seeing* derives from the words Jesus speaks to Lazarus's sister, Martha, when she warns him not to open her brother's tomb. Jesus says, "Did I not tell you that *if you would believe you would see the glory of God*?" (11:40). John summons us to believe in God's incarnate Word, opens our eyes to see him as the light of the world, and calls us to conduct our lives illuminated by the truth enfleshed in Jesus. Trust in the Son of God provides us a way of understanding our relationship to God our Father, the life we share as sisters and brothers, and our place in the universe. *Believing* in Christ empowers us to *see* through our Lord's own eyes.

Bruce McNab
Bozeman, Montana
Ascension Day
May 5, 2016

Chapter One

1:1–18. The Prologue: "In the beginning was the Word."

Vv. 1–5. "In the beginning was the Word . . . In him was life, and the life was the light of men."

INTRODUCTION. The first eighteen verses of John are the prologue to the gospel. It provides readers an essential tool for identifying the deep significance and timeless meaning of the episodes from the life of Christ this gospel narrates—the truth about God and humankind disclosed in the words and works of Jesus of Nazareth, his Son. The prologue is a meditation on Genesis 1, probably added to the finished manuscript by an editor before the gospel begins to be copied and distributed.[1]

These initial verses function as a theological introduction or "overture to the narrative," written from a post-Easter perspective.[2] The prologue introduces themes that will reappear at various points later in the book. Among the melodies we will hear played again are these: the re-creative, life-giving power of the incarnate Word; the invincibility of the true light that God sent into the world to enlighten and enliven everyone; the ability of faithful, eyewitness testimony to bring others to believe in God's Son, through whom alone can we come truly to know the Father; the inevitable rejection of the Son's truth by those who are not really children of God, although they masquerade as such; the ultimate, perfect revelation of the glory of God in the person of his Son, who takes mortal flesh and chooses to abide with human beings; and, finally, the abundance of grace, truth, and blessing which is poured out for all who believe in the One whom the Father sent.

To shift the metaphor, we may think of the prologue as a poetic lens through which the gospel's editor wants us to read the personal testimony of "the disciple Jesus loved." The prologue takes the story of Jesus back before his conception and birth, which are

---

1. Some commentators think the author of the prologue appended an epilogue (ch. 21) at the same time. First John 1:1–4 seems to reflect the prologue. This, coupled with the consistent literary style, may indicate that 1 John was written by the gospel's final editor.

2. Brown, *John I–XII*, 3.

described in Matthew and Luke, back beyond the dawn of history itself, and identifies Jesus as God's "Word," by whom and for whom all things came to be. The prologue tells us that Jesus is God's Word incarnate as a human being, sent into the world so that those who receive him and believe in him might become children of God. *Logos* is the Greek term that our English-language Bibles translate as "Word." Since ancient Greek philosophers utilized *logos* as a technical term,[3] some commentators treat its appearance in the prologue to John as an example of how Greek philosophy came to influence early Christianity. In recent years, however, Jewish scholars have pointed out that John's idea of the *Logos* more likely derives from pre-Christian Jewish reflection on the creation story in Genesis and Hebrew Wisdom literature rather than from Greek philosophy. They observe in pre-Christian Palestinian Judaism a tendency to treat the Word of God sometimes as a theological being, virtually "a second God," not unlike the way Christians ultimately come to regard the three "persons" of the Trinity.[4] The rabbis of Jesus's time closely connected Torah with Wisdom and spoke of both as pre-existent. Many scholars comment that when the prologue refers to the *Logos* as being "with God" (vv. 1–2) and later as becoming "flesh" and dwelling (literally "pitching his tent") among us, he is using the same Torah/Wisdom imagery.[5]

In the body of his gospel John makes theological use of a number of terms initially presented here in the prologue. Readers should notice how the following words are used:

(nouns) word, life, light, darkness, truth, glory, hour, and world;

(verbs) believe, bear witness (testify), know, abide (dwell), come, see, follow, and live.

However, as we read John it is important to keep in mind that the author is not striving for rigorous semantic precision. His vocabulary is frequently ambiguous, and sometimes he deliberately uses double entendre. Since sentences with multiple layers of meaning appear regularly in John, careful readers will remain alert for them.

As we begin to read John, we should take care to recognize the weight the author gives to the function of witnesses, and in particular to eyewitnesses. John writes, "No one has ever seen God; the only Son, who is in the bosom of the Father, he has made him known" (v. 18). Later, in his sermon to the crowd in the Capernaum synagogue, Jesus tells them, "Everyone who has heard and learned from the Father comes to me. Not that anyone has seen the Father except him who is from God; he has seen the Father" (6:45*b*–46). The Fourth Gospel portrays Jesus, the unique Son of God, as the only human being qualified to offer eyewitness testimony about God and it offers

---

3. Various Greek philosophers use *logos* in different ways—e.g., to identify divine reason or the generative principle of the universe.

4. Boyarin, *Border Lines*, 89. Part 2 (89–147) of Daniel Boyarin's book describes the role *Logos* theology once played in non-Christian Jewish thought. See also Dunn, *Did the First Christians Worship Jesus*, 120.

5. Keener, *Gospel of John*, 1:364–74, 408–10.

readers "the disciple Jesus loved" as the ideal eyewitness, the one whose testimony concerning Jesus is "true" (21:24*b*).[6]

> **[1:1–5]** *¹ In the beginning was the Word, and the Word was with God, and the Word was God. ² He was in the beginning with God; ³ all things were made through him, and without him was not anything made that was made. ⁴ In him was life, and the life was the light of men. ⁵ The light shines in the darkness, and the darkness has not overcome it.*

RESPONSE. Everyone and everything has a history—individuals, families, nations, cultures, species, planets, stars, even the universe. We're naturally curious about beginnings, especially our own. When I was little, I'd sit on my mother's lap and say, "Tell me about when I was a baby." Then she would tell me stories, filtered through her memories and molded by her emotions. My mother's stories were not clinical reports, certainly not what my teachers many years later would label "scientific history." But they were *true stories* about her and about me—what I might call "the truth according to Mom."

I grew up across the street from my father's parents, which doesn't happen often for children growing up in America these days. When I was in junior high, I'd sit on their front porch and listen to Pappy talk about things he remembered from long ago. He'd suffered a stroke and wasn't able to work for as long in his garden as he once did, so he'd sit on the shady porch in the late afternoon, enjoying the occasional east Texas breezes, waiting for his only grandchild to wander over and sit with him. Pappy required little prompting to re-tell tales he once heard from his own grandfather along with his personal stories about growing up in rural Arkansas during the last decades of the nineteenth century, the grandson of an immigrant Scottish carpenter. It wasn't until I was a few years older that I realized the parts about him fighting with Indians and wrestling alligators were probably just a bit of fancy meant to entertain a youngster. But oral history is full of that sort of thing. He could have been a Hebrew patriarch telling stories to a circle of wide-eyed boys around a campfire in the century after the conquest of Canaan. But, unlike his ancient predecessors, my grandfather *did* have documentary evidence to back up at least one of his claims: a dog-eared old Kodak photo of himself and another man holding between them a rope from which hung the carcasses of several alligators.

The stories we tell about our beginnings reveal something of how we think about ourselves, our place in the world, and our future. "*In the beginning was the Word* . . ."—How far back in time do we set "the beginning"? Which of a number of possible beginnings did the author of the prologue have in mind?

---

6. Bauckham, *Jesus and the Eyewitnesses*, 127–29. Bauckham notes that in the Fourth Gospel, Jesus himself lays down the qualification for those who are to be witnesses to him: "You also are to testify because you have been with me from the beginning" (15:27). According to the Fourth Gospel, the Beloved Disciple began to follow Jesus slightly earlier than did Peter (see 1:35–42); therefore, his eyewitness authority is slightly better even than Peter's.

In the beginning was the Word.

At the beginning of God's self-disclosure, God spoke to Abraham, "Leave your native land and your family home, and go to a place that I will show you" (paraphrase of Gen 12:1).

In the beginning was the Word.

At the beginning of Israel's history as a people, God spoke to Jacob, "Your name shall no longer be called Jacob. Israel shall be your name—'the one who wrestles with God'" (paraphrase of Gen 32.28).

In the beginning was the Word.

At the beginning of Jesus's ministry, God spoke to him, "You are my Son, my Beloved. I delight in you" (paraphrase of Mark 1:11).

In the beginning was the Word.

At the beginning of the church's mission to the world, the risen One spoke to his disciples, "You will receive power when the Holy Spirit comes to you, and then you'll be my witnesses—in Jerusalem and all Judea and Samaria, and even to the ends of the earth" (paraphrase of Acts 1:8).

In the beginning was the Word.

At the beginning of my personal awareness of the reality of God, when I was a very little child, my mother read Bible stories to me. She told me, "These aren't just stories. They're the Word of God."

Being reared on Bible stories did something important for me and many other children of my generation: *it prepared us to expect that God was going to be involved in our life.* Our mothers and fathers taught us that what we read in the Bible was "God's Word" as it was once spoken to Abraham, or Moses, or the Hebrew people, or Jesus's disciples. And they made it clear that God's message to those biblical characters was also a word spoken to us. That idea created for us a degree of expectancy, a context in which everything we might read in the Bible had the potential of touching and affecting our own lives.[7]

"In the beginning was the Word, and the Word was with God, and the Word was God. He was in the beginning with God; all things were made through him, and without him was not anything made that was made" (v. 1). Our author launches his gospel by echoing the story of beginnings found in the first book of the Bible. Genesis starts: "In the beginning, God created the heavens and the earth. The earth was without form and void, and darkness was upon the face of the deep; and the Spirit of God was moving over the face of the waters. And God said, 'Let there be light;' and there

---

7. McNab, *Finding the Way*, 25.

was light. And God saw that the light was good; and God separated the light from the darkness. God called the light Day, and the darkness he called Night" (Gen 1:1). God, the Creator, spoke a command, and there was light. The Creator's power is exercised with words of command and with words that impose *names*. Names give identity to things and to people. Names have the power to shape how we think.

Whether we're thinking about the world's beginning, or a nation's beginning, or a family's beginning, or a single individual's beginning, *words* come into play. Stories. Explanations. As far as we can tell, the way humans use language sets us apart from other animals. Zoologists say animals communicate with one another, and each species has its own language, its own set of sounds or symbolic behaviors used to communicate with others of its kind—and some of these non-human languages are quite complex.

But, as best we're able to judge, no animal language is as highly developed as human language. Eons ago our prehistoric ancestors learned to speak to one another, and as the ages passed they learned to speak in ever more complex ways. They figured out how to do more than ask for directions to the nearest food supply, or to the river, or to where a mate might be found. They learned how to say something beyond "This antelope meat is spoiled," or "No berries grow around here." At some point our forebears learned how to ask more complicated questions than inquiries about the availability of food and drink or a mate. They learned how to ask the first intelligent question: "*Why?*"

Children learn how to speak from their parents, and their use of words almost always begins with names. First, a baby names Mama and Dada, then big sister, Grandma, and the family dog. She learns what to call food items and colors. But in an amazingly short time, the little one will begin to ask, not just "What's that," but also "Why?"

We may think of "Why?" as the first intelligent question because it can be employed to demand a *reason*, a justification for the reality we see. The answer to a child's question, "Why does water run out of the tub when I pull the plug," or "Why is the sky blue?" is going to be qualitatively different from an answer to "Why can't I take Suzy's dollhouse home with me," or "Why did my puppy die?" A truly curious child may grow up to ask the big question that Christianity and other religions offer to answer, but which science does not regard as meaningful because science has no way to answer it: "*Why is there something rather than nothing?*" When science tries to explain *why*, it usually ends by telling us *how*, describing the physical mechanics of the natural order. "How?" is a different question from "Why?"

Communication is probably the most important activity in which human beings engage. (It's even more important than procreation, since—for humans at least—some level of communication has to precede procreation.) Consider all the aspects of human society and civilization that would be impossible if people weren't able to communicate with one another in complex ways. Obviously there would be no culture: no religion, no philosophy, no literature, and no art. But there would also be no social organization—no agriculture, no towns, and no commerce.

We have faster, farther-reaching, more universally accessible communication technology today than ever in history: namely, the world-wide web and the various electronic devices that permit access to it. The power of the internet now exceeds television, radio, and all forms of printed media put together. And that power is only going to grow in the future.

However, there's something even more essential to communication than the latest electronic wizardry—something very old, very primitive: *language*. In certain circumstances, a picture might be worth a thousand words, but if we didn't have words it would take a lot of pictures to convey all but the simplest message. Language is indispensable, but we always communicate in *a* language or at least one language at a time. We cannot simply speak "language," we must speak English, Spanish, Mandarin, Zulu, or some other specific tongue—unless we're Pentecostals who speak in "tongues" which are only understood by a gift of the Holy Spirit. People who are adept in the use of multiple languages tell us that there are certain things one simply cannot easily translate from language A to language B.[8]

We human beings have a built-in need to communicate. We're social creatures, and we feel compelled to tell our stories, share our gossip, make our point, and join the debate. If we're normal people, we just *have* to make our feelings, wants, needs, and hopes known. If we have a good idea, we can't just sit on it, we have to tell somebody. When we can communicate, then we feel human. When we can get our message out to people that matter to us, then we feel fulfilled.

Highly influential photographs, video clips, and music are regularly posted on the internet, but the medium's greatest potency depends not on any of these, but on language. *Words are crucial.* It's with words that we connect with one another. Through words we arrive at understanding, make peace, share joy, plan celebrations, and organize productive work.

But there's a darker side to language. Because messages composed of words are always our creations, crafted for the moment, and because we're imperfect speakers—as well as imperfect listeners—our words can be misunderstood. And because we are not only imperfect but sometimes actively evil, our messages can be calculated to deceive, confuse, control, or manipulate—to tear down rather than build up. To put it simply, we can tell lies.

---

8. In the mid-1990s, I knew a man who was working on a translation of the Bible into a language spoken by a very small ethnic group living on a few islands in the South Pacific. These people had no herd animals of any kind and their principal source of protein was seafood. Translating all the biblical references to sheep (as well as other large four-footed mammals) into this language was presenting an obstacle difficult to overcome. The last time I spoke with him about the subject, he and his colleagues were thinking about experimenting with analogies that made use of fish in some way. This sent biblical stories off on strange tangents, since there is no marine-life counterpart to a shepherd.

I'm a preacher, and I have thought a great deal about the business of preaching—communicating the Word of God. It's what I do, or what I used to do every Sunday until I retired. You can sit in a pew and listen to sermons on Sundays and never be completely sure, unless you have some other, corroborating input, whether or not the preacher is telling you truth or just spinning a metaphysical spider web.

To be trustworthy, to be effective in the long run, the words of a preacher—or of a salesman, or of a spouse—must be substantiated by *deeds*. Talking is not enough. Words are not enough, whether they're words about God or words about the car I want you to buy from me, or words that are intended to convey how much I love you.

Vv. 6–18. "The Word became flesh and dwelt among us . . . We have beheld his glory."

INTRODUCTION. The baptizing prophet is the only person named John to whom the Fourth Gospel ever makes reference. He is never identified as "John the Baptist," as in the Synoptics, but simply as "John." The author of the prologue—writing many years after the events described in the Fourth Gospel's narrative—knows how important the Baptizer was during his own lifetime and afterwards. John has a huge following, perhaps numbering in the tens of thousands, at the time when Jesus first begins a public ministry. The prologue recognizes the importance of the Baptizer as a prophet sent from God, but also makes clear that he should be understood only as a precursor and witness to the Messiah, not as a figure equal in any way to Jesus, the Son of God.

The crucial verses of the prologue are 9–14, describing the incarnation of the divine *Logos,* who comes to his own people and dwells among them, but is rejected by them. Because the Fourth Gospel's first readers are serious-minded Jews, they easily recognize the prologue's Old Testament allusions. (Contemporary Christian readers of John do not as readily spot these references.) In addition to associating the *Logos* with both Torah and Wisdom, as mentioned above, reading that the incarnate *Logos/Torah/Wisdom* "pitched his tent among us" (v. 14) automatically brings to the mind of John's earliest audience the Tabernacle in the wilderness, the Lord's abiding place in the midst of Israel as God's people journey to the Promised Land. To read "we beheld his glory" (v. 14) offers an additional connection with the same Exodus imagery, since the rabbis always identified the presence of the Lord with his glory. The prologue invites John's readers in every era to see that Jesus of Nazareth is the final and perfect revelation of God's Word and presence among his people.[9]

Though "his own" will repudiate him, the *Logos* will give to all who choose to "receive him" the power to become God's children. Believers will become children of God through union and likeness with God's unique Son, Jesus. The prologue concludes with the statement, "No one has ever seen God; the only Son, who is in the

---

9. Keener, *Gospel of John*, 1:408–11. The Greek word translated "dwelt" by the RSV in v. 14 literally means "pitched his tent" (*eskēnōsen*).

bosom of the Father, he has made him known" (v. 18).[10] The theme of Jesus as the unique representative of God, speaking only what his Father says and doing only what his Father does, will be increasingly emphasized through the gospel until in the Farewell Discourse we hear Jesus say to Philip, "He who has seen me has seen the Father" (14:9*b*). Jesus is "the human face of God;" those who come to believe in him will identify Jesus with God. The incarnation of the Son of God, his ministry in the world, his gathering of a community of people who believe in him, and his self-offering on the cross, are portrayed as a single, unified revelation of God's saving love and glory.

In v. 9 we encounter the second instance of the word "world" in the Fourth Gospel. It is important to recognize that for this gospel the "world" (*kosmos*), which God made through the agency of the Word (v. 10), is the stage on which the cosmic drama of conflict between God and the Evil One is being played out. Modern readers should take care not to misunderstand the use of "world" here and imagine it in a twenty-first century environmentally/ecologically-focused way. It is not a reference to the whole created order. The gospel writer portrays the world as a creation at odds with its Creator. God loves his world (as we are famously told in 3:16), and because of that love, he sends his Son to save it.[11]

> [1:6–18] *6 There was a man sent from God, whose name was John. 7 He came for testimony, to bear witness to the light, that all might believe through him. 8 He was not the light, but came to bear witness to the light. 9 The true light that enlightens every man was coming into the world. 10 He was in the world, and the world was made through him, yet the world knew him not. 11 He came to his own home, and his own people received him not. 12 But to all who received him, who believed in his name, he gave power to become children of God; 13 who were born, not of blood nor of the will of the flesh nor of the will of man, but of God.*
>
> *14 And the Word became flesh and dwelt among us, full of grace and truth; we have beheld his glory, glory as of the only Son from the Father. 15 (John bore witness to him, and cried, "This was he of whom I said, 'He who comes after me ranks before me, for he was before me.'") 16 And from his fullness have we all received, grace upon grace. 17 For the law was given through Moses; grace and truth came through Jesus Christ. 18 No one has*

10. There is interesting congruency between "No one has ever seen God; the only Son, who is in the bosom of the Father, he has made him known" (v. 18) and Paul's description of Christ as "the image of the invisible God" (Col 1:15). Indeed, the prologue demonstrates a theological perspective akin to the perspective of Paul in Col 1:15–20.

11. See O'Day, *Gospel of John*, 792, 796. Malina and Rohrbaugh, *Social Science Commentary*, 246, assert that for the Fourth Gospel "the world" must be understood as a reference only to the chosen people of God, Israel, who constitute "the world" of Jesus, and any other way of explaining the term is anachronistic. According to Malina and Rohrbaugh, "world" in John "never refers to . . . all human beings, the whole human race" (*Social Science Commentary*, 246). This is a view not widely asserted by other commentators, but it is a possible way of reading the text.

ever seen God; the only Son, who is in the bosom of the Father, he has made him known.

RESPONSE. These verses from John are like costly treasures which we usually take out of their box and contemplate only at Christmas—like special antique ornaments for the tree. We treat them like unusual, fragile pieces of art, and often we admire them without fully grasping what they mean and what their purpose is.

The "Word" that "was in the beginning with God," and indeed "was God," is not like a single part of speech, a noun or a verb or an adjective. The Word was and is a whole message, *the* message God wanted to communicate to his world from the very first moment of the world's existence: the message of God's own being, purpose, and work—everything that finite human beings might be able to comprehend about the infinite God. Since language is inadequate to communicate truth at such a profound level, that divine "Word," that message, that love-letter from God to God's needy, sin-filled world, becomes a *person*—one particular man, a Jew named Jesus. God's message to his world comes to life in Mary's baby boy. The Lord of history comes into the world of human beings as a helpless, dependent infant, in order that we mortals might ultimately *know* God just as we know our own mothers and fathers. God sends his Son into the world in order to create an intimate bond between human beings and our Creator. Pretty amazing, isn't it?

That's why when—at the end of Jesus's ministry on earth—his dear friend Philip says to him in exasperation, "Look, Master, if you would just show us the Father, then we'll be satisfied," Jesus answers, "Oh, Philip, have I been with you all this time and you still don't get it? Don't you know me yet? Listen: whoever has seen me has seen the Father. I am in the Father, and the Father is in me. The Father and I are one" (paraphrase of John 14:8–10 and 10:30 combined).

Beyond every form of persuasive discourse, every artful pattern of words, every skillful intellectual proposition, is the raw stuff of human experience, of encounter, of flesh disclosing God—so that we mortals might know even as we are known and understand even as we have been understood. The prologue to John tells us that in Jesus God's message of truth, light, life, power, hope, and unconditional love meets us on our own ground, comes to live among us, even in our house. He comes to live within us, to make us children of God just as he is.

The Law—words of judgment, of right and wrong, good and evil, clean and unclean, of "do" and "do not"—came to people through Moses. But those Laws could not change hard human hearts. The best they could do was to make us aware of how often and how badly we fail. (It's true that guilt does have a useful place in the grand scheme of things.) However, when God's grace and truth come through Jesus Christ, our stone-hard hearts melt. God's only Son, the one closest to the Father's heart, still comes into the society of mortals and makes God known. In making God known, he reveals to us our own identity and destiny as God's children. Therefore,

. . . when we touch and heal each other, in our brokenness and grief;

. . . when we make peace in the chaos of an angry world;

. . . when we laugh, or weep, or work together as sisters and brothers, members of one family;

. . . when a mother tends her newborn with love in her eyes or a father snuggles his weeping, frightened toddler against his shoulder;

. . . and when we come to a table like the one around which Jesus gathered with his friends on the last night of his earthly life to eat the Bread and share the Cup, then we know he's here among us.

The One who reveals the heart of God now lives among us, and he will never abandon us to face the future alone. We are able to reach out and touch him in the flesh of our sisters and brothers.—Because we can do that, we know why there's something rather than nothing. We, insignificant organisms on a speck in the immeasurably vast universe, can reach out to our equally insignificant fellow mortals and, in touching our neighbor, touch the face of God. This is the reason why there's *something* rather than nothing.

John's Gospel says, "We have beheld his glory, glory as of the only Son from the Father." I think most of us are so captured by our contemporary American culture that we reflexively identify *glory* with the fame generated by media-driven celebrity. For us, glory means adoring public recognition of an achievement, pictures on magazine covers, and appearances on television talk shows. It's what comes to those who succeed in winning the Oscar for Best Actress in a Leading Role or the Nobel Prize for Medicine or the Masters' Golf Tournament. That, however, is merely the acclaim of the fickle public, a pseudo-glory that quickly fades. Jesus receives this kind of glory from the palm-waving crowds as he rides into the Holy City on Sunday morning, though in five days' time the cries of "Hosanna, Lord" will morph into angry demands for his death.

The author of the prologue means something quite different when he says, "we have beheld his glory." He is not referring to the praise God receives from mortals. The glory of which he writes is an unmistakable, clearly discernible manifestation of the presence and power of the holy One. Such glory is a property of the Divine nature, and on rare occasions God allows his children to see it. Since it is impossible for mortals to see God's glory without God's help, the Almighty—at very special moments—reveals that glory to us through what he does. Such moments are rare and come only when God chooses. The Fourth Gospel contains no story of the transfiguration, but the narrative of that episode in the Synoptics provides a paradigm for the revelation of the glory of the Son of God, a revelation which is made complete only in his cross and resurrection.[12] The word *glory* has a variety of meanings in the Fourth Gospel. Sometimes it refers to the praise that human beings give to God (and to one another), but the glory that the Son comes to reveal to us is the truth of God's presence and the reality of God's life-giving purposes.

When the prologue says "we have beheld his glory," I think its author writes as spokesman of a community drawn together by the magnetic quality of the Beloved Disciple's testimony. He recalls his teacher's stories of standing as a young man in the presence of Jesus of Nazareth, the Word made flesh, listening to Jesus's wisdom, becoming his friend, eating and drinking with him, touching him and being touched by him (especially when his Master washes his feet), sadly seeing him die on a Roman cross, then joyfully meeting him again after he rises from the dead. The community of believers for whom John's Gospel is written can say "*we* have beheld his glory" because all of them see Jesus through the trustworthy testimony of one man, "the disciple Jesus loved," whose words and actions inspire them to believe. Members of the Beloved Disciple's community may never have observed the risen One with their physical eyes, but they do believe (20:29), and because they believe they too can "see." For them, *believing is seeing.* Thus, even the editor who writes down the stories and memories of the Beloved Disciple is able to inscribe with personal conviction the words, "*we* have beheld his glory, glory as of the only Son from the Father." This remains the cry of the faithful, even in this third millennium of the Jesus movement: *We have seen his glory! We too are witnesses.* The testimony of witnesses is crucial in John.

Jesus alone reveals the human face of God, and the man whose personal testimony is the foundation of this gospel once beheld that face. In his heart, he sees it still. When we hear the account of Jesus giving sight to the man born blind, we really perceive the attitude and viewpoint of the Beloved Disciple himself: "One thing I know, that though I was blind, now I see." (9:25*b*) In a sense the gospel writer himself is one who was born blind.—So am I. And so are you.

---

12. I suggest in chapter 13, below, that we might regard the Fourth Gospel's portrayal of Jesus taking off his formal attire, wrapping around himself the towel of a servant, and kneeling to wash his disciples' feet as a theophany comparable in its own way to the Synoptics' transfiguration story.

A General Introduction to John 1:19—12:50.
"The Book of Signs" Begins

Coming to believe in Jesus is a life-or-death decision in the Fourth Gospel. The author recognizes that one's attitude toward Jesus is the crucial factor in determining whether a person will choose to believe. John intends for his gospel to be an instrument that will shape readers' attitudes. The narrative portion of John begins with 1:19. This verse was probably the beginning of the gospel until the prologue (1:1–18) was added as a theological overture to the work by its final editor. I adopt Raymond E. Brown's scheme of labeling 1:19 through 12:50 as the "Book of Signs," since the narrative is constructed around the explication of seven or eight signs (miracles), by which the Son of God discloses his identity.[1] Except for his trip to Samaria in chapter 4, Jesus's ministry in the Book of Signs focuses for the most part on his own people, the Jews, and much of his teaching is public, including addresses to crowds and public debates in the temple with representatives of the chief priests and the elders. John's stated purpose for writing is "that you *(plural)* may believe that Jesus is the Christ, the Son of God, and that believing you *(plural)* may have life in his name" (20:31).

John does not write about all the healings, exorcisms, and nature miracles detailed in the Synoptics. He even declines to use the word "miracle" (literally, "act of power" in Greek) which the other gospels apply to these deeds. In the Book of Signs, the gospel writer and bystanders in the narrative speak of Jesus's miracles as "signs," though Jesus himself—for reasons which are uncertain—calls them his "works." John does not discount the power of God which is always active in Jesus, but his intent is to draw readers' attention to the spiritual significance of a few carefully selected specimen miracles rather than to the dramatic impressiveness of a large number of them. Although the Beloved Disciple describes relatively few signs, he intends for readers to understand that Jesus's ministry is characterized by numerous such events. For example, Nicodemus says, "Rabbi, we know that you are a teacher come from God; for

---

1. The seven are: (1) changing water into wine (2:1–11); (2) healing the official's son (4:46–54); (3) healing the paralyzed man at the pool called Bethzatha or Bethesda (5:1–11); (4) the feeding of the five thousand (6:1–15); (5) walking on the water through the storm, a theophany (6:16–21); (6) giving sight to the man born blind (9:1–7); and (7) raising Lazarus from the dead (11:1–44). Wright, *Resurrection*, 669, proposes a list of *eight* signs—identical to the list above through the first four, but continuing with (5) the man born blind (9:1–7); (6) the raising of Lazarus (11:1–44); (7) the crucifixion (19:1–37); and (8) the resurrection (20:1–29). Wright sees the signs as continuing throughout the gospel and does not restrict them to the first half of the gospel. A few writers believe John may have made use of a very early "signs gospel," a lost document that recorded seven or eight stories of miracles performed by Jesus, with an account of the passion and resurrection attached. See Brown, *John I–XII*, xxxi–xxxii; Martyn, *History*, 150–51; Powell, *Gospels*, 114–15.

no one can do *these signs* that you do, unless God is with him" (3:1). Immediately before the epilogue, the narrative says, "Jesus did *many other signs* in the presence of the disciples, which are not written in this book" (20:30). Many commentators identify seven miracles described in the first eleven chapters of John which appear to function as signs, though the author himself only labels two of them specifically as "signs," the changing of water into wine (2:1–11) and the healing of the official's son (4:46–54).

The Book of Signs concludes on a somber, wistful note with a meditative coda in 12:37–50. This coda is a collection of Jesus's sayings which acknowledge that although his people and their leaders hear his words and see his signs, most of them reject him. Nothing he does can convince them; their hearts are hard, and they have become implacably hostile to him. Finally, they decide that he must die.

John 1:19–50. John the Baptist bears witness to Jesus.

Vv. 19–28. John testifies, "Among you stands one whom you do not know."

INTRODUCTION. Mark, generally regarded as the oldest of the four gospels, begins with an account of the ministry of John the Baptizer. Christians today are generally unaware of the essential role that ritual bathing (what we call "baptisms") played in first century Jewish religion—and that such baths still play in orthodox Judaism. Jewish Law requires ritual bathing for a variety of reasons. Mark 1:4–5 says, "John the baptizer appeared in the wilderness, preaching a baptism of repentance for the forgiveness of sins. And there went out to him all the country of Judea, and all the people of Jerusalem; and they were baptized by him in the river Jordan, confessing their sins."[2] Although the Fourth Gospel quotes the Baptizer's self description as one who prepares the way for the Messiah (see v. 23)—a role many Jews expected to be fulfilled by a return of the Prophet Elijah—it does not describe the Baptizer's Elijah-like attire the way Matthew does (Matt 3:4). However, John does draw a connection between the Baptizer and Elijah by telling us that his baptizing ministry takes place at a site called Bethany beyond the Jordan (v. 28), a spot on the east side of the river near where Elijah had been taken up into heaven (2 Kgs 2:1–14).

An obviously unusual thing about the Fourth Gospel is how it uses the expression "the Jews," which occurs first here in v. 19. (See Appendix Two, pp. 353–59, below, for a detailed discussion of this aspect of John's rhetoric.) John's style seems odd to modern readers because Jesus and his disciples are all Jews, as are all the people mentioned in the gospel, except for the Samaritans to whom he reaches out (4:4–42) and the Gentiles who conduct his trial and crucifixion (18:28–19:38). John appears to use "the Jews" in three distinctly different ways, but it is impossible to discern precisely which use is intended in every context. The most frequent use of the expression is also the

2. Among first-century Jews, washing in water was a token of repentance and a desire for closer communion with God. (See Kohler and Krauss, "Baptism.")

most surprising. It applies to the religious authorities who demonstrate hostility to Jesus—the chief priests, elders, and Pharisees. This is what we encounter in v. 19. A second use of "the Jews" is to indicate the people of Judea and Jerusalem, as opposed to Jesus's Galilean countrymen or Jews who reside elsewhere in the Mediterranean world. The final way the Fourth Gospel uses "the Jews" is the way that seems most logical to us, i.e., referring to people who are ethnically and religiously Jews.[3]

> **[1:19–28]** *19 And this is the testimony of John, when the Jews sent priests and Levites from Jerusalem to ask him, "Who are you?" 20 He confessed, he did not deny, but confessed, "I am not the Christ." 21 And they asked him, "What then? Are you Elijah?" He said, "I am not." "Are you the prophet?" And he answered, "No." 22 They said to him then, "Who are you? Let us have an answer for those who sent us. What do you say about yourself?" 23 He said, "I am the voice of one crying in the wilderness, 'Make straight the way of the Lord,' as the prophet Isaiah said."*
>
> *24 Now they had been sent from the Pharisees. 25 They asked him, "Then why are you baptizing, if you are neither the Christ, nor Elijah, nor the prophet?" 26 John answered them, "I baptize with water; but among you stands one whom you do not know, 27 even he who comes after me, the thong of whose sandal I am not worthy to untie." 28 This took place in Bethany beyond the Jordan, where John was baptizing.*

RESPONSE. If there is anyone in Jewish society at the time Jesus begins his ministry that Americans might call a "celebrity" today, that person is the priest named John the son of Zechariah, whom the Synoptic gospels call "John the Baptist." He is probably the most famous living Jew, a prophet the like of whom Israel has not seen since the time of Malachi, four hundred years earlier. The eyes of the nation are upon him—a reality of which he must be aware. People in the villages of Galilee and Judea who might not know the names of any elders of the Great Sanhedrin[4] know something about John.

In this opening narrative we encounter John in a place called Bethany on the east side of the Jordan, where a delegation of official representatives from Jerusalem is interviewing him.[5] John is a member of the hereditary temple priesthood, but he is also acclaimed by the common people as a new prophet sent by God. Nevertheless, the ritual bath he proclaims and administers to masses of people in the waters of the

---

3. See Culpepper, *Anatomy*, 125–32.

4. *Sanhedrin* is a Greek word that means "assembly" or "council." The Great Sanhedrin was the highest council and supreme court of the Jews. In every town and region there were lesser sanhedrins that rendered decisions in local affairs. Appeals from lesser sanhedrins went to the Great Sanhedrin which met in the Hall of Hewn Stone in the temple. (The word *Sanhedrin* used without a modifying adjective always refers to the Great Sanhedrin in Jerusalem.)

5. This episode in Bethany beyond the Jordan (ch. 1) and the later one in Bethany on the Mount of Olives (ch. 11) bracket the Book of Signs.

Jordan is unusual from the authorities' point of view. It looks more like a dramatic prophetic gesture than a version of the ordinary Jewish penitential purification rite. Keep in mind that in the Fourth Gospel, whenever representatives of the Jewish establishment ask questions of anybody, their intentions are invariably hostile, and any politeness or language of respect they offer is merely a ruse.

The powers-that-be demand that this new Elijah-like character explain himself. "Who are you?" their emissaries ask. "Let us have an answer for those who sent us. What do you say about yourself?" (v. 22). The common people regard the charismatic son of Zechariah as a heaven-sent prophet. But it's unlikely that the aristocrats of the Sanhedrin are wondering if John might truly be one of the apocalyptic figures their traditions say will appear before the Day of Judgment—Elijah, or the prophet-greater-than-Moses, or the Messiah. These minions of the temple hierarchy have not come with friendly greetings from the high priest and his colleagues; they have come to give the Baptizer a grilling. Later we'll see the same kind of people aiming their hostile queries at Jesus. In every instance, the questioners' objective is not to learn God's will but to discredit those who seem to threaten their leadership.—This sort of thing happens in our own day, does it not? Even among ordinary Christians such as we are. Sometimes we're assailed by clever adversaries, incorrigible skeptics whose questions arise, not from a sincere desire to know God's truth, but from a wish to ridicule or defame those who believe in Jesus.

We realize that the temple authorities' questions to the Baptizer are antagonistic and unsympathetic, but John's Gospel also poses an implicit question for its readers to ponder. Behind the prologue, behind the narrative accounts of Jesus's signs, behind the wise teachings of the Son of God, behind the depiction of the Lord's crucifixion and resurrection, John's Gospel continuously asks us: *"Who are you?"*—Where are you coming from, you who read this gospel? Are you a truth-seeker? Do you love the Lord Jesus? Do you want to believe?

The gospel writer intends for his community to understand that the Baptizer, although an authentic prophet of God, nonetheless has only a preparatory role in the history of salvation. He quotes the prophet's self-identification, "I am the voice of one crying in the wilderness, 'Make straight the way of the Lord,' as the prophet Isaiah said" (v. 23). Augustine of Hippo in the early fifth century noticed the comparison of the Baptist's claim to be merely a prophetic "voice" with the Fourth Gospel's identification of Jesus as the incarnation of the pre-existent "Word" of God, the source of Isaiah's own enlightenment (see 1:9). Concerning the Baptizer, Augustine said in one of his sermons, "John is the voice, but the Lord is the Word who was in the beginning. John is the voice that lasts for a time; from the beginning Christ is the Word who lives forever."[6]

The Fourth Gospel identifies the Baptist's main mission as the calling of Israel's attention to Jesus, who outranks him even though he *"comes after"* him—using an

---

6. Augustine of Hippo, *Sermo* 293, quoted in Walsh, "Witness," 275.

expression that seems to mean that Jesus is one of the prophet's own followers. John attests that Jesus is more important than he. The son of Zechariah is indeed a prophet sent by God, but Jesus is the *Son* of God. John's Gospel gives us a picture of the Baptizer as God's faithful servant, manifesting perfect humility, recognizing his own secondary place in God's plan for Israel and happily accepting that lesser place. He tells the questioning Pharisees, "I baptize with water; but among you stands one whom you do not know, even he who comes after me, the thong of whose sandal I am not worthy to untie" (v. 27). A disciple would do any servile task for his teacher except unfasten his sandals (and wash his feet). John acknowledges that Jesus is his disciple, but asserts this particular disciple's inherent superiority. The prophet is not worthy even to untie Jesus's sandals. The bold Baptist is both wise and shrewd in dealing with the emissaries from the Sanhedrin, but he is free of vanity. Praise from high-ranking officials, something all-important to the priests, Levites, and Pharisees who are interrogating him, is not important to the Baptizer. He cares only about fulfilling his mission. In this respect he resembles the one for whom he was sent to prepare the way. (See 5:41–44)

Vv. 29–34. John points to Jesus: "Behold, the Lamb of God."

INTRODUCTION. John describes Jesus as "the Lamb of God, who takes away the sin of the world" (v. 29). Keep in mind that, for John, "the world" is the realm of humankind, beleaguered by sin and evil, the stage on which the conflict between God and the Evil One is played out. Commentators propose various ideas about what "Lamb of God" the Baptizer might have in mind. The most likely Old Testament antecedent is the Passover lamb.[7] At the exodus the blood of the Passover lamb is the sign that marks the homes of the Hebrews, so that the Lord passes over them, leaving them safe on the night when he slays the first-born of the Egyptians (see Exod 12:12–13). The Passover lamb is not technically a sacrificial lamb. However, by the time of Jesus Passover lambs are only slaughtered by priests in the temple and are commonly spoken of as sacrifices. For example, the apostle Paul writes to the Corinthian church, "Christ, our paschal [Passover] lamb, has been sacrificed" (1 Cor 5:7). His identification of Christ as the Passover lamb confirms the likelihood that this is the lamb to which John refers.

It's worth noting that although John speaks of the descent of the Spirit upon Jesus in the form of a dove—which the other gospels tell us happens at the time of his baptism in the Jordan—it never mentions the actual baptism itself. That is probably because John wishes to portray the prophet-baptizer as clearly subordinate to Jesus, the Son of God. (We are, however, safe in assuming that the entire story of Jesus's baptism is familiar to the Fourth Gospel's original audience.)

---

7. Brown, *John I–XII*, 58–63.

It is significant that John not only sees the Spirit as descending upon Jesus, but also observes that the Spirit *remains* on him (v. 32). To speak of the Spirit remaining on Jesus (or "abiding with" him) draws a contrast between Jesus and various Spirit-anointed prophets and rulers in the Old Testament.[8] Such figures were filled with the Spirit, but Jesus is the only one upon whom the Spirit descends and abides always. John shows us in later chapters that Jesus has power to bestow the Spirit on his disciples after he is glorified (7:39; 20:21). The Baptizer tells his audience by the Jordan that God has revealed these things to him. He proclaims, "He who sent me to baptize with water said to me, 'He on whom you see the Spirit descend and remain, this is he who baptizes with the Holy Spirit'" (v. 33). Acts shows the earliest Christians expected that believers baptized in the name of Jesus would also receive the Holy Spirit, either at the same time or soon after (see Acts 19:1–7).

> **[1:29–34]** [29] *The next day he saw Jesus coming toward him, and said, "Behold, the Lamb of God, who takes away the sin of the world!* [30] *This is he of whom I said, 'After me comes a man who ranks before me, for he was before me.'* [31] *I myself did not know him; but for this I came baptizing with water, that he might be revealed to Israel."* [32] *And John bore witness, "I saw the Spirit descend as a dove from heaven, and it remained on him.* [33] *I myself did not know him; but he who sent me to baptize with water said to me, 'He on whom you see the Spirit descend and remain, this is he who baptizes with the Holy Spirit.'* [34] *And I have seen and have borne witness that this is the Son of God."*

RESPONSE. For a second day the personal testimony of John the Baptist continues with an invitation for his audience to see what he sees. "*Behold!*" is an imperative that appears repeatedly in the Fourth Gospel. "Believing" and "seeing" are intimately connected for John. The author constructs his narrative in such a way that the identity of the Baptizer's audience in vv. 29–34 is not completely clear. We wonder: Is he speaking to the representatives from the Jerusalem authorities, as in vv. 19–27? Not anymore.—Is he speaking to his own disciples? Possibly, but probably not yet, since he addresses them the next day, in vv. 35–36.—Is he speaking to the crowd of people who have gathered at the Jordan to hear him preach? This seems the most likely answer; however, I believe John intends that his readers envision an even wider audience.

Our gospel writer wants everyone who reads or hears his message—including us, two thousand years later—to be part of the audience that listens to the Baptist's exhortation. In effect, he's telling us, "All you who are listening to the Baptizer, open

---

8. Isa 11:1–2a is often interpreted by Christians as a messianic prophecy and applied to Christ: "There shall come forth a shoot from the stump of Jesse, and a branch shall grow out of his roots. And the Spirit of the Lord shall rest upon him." However, the Hebrew phrase "rest upon him" is not the same as "remain upon him." See Burge, *Anointed Community*, 50–62, which also offers a discussion of the Fourth Gospel's connection between the descent of the Spirit upon Jesus at his baptism and Jesus as the bestower of the Spirit after his resurrection.

your eyes to the truth he recognizes. Look! Jesus is the Son of God, the Lamb who takes away the sin of the world." Although the Fourth Gospel inserts the prophet's speech into its narrative before the beginning of Jesus's active ministry, we notice that the Baptizer says Jesus is "the Lamb of God who takes away the sin of the world," not "the Lamb of God who *will* take away the sin of the world." Use of the present tense may not be syntactically significant, but this choice of language tells us that the work of the Lamb of God is already going on. Our author is writing for the post-Easter church—including both his initial audience and us who read it today. John always employs his personal post-Easter perspective, even when he's telling stories about his Master's earliest days of ministry.

John the Baptist points to Jesus and says, "Look! There's the one who takes away the sin of the whole world." These words inspire John's readers to appeal for Jesus's help. Surely, he can take away the burden of guilt we feel. However, the redemptive work of the Lamb of God is much broader than simply providing a remedy for our personal guilt issues. Unfortunately, because we live in the Age of Therapy some third millennium Christians reflexively treat the Lamb of God merely as if he were a wise therapist whose good counsel can liberate us from our neuroses and make us feel better about ourselves.

Christ's taking away the *sin* of the world is not simply a matter of tending to our personal feelings of moral failure. Christians, Jews, Muslims and even atheists suffer from moral guilt. Anyone who is in touch with reality knows that we will often do bad things we ought not to do and frequently leave undone good things that we ought to have done. We typically label those moral shortcomings as "sins." We want to do good and not evil, but we'll never escape the need to acknowledge and seek pardon for our sins, our moral and ethical lapses. We'll always need forgiveness—from others, from ourselves, and from God.

The capacity to feel guilt is connected with the ability to distinguish between good and evil, between right choices and wrong choices. Only sociopaths never feel guilt. Of course, there is *authentic* guilt, arising from awareness of a genuine moral failure on our part. There is also *false* guilt, arising from our failure, say, to live up to our mother's expectation that we would get married, have a family, and live down the street from her for the rest of her life. Repentance is the New Testament cure for authentic guilt. For false guilt, we can turn to therapy.

What we need more than balm for our guilty conscience is a way to know God— a way to experience unity with God, a way to find the peace the world cannot give. "Sins" (plural) like the ones I have described are moral lapses. "Sin" (singular) is a state of being, a life oriented away from the true God and towards a substitute—a false god. (Yes, we do have idols in the twenty-first century, but they're not as simple as statues in shadowy temples once were.) Sin, the state of being oriented *away* from God, results in an ever-widening breach between us and God, the source of life. Therefore, sin is much more serious than the sum of all the moral failures that burden us with guilt feelings. Immoral or wicked behavior—things we ought to know better than to do—will inevitably be a fact of human life. But the "sin of the world" the Lamb of God takes away is the disorientation of souls which keeps us moving further and further from God, the canyon we ourselves dig to keep God out of our lives. It is an abyss the Lamb of God bridges over so that we might be able to follow him home to the Father.

The eternal Word became a human being to communicate the love of God to us. Jesus "takes away the sin of the world" by coming into our world and into our lives to reveal his Father as *our* Father (see 20:17): ever-present, always loving, and unfailingly merciful. He knows that we, like all children, will break some rules, maybe a lot of rules. We will make mistakes. We will do some things that we can only perceive afterwards as embarrassing moral lapses. We will need to express our sincere remorse for these and commit—with God's help—to make a fresh start. Nevertheless, because Jesus "takes away the sin of the world," our moral failures will not cut us off from God any more than the misbehavior of a child can nullify his mother's love.

John says, "I myself did not know him; but for this I came baptizing with water, that he might be revealed to Israel" (v. 31). Aren't there times when our eyes are opened to know someone in a new way, even someone who has been a friend for years? The Baptist has probably been familiar with Jesus since they were boys, but when he sees the Spirit descend like a dove and remain on him, John's eyes are opened to a reality that has until then been hidden. And God whose Voice has called John to his own prophetic ministry of cleansing Israel in the waters of the Jordan identifies this man, Jesus, his own disciple and kinsman, as the Son of God who is to wash all humanity with the cleansing energy of the Spirit.

Vv. 35–42. Jesus's first words: "What do you seek?"

INTRODUCTION. It may have been common knowledge in the earliest Christian communities that Jesus himself was originally associated with the prophet John, the son of Zechariah, and that Jesus's first followers came to him from the Baptizer. This section describes an occasion when two of John's followers leave their master and begin to follow Jesus. Verse 38 gives us the first words spoken by Jesus in the Fourth Gospel, "What do you seek?" This is a very important question, and it should linger in the minds of all who read this gospel. One of the two disciples of the Baptizer is Andrew, the brother of Simon; the other is unnamed. However, tradition says the unnamed one is, in fact, the disciple whose testimony is enshrined in this gospel, "the disciple Jesus loved."

It's worth noting that in a number of instances John gives his readers the Greek equivalent for a common Aramaic word, such as *rabbi* (v. 38). This tells us that the original audience for John's Gospel is not only composed mostly of Hellenistic Jews, but also includes Gentile converts who do not automatically understand even the basic Aramaic or Hebrew vocabulary familiar to all Greek-speaking Jews.

[1:35–42] *³⁵ The next day again John was standing with two of his disciples; ³⁶ and he looked at Jesus as he walked, and said, "Behold, the Lamb of God!" ³⁷ The two disciples heard him say this, and they followed Jesus. ³⁸ Jesus turned, and saw them following, and said to them, "What do you seek?" And they said to him, "Rabbi" (which means Teacher), "where are you staying?" ³⁹ He said to them, "Come and see." They came and saw where he was staying; and they stayed with him that day, for it was about the tenth hour. ⁴⁰ One of the two who heard John speak, and followed him, was Andrew, Simon Peter's brother. ⁴¹ He first found his brother Simon, and said to him, "We have found the Messiah" (which means Christ). ⁴² He brought him to Jesus. Jesus looked at him, and said, "So you are Simon the son of John? You shall be called Cephas" (which means Peter).*

RESPONSE. Now comes a key moment. The incarnate Word speaks for the first time with a human voice. The narrator sets the stage for us to imagine it. The Baptist stands beside a path near the Jordan along with two of his disciples, one of whom is Andrew and (according to tradition) the other is the man who will later be known to us as Beloved Disciple. Jesus walks past, and the prophet says to Andrew and his companion, "Behold, the Lamb of God!" This is the second time the Baptist compares Jesus to the Passover lamb.[9]

When his two disciples hear these words, they leave their master and begin to follow Jesus. Hearing their footsteps, Jesus turns around and speaks his first recorded words in John's Gospel, "What do you seek?" (v. 38a). These words frame a question the gospel writer wants its readers to understand as being addressed not just to Andrew and his companion, but to every one of us: *What are you looking for?* John wants us to ponder this as we read the rest of his book. To make the question personal, let's place the emphasis on the pronoun, "What are *you* looking for?"

. . . It could be that you're a well-off retired person. For you, life is good. You've achieved all your life goals, and there's nothing significant you're looking for anymore. However, your comfortable existence, though worry-free, feels stale. Golf, skiing, and foreign travel no longer are fulfilling. Perhaps you need to find a deeper purpose for what is left of your life than simply enjoying your leisure.

. . . Maybe you're out of work and looking for a job, or for a life partner, or for help in raising children. Maybe you have experienced a great loss and are looking for healing or consolation. Maybe you feel deep personal needs and wonder whether they will ever be met.

9. Because the blood of the Passover lamb had a saving effect, the lamb came to be regarded as a prefiguration of Christ. In 1 Cor 5:7 Paul writes, "Christ our paschal lamb has been sacrificed." And John tells us that Jesus was condemned to death at noon on the day of preparation for the Passover, which was the exact hour that the sacrifice of the Passover lambs began in the temple (19:14).

. . . Perhaps you're a serious Christian, seeking to grow in your relationship with Jesus, or for an answer to prayer, or for discernment in using your gifts in service to God.

. . . Or you might be among the large number of people who are still searching for answers to the two classic existential questions: *"Who am I,"* and *"What is my life supposed to be about?"*

Jesus asks the men following him, "What are you looking for?" And they answer with a question of their own: "Rabbi . . . where are you staying?" (v. 38*b*). You and I might translate their question as, "Where do you live?" or "Where will we be able to find you?"[10] Their question tells Jesus an essential fact about them. They want to get to know him; they want to have a deep connection with him. *They want to be with him.* If they're merely seeking information they will answer him differently. They'll say, "We're seeking the Messiah," or "We're looking for the kingdom of God." Yes, they're seeking the Messiah and the kingdom, but they're really looking for something else, something even more important. The placement of this episode in John's narrative and the meaning of the question, "Where do you live," tells readers that having a living relationship with Jesus is an end in itself, not a means to some other end. In truth, such a living relationship is the most desirable objective for every human soul, because to know the Son is to know his Father also. Nothing could be more important. Recall the concluding sentence of the prologue: "No one has ever seen God; the only Son, who is in the bosom of the Father, he has *made him known*" (v. 18).—Jesus enables us to know God.

To be able to share the life of God is better than learning the correct answers to all the possible big questions of life. Indeed, it makes those questions moot. The two ask Jesus, "Where do you live?" (That is, "Where can we find you?") And he replies, "Come, and see" (v. 39). Our gospel writer delights in using expressions which his readers can understand in more than one way. "Come and see," the second thing we hear from the lips of Jesus in this gospel, just like "what are you seeking," must also be understood as an invitation to John's readers. We're being challenged to enter further into the story, into the ongoing revelation described in this gospel, where we'll see the living Word, learn of his works, and be transformed as he teaches us. We're being invited to live our lives with awareness that God has more truth to reveal.[11] You and I ask, "Where can I find Jesus today?" And the Lord answers, "Come, and see." In John's story world, the two former disciples of the Baptizer walk with Jesus, stay with him that day, that night, the next day, and the next night—and the rest of their lives.

10. The Greek word *menō*, meaning "remain," "stay," "abide," or "dwell," is an important word in John's vocabulary of symbolic expressions.

11. In 16:13, Jesus tells the disciples, "When the Spirit of truth comes, he will guide you into all the truth; for he will not speak on his own authority, but whatever he hears he will speak, and he will declare to you the things that are to come." The author of John writes as one to whom the Spirit has already revealed profound truth about Jesus.

We must not overlook Andrew's eagerness to find his brother Simon and bring him to meet Jesus—either later that afternoon or the next day. He says to Simon, "We have found the Messiah!" (v. 41). Unlike the Synoptics, the Fourth Gospel presents Jesus as Son of God and Messiah from its beginning, and Andrew is first among the disciples to name Jesus as Messiah. John clearly presents Andrew's act of bringing his brother to Jesus as an example for us to imitate. But correctly labeling Jesus as Messiah or even as Son of God does not mean that the disciples yet understand the true significance of either title. Recognizing Jesus's proper titles is a step in the right direction, but John will show us that the disciples have a lot yet to learn about how Jesus understands both his messianic identity and his mission as the Father's unique Son.

When the men ask Jesus "Where do you live?" he doesn't offer them a banal answer, such as, "I live with my mother and family in Nazareth, but I'm thinking about moving down to Capernaum." Neither does he say, "I'm on the move a lot these days, going here and there, so it's hard for me to tell you where to find me." In a purely ordinary sense, either of those answers would have been accurate. But the two men aren't asking for Jesus's place of residence—at least not in the ordinary sense. When Jesus says, "Come, and see," he invites them to accompany him and, through the experience of being his companions, they learn not just who *he* is, but who *they* are and what their lives are going to be about. Jesus will finally give his friends a clear answer to the question, "Where do you live," on the night before his death. After the Supper he will tell them, "If a man loves me, he will keep my word, and my Father will love him, and we will come to him and *make our home with him*" (14:23).

These first disciples will come to see Jesus and share his life in many different contexts, which John will describe. And we who read will see and learn along with the disciples that "the dwelling place of God" is not a location on a map, like a temple or a holy mountain. God's dwelling place is situated in the geography of human relationships. One of these first disciples may be the one who later writes, "God is love, and he who abides in love abides in God, and God abides in him" (1 John 4:16). These two men will come to know Jesus, and as they do, they will discover their own true selves. In time, after Jesus is crucified and raised from the dead, they will realize that they're able to see him in one another. They'll see that he is living in them, abiding with them, and will never leave them. By the grace of God, the same thing happens for twenty-first century Christians.

Vv. 43–51. Jesus calls Philip and Nathanael.

INTRODUCTION. Jesus goes up from the Jordan valley to Galilee, where the number of his disciples begins to grow beyond the Beloved Disciple, Andrew, and Simon Peter. Jesus calls Philip, a friend of Andrew and Simon, to follow him (v. 43) and then Philip recruits Nathanael, who is not mentioned in the Synoptic gospels. It's possible that John might intend us to perceive Jesus's description of Nathanael as "an *Israelite* in whom there is no guile" (v. 47) as a contrast with "the *Jews*" who prove to be his constant adversaries and whose words and behavior are regularly characterized by guile.

> **[1:43–51]** *⁴³ The next day Jesus decided to go to Galilee. And he found Philip and said to him, "Follow me." ⁴⁴ Now Philip was from Beth-sa'ida, the city of Andrew and Peter. ⁴⁵ Philip found Nathan'a-el, and said to him, "We have found him of whom Moses in the law and also the prophets wrote, Jesus of Nazareth, the son of Joseph." ⁴⁶ Nathan'a-el said to him, "Can anything good come out of Nazareth?" Philip said to him, "Come and see." ⁴⁷ Jesus saw Nathan'a-el coming to him, and said of him, "Behold, an Israelite indeed, in whom is no guile!" ⁴⁸ Nathan'a-el said to him, "How do you know me?" Jesus answered him, "Before Philip called you, when you were under the fig tree, I saw you." ⁴⁹ Nathan'a-el answered him, "Rabbi, you are the Son of God! You are the King of Israel!" ⁵⁰ Jesus answered him, "Because I said to you, I saw you under the fig tree, do you believe? You shall see greater things than these." ⁵¹ And he said to him, "Truly, truly, I say to you, you will see heaven opened, and the angels of God ascending and descending upon the Son of man."*

RESPONSE. Accompanied by three disciples, Jesus leaves the Jordan valley and goes up to Galilee. There he finds Philip—fellow townsman of Andrew and Peter—and invites him to become one of their number. Philip in turn seeks out Nathanael, announcing, "We have found him of whom Moses in the law and also the prophets wrote, Jesus of Nazareth, the son of Joseph" (v. 45).

John shows us that disciples come to Jesus by different routes. Some are directed to him by John the Baptist; some are personally called by Jesus himself; and some are brought by friends who are already his followers. There is no single pattern. In similar fashion, people in our day come to Christ in many different ways and at different points in life. Some are younger; some are older. Some are actively seeking God; others are engaged by friends or acquaintances that arouse their curiosity by saying, "Let me tell you what happened to me."

The narrative tells us that Nathanael is occupied with some kind of personal pursuit when Philip finds him. Whether he's tending a fig tree or studying the Torah is difficult to know, but Nathanael is skeptical about whether this man called Jesus of Nazareth is worth his attention. After all, Nathanael is a busy man. But Philip perseveres, saying to him exactly what Jesus himself said earlier, "Come and see" (v. 46). So Nathanael comes and is greeted by Jesus, who—though he has never met him before—discerns Nathanael's true character, "an Israelite, indeed, in whom is no guile" (v. 47). This means he knows Nathanael is a man who "tells it like it is," who speaks his mind without dissimulation. Jesus even knows what Nathanael was doing at the time Philip found him. When Jesus displays such a miraculous gift of insight, the new recruit is astounded. He overreacts and wildly exclaims, "Rabbi, you are the Son of God! You are the King of Israel!" (v. 49).

It's right to say that Jesus seems amused by Nathanael's quick, enthusiastic affirmation of his true identity. He answers, "Is that all it takes? I just have to say 'I saw you when you were under the fig tree,' and all of a sudden you're a true believer?" He promises Nathanael more impressive revelations are yet to come, reminding him of Jacob's dream about the ladder leading up to heaven (Gen 28:10–17), and telling him (and us, too, since the pronoun "you" is plural), "Truly, truly, I say to you, you will see heaven opened, and the angels of God ascending and descending upon the Son of Man" (v. 51).[12] In this encounter, Jesus calls himself "Son of Man," the name he most frequently uses for himself in all the Gospels. He says that in days to come those who share Nathanael's faith will recognize that the link between earth and heaven is not located in a physical place, like Herod's temple, but in the human person of Jesus himself. The Son of Man will open heaven for his disciples to enter; he is now the world's "ladder to God."

Doing Your Own Theology

Questions for reflection after reading John 1.

- The author of the prologue writes, "The Word became flesh and dwelt among us, full of grace and truth" (v. 14). The eternal *Logos*, who was present with God "in the beginning," God's agent in the creation of all things, enters the created order as a fleshly participant in it. He becomes a particular, ordinary human being, born into a normal human context, living and dying surrounded by family and friends. When the author says the incarnate Word "dwelt among us," he writes as spokesman of those who knew him, who can attest to what "we have heard, which we have seen with our eyes, which we have looked upon and touched with our hands, concerning the word of life" (1 John 1:1). One cannot be human except as a particular human being living in a particular social order, just as one cannot speak "language," but must speak a language. The claim that God chose to be uniquely embodied in Jesus of Nazareth, a Jew from an inconsequential village in a minor province of the first century Roman Empire, created division among his contemporaries, and still challenges people today. The challenge is often called "the scandal of particularity."—*What does the idea that God chose to became incarnate uniquely in Jesus of Nazareth teach us about the nature of God? What might it teach us as believers concerning ourselves?*

12. Use of the double *amen* by Jesus to introduce a solemn pronouncement is unique to John, occurring twenty-five times in the Fourth Gospel. (*Amen* is translated "truly" in the RSV.) In the Synoptics, Jesus uses a solitary *amen* at the beginning of such declarations; but, whether single or double, this unusual usage is very likely an authentic reminiscence of Jesus's way of speaking.

- The Fourth Gospel is tightly written. What we read in the opening chapter of the book connects directly with what we will read later in the narratives of Jesus's passion and resurrection. The Baptizer first identifies himself, and then we hear him identify Jesus. He proclaims Jesus as "the Lamb of God who takes away the sin of the world" (v. 29); he also says that Jesus is "he who baptizes with the Holy Spirit" (v. 33) and, finally, that Jesus is "the Son of God" (v. 34).—*Which of the three ways that John identifies Jesus has the most powerful personal meaning for you right now? Why?*

- Pointing to Jesus walking past, John tells two of his own disciples, "Behold, the Lamb of God!" (vv. 35–36). The two men leave John and go off to follow Jesus. When Jesus turns around and sees them walking behind him, he asks, "What are you looking for?" (v. 38). These are the first words Jesus speaks in John's Gospel, which makes them extremely important. Like the question the priests and Levites ask John the Baptist earlier, the question, *"What are you looking for,"* is asked of us who read the gospel. The two men following Jesus answer him with a question of their own, "Rabbi, where are you staying?" Jesus replies, "Come and see" (v. 39), an answer we can understand as an invitation to keep reading the gospel!—*What are you looking for as you read John? What are you looking for in your life? Are you, like the two disciples, seeking to know Jesus? Are you also seeking to make him known to others who are seeking him?*

Figure. 1. Aerial view of the Temple Mount in 2013 looking from south to north. The Muslim Dome of the Rock (completed in 691 CE) is located where both Solomon's and Herod's temples stood. The busiest public entrances to the temple enclosure were from the south, and the original stairs may still be seen.

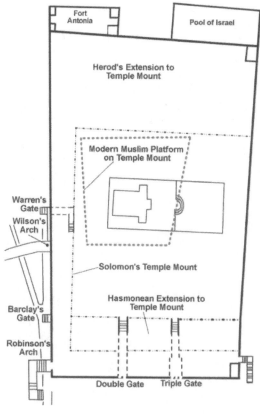

Figure 2. Diagram of Herod's Temple Mount. *(Compare to the photograph above.)* Herod's reconstruction of the temple began ca. 19-20 BCE and ended ca. 60 CE. Herod's engineers built a vast masonry box around the summit of Mount Moriah and filled it with vaulted substructures and rubble in order to expand the area of the enclosed temple platform by nearly fifty percent. The new area, not part of Solomon's temple platform, was not considered sacred and, therefore, was open to non-Jews. The market for sacrificial animals and money changers (see John 2:13–16) was likely in this area. Tunnels led upward to this outer court from the busy southern entrances.

Figure 3. Israel Museum scale model of the Temple Mount, viewed from the east. The entire temple enclosure was surrounded by a colonnade. (To compare the size to human scale, these columns were over fifty feet high, while a typical person was under six feet tall.) The portion of the colonnade along the east side was known as the Portico of Solomon, although it did not date from Solomon's time (see 10:22–23). The Shushan Gate in the east wall was not used by worshipers entering the temple. The tall Royal Stoa on the south side of the enclosure was a large basilica 108 ft. wide, 108 ft. high, and 788 ft. long, open on the north side. Two stories tall, it included the meeting hall of the Sanhedrin, areas where Jewish sages taught, and various commercial establishments. It was not a ritually "clean" area. Exits from the tunnels that led up to the temple enclosure from the southern entrances are visible immediately north of the Royal Stoa in the Israel Museum scale model.

Figure 4. Israel Museum scale model of the Temple Mount, viewed from the west. From south to north (*r.* to *l.*) there were four entrances to the temple (see Fig. 2, above). The northernmost, now called Warren's Gate, is concealed by the bridge now called Wilson's Arch. The double entrance at the south end of the western wall, at the point now known as Robinson's Arch, led into the Royal Stoa. An elevated walkway (not shown in the scale model) possibly led from it to the high priest's palace.

Figure 5. Israel Museum scale model of the temple, viewed from the northeast. The wall around the base of the stairs leading up to the temple is the *soreg*, beyond which only Jews could pass. (Stone tablets engraved in Greek were posted along the *soreg* wall warning non-Jews not to enter on pain of death.) Everything outside the *soreg* is the so-called court of the Gentiles. The first court inside the temple, open to all Jews, was commonly called the court of the women because it was the only area in the sacred space where women were allowed. This court was a scene of constant singing, dancing, and music. The treasury of the temple was located here, as were the four monumental lampstands lighted at the Feast of Tabernacles (see p. 128, below). The elevated ornamental gateway visible on the west side of the court of the women is the Nicanor Gate, also called "the Beautiful Gate" (see Acts 3:2, 10), where the Levite choirs stood to sing.

Figure 6. Fragment of stone-work from Herod's temple. Herod was of Edomite ancestry, raised as a Jew but thoroughly Hellenized. His new temple was Hellenistic in style, with stonework displaying rosettes and Greek-key patterns *(visible here)*, acanthus leaves, and utilizing columns of the Corinthian order.

Figure 7 and Figure 8. Two examples of first century *opus sectile* marble pavements from Italy, roughly contemporary with Herod's temple. The entire temple enclosure was paved with multi-colored marble, probably employing simpler patterns (as on the *l.*) in the outer court and increasingly more elaborate patterns (as on the *r.*) within the sacred space. The Temple Mount Sifting Project has recovered numerous fragments of the marble tiles used to pave the temple area.

Figure 9. Israel Museum scale model of the Bethesda Pool (see John 5:2–9). The text of the gospel describes it as a pool with five porticoes (v. 2). Archaeological excavation "indicates the existence of a pool with two basins, lying one to the north and one to the south, in trapezoidal form, surrounded on four sides by porticoes, with an additional portico dividing the pool from west to east."[1] The northern pool (*r.* in the photo) was larger and higher. Water was released from it into the southern pool by a small opening in the transverse wall. There were steps and landings leading down to the more southerly pool on its west side. This was probably the scene of Jesus's healing of the paralytic, described in 5:2–9.[2]

1. Von Wahlde, "Archaeology," 563.
2. Ibid., 564.

Chapter Two

2:1–12. The first Sign: Jesus changes water to wine at a marriage feast.

Vv. 1–12. Jesus "manifested his glory, and his disciples believed in him."

INTRODUCTION. The Fourth Gospel portrays a quite different start to Jesus's ministry from what the other gospels describe. Instead of showing him going to synagogues, teaching, healing, casting out demons, and attracting wide attention, John tells the story of Jesus and his disciples sharing a traditional family wedding celebration—the happiest event known in Galilean village society. We may safely presume that Jesus and his disciples, along with his mother and brothers, are invited to this wedding in the little village of Cana near Nazareth because the bridegroom is their kinsman. (A pious legend says the groom is none other than John, the son of Mary's sister Salome and her husband, Zebedee. If so, that would make the Cana celebration the wedding of the Beloved Disciple himself.) John's story of Jesus's first miracle, which the author says is his first "sign," functions both as a conclusion to the gathering of Jesus's disciples and as a transition to the narrative of his public ministry. (See A General Introduction to John 1:19–12:50, p. 12, above.)

In comparison to the Synoptics, John does not portray spectators as awestruck or amazed by Jesus's deeds. Popular response is sometimes noted, but invariably muted (e. g. , 7:31) except in the case of the feeding of the five thousand, when Jesus has to withdraw in order to prevent the crowd from taking him and making him king (6:14–15). The first of his signs, which we read about here, is noticed and understood only by his disciples; it reveals Jesus's glory (v. 11) and leads to a new level of faith in these disciples—who already have begun to believe in him (1:35–51). This points to how John would have readers understand the purpose of all Jesus's signs (20:31). The Fourth Gospel will show that a belief in Jesus which is wholly dependent on seeing signs is less valuable than belief grounded in trusting Jesus's words. It is, however, a starting point, and that is what we see in John's account of Jesus's first sign.[1]

This narrative introduces the concept of Jesus's "hour"—the moment when his glory is fully revealed in death and resurrection. When his mother tells Jesus that there is no more wine for the wedding celebration, he says to her, "O woman, what have you to do with me? My hour has not yet come" (v. 4). Because John tells us that the marriage at Cana was "on the third day," he may intend for readers to make a connection between this, the first of his signs, and the glory that will be entirely disclosed at the arrival of his hour. We note that just as John does not give a name to Jesus's mother, who appears only here and in 19:25–27 at the foot of the cross, neither does he give a name to the Beloved Disciple, although both characters have tremendous symbolic importance in his gospel story.

Many commentators see the miracle at Cana as a display of John's theology of fulfillment and replacement. Superabundance of wine was an expected mark of the coming messianic age. Jesus's replacement of the water intended for Jewish rites of purification (v. 7) with the messianic banquet's wine of gladness and celebration may be read as asserting that the traditional rites of purification have now served their purpose and the age of messianic joy is breaking in.[2] In this new age, the Spirit will be the cleansing agent, not water; and as John the Baptizer has told us, the Son of God is the one who washes God's people with the Spirit (1:29–34).

> **[2:1–12]** [1] *On the third day there was a marriage at Cana in Galilee, and the mother of Jesus was there;* [2] *Jesus also was invited to the marriage, with his disciples.* [3] *When the wine failed, the mother of Jesus said to him, "They have no wine."* [4] *And Jesus said to her, "O woman, what have you to do with me? My hour has not yet come."* [5] *His mother said to the servants, "Do whatever he tells you."* [6] *Now six stone jars were standing there, for the Jewish rites of purification, each holding twenty or thirty gallons.* [7] *Jesus said to them, "Fill the jars with water." And they filled them up to the brim.* [8] *He said to them, "Now draw some out, and take it to the steward of the feast." So they took it.* [9] *When the steward of the feast tasted the water now become wine, and did not know where it came from (though the servants who had drawn the water knew), the steward of the feast called the bridegroom* [10] *and said to him, "Every man serves the good wine first; and when men have drunk freely, then the poor wine; but you have kept the good wine until now."* [11] *This, the first of his signs, Jesus did at Cana in Galilee, and manifested his glory; and his disciples believed in him.* [12] *After*

---

1. Keener, *Gospel of John*, 1:492.

2. A similar set of ideas is conveyed by the Synoptics in their accounts of Jesus's "new wine" rejoinder to the Pharisees who criticize him for eating and drinking with sinners (see Matt 9:14–17; Mark 2:18–22; Luke 5:30–39). Interestingly, in Luke 5:38–39, Jesus says, "New wine must be put into fresh wineskins. [But] no one after drinking old wine desires new, for he says, 'The old is good.'"

this he went down to Caper'na-um, with his mother and his brothers and
his disciples; and there they stayed for a few days.

RESPONSE. The common practice in Jesus's day was for a groom and his entourage to fetch the bride and her attendants from the bride's family home and bring her in procession to the groom's family home, where the couple would feast with relatives and friends from the village and thereafter consummate their marriage in a tent erected in the courtyard. After the wedding night, the groom's family would hold open house for six more days and nights.[3] The family of the groom would host this week-long party, and each day there would be food and drink, singing and dancing—lots of food, and lots of drink. And they didn't drink fruit juice or the ancient equivalent of Perrier. The rabbis said, "Where there is no wine, there is no joy." Most guests at a village wedding would be from the least affluent stratum of Galilean society, and a wedding was one of only a few times in the year that poor people drank wine and ate meat. Except for Passover and weddings, luxuries like wine and roast meat were enjoyed only by the rich.

The New Testament shows that the wedding feast was a common metaphor for life in the kingdom of God.[4]—And why not? A wedding was the most fun, the most joy, the most delight, and the greatest degree of togetherness that ordinary people in that age and place could imagine. It was as close to heaven as mortal life would allow them to get. A wedding party with God himself as host is the image of the kingdom of God, the icon of eternal life.[5]

I trust this sets the stage well enough to show what's going on when Jesus's mother takes him aside from the other guests and tells him, "They have no wine." If the wine is gone, this party will be over quickly. The joy will evaporate. We can't know for sure whether this is near the last day of the week-long festivities, yet since it is the marriage feast of a close relative, Jesus's mother can't stand aside and permit her family to be shamed by their inability to provide enough wine to last the full week. So, she does what comes naturally to widows under those circumstances and in that society; she passes the problem along to her eldest son. Notice, she doesn't say, "Son, why don't you borrow a donkey and ride over to Nazareth and get us a few more skins of wine?" Jesus's mother doesn't ask him for anything specific, she simply tells him, "They're out of wine." She trusts Jesus to address the matter in whatever way he thinks best. That's good thinking for us, too, as we present our needs to the Lord. It's enough merely to

---

3. Malina and Rohrbaugh, *Social Science Commentary*, 66–71, describe the social details of a village wedding.

4. See, e.g., Matt 22:1–2 and Rev 19:6–9.

5. N. T. Wright explains the connection between "the kingdom of God" and "eternal life," pointing out that the Greek expression *zōē aionios*, usually translated "eternal life," literally means "life of the age," meaning "life of the age to come," the messianic age that would bring God's justice, peace, and healing to the world. Wright, *How God Became King*, 44–45.

turn over to God the matters that trouble us and leave them with him. It isn't necessary for us to suggest a course of action to the Almighty.

Jesus's response to his mother does sound harsh in the RSV translation, "O
woman, what have you to do with me? My hour has not yet come" (v. 4). Although
a son addressing his mother this way would have seemed unusually formal, it would
not have sounded impolite to anyone who overheard their conversation. We might
better read the remainder of his words as "What is that to you and me? My hour has
not yet come." This is the first mention of Jesus *hour*, a significant expression in John's
Gospel. His "hour," what we Americans would likely call his "time," will come at last
in his passion and resurrection. It's only in his death and his rising from the tomb that
the glory of the divine Son is to be fully manifested. So he signals to his mother that
he's not yet ready to go public. However, Jesus is a loving and dutiful son, and he takes
action to meet what his mother perceives as a need.

There are six oversized stoneware jars set into the ground in the courtyard. Before
the wedding, they provide water for the rituals of purification required for a devout
Jewish household. Now they stand empty. Those purificatory rites already have been
performed; the requirements of the Law are fulfilled. Jesus tells the waiters to fill the
empty *amphorae* again to the brim with water. The servants must make many trips to
the well, because the six jars each hold about 30 gallons. Then he tells them to take a
dipper of the water to the master of ceremonies for the feast. When that man tastes it,
it is no longer water, but wine—and better wine than has been served until now. He
assumes the bridegroom has done the unexpected and saved the best vintage for last.

John tells us this: near the end of a full week of eating, drinking, and dancing—
what we moderns would describe as "partying"—Jesus provides a wedding celebration with 180 gallons of Dom Pérignon 1948, and the merrymaking takes on new
life. That's an instance of what we should call "radical grace." Nobody except Jesus's
mother, the table servers (and later his disciples) knows what really has transpired;
the bridegroom and his father receive all the credit. Yet, as Revelation says, Jesus is the
true Bridegroom, and he is among us to do his heavenly Father's will.

If Jesus does not intervene, the wedding feast will be cut short, and the villagers
will go home and gossip for months about the fiasco. The groom and his family are
not wealthy people, and they will be publicly humiliated if the wine runs out before
the last day of the feast. Everyone in the village will know that they tried to put on a
proper wedding bash and failed. However, Jesus is there, and as the gospel writer tells
us in his prologue, "from his fullness have we all received, grace upon grace" (1:16).
Jesus meets their need without drawing attention to his behind-the-scenes role in
providing an abundance of vintage wine; he stays in the background. This is how God
does things. Most beneficiaries of divine grace are unaware of what's really going on,
because Christ shines his light in our darkness by reflecting it off his disciples.

John's Gospel discloses—in one episode after another—the overflowing love of
God, who delights in providing gifts for his children. Mark pictures Jesus beginning

his work with a rousing sermon, "The time is fulfilled, and the kingdom of God is at hand. Repent, and believe the gospel!" (Mark 1:15). John shows the incarnate Son starting his ministry among his own family and their neighbors, not with a sermon or miracles to amaze a multitude, but by attending a wedding party and providing a simple sign—abundant and delicious wine for all. The wedding at Cana is a foretaste of good things to come, a sign for those who have eyes to see and hearts prepared to trust in the love of God. Later in the Fourth Gospel, Jesus will say, "I came that they may have life, and have it abundantly" (10:10). The six jars that once held water for the Law's rites of purification now hold the wine of joy and gladness, because the One for whom the Law was a preparation has arrived at last.

Jesus's provision of wine for the wedding is a wonderful sign for Christians and for those in our day who take pleasure in portraying Christians as party-poopers, wet blankets, and kill-joys. The story of the wedding at Cana says, "Not so!" God does not mean the community of his Son's disciples to be an assembly of unsmiling faces, stingy dispositions, and no fun. Jesus shows that life among the saints is meant to be full of gladness, delight, and abundance—laughter, wine, and dance music, where a good time is had by all. Jesus displays at the outset of his mission an open-handed, generous, gracious approach to the world, drawing into the celebration of divine abundance all that, like the humble villagers of Galilee, are poor, marginalized, and lowly. At Cana, Jesus gives the sign that God is now among us, one of us. His light is shining.

2:13–25. Jesus issues his first challenge to the temple authorities.

Vv. 13–16. In the temple Jesus finds money-changers and sellers of sacrificial animals.

INTRODUCTION. We come now to the first of three Passovers mentioned in the Fourth Gospel (for the other two, see 6:4–65 and 11:55–20:29). Hostility to Jesus begins at this first Passover, when the temple authorities identify the man from Nazareth as a danger to them. Hostility to Jesus increases after the second Passover, when it is evident that not only is the Son of God misunderstood and unrecognized by the chief priests and elders but also by the crowds who have been following him and have seen his signs. The hostility reaches its climax at the time of the third and final Passover, when Jesus is betrayed, arrested, crucified, and raised from the dead.

With 2:13–25, John begins to show Jesus as a radical disturber of the temple establishment, a figure as unwelcome to the high priest and his associates as the prophet Jeremiah had been to their predecessors six hundred years earlier, or as Martin Luther would be to the Pope fifteen hundred years later. John tells us that after a brief visit to Capernaum (2:12), Jesus goes up to Jerusalem for the Passover. Other than Luke's descriptions of Jesus presented in the temple as an infant and taken there as a twelve-year old, the Synoptic gospels tell of only one Jerusalem visit—at the Passover season of his death and resurrection. The common assumption that Jesus has a three-year ministry is based on John's chronology.

All four gospels describe Jesus overturning the money changers' tables and driving out those who sold sacrificial animals. However, only John places the incident at the beginning of Jesus's ministry—the first thing he does on his first recorded visit to Jerusalem. The other gospels locate the event immediately after the triumphal entry.[6] John's decision to place the episode early, rather than being a correction of the Synoptic chronology, is more likely a theological choice, inspired by the way John wants to tell Jesus's story. John's structure allows readers to see much of what follows as the working out of a process which the Son of Man initiates during this first Passover and which he concludes at his final Passover in Jerusalem, when he offers himself as the Lamb of God who takes away the sin of the world.

It is important for modern readers to recognize that when the Roman armies destroyed Jerusalem and leveled its temple in 70 CE, the traumatic impact on all Jews was both personally devastating and spiritually disorienting—for those who rejected Jesus as Messiah as well as for those who followed him. The center of their religious world, the place God had chosen to be "the dwelling place of his name," was obliterated. It was not only the holiest spot on earth for the people of Israel, the dazzlingly beautiful temple was new. Its construction ended only a short time before its destruction. Jews needed to find some way to understand why the Almighty had allowed such a thing to happen.

It is possible the author of the Fourth Gospel intended his original audience to interpret Jesus's behavior in the temple as a symbolic rejection of the entire existing sacrificial system. Since the temple had been destroyed 20–25 years before John's Gospel began to circulate, and no rebuilding plans were under way, it would be comforting for Jewish believers to know that Jesus himself had abolished the temple sacrifices. This is the position taken by the anonymous author of the Letter to the Hebrews, which scholars date to the late 60s CE. The writer of Hebrews paraphrases Ps 40:6–8, regarding the psalm as Christ's own words, "when he came into the world" (Heb 10:5).[7] Then he comments, "When he [Christ] said . . . 'Thou hast neither desired nor taken pleasure in sacrifices and offerings and burnt offerings and sin offerings' (these are offered according to the Law), then he added, 'Lo, I have come to do thy will.' He abolishes the first in order to establish the second. And by that will we have been sanctified through the offering of the body of Jesus Christ once for all" (Heb 10:8–10).

If John's readers understand Jesus as declaring that the temple sacrifices are now superseded, they are prepared for what Jesus will say later to the woman at the well in Samaria, "Woman, believe me, the hour is coming when neither on this mountain nor

---

6. Keener, *Gospel of John*, 1:518.

7. Heb 10:5b–7: "Sacrifices and offerings thou hast not desired, but a body hast thou prepared for me; in burnt offerings and sin offerings thou hast taken no pleasure. Then I said, 'Lo, I have come to do thy will, O God,' as it is written of me in the roll of the book." (See Ps 40:6–8.)

in Jerusalem will you worship the Father. You worship what you do not know; we worship what we know, for salvation is from the Jews. But the hour is coming, and now is, when the true worshipers will worship the Father in spirit and truth, for such the Father seeks to worship him. God is spirit, and those who worship him must worship in spirit and truth" (4:21–24).

Elimination of animal sacrifices is not a novel idea; it appears frequently in the prophets.[8] John intends his audience to understand that when Jesus refers to the temple as "my Father's house," he is stating the basis of his authority to make pronouncement about how God's people should worship. For the first time in John's Gospel, Jesus explicitly identifies himself as Son of God. It's a little surprising that when "the Jews" later confront him concerning his behavior they make no comment about this claim. However, even though they do not mention it now, they will not forget it. At his trial before Pilate, the elders of the people say to the Roman governor, "We have a law, and by that law he ought to die, because he has made himself the Son of God" (19:7).

> **[2:13–16]** *13 The Passover of the Jews was at hand, and Jesus went up to Jerusalem. 14 In the temple he found those who were selling oxen and sheep and pigeons, and the money-changers at their business. 15 And making a whip of cords, he drove them all, with the sheep and oxen, out of the temple; and he poured out the coins of the money-changers and overturned their tables. 16 And he told those who sold the pigeons, "Take these things away; you shall not make my Father's house a house of trade."*

RESPONSE. Although this is the first visit of Jesus to the temple described by John, it is not Jesus's first experience as a Passover pilgrim. The Law requires all adult Jewish males to assemble before the Lord three times a year—at Passover, at Pentecost, and at the Feast of Tabernacles. Most Jews who live a significant distance from Jerusalem can't get there three times a year, but those within a week's journey by foot are sure to make the trip. Jesus arrives slightly in advance of the feast, as many Passover pilgrims do, in order to undergo any rites of purification that might be necessary to prepare for the feast.

Since it's impractical for most worshipers to come to Jerusalem carrying a lamb or leading an ox during a week on the road, a bazaar or animal market is provided for the sale of unblemished animals and birds suitable for sacrifice. In Jesus's time this bazaar is found in the newly-enlarged outer court of the temple, the only area of the vast enclosure to which non-Jews are admitted. This strategic placement makes it

---

8. See Powell, "Deal-Breakers," 277–82. Jesus's prophetic gesture could be seen as a protest against the cult of sacrifice similar to those recorded in the books of Amos, Hosea, Isaiah, Jeremiah, and Malachi. For example, in Isa 1:11, the Lord says, "I have enough of burnt offerings of rams and the fat of fed beasts; I do not delight in the blood of bulls, or of lambs, or of he-goats." Hosea 6:6 is equally familiar, "I desire steadfast love and not sacrifice, the knowledge of God, rather than burnt offerings." Psalm 50 proclaims that "a sacrifice of thanksgiving" (v. 14) is what the Lord desires rather than animal offerings, for God does not "eat the flesh of bulls or drink the blood of goats" (v. 13).

accessible to Gentiles as well as Jews who want to buy animals for offerings. Indeed, many private sacrifices are offered by non-Jews each day. Even the Roman emperor endowed a daily sacrifice to be offered in his name.

Jesus tries to expel the animal sellers and money changers from the outer court of the temple, but why? We want to understand the real reason behind his act. Is it because the sale of animals and the changing of money pollutes the sacred space? Surely not. The huge outer court of the temple—newly enlarged by Herod's expansion of the Temple Mount—is a profane zone by definition, even by name, not technically part of the sacred space of temple proper. The so-called Court of the Gentiles is meant to be a place where unclean people might come. Jesus's expulsion of the money changers and animal sellers can't have been meant as a "cleansing," since nobody—including Jesus—expects the outer court to be ritually pure.[9]

Our next tendency is to assume that the sale of sacrificial animals in the temple is a racket, a form of profiteering against which Jesus is objecting. This accusation shows up in the writings of the rabbis and is repeated in many Bible commentaries. Yet the temple is also the center for Jewish charitable giving, and there's evidence that some wealthy Jews are glad to buy up sacrificial animals and offer them for resale in the temple's animal bazaar at prices their poorer co-religionists can afford. (By law, no sacrifice is acceptable if the one who offers it acquires it at no cost.) It seems that although sometimes animal sellers extort high prices, at other times the prices are fair. The animal market is probably a typical oriental bazaar where a number of competing vendors occupy their own stalls. Buyers find an animal and negotiate with the vendor over the price. This still goes on in public markets all over Asia and Africa. Price-fixing is difficult in such settings.

The money-changing business is different. It is seasonal, operating in the temple only right before Passover, when the half-shekel temple tax is due. Money changers swap other coins for Tyrian silver shekels, the only money acceptable under rabbinical law for payment of the temple tax or monetary donations.[10] Money changers charge a commission fixed by law. It's handsome but not unreasonable. The Sanhedrin does not countenance fraud or dishonest business practices. The temple itself receives a financial benefit from the money changers, income essential in order for the temple to continue its function as the initiator of public works.[11]

9. John uses the Greek word *hieron* for the entire temple area, including the outer court (the so-called Court of the Gentiles), and the word *naos* for the sacred space. The RSV translates both Greek words as "temple." Bahat, "Jesus and the Herodian Temple Mount," 303–7, gives a careful description of the large area of landfill which Herod added to the original Temple Mount. This expanded area, while part of the *hieron*, was outside the *naos* (the sacred enclosure) and could be used for secular activity. The laws of ritual purity did not apply to it.

10. The Tyrian coins were of pure silver and the very best weight, which seems to be why the temple rules required that they alone be used. Oddly, these coins were marked on one side with the image of the Tyrian god, Melqart-Herakles, and on the other with an eagle, two "graven images" otherwise forbidden under Jewish law. See Franz, "Tyrian Shekel."

11. Bahat, "Jesus and the Herodian Temple Mount," 306.

What Jesus does in the outer court of the temple is a *prophetic act*. In John's Gospel, Jesus is Son of God and also a prophet whose mission is to proclaim God's living word to his people. Jesus not only speaks this word, but embodies it. Indeed, he *is* the living Word. In the Old Testament we see prophets making public pronouncements in God's name and acting out God's messages through symbolic gestures. For example, Ahijah tears a garment into twelve pieces (1 Kgs 11:30); Hosea marries a prostitute (Hos 1:2); Jeremiah wears an ox-yoke (Jer 27:2); and Ezekiel eats a scroll (Ezek 3:3). Going to the temple as a Passover pilgrim and expelling the sellers of sacrificial animals and money changers is a classic Old Testament-style prophetic gesture. It doesn't matter whether Jesus actually manages single-handedly to expel from the outer court all the lambs and goats and oxen with their wranglers, all the dove sellers with their birds, and all the money changers. That would have been virtually impossible for one man, and it wasn't necessary under the circumstances. Jesus brandishes a whip of cords and creates a public scene. He pours out bags of coins and turns over some money changers' tables, shouting, "Take these things away; you shall not make my Father's house a house of trade." The prophetic point is made. A number of bystanders see, hear, and take notice, and a report goes immediately to the highest authorities.[12]

If it is unlikely that Jesus is trying to turn an intentionally profane area into a part of the sanctuary, and if he is not troubled that some vendors in the bazaar might be taking a profit, what else could be motivating him to perform this dramatic gesture? The answer is found in what he cries out, "Take these things away; you shall not make my Father's house *a house of trade*." Those who make offerings in the temple (not all of which are animal sacrifices) do so for a variety of reasons, e. g. , thank offerings, expiatory offerings, purificative offerings, or votive offerings (i.e., offerings made in fulfillment of a vow). The latter category of offering is by far the most common. Jesus knows that many worshipers assume that in presenting sacrificial offerings they are making a *material transaction* with God—that is to say, a "trade."[13] This would be particularly true in the case of the many sacrifices presented in fulfillment of vows. For example, a sheep owner whose flock is dying of disease might make a vow like this, "Lord, if you cure the murrain that is killing my sheep, I will offer you a dozen lambs next spring." Such thinking turns worship into a business arrangement with the Almighty. If the Lord gives me what I want, then I will give him something valuable in return. This is a "Let's make a deal" approach to God—bargaining for God's favor. Kings would take a line like this, "O God, if you give me victory over my enemies, I will give ten thousand shekels of gold to your temple and offer five hundred bulls on your altar."

Transactional materialism like this is the rule in pagan religion. In paganism, the gods are regarded as powerful and immortal, but otherwise assumed to be quite

12. Keener, *Gospel of John*, 1:522–27.

13. Powell thinks Jesus objects not to all sacrifice, but to offerings by those who regard God's house as "a place of commerce, where the forgiveness of sins can be purchased by the unrepentant." Powell, "Deal-Breakers," 277–78.

like human beings. They have no love for mortals. Their aid can only be purchased by gifts and sacrifices. Although the God of Abraham, Isaac, and Jacob reveals himself as a God of covenant love and faithfulness, wholly unlike the divinities of the Gentiles, the pagan "commercial" attitude toward God is common in ancient Judaism. Unfortunately, it can also be found in contemporary Christianity. Both consciously and unconsciously we frequently behave as if we could negotiate a deal with God, particularly if we're afraid of dying. This transactional approach denies both God's sovereignty and God's grace.

Jesus proclaims that God deals with his children as a loving and compassionate Father, not as a provider of services in the spiritual commodities market, looking for the most profitable exchange. God has no needs of any kind. God is always a giver, never a seller. There is nothing we have that does not come to us as God's gift; thus, we have nothing to offer him in trade. God doesn't want offerings from us; he only wants us to imitate him, as beloved children imitate their Father. (See Eph 5:1–2.) God is gracious, merciful, and generous. He wants us to be the same.

Recognition of this truth inspired some Hebrew prophets to inveigh against the role that burnt offerings played in their people's worship. To reverse a modern expression, such sacrifices are easily identified as "religious," but are not necessarily "spiritual." Jesus's expulsion of the sellers of sacrificial animals and money changers reminds us of the truth of David's words, "Thou hast no delight in sacrifice; were I to give a burnt offering, thou wouldst not be pleased. The sacrifice acceptable to God is a broken spirit; a broken and contrite heart, O God, thou wilt not despise" (Ps 51:16–17). As Jesus later tells the Samaritan woman, "God is spirit, and those who worship him must worship in spirit and truth" (4:24). It is reasonable for us to imagine that Jesus would have gladly purified temple worship by eliminating animal sacrifices.

Vv. 17–22. "The Jews" want to know the source of Jesus's authority.

INTRODUCTION. Our author puts his narrative together purposefully. John uses this episode in the temple and Jesus's dialogue with the Jewish authorities as a dramatic, public illustration of what Jesus says to Nathanael in 1:51—the person of the Son of God will hereafter be the point of communication and communion between God and humankind. It also sets up Jesus's first confrontation with agents of the temple authorities. Starting here, readers will observe the growing mistrust, misunderstanding, and hostility of the priestly hierarchy, which will culminate in the Sanhedrin's perverse response to the raising of Lazarus from the dead: the decision that Jesus must die (11:47–53).

John's audience will grasp that they are now meant to understand their risen Lord as both the replacement of the now-destroyed temple itself (2:22) and as the perfect oblation for which the many former sacrifices were only an anticipation. Jesus is "the Lamb of God who takes away the sin of the world." What Jesus says and does in 2:13–25 has significance similar to the changing of water to wine at the wedding feast. The theme of replacement is illustrated here for a second time in chapter 2. We will note its appearance later in other settings. The Jewish authorities in the narrative have no idea what Jesus is talking about when he tells them, "Destroy this temple, and in three days I will raise it up" (2:19). His disciples ultimately will understand, and so will believers who read John's Gospel.[14] N.T. Wright describes the gospel writer's intent this way,

> John's Jesus is saying that the resurrection will be the ultimate sign that demonstrates both his right to do what he has done and the meaning he gives to it. The present temple system is corrupt and under divine judgment; Jesus's own death and resurrection will be the means of the true God doing the new thing through which . . . that which was hitherto accomplished through the temple would from now on be accomplished through Jesus himself. The resurrection will inaugurate a new world in which temple-worship will be thrown open to all and sundry, irrespective of geography and ethnic backgrounds.[15]

When Jesus's reply is reported to the high priest and his colleagues, they imagine this man is an upstart, self-proclaimed prophet threatening to destroy the temple. Such people come along from time to time. They may be crackpots, but they might also be dangerous; therefore, the authorities always treat their threats seriously. In Mark's version of Jesus's hearing before the Sanhedrin on the night before his crucifixion, witnesses accuse him of saying, "I will destroy this temple that is made with hands, and in three days I will build another, not made with hands" (14:58; Mark also quotes something similar being voiced by bystanders on Golgotha, 15:29).

John makes clear in vv. 17–22 that his interpretation of what Jesus means by "Destroy this temple, and in three days I will raise it up," arises from extended post-Easter reflection by the disciples. It's something no one understands until after Jesus is raised from the dead. The idea that the Messiah, when he comes, will purify or even rebuild the temple is an old one. But if Jesus simply means to give the priestly authorities a version of this old messianic claim, why does he introduce the phrase "in three days"? Even if we concede that John substitutes the word "raise" for the word "build" (used in Mark 14:58 and 15:29), the modifying phrase "in three days"—which occurs in all three gospel versions of the saying—still looks like a resurrection prediction, one not very different from those occurring in the Synoptics (e.g., Mark 8:31; Matt 17:22–23; Luke 9:22).[16]

In John's Gospel the temple authorities now begin paying close attention to what Jesus says and does. The high priest will be advised of his presence the next time Jesus

14. John's apocalyptic vision of the heavenly Jerusalem echoes the idea that Jesus, the Lamb, replaces the temple, "I saw no temple in the city, for its temple is the Lord God the Almighty and the Lamb" (Rev 21:22).

15. Wright, *Resurrection*, 441. See, e.g., 4:19–24.

16. Smith, *John*, 90–91.

appears in the temple. Every time Jesus shows himself in the House of God hereafter, he will face a challenge from the Jewish hierarchy.

It is important for modern readers to keep in mind that the devastating war with Rome in 66–73 CE, which one author describes as "the first holocaust," results not only in the leveling of the temple (in the year 70), but in the annihilation or enslavement of every Jew found in the fallen city. A total of more than 1.1 million perish in the First Jewish War, representing a larger percentage of the entire Jewish population than the number killed in the twentieth century by the Nazis.[17] This terrible event takes place a generation before John's Gospel is published. Therefore, John's original audience reads Jesus's words, "Destroy this temple, and in three days I will raise it up" (v. 19), with the knowledge that the temple was indeed destroyed. That it has not yet been rebuilt, nor the former sacrificial system restored, does not eliminate every hope for a re-establishment of temple worship. However, it does create an environment in which other possibilities for the future of God's people must be considered—including a new understanding of the worship God desires.

> **[2:17–22]** *17 His disciples remembered that it was written, "Zeal for thy house will consume me." 18 The Jews then said to him, "What sign have you to show us for doing this?" 19 Jesus answered them, "Destroy this temple, and in three days I will raise it up." 20 The Jews then said, "It has taken forty-six years to build this temple, and will you raise it up in three days?" 21 But he spoke of the temple of his body. 22 When therefore he was raised from the dead, his disciples remembered that he had said this; and they believed the Scripture and the word which Jesus had spoken.*

RESPONSE. The temple authorities, "the Jews" as John often calls them, see what Jesus does as an unwarranted interruption of an entirely proper business being conducted in a part of the temple precincts where they could not violate the sanctity of the House of God. What Jesus does seems a challenge to their authority. They wonder what right this Galilean has to create such scene. And what does he mean by describing the temple as "my Father's house"? What kind of authority does he claim to have?

The angry priests have many questions, which is why they ask what "sign" Jesus can show them that might signify authority for him to do what he has done. They want to see divine credentials from this Galilean disturber of the Passover peace. However, instead of providing the kind of miraculous sign they'd like to see, such as making the sun move backwards on the sundial the way Isaiah did for King Hezekiah (Isa 38:8), Jesus makes an assertion both incomprehensible and unforgettable, "Destroy this temple, and in three days I will raise it up." John intends us to hear this as a prediction of Jesus's death and resurrection, *the* ultimate sign he will give. Naturally, "the Jews" don't get it, and so they make a sarcastic rejoinder. The gospel writer employs a technique of misunderstanding repeatedly, often in situations where Jesus is face-to-face

---

17. Carroll, *Christ Actually*, 46–53.

with his enemies, as here. This is sometimes a literary device which allows John to insert Jesus's explanation, though that does not occur here.

When the first audience for John's Gospel reads the story of Jesus's prophetic act in 2:13–17, most of them understand it as a sign that God has replaced the old perpetually offered sacrifices of the temple rites with the once-for-all self-oblation of Jesus, "the Lamb of God who takes away the sin of the world." This is underscored when John tells of Jesus being sentenced to death by Pilate on the day of preparation of the Passover at the precise time the sacrifice of the lambs is beginning in the temple (19:14).

John's community has learned to hear Jesus's words in 2:19 as meaning that just as in the rabbinical Law with its many sacrifices is now superseded, so also its temple is now replaced. Herod's beautiful temple lies in ruins and there have been no sacrifices for a quarter of a century. Jesus's body is now the "temple" where God abides. Those who listen as John's Gospel is read aloud in their Christian gatherings may also hear from time to time some of the letters of Paul and Peter. Perhaps they're starting to envision themselves as the Body of Christ—a holy temple built of "living stones" (1 Cor 12:12–27; Eph 2:14–21; 1 Pet 2:4–10).[18]

If Christ himself—in the sense of the "Body of Christ," Paul's name for the church (see, e.g., 1 Cor 12:12–27)—has now replaced the ruined Jerusalem temple as the proper locus for worship, this suggests how twenty-first century readers of John might think about our own ways of worship. Human beings instinctively grow attached to holy places. We see this phenomenon in every age, from prehistoric times down to the present. There is nothing objectionable about having emotional attachment to the church where we have worshiped for many years or reverence for a special place where we have experienced God's closeness. (It's clear in the Fourth Gospel that Jesus has both respect for and attachment to the Jerusalem temple, even though he is announcing its replacement.) Worship in the sense of an *encounter* between God and God's people, the experience of "meeting the Lord," happens in the context of community with one another in Christ. This is the message of the Fourth Gospel. This encounter depends in no way on a physical, geographical setting. It *does* depend on the assembled worshipers' shared sense of union with Jesus. This will be implied by Jesus in his conversation with the woman of Samaria (4:21–24) and is what he seems to mean in Matt 18:20, when he tells his disciples, "Where two or three are gathered in my name, there am I in the midst of them."

Vv. 23–25. Jesus does not trust those whose belief is based only on miracles.

INTRODUCTION. Although signs play an important role in John's Gospel, he is careful to tell his readers that Jesus does not fully trust those who "believe in his

18. See Keener, *Gospel of John*, 1:526–27.

name" only because they have seen miracles, which are the sort of "signs" alluded to in v. 23.[19] Their "believing" is of a preliminary and lesser quality than believing based on confidence in the truth of Jesus's words. John never uses the Greek noun usually translated as "faith" or "belief" in English. For the author of the Fourth Gospel, believing is something one *does*, and he invariably expresses it as an active verb implying a relationship between the believer and the one in whom he believes. John knows no such phenomenon as a "faith" which someone possesses.

> **[2:23–25]** *²³ Now when he was in Jerusalem at the Passover feast, many believed in his name when they saw the signs which he did; ²⁴ but Jesus did not trust himself to them, ²⁵ because he knew all men and needed no one to bear witness of man; for he himself knew what was in man.*

RESPONSE. John does not describe the "signs" which "many" saw when Jesus "was in Jerusalem at the Passover feast," prompting them to "believe in his name." Perhaps the author wants his audience to regard Jesus's expulsion of the money changers and sellers of sacrificial animals as a certain *kind* of sign, albeit not a miraculous one. We will note other places where this gospel makes indefinite references to "signs" beyond the seven the author describes in detail. John's audience undoubtedly knows at least one other written gospel and is probably aware of more miracle stories, so it's enough for the author simply to allude here to other signs. His readers' imaginations will fill in the blanks.

John tells us that although there are people who after seeing Jesus's miracles demonstrate a certain kind of "belief in his name," their belief is inadequate. It may lead them to follow Jesus from place to place for a time, but only because they hope to see him perform more miraculous healings. They do believe he's a miracle-worker; they may even believe he is sent by God; however, they haven't seen his glory and don't know him. For the Fourth Gospel, as we see from Andrew's and the Beloved Disciple's response to Jesus's question "What do you seek" (1:38–39), true and trust-worthy believers are *those who seek to know Jesus.* Therefore, Jesus—who discerns the thoughts of everyone—does not "trust himself" to people who only seek "signs and wonders"(4:48). The multitude he feeds in chapter 6 will be composed of such people, opportunists who want to use Jesus for their own ends. (See 6:22–27.)

We will not see Jesus fully trust himself to anyone until his hour comes and he tells his beloved brothers, "If you had known me, you would have known my Father also; henceforth you know him and have seen him" (14:7); and "No longer do I call you servants, for the servant does not know what his master is doing; but I have called

---

19. In biblical language, to speak of the "name" of God (or the "name" of any human being), was a reference to what we today would call the *person* of God and sometimes the *presence* of God. To believe in Jesus's "name" is to believe in the reality of what Jesus can do—i.e., his wonder-working power. See Malina and Rohrbaugh, *Social Science Commentary*, 247.

you friends, for all that I have heard from my Father I have made known to you" (15:15).

Doing Your Own Theology

Questions for reflection after reading John 2.

- The miracle at Cana is often treated as an illustration of John's theology of fulfill-ment and replacement. Jesus replaces the water intended for Jewish rites of puri-fication with the messianic banquet's wine of gladness and celebration, marking the arrival of the New Age.—*As you reflect on your own life, can you see where Christ has replaced something you formerly depended on? What did he replace? How did this come about?*

- It is essential for us to keep in mind that at the time John's Gospel was first distributed, the temple in Jerusalem had been in ruins for over twenty years. It would never be rebuilt. Loss of their temple, the sacred and traditional "point of contact" between God and his chosen people, was spiritually and psychologically devastating to all Jews, even if they lived far from the Holy Land. Both Jesus's friends and his enemies recalled that Jesus had said something like "destroy this temple and in three days I will raise it up" (2:19). Jesus's followers had to grapple with what he meant by that, and they did not understand it until after Easter.—*For Christians in our own day, what kind of loss might we experience that would be comparable to the Jews' loss of their temple in the first century? What is our "point of contact" with God?*

- Religious people in every culture known to history have tried to bargain with God, to buy God's favor, either with votive offerings or pledges to change their behavior or undertake some heroic endeavor. These people hope to "make a deal" with God.—*If we cannot win God's favor by votive offerings or promises, how can we please God? What does God seek from those who believe in his Son?*

Chapter Three

3:1–15. Jesus teaches Nicodemus about new birth.

Vv. 1–6. "Unless one is born anew, he cannot see the kingdom of God."

INTRODUCTION. John introduces us to Nicodemus, who—like Nathanael—appears only in the Fourth Gospel. He describes Nicodemus as a "ruler of the Jews," meaning a member of the Great Sanhedrin, surely a scribe and a Pharisee.[1] All we know about Nicodemus is what we read in John, although there is some historical information about the prominent family of which he might possibly be a leading member.[2] If Nicodemus is indeed the patriarch of the Bet Gurion family, he is one of the wealthiest men in Jerusalem. Like the Rich Ruler in Luke 18:18–23, he is an affluent, important man who is drawn to Jesus, even though most of his peers are not. John intends for us to recognize Nicodemus as someone who has seen Jesus's "signs" (v. 2) and has come to "believe in his name" (2:23), though belief merely based on witnessing miracles is less than what Jesus wants from people. He calls Jesus "Rabbi," the way his first disciples do (1:38). We'll encounter Nicodemus again twice, at 7:50 and at 19:39. In his final appearance, publicly associated with Joseph of Arimathea in the burial of Jesus, Nicodemus seems to have become a trustworthy and true disciple, whose "deeds have been wrought in God" (3:21).

Jesus's conversation with Nicodemus is a dialogue which leads to the first of a number of theological teachings in John (which scholars often call *discourses*). Its setting, as part of a conversation between Jesus and this seeker who comes out of the darkness of the world to find the light of Christ, allows John to provide basic counsel

---

1. Jeremias, *Jerusalem*, 237, 255.

2. See Bauckham, *Testimony*, 137–72. Keener, *Gospel of John*, 1:535, dismisses identification of Nicodemus with the famous Naqdimon ben Gurion (sometimes spelled *Gorion*), who would have been a young man at the time of Jesus. Jeremias, *Jerusalem*, 95–96, comments on the wealth of the scribe Nicodemus, whose family was most likely part of the rich Jerusalem merchant class.

for readers whose faith needs to grow deeper. The substance of this and later dialogues and discourses in the gospel may be formulated from teachings the Beloved Disciple gave to his own followers in the first Christian generation, grounded in his memory of the way Jesus himself spoke to those around him but probably not offering verbatim quotations, except when a saying is introduced by "Truly, truly, I say to you," as in v. 3.

Jesus's vocabulary in vv. 3–8 is marked by use of Greek words that have multiple meanings: anew/again/from above, see/perceive/recognize, wind/breath/spirit, and sound/call/voice.[3] "Unless one is born anew, he cannot see the kingdom of God" (v. 3) is a well-known and frequently-quoted saying of Jesus. The Greek version is perhaps intentionally ambiguous in one further way, since the verb translated "born" is a form that can equally apply to the role of the father in the birth of a child. Because the word translated "again" also can be translated "from above," we may legitimately translate the sentence as, "No one can see the kingdom of God without being begotten from above."[4] John emphasizes that those who believe in God's Son receive power to become God's children. Therefore, Nicodemus should understand "being begotten from above" as describing the experience of becoming God's child, entering a relationship of such closeness with God that he acquires a level of insight into the Father's purposes—begins "to see the kingdom of God." Later in the gospel, in the scene that describes the trial before Pilate, Jesus's explanation of the nature of his kingship—which is "not of this world" (18:35–37)—enables readers to grasp more fully what he means by "the kingdom of God" in this dialogue with Nicodemus. Unfortunately, despite his great learning, the elderly scribe does not grasp what Jesus wants to teach him.

> [3:1–6] *¹ Now there was a man of the Pharisees, named Nicode′mus, a ruler of the Jews. ² This man came to Jesus by night and said to him, "Rabbi, we know that you are a teacher come from God; for no one can do these signs that you do, unless God is with him." ³ Jesus answered him, "Truly, truly, I say to you, unless one is born anew, he cannot see the kingdom of God." ⁴ Nicode′mus said to him, "How can a man be born when he is old? Can he enter a second time into his mother's womb and be born?" ⁵ Jesus answered, "Truly, truly, I say to you, unless one is born of water and the Spirit, he cannot enter the kingdom of God. ⁶ That which is born of the flesh is flesh, and that which is born of the Spirit is spirit.*

RESPONSE. We can only make an educated guess about what kind of person Nicodemus was, but an informed imagination can sometimes lead to deeper understanding. In this reflection I picture Nicodemus as an insider, a prominent older man, a scribe of great dignity and status, a man with a reputation of which he is duly proud.[5] A very

---

3. The four Greek words with multiple meanings are *anōthen, idein, pneuma,* and *phōnē.*

4. Brown, *John I–XII,* 128; Keener, *Gospel of John,* 1:537.

5. A Jewish "scribe" in this period (*grammateus* in Greek) is an expert in interpretation of the Law—a jurist, theologian, and teacher. Contemporary Bibles that translate the word as "lawyer" give

wealthy man, he's also a member of the Great Sanhedrin. Nicodemus's status does not derive from his political connections, but from the fact that he's an authentically holy man, a *rabbi* worthy of the title—a judge, theologian, and teacher. In fact, Jesus calls him "*the* teacher of Israel" (v. 10).[6] Scribes of Nicodemus's stature are accorded greater public honor than any other figures in Jewish life, even high priests.[7]

From what he has seen of Jesus thus far, Nicodemus concludes that this Galilean villager is a true prophet, called by God from the practice of his trade to preach to Israel much the same way God called Amos "the herdsman and dresser of sycamore trees" seven and a half centuries before. (See Amos 7:12–15.) Because he has sincere regard for Jesus, Nicodemus starts their conversation by offering the prophet from Nazareth a compliment, even treating him as a peer: "Rabbi, we know that you are a teacher come from God; for no one can do these signs that you do, unless God is with him" (v. 2). Although he's a colleague of the elders and most prominent wise men of Israel, Nicodemus might not be willing to describe any of them as having "come from God." He knows them too well. Jesus is different; Jesus is clearly special, although Nicodemus doesn't yet realize how special he is. "Prophet" is a category this Great Sanhedrin member understands, a category most Jews deeply respect, even though the chief priests and their fellow Sadducees do not recognize the spiritual authority of prophets in the way Nicodemus and other Pharisees do.

Commentators and preachers have customarily treated this prominent scribe's visit to Jesus at night as a clandestine meeting—arranged to take place after dark so the great man might not suffer public embarrassment while calling on a Galilean tradesman-turned-prophet who has drawn critical attention from the high priest and his associates. I imagine a rather different scenario for the occasion, however. Jewish sages were reputed to discuss the Torah by lamplight late into the night; therefore, a night-time visit to Jesus by a great teacher like Nicodemus might be treated as a gesture of admiration from the old theologian to the young prophet, whom he generously and kindly addresses as "rabbi" even though he knows Jesus has no formal rabbinical standing.[8]

If, in fact, Nicodemus the eminent scribe is also a prominent member (or perhaps even the patriarch) of the rich Bet Gurion clan, he is a person of the highest social and economic status. Such a gentleman will be carried through the Jerusalem streets in a

---

readers the best sense of the actual role of scribes. The respectful title *rabbi* ("great one") is usually accorded only to scribes. Scribes regularly teach in synagogues. The Great Sanhedrin is made up of representatives of three groups, chief priests, elders (heads of aristocratic families), and scribes. Scribes in the Sanhedrin are the most senior, most renowned teachers and interpreters of the Law in the land. Scribes can be either Pharisees or Sadducees, but in the time of Jesus the scribal members of the Sanhedrin are all Pharisees. See Reicke, *New Testament Era*, 124, 146, 150–63; Jeremias, *Jerusalem*, 233–45.

6. The RSV translates with the indefinite article, "a teacher," but the Greek is clearly "the."

7. Jeremias, *Jerusalem*, 243–44.

8. Malina and Rohrbaugh, *Social Science Commentary*, 81. See Bauckham, *Testimony*, 165–66.

sedan chair borne by servants, accompanied by an entourage including torch-bearers and armed retainers.[9] Furthermore, since Nicodemus is going as a well-known scribe to visit a man he wishes to treat as a fellow-teacher, he will also be accompanied by his own disciples, since that is the custom. He's a person of such wealth and rank that he can pay a visit to whomever he chooses, without concern for what other people might think. Nicodemus has the sort of social standing that insulates a person against embarrassment. If his visit to Jesus of Nazareth attracts attention, so what? The great man's high regard for Jesus is more likely to elevate the unknown Galilean in the eyes of others than to lower their opinion of Nicodemus. We don't know in whose house they meet, but it is probably a substantial household, and Jesus's disciples will certainly be present with their Master to receive this eminent "teacher of Israel" and his disciples.

Many Jews are anticipating the day when "the kingdom will be restored to Israel," meaning a kingdom like that of David and Solomon.[10] This restored kingdom will be indisputable proof of God's power, displayed in a form that the Romans cannot fail to acknowledge—military power. First century Jews of every party are aware of something twenty-first century Christians often don't know: God's ancient title, *Yahweh Sabaoth*, "Lord of Hosts," acclaims him as Lord of Armies, the King of Heaven, and a God of war with countless fighting angels at his disposal. This confidence helps give spiritual energy to two great, virtually suicidal armed rebellions against Rome, first in 66–73 and again in 132–5. At the time John's Gospel is ready to be published, the first of these wars has already taken place, and its devastating consequences weigh on every Jewish mind.[11] This war is *the* pivotal event of Jewish history. If we ignore this fact, we overlook an essential element of the background against which the Fourth Gospel is set.

As their talk begins, Jesus doesn't respond diplomatically to Nicodemus's flattering salutation. Instead he says, "Truly, truly, I say to you, unless one is born anew, he cannot see the kingdom of God" (v. 3).[12] "Born again" is how the King James Version translates this. People make jokes about born-again Christians. We've all seen the bumper stickers that say, "Being born once is enough." We've heard the jokes—maybe even told a few ourselves. Despite the ridicule, everybody understands at least a little bit about what it means to be "born anew." Jesus is saying Nicodemus needs a fresh vision of God's work in the world. Jesus tells this venerable "teacher of Israel" that unless he becomes a new creation—"born anew" or "begotten from above"—he will never

9. Jeremias, *Jerusalem*, 92–99, describes the opulent lifestyle of Jerusalem's wealthy class in the time of Jesus.

10. See Acts 1:6 and Mic 4:8–13.

11. According to Josephus, *Wars*, VI.ix.3, 587–88, more than 1,000,000 Jews died and 97,000 were sold into slavery.

12. The two Greek words used here can be translated into English as "born (or begotten) anew," "born (or begotten) again," or "born (or begotten) from above." Many modern translations include at least one or more of the variations in marginal notes.

perceive the truth of God's kingdom. He will never see the world through God's eyes. When we think of Nicodemus as an old man, perhaps well into his seventies, Jesus's admonition to him to be "born anew" acquires a new and paradoxical character.[13] The elderly aristocrat is nearing the end of a long life. What can the young prophet mean by telling him that he now needs to be "begotten from above"?

Nicodemus does believe that Jesus has come from God, but the older man has trouble understanding what he's saying. John describes this grey-bearded gentleman as locked into very firm presuppositions about the Almighty and about human life. If one is born a member of the Covenant People and one keeps the Law with pure devotion, what kind of advantage could come from some "new birth"? He treats Jesus's language about being born anew literally, missing both the metaphor and the double entendre, and asks, "How can a man be born when he is old? Can he enter a second time into his mother's womb and be born?" (v. 4). Readers of John's Gospel understand that Jesus is talking about a heavenly begetting, a transformed perspective that can only be attained when one becomes (as Paul had already put it in 2 Cor 5:17) "a new creation." Regardless of his status as a child of Abraham and a keeper of the Law, for old Nicodemus to gain this new perspective and experience of being "begotten from above," making God his Father, he needs to be *"born of water and the Spirit"* (v. 5).

John's readers already grasp what this means: Nicodemus—even though he's an elder of the Great Sanhedrin and a famous teacher of Torah—can't truly perceive spiritual reality until he's baptized as a disciple of Jesus and moves fully into the light of Christ.[14] The combination of "water" with "Spirit" in v. 5 is an acknowledgement that John understands the bath of baptism as an essential experience for those who would be disciples of Jesus. But it is the Spirit of God moving with mysterious power that makes the disciple a "new creation," a child of God, and puts him for the first time in a position to see as God sees. We twenty-first century Christian readers of the gospel have been baptized, but has anything made us feel literally reborn by the work of God's Spirit? The New Testament elsewhere presumes that those who are reborn by the Spirit will have experiences that demonstrate evidence of this new life (see, e.g., Acts 19:1–7; Rom 8:2–17; 1 Cor 12:1–14:5).

Vv. 7–15. Jesus explains the life-giving work of the Spirit.

INTRODUCTION. Nicodemus disappears from the text after his question in v. 9. It's difficult to discern what part of vv. 10–15 is a direct quotation of Jesus and what part is the gospel writer's own narrative. In v. 13 there's a reference to the ascension

13. There is no certain information from the time of Jesus, but later rabbis indicate that scribal members of the Great Sanhedrin had to be of advanced age. Only such were eligible as had filled three offices of gradually increasing dignity, namely, those of local judge, and member successively of two magistracies at Jerusalem. See Bacher and Lauterbach, "Sanhedrin," 43.

14. See McGowan, *Ancient Christian Worship*, 143.

of the Son of Man, which suggests an observation from the Beloved Disciple's own experience, demonstrating his post-Easter perspective. However, v. 12, "If I have told you earthly things and you do not believe, how can you believe if I tell you heavenly things," is surely meant to be the voice of Jesus. John's Gospel is written consistently in one "voice," without obvious rhetorical differences between the speeches of Jesus and the commentary of the narrator.

Readers need to keep John's habitual use of double entendre in mind. The word for "wind" and the word for "spirit" are identical in Greek and Hebrew. Nicodemus cannot hear Jesus say "wind" without also hearing him say "spirit." To be *begotten from above* is to be born of the Spirit. This birth is heavenly, not earthly or fleshly. It is mystical, "from above."[15] The Greek word translated "sound," also means "call" or "voice." Those who are born of the Spirit will have ears attuned to the Spirit's call. That is to say, they will be open to *inspiration*—an idea which would probably seem strange to an elderly scribe whose life-long approach to understanding the will of God is rooted in the study of oral traditions handed down from earlier generations of Jewish wise men. The idea that the Spirit of God will speak directly to the children of God, providing them with direct guidance and encouragement, is essential to John's theology. Jesus will expound this theme later in his Farewell Discourse (see 14:16–17, 25–26; 15:26; 16:7–15).

Scribes in this era are revered among Jews as custodians of an esoteric tradition, a level of wisdom concerning the works of God which is passed along to only a few men in each generation.[16] By rights, such a prominent teacher should be precisely the kind of man who could grasp what Jesus means regarding the importance of a new birth "from above." Nicodemus, alas, fails to understand Jesus—at least for now.

> [3:7–15] ⁷ *Do not marvel that I said to you, 'You must be born anew.' ⁸ The wind blows where it wills, and you hear the sound of it, but you do not know whence it comes or whither it goes; so it is with everyone who is born of the Spirit." ⁹ Nicode'mus said to him, "How can this be?" ¹⁰ Jesus answered him, "Are you a teacher of Israel, and yet you do not understand this? ¹¹ Truly, truly, I say to you, we speak of what we know, and bear witness to what we have seen; but you do not receive our testimony. ¹² If I have told you earthly things and you do not believe, how can you believe if I tell you heavenly things? ¹³ No one has ascended into heaven but he who descended from heaven, the Son of man. ¹⁴ And as Moses lifted up the serpent in the wilderness, so must the Son of man be lifted up, ¹⁵ that whoever believes in him may have eternal life."*

RESPONSE. Jesus tries to help Nicodemus understand. He tells him, "The wind blows where it wills, and you hear the sound of it, but you do not know whence it comes or

---

15. See Burge, *Anointed Community*, 158, 168–69.

16. Jeremias, *Jerusalem*, 237–42.

whither it goes; so it is with everyone who is born of the Spirit" (v. 8). Meteorologists can explain how much wind we're going to have and from what direction it will be blowing any time of day. However, most of us are as ignorant about these things as Nicodemus was. Unless I look at a weather app on my smartphone, I have no idea where the wind is going to come from, or how hard it's going to blow. I only hear it and feel it on my skin. And I see tree limbs swaying or sometimes breaking in a storm.

But I do know this much: the wind *is* going to blow. Although there may be hours of calm, the wind is certain to blow every day, either in soft breezes or a gale. Sometimes the wind will whisper, and at other times it will roar.[17] Nicodemus—despite his mastery of esoteric Jewish lore—has a difficult time understanding metaphors. Readers of John, however, need to be prepared for them. Jesus says the wind of God, the Spirit of God, is always blowing—first over here and then over there, sometimes like a tornado and sometimes like a zephyr. The Spirit is always speaking to the ears of the soul, sometimes with only a whisper and at other times with a shout. One day the Spirit blows and pushes a person to a new place, a new life, a new birth, a new way of perceiving God as Father and other people as sisters and brothers. When this happens, you understand the whole business about being "born again." The world has not changed, but your way of perceiving the world, yourself, God, and other people is changed decisively. Transformed. It happened to me. It has happened to many of you who read this book. It's not an experience meant for only a few specially-chosen individuals. It's what God wants for everyone who loves him and seeks his face.

Furthermore, the new birth that Spirit brings can happen more than once. Yes, I'm saying you can be "born again" again. Remember, it's a metaphor, not a scientific aspect of human biology. Jesus says, "The wind blows where it wills." I doubt that I'm the only person who can look back on a long life and see more than a single occasion of God giving me amazing new life, fresh insight, altered perspective, and transformed understanding.

The wind of the Spirit blows when and where God chooses. The Spirit is not under my control, though I *can* try to run away from him. I can hide in a sealed tunnel underground (metaphorically-speaking) where no outside breeze may be felt, but only the mechanically controlled air conditioning I have installed. If I insulate myself from the Spirit in this way, I will be hiding from exactly what God wants to give me. Churches sometimes become such "sealed tunnels," and their rules and forms of worship become like air conditioning—simulations of the wind of the Spirit rather than the real thing. The sound of air conditioning is always the same, an on-and-off, monotonous whir passing through controlled vents—easy to ignore.

The last words we hear from Nicodemus in this chapter are in v. 9. We can imagine the perplexed look on his face as he plaintively asks Jesus, "How can this be?" In John's story, Nicodemus seems incorrigible—an apparently unteachable old teacher. This is probably how members of the Johannine communities felt about their

---

17. See 1 Kgs 9:11–13.

well-intentioned fellow Jews who simply could not, would not, understand the Christians' message about the Messiah, the Son of God, and the ongoing work of the Spirit.

Although John starts quoting Jesus directly, he slips into the first-person plural as he gives Jesus's response to Nicodemus. This is understandable if we consider the hypothetical setting: a meeting of two rabbis and their respective disciples for discussion of Torah. When Jesus says "we" he speaks for himself and his followers, and his use of the second person plural "you" refers to Nicodemus and his disciples (and to those in the Great Sanhedrin who have already decided Jesus is a dangerous and misleading teacher): "Truly, truly, I say to you, we speak of what we know, and bear witness to what we have seen; but you do not receive our testimony" (v. 10). The experience of new birth by water and the Spirit is something that happens in this life; it is—to use Jesus's Fourth Gospel vocabulary—paradoxically "earthly." If we can't grasp the meaning of something rooted in ordinary experience like the metaphor of "new birth," then we will never understand what the One who came down from heaven teaches about the kingdom of God or eternal life. Nicodemus does not understand, at least not yet. When he leaves Jesus, he goes back into the darkness—a metaphor for his unenlightened state.

3:16–21. "God so loved the world that he gave his only Son."

Vv. 16–18. God sent his Son into the world to save the world.

INTRODUCTION. This chapter of John contains two of the most familiar verses in the New Testament, "Truly, truly, I say to you, unless one is born anew, he cannot see the kingdom of God" (v. 3) and "God so loved the world that he gave his only Son, that whoever believes in him should not perish but have eternal life" (v. 16).

As pointed out in the introduction to 1:6–18, for John, "the world" (*kosmos*) is the scene of dramatic conflict between God and the Evil One (see p. 8, above). Often John uses "world" to mean, not the whole created order, but particularly the human beings within that order who are now at odds with God and with Jesus, people who prefer to linger in the darkness rather than come to the light (v. 19).[18] Nevertheless, God loves his world (v. 16) in spite of its rebellion, and because of his love for the world he gives his Son to save it. The Baptizer describes Jesus as "the Lamb of God who takes away the sin *of the world*" (1:29). Only in v. 16 does John speak of God "giving" his Son for the salvation of the world; the usual expression is that God *sends* his Son into the world (v. 17).[19] Although God gives his Son in love for all people, only those who believe in Jesus accept the Father's gift.[20]

18. See, e.g., 3:19; 7:7; 8:23; 12:25, 31; 14:17, 27, 30, 31; 16:8, 11, 20; 17:6, 9, 13–16, 25; 18:36.

19. See also, e.g., 4:34; 5:23–24, 30, 30–37; 6:38; 10:36.

20. O'Day, *Gospel of John*, 552–53.

Being "born anew"—which we know can also be read as "begotten from above"—and entering eternal life are essential elements in John's theology. 3:16–21 is most easily understood as the voice of the narrator, though some English translations treat it as Jesus's own words. We misunderstand the word *believe*, as used in John, if we treat believing in Jesus as simply the affirmation of some theological propositions about him. In the Fourth Gospel, affirmation of Jesus's titles is merely a preliminary level of belief. Most Christians in our time hold to some form of what we might label as "a belief system," meaning a collection of ideas (which may, in fact, not be systematic at all) about, say, the Trinity, christology, sin and grace, word and sacrament, justification by faith, and the church. "Believing in God's only Son," however, is not about doctrines or the theological definitions that compose belief systems. *Believing* is a personal posture in relationship to another person, Jesus of Nazareth. It's a stance of *trust* in Jesus, a choice to stand with him come what may.

The Fourth Gospel has a great deal to say about "eternal life," and the first occurrences of that expression are found here in vv. 15–16. It occurs in the other gospels only eight times, six of which come from repetitions by Matthew and Luke of the account of an event described originally in Mark—the visit to Jesus of a so-called "Rich Ruler" (Mark 10:17–31; Matt 19:16–30; Luke 18:18–30). John, however, has almost nothing to say about "the kingdom of God." The phrase "kingdom of God" is found in the Fourth Gospel only in Jesus's dialogue with Nicodemus (3:3, 5). Might it be possible that Nicodemus's visit to Jesus is what lies behind the Synoptic accounts of the visit of the "Rich Ruler" who wants to "inherit eternal life" (Mark 10:17)?[21] Some biblical scholars regard the message of eternal life in the Fourth Gospel as the Johannine counterpart to what the Synoptics call the kingdom of God, understanding that the Greek expression our Bible usually translates as "eternal life" literally means "the life of the age." Jewish thought divided time into two ages—the present age and the age to come. The age to come will be "the age of the King Messiah," which is to say, the kingdom of God.[22]

> **[3:16–18]** *16 For God so loved the world that he gave his only Son, that whoever believes in him should not perish but have eternal life. 17 For God sent the Son into the world, not to condemn the world, but that the world might be saved through him. 18 He who believes in him is not condemned; he who does not believe is condemned already, because he has not believed in the name of the only Son of God.*

RESPONSE. There's one Bible verse everybody in America must know about, even if some people don't know exactly what it says, John 3:16. We could call it "the sports fan's verse," because it seems that in our country at most televised sports competitions

21. Nicodemus was probably elderly, but the Synoptics' "Rich Ruler" is described as a "young man" only in Matthew's version (19:22), not in Mark or Luke.

22. Wright, *How God Became King*, 44–45.

there's at least one person in the bleachers holding up a sign that reads, "JOHN 3:16." That's why everybody knows about it. It would take a big piece of poster board to print out in sufficiently large letters the sentence, "God so loved the world that he gave his only Son, that whoever believes in him should not perish but have eternal life."

When I was a child going to Sunday School in east Texas back in the early 1950s, we memorized John 3:16 and added verse 17: "For God sent the Son into the world, not to condemn the world, but that the world might be saved through him." There are many things I could say about John 3:16–17, but mostly I want to say something about what those two verses have meant in my own life. That's appropriate, since—as I wrote in the preface—this book is as much a testimony of faith as an exercise in scholarship. These two verses taken together promise peace, joy and hope to the world, and what could be more desirable than that?

The author writes, "God so loved the world," not "God so loved the church." Not "God so loved Israel." Not "God so loved the righteous." John says, "God so loved the *world*." Our inclination, because we are twenty-first century believers with an eco-logically-sensitive, creation-oriented spirituality, is reflexively to think of the world here as the organic, created order. While affirming a theological understanding of the created universe itself as a product of God's love and an object of God's care, we must observe that John never refers to the world in that context. For him, the world, is specifically the realm of human beings and human history. Despite being God's own handiwork (1:9), the world is filled with darkness, corrupted by human sin. The world is God's good creation, but that creation now leans away from its Creator. First John says, "the whole world is in the power of the evil one" (5:19).

John 3:16 says that because God "so loves the world"—or, as we would probably phrase it today, "God so loves humankind"—God gave his only Son. A fact of human experience is that we save our best gifts for those we love the most. We make our greatest sacrifices for them. I'm sure that's what you do; I know I do. God gave his Son to the world God loves, the society of human beings. The first words of John's Gospel, 1:1–3, say the Son was always with the Father and was the Father's agent in the creation of the world: "In the beginning was the Word, and the Word was with God, and the Word was God. He was in the beginning with God; all things were made through him, and without him was not anything made that was made." Ultimately, the Son of God is sent as the Creator's gift to the world of humankind, to be the Son of Man, our brother, so that we can share the very life of God. Salvation is for the whole world. The Fourth Gospel proposes that salvation for humanity will follow when all choose to trust in the only Son of God who came among us as Jesus of Nazareth, a man who lived and died and rose from the dead more than twenty centuries ago. (The same principle is enunciated by Paul in Rom 8:14–23, written about forty years before John's Gospel.)

I don't think *believing in* Jesus requires me to give intellectual assent to any of the various doctrinal propositions about him that history has produced. Creeds and doctrines are interesting and often helpful, but mere doctrine has no power to save. We're not going to be rescued from despair, existential anguish, and the fear of death by affirming "correct" theological definitions. In fact, the correctness of our doctrinal definitions is open to question. What qualifies a creature to describe the Creator? Our doctrinal propositions may at best be eighty percent accurate. Or fifty percent. Or maybe only ten percent. Our dogmas are no more than educated guesses, made with the most honorable and holy of intentions.

Frankly, it's presumptuous of human beings to imagine our limited intellect is sufficient to provide us with a complete understanding of God or even a wholly adequate working definition of God. Mortals can only know what God has revealed of Godself, and I don't think God has revealed everything. Not yet, probably not ever. So, asking a human being to explain what God is doing is like asking your golden retriever to explain electric lights. She can't explain them, but she has come to know that not long after your bedroom light comes on in the morning and she hears you thumping around, there will be breakfast in the doggie dish and then you will have a romp with her in the back yard. Intellectually speaking, that's about where we mortals stand, relative to God. (I mean no disrespect to great theologians like Origen, Augustine, and Aquinas or Luther, Calvin, and Barth. Since those great souls now behold the Beatific Vision, I suspect they would not disagree with my assessment.) If we love God, and if we listen to God and walk with God as Jesus taught us, we can make some pretty good observations about how God is going to deal with us.

Here's what I mean when I tell you "I believe in Jesus." I'm telling you I freely and completely trust my present and my future to this singular being, Jesus Christ, who is the central figure of the New Testament, whom I encounter in the Spirit and whom I also experience in the fellowship of others who trust him. You see, for me, believing in Jesus is all about *trust*. It's relational, not intellectual. It's about the heart more than the head. It's about trusting. It's about risking. It's about loving. There's always a leap in faith, and there's always a risk in loving. It's a posture, as I write in the introduction to this section, a "stance"—one that calls for courage from us who believe.

"God so loved the world that he gave his only Son, that whoever believes in him should not perish but have eternal life." When people decide to trust Jesus—not just say they trust him, but actively do so—they move from the Community of the Dying to the Community of the Living. I'm using language metaphorically here, theologically, perhaps even mystically. I'm not referring to literal, biological death or biological life. Biologically, all of us are dying. We started dying at exactly the same time we started living. We're creatures, and our creatureliness makes us subject to the cycle of nature: birth, growth, maturity, reproduction, decay, and death. In my church on the first day of Lent every year, the officiant marks a cross with ashes on worshipers' foreheads and says to them, "Dust you are, and to dust shall you return." John 3:16 is about spiritual life and spiritual death. Eternal life is not simply endless ordinary existence, but neither is it the same thing as "going to heaven." It is an experience of the kingdom of God.

Eternal life means living in a state of communion with our Creator, our Father, and our God. That communion begins as soon as we trust our today, and our tomorrows, and our forever to Jesus, and it continues always—up to, through, and on the other side of the certain demise of our fragile, physical bodies. In the sense of John 3:16, to "perish" means to cut ourselves off from God, turn our backs on Jesus, and spurn the Father's outstretched hand. To live is to trust the Son of God, and to be dead is to refuse to let the Spirit move us to that trusting relationship. (Heartbeat and respiration are purely incidental.)

Christians should be people who know how to love others because we are loved by God. Most of us know people who have been hurt by the church or wounded by well-intentioned but insensitive Christians. Jesus, however, was not in the business of judging or condemning or pronouncing doom on anybody, and neither should we be. That's not our job. John 3:17 says, "For God sent the Son into the world, not to condemn the world, but that the world might be saved through him." Jesus came to bring *salvation* to the world. To experience salvation means to be rescued from disaster, or to be healed, made whole. I think we'd all agree that to be safe and whole is better than to be in danger, diseased, or disintegrated—in mind, body, or spirit. The Son of God was born into the world of human beings—a world marked by the struggle with sin—to bring life and hope not only to God's ancient covenant people, descendants of Abraham according to the flesh, but to every living soul. John tells us that Jesus the good shepherd "came that they may have life, and have it abundantly" (10:10).

Vv. 19–21. The light streams out from Jesus.

INTRODUCTION. Vv. 20–21 bring to a close the story of Nicodemus's visit to Jesus and reiterate John's understanding of Jesus as the one who has been sent from God to give light to the world (1:4–5, 9), a theme that will be elaborated in chapter 8. Although his dialogue with Jesus in chapter 3 ends with Nicodemus remaining stuck in an earthly and unspiritual perspective, the elderly scribe and Sanhedrin member has come through the darkness to meet with Christ, and we will learn more about him later in the gospel (see 7:50 and 19:39). "He who does what is true comes to the light, that it may be clearly seen that his deeds have been wrought in God" (v. 21). Nicodemus serves as an example of how one may grow, by stages, from curiosity about Christ to ardent commitment.

> [3:19–21] *¹⁹ And this is the judgment, that the light has come into the world, and men loved darkness rather than light, because their deeds were evil. ²⁰ For every one who does evil hates the light, and does not come to the light, lest his deeds should be exposed. ²¹ But he who does what is true comes to the light, that it may be clearly seen that his deeds have been wrought in God.*

RESPONSE. I see it like this: Jesus is holding the door of life open for us. In fact, John's Gospel tells us Jesus even calls himself "the door" (10:7). Light streams out through the door to drive away the darkness. We can choose to trust him and go through that door, or we can choose to say, "No thanks, I'm looking for a different door." Or even, "I think I'd prefer a different 'life,' one where I don't have to trust any power greater than my 'sacred self.'" Someone might even say, "I don't think there could be a life more fulfilling than the one I'm already living. I have all I could possibly want!" To such people I say, "OK. That's your choice. Peace be with you. Be happy."

As for me, I've put my hand in Jesus's hand, and this is how I would describe it: I have gone through his door, and now I'm walking where he leads me. I stumble and fall often. And I pull away from him to go investigate something off the road far more often than I should, like the golden retriever I mentioned earlier. But Jesus stands there and waits patiently for me to come back to him. When I'm so distracted that I don't come back, he comes looking for me, and he always finds me. He knows I'm really still just a curious puppy and easily sidetracked. I wish I could describe for you exactly what our destination will be like—either tomorrow or at the end of the road. But I don't know. All I really know is this: I'm glad to be on the road with Jesus. Gladness is precisely the emotion I feel. I trust him. And I hope that reading John with me will help you trust him too.

3:22–36. John appears for the last time.

Vv. 22–36. John says, "He must increase, but I must decrease."

INTRODUCTION. The last section of chapter 3 touches on some of the same topics as Jesus's conversation with Nicodemus: contrast between the one who is "of the earth" and the one who is "from above," the giving of the Spirit, and eternal life. This is the only place in the New Testament where we're told Jesus and his followers began their ministry by administering a baptism similar to that of John. The editor modifies this by adding in 4:2 a parenthetic qualification, "Jesus himself did not baptize, but only his disciples." He wants to make Jesus's superiority to his forerunner explicit; agreeing that Jesus also baptized people makes the distinction between the two less sharp. However, the community for which the Fourth Gospel was written may have retained memories of Jesus's own baptismal activity, so that omitting mention of it could raise questions.

Although Mark 1:14 says Jesus begins his ministry after John the Baptist is arrested, John 3:25 states the opposite, and vv. 22–24 describe overlapping ministries. It should not surprise us to be told there was continuity between the baptizing ministry of John and the early ministry of Jesus, especially since the Fourth Gospel implies Jesus was once one of the Baptist's own followers (1:26–27, 30).[23] John 3:22–30 reminds

23. Although they do not say Jesus baptized anyone, Mark and Matthew suggest continuity

us there are many details about the historical Jesus concerning which we are simply ignorant. Did the practice of Christian sacramental baptism have its origin in a bathing rite, similar to and yet distinctly different from that of John, which Jesus himself once administered for at least a short time at the beginning of his ministry? Is this why John describes Jesus in 1:33 as "he who baptizes with the Holy Spirit"? It is possible. In which case it may be this baptism to which Jesus refers in 3:5 when he tells Nicodemus, "Unless one is born of water and the Spirit he cannot enter the kingdom of God."

In the broader context of John, the point of vv. 22–36 is to emphasize that despite their history and some obvious similarities between the two, Jesus is the Messiah, the Son of God, while the Baptist, albeit a prophet sent from God, is merely an advance man for the Messiah. In Old Testament tradition, Israel is the bride of Yahweh. Here, the Baptist says Jesus is the bridegroom while he is only the best man: "He must increase, but I must decrease" (v. 30).

There are a variety of opinions regarding whose voice is heard in vv. 31–36, since the RSV text shows v. 30 as the last word of John. Some scholars propose that the Baptist's voice continues to the end of the chapter, while others argue these verses should be considered as a formal theological teaching by Jesus. I read vv. 31–36 as the narrator's commentary, similar in literary form to 3:16–21.

[3:22–36] *²² After this Jesus and his disciples went into the land of Judea; there he remained with them and baptized. ²³ John also was baptizing at Ae'non near Salim, because there was much water there; and people came and were baptized. ²⁴ For John had not yet been put in prison. ²⁵ Now a discussion arose between John's disciples and a Jew over purifying. ²⁶ And they came to John, and said to him, "Rabbi, he who was with you beyond the Jordan, to whom you bore witness, here he is, baptizing, and all are going to him." ²⁷ John answered, "No one can receive anything except what is given him from heaven. ²⁸ You yourselves bear me witness, that I said, I am not the Christ, but I have been sent before him. ²⁹ He who has the bride is the bridegroom; the friend of the bridegroom, who stands and hears him, rejoices greatly at the bridegroom's voice; therefore this joy of mine is now full. ³⁰ He must increase, but I must decrease." ³¹ He who comes from above is above all; he who is of the earth belongs to the earth, and of the earth he speaks; he who comes from heaven is above all. ³² He bears witness to what he has seen and heard, yet no one receives his testimony; ³³ he who receives his testimony sets his seal to this, that God is true. ³⁴ For he whom God has sent utters the words of God, for it is not by measure that he gives the Spirit; ³⁵ the Father loves the Son, and has given all things into his hand.*

---

between the preaching of the Baptist and Jesus's own gospel. Mark 1:15 quotes Jesus's proclamation at the beginning of his ministry as: "The time is fulfilled, and the kingdom of God is at hand; repent and believe in the gospel." This is essentially the same message Matt 3:2 attributes to John the Baptist, "Repent, for the kingdom of heaven is at hand."

³⁶ He who believes in the Son has eternal life; he who does not obey the Son shall not see life, but the wrath of God rests upon him.

RESPONSE. If we accept the picture of the two men that Luke's gospel offers—a picture regarded as legendary by some scholars—we see Jesus and John are close relatives, almost the same age (see Luke 1:1–38). The Fourth Gospel doesn't tell us how long John has been preaching and baptizing before the official investigating committee from Jerusalem arrives to confront him (see 1:19–28). Since apparently the baptizing prophet has only recently come to the authorities' attention, it must be relatively early in his ministry. Even so, he already has established a reputation and is drawing huge crowds. John is a young man, about thirty years old, not an elderly teacher like Nicodemus with a cluster of younger disciples in his train. He's a brave young firebrand of a preacher, addressing himself to a religious community that doesn't usually regard the ideas of men under age forty as worth much. The disciples gathered around him are probably men as young as he or even younger. Like him, they're full of righteous zeal, eager for what we'd call "a reformation" in Israel.

How do you think John might feel, at this early stage in his own work of prophetic witness, to see Jesus, probably a kinsman—a man who, until a short time before, stood among John's own followers—not only replicating part of John's own preaching but launching into a personal ministry of his own that presents the same experience John offers, a new, unorthodox ritual bath (baptism) signifying both spiritual cleansing and new birth? Not only does John's former disciple seem to be copying him, but the crowds that until recently were streaming to John now seem to prefer the new prophet. Some of John's followers arrive with the report, "Rabbi, he who was with you beyond the Jordan, to whom you bore witness, here he is, baptizing, and all are going to him" (v. 26).

In the world most of us inhabit, a teacher or mentor hopes for a protégé to succeed, but not necessarily so quickly as to become a competitor to his master. The ideal order of things is for one's students to flourish, do well, and build a reputation about the time their elderly mentor is ready to move offstage. However, Jesus and John are the same age, and John's own ministry to Israel has but recently begun. Yes, John has already told the investigating committee from Jerusalem, and the crowds, and his followers that he is not the Messiah, not Elijah returned from heaven, and not the "prophet-greater-than-Moses." Yes, John has called attention to Jesus and described him as "the Lamb of God who takes away the sin of the world." John has demonstrated deep personal humility, announcing he's not even worthy to untie Jesus's sandals. Still, John might well expect that Jesus, the Lamb of God, will do something more dramatic than set up shop just up the Jordan Valley and start baptizing people.

John is cut from different cloth than most people we know. He is truly a prophet, a man who hears the Voice of God and obeys what he hears God telling him. He is totally invested in seeing God's will done and trusts God's ways. If the anointed one, the Messiah, happens to be his own former follower, the prophet is content to see his ex-disciple's name exalted above his own. John does not feel the need to have top billing. His young disciples might be jealous for their master's honor or status, but the prophet himself is not. If his moment in the sun is to be brief, so be it. He tells them, "No one can receive anything except what is given him from heaven. . . . He must increase, but I must decrease" (vv. 27, 30). John understands himself as playing the role of friend of the groom at a wedding. He handles all the wedding arrangements, invites the guests, and even stands guard outside the wedding tent, waiting until the groom arrives to join his bride for their wedding night. But the bride—Israel in this case—belongs to her rightful bridegroom, the Son of God. The friend of the groom is delighted to be a key member of their wedding party. But now that the groom has arrived to claim his bride, the wedding-arranger's work is done.

Contemporary Christians should take a lesson from John, the friend of the groom. Are we able to content ourselves with being agents of grace, dispatched here or there to do God's bidding, and find our fulfillment in seeing our small piece of the Lord's great work accomplished? Or do we hanker for recognition, eager that our small contribution to the grand project should be duly recognized? Are we among those who check carefully to make sure our names are included in the published list of members being thanked for serving on the parish outreach committee? And if we have been accidentally (or even deliberately and unkindly) overlooked, does it matter very much to us? The same principle applies to churches. Does it ever occur to us that the existence of our local congregation or even our denomination might be purely provisional in the larger plan of God, merely the precursor of a holier entity, some future community of faith that will have more enduring significance in the divine economy? John the Baptist was content to "prepare the way of the Lord," to be of merely transient significance in God's great plan. "He must increase, but I must decrease."

The narrator tells us, "He who comes from above is above all; he who is of the earth belongs to the earth, and of the earth he speaks; he who comes from heaven is above all" (v. 31). John is a prophet, but he is still a man "of the earth." John's baptism is only a baptism in water, a baptism of earthly purification, a preparation for the revealing of the Lamb of God. Jesus's baptism is in water *and* Spirit (3:5), and the Spirit gives new life, eternal life to those who put their trust in God's Son. John, like the prophets of old, has a share of God's Spirit. This enables him to speak for God. But upon his Son, sent from heaven to earth, God has poured out his Spirit without limit. The Son alone is able to witness concerning things that are above. Yet, as the narrator wistfully notes in v. 33, "no one receives his testimony." He comes to his own home, to his own people, Israel, but they "receive him not" (1:11).

Chapter Three

Doing Your Own Theology

Questions for reflection after reading John 3.

- The first thing Jesus tells Nicodemus when the elderly teacher comes to call on him is this: "No one can see the kingdom of God without being begotten from above" (v. 3).[24] Jesus says that Nicodemus will not perceive what God is doing at the moment (i.e., the significance of Jesus), regardless of how many years he has spent studying the Scriptures, unless he enters into a completely new relationship with God. The old man must have a new birth, with God as his Father. Jesus then repeats himself in a slightly different way, saying, "Truly, truly, I say to you, unless one is born of water and the Spirit, he cannot enter the kingdom of God. That which is born of the flesh is flesh, and that which is born of the Spirit is spirit" (vv. 5–6). In other words, to become actively involved with what God is doing in the world (i.e., not only perceive but actually enter the kingdom of God) Nicodemus must have a new birth from "water and the Spirit." The great teacher must become a disciple of Jesus. It's painful to be told we must begin again, go back to square one, especially if we have been working on something for a long time; and it's particularly unpalatable when we're proud of our achievements. For a respected rabbi to hear that he must literally become a child again seems like madness.—*What gives us strength to start over? How does God make us willing to be "born again," ready to return to being a child? How can we know whether we have been "begotten from above"?*

- John 3:16 is probably the best-known verse in the New Testament: "God so loved the world that he gave his only Son, that whoever believes in him should not perish but have eternal life." God's love for the world is all the more meaningful when we perceive that for John the world is the realm of humankind in rebellion against God, under the sway of the Evil One, choosing to live in darkness rather than light. The world deserves punishment, yet God loves the world so much that he sends his own Son into the world, not to condemn it and punish it, but to save it (v. 17), to be "the Lamb of God who takes away the sin of the world" (1:29). One of the interesting characteristics of John, in comparison with the Synoptics or the letters of Paul, is that the Fourth Gospel does not urge its readers to repent; it simply calls them to *believe.*—*What, in your own experience, has most clearly demonstrated God's love for you? What shows that you believe in Jesus? How would you explain to a curious, non-Christian friend the difference between "believing that" Jesus was a real, historical person and "believing in" Jesus?*

- The Fourth Gospel will have a great deal to say about eternal life, and the first occurrence of that expression is here in v. 16, where we are told whoever believes in Jesus "should not perish but have eternal life." It seems obvious Jesus is using

24. Author's translation, Brown, *John I–XII,* 128.

metaphoric language; he is not proposing that those who believe in him will be spared physical death. Eternal life does not refer to immortality, an indefinite extension of ordinary human existence. The introduction to vv. 17–18 suggests that eternal life may be understood as a reference to the Jewish idea of life in the age to come, the Messianic age, the kingdom of God.—*We will reflect on our understanding of eternal life again as we read John, but on the basis of the first three chapters, how do you understand it? People sometimes speak about "going to heaven" when they die (an expression that does not occur in the Bible). What is the difference between going to heaven and having eternal life?*

Chapter Four

4:1–42. Jesus meets a woman at a well in Samaria.

Vv. 1–18. Jesus asks a Samaritan woman for a drink of water.

INTRODUCTION. Concerning the incarnate Word John says in the prologue (1:11–14), "He came to his own home, and his own people received him not. But to all who received him, who believed in his name, he gave power to become children of God; who were born not of blood, nor of the will of the flesh nor of the will of man, but of God." In chapter 2, the Son of God comes to the temple and meets with hostility; in chapter 3, he enters into dialogue with a well-intentioned, but confused and hesitant prominent Jewish elder, the aristocrat Nicodemus, who simply doesn't "get it" when Jesus tells him that he needs a "new birth from above." The Lord has indeed come to his own people, and he has not been received by those who should recognize him.

Jesus, who has been baptizing in the Jordan Valley, is returning to Galilee, and John tells us to get there he has to pass through Samaria (v. 4). This is not true in terms of geography; there is a shorter route to Galilee. But it *is* true in terms of a divine imperative and for the sake of the story which John wants to tell. Samaria is a land whose people are despised by Jews as heretical half-breeds. In contrast to his night-time dialogue with the wise and learned Nicodemus, Jesus has a noonday conversation with a person who is Nicodemus's total opposite, a Samaritan village woman whose personal life seems to be in disorder. This humble woman will "receive him." She will believe. She will "get it."

> **[4:1–18]** *¹ Now when the Lord knew that the Pharisees had heard that Jesus was making and baptizing more disciples than John ² (although Jesus himself did not baptize, but only his disciples), ³ he left Judea and departed again to Galilee. ⁴ He had to pass through Samar'ia. ⁵ So he came to a city of Samar'ia, called Sy'char, near the field that Jacob gave to his son Joseph. ⁶ Jacob's well was there, and so Jesus, wearied as he was with his journey, sat down beside the well. It was about the sixth hour. ⁷ There came*

a woman of Samar'ia to draw water. Jesus said to her, "Give me a drink."
8 For his disciples had gone away into the city to buy food. 9 The Samari-
tan woman said to him, "How is it that you, a Jew, ask a drink of me, a
woman of Samar'ia?" For Jews have no dealings with Samaritans. 10 Jesus
answered her, "If you knew the gift of God, and who it is that is saying
to you, 'Give me a drink,' you would have asked him, and he would have
given you living water." 11 The woman said to him, "Sir, you have nothing to
draw with, and the well is deep; where do you get that living water? 12 Are
you greater than our father Jacob, who gave us the well, and drank from it
himself, and his sons, and his cattle?" 13 Jesus said to her, "Every one who
drinks of this water will thirst again, 14 but whoever drinks of the water
that I shall give him will never thirst; the water that I shall give him will
become in him a spring of water welling up to eternal life." 15 The woman
said to him, "Sir, give me this water, that I may not thirst, nor come here
to draw." 16 Jesus said to her, "Go, call your husband, and come here." 17 The
woman answered him, "I have no husband." Jesus said to her, "You are
right in saying, 'I have no husband'; 18 for you have had five husbands, and
he whom you now have is not your husband; this you said truly."

RESPONSE. Although John consistently sees Jesus from a post-Easter perspective, the physical reality of the Son of Man—his true humanness—is never denied. It's a long road up from the Jordan and it's high noon on a hot day in Samaria. Jesus is tired, hungry, and thirsty. His disciples go into the town of Sychar to find something to eat, while Jesus sits on the coping of an ancient well to rest. While he's sitting there, a woman from the town comes out to draw water.

Going to the well to draw water is woman's work in first century Palestine. Every village household rises with the sun, and as soon as they can get going in the morning, the women take clay jugs with long cords attached to the handles and walk to the town well. Their job is to bring back enough water to meet the needs of their households for that day. It's burdensome labor, but it has an aspect that makes up for the daily tedium. Except for the Sabbath, it provides a time each morning for the women to socialize with one another.

We can safely assume that most days the women linger at the well to swap stories about their children, complain about their husbands, and gossip about their neighbors. If we were listening to them chatter we'd probably hear things like this: "Did any of you know old Samuel the rug merchant is now going to take a second very young wife, all the way from Damascus? And, get this: her father is a Greek!" . . . "I see that Deborah isn't here this morning. My guess is she's with child—yet again, and at her age!" . . . "My, my, my! You don't say? Children are a blessing from Heaven, of course, but Deborah already has eight. One of her girls should be coming soon for the water."

Fetching several heavy jugs of water is hard work, but fellowship around the well-head in the coolness of dawn gives it a pleasant convivial dimension, except for women whose company at the well in the morning might be unwelcome, women whose behavior has offended the sensibilities of the proper ladies of the village, women such as the one who meets Jesus at the well at noon. It's reasonable to suppose that she comes then rather than at dawn because there's a reason she wants to avoid the others. Perhaps a scandal has been attached to her, something that calls her virtue into question in the eyes of the other women. Maybe she suspects the others' morning water-drawing gossip might be about her, so she chooses to draw her household's water later, at the hottest time of day. We shouldn't picture this Samaritan woman as a prostitute, as some do. That's reading our own prejudices into the text. She is a village woman who has lost face with her peers, however, and wants to evade their scornful stares and whispering behind her back. All of us have times when we want to sidestep situations that force us to be around other people—especially if we might be embarrassed, shunned, or called names. Anybody who has felt that way, female or male, can identify with the Samaritan woman, who shares center stage with Jesus in the meaningful drama John presents in chapter 4.

As the woman comes up to the well, Jesus says, "Give me a drink." This is a bold move on his part, and the woman is surprised. Jesus is obviously a Jew, and Jews despise Samaritans. They will not give them the time of day or do any business with them, if it can be avoided. The feeling is mutual; the two people groups—though we might call them "cousins"—each despise the other. But also, among both Samaritans and Jews, pious men do not engage in conversation with women in public, even their own wives or daughters. The woman, however, doesn't act shocked that a man is speaking to her in public; maybe she assumes he takes her to be a woman of loose morals, since everyone knows decent women always go to the well at first light. Nevertheless, she's surprised a Jew is taking the initiative to address a Samaritan and even ask her for a favor.

This noontime encounter with a Samaritan woman of dubious repute is an artful counterpart to Jesus's nighttime meeting with Nicodemus, a Jewish man of the highest standing, a member of the Great Sanhedrin who is attracted to Jesus, regardless of the opinion of his Pharisee peers. Nicodemus comes to Jesus at night—and his coming in the darkness may also be a metaphor for the darkness that still clouds his thinking even after he has spoken with Jesus. The Samaritan woman meets Jesus at the well by accident in the bright light of mid-day because she wants to avoid coming face-to-face with female fellow villagers. But their meeting in the daylight could also be a metaphor for the woman's readiness to be illuminated by Jesus. Just as with Nicodemus, Jesus's encounter with the Samaritan woman gives rise to another theological dialogue, one which also deals with the Spirit.

Jesus, a Jew and therefore a person whom any Samaritan (either male or female) would have avoided, reaches out to a humiliated Samaritan woman, scorned by her neighbors, and asks her to help him in a simple way, by providing him a drink of water.—Does John offer counsel here for attentive readers? This encounter between Jesus and the Samaritan woman tells us that no matter how unloved we might be, no matter how disordered our lives, no matter how spurned by our peers or disappointed in ourselves, *God identifies with us.* God reaches out to us. God takes the initiative. Regardless of who else might assume that we're unpardonable, God thinks otherwise.

The woman says, "How is it that you, a Jew, ask a drink of me, a woman of Samaria?" (vs 9). Jesus replies, "If you knew the gift of God, and who it is that is saying to you, 'Give me a drink,' you would have asked him, and he would have given you living water" (v. 10). The two engage in playful repartee about where and how Jesus might get hold of this "living water"—which ordinarily means running water from a spring or stream, rather than from a cistern. The woman's failure to grasp that Jesus is speaking metaphorically resembles Nicodemus's earlier misunderstanding when Jesus spoke of being born anew.

Living water sounds much more refreshing to this woman than the flat-tasting water she draws from Jacob's ancient well. She'd love to have some right now. But how and from what source could this out-of-place Jew who lacks even a goatskin bucket dip living water? We're accustomed to John's metaphoric devices and his irony by now. Though the woman doesn't yet understand, we know Jesus isn't talking about water scooped from a spring with a clay pot. This living water isn't H2O. It's the water of God's Spirit, water for the soul, water for the inner thirst, the deepest need of every human being—the need for unconditional love, forgiveness, mercy, hope, and a second (or third or fifty-fourth) chance. Jesus tells the woman, "Everyone who drinks of this water will thirst again, but whoever drinks of the water that I shall give him will never thirst; the water that I shall give him will become in him a spring of water welling up to eternal life" (v. 14).

Who among us wouldn't want something like that—a fountain of eternal life bubbling up from within our soul? (We'll hear Jesus saying almost the same thing again in 7:37–38, and the narrator will inform us that he is speaking of the Spirit.) The woman is beginning to catch Jesus's meaning, so she says, "Sir, give me this water, that I may not thirst, nor come here to draw." Then Jesus replies, in effect, "First, go get your husband and bring him here to me."—Oops. That is not possible, of course. Then it all comes out, her whole sad story. Though the gospel spares us the details, we can imagine them: the five marriages (and maybe five divorces), the man she's living with now (but not married to), and all the hurts and rejection she has experienced. She sobs with disappointment at the wreck her life has become, when all she ever really wanted was a little house, a kind husband, and babies. The woman tells Jesus all about it, or maybe he tells her "all that I ever did" (v. 29).[1] Whatever she might have done, Jesus speaks not a single word of judgment. He accepts her.

Vv. 19–26. Jesus tells the woman he is the Messiah.

INTRODUCTION. Jesus's partner in dialogue, the woman of Samaria, shows herself to be quite perceptive. She recognizes Jesus as a prophet who might give a definitive answer to the decisive question that divides Jews from Samaritans, "Where is the right place to worship?" He answers her question by proposing a new understanding of worship (vv. 21–24), although he states, "You worship what you do not know; we worship what we know, for salvation is from the Jews" (v. 22). Then Jesus does something for this woman which he has not done and will not do for anyone else; he explicitly identifies himself as the Messiah (v. 26). This is also the first of numerous instances in which John shows Jesus associating himself with the sacred Name of God, "I Am." In Exod 3:15, when Moses at the burning bush asks God to tell him his name, God says his name is "*I AM WHO I AM*" (which may also be read as "*I will be who I will be*"). "I AM" is the Hebrew divine name, usually transliterated as *YAHWEH*, and translated as LORD (always in upper case letters) in English language Bibles.[2]

Jesus's conversation with the Samaritan woman reiterates for readers of John some points already made by this gospel—in chapter 1, about the grace and truth of God which are revealed only in his Son; in chapter 2, concerning the earthly temple and its repeated sacrifices now being replaced in the person of the Lamb of God, whom the Father has sent into the world to take away the sin of the world; and in chapter 3, about the gift of new birth in the Spirit, mediated by God's Son, a gift which is essential for anyone to know God and see what God is doing. In this chapter, Jesus tells his dialogue partner that God is spirit and must be worshiped in Spirit and truth.[3] John may want to show Jesus here as contrasting true worship in the Spirit with the

1. Since Origen (185–254), various writers have proposed an allegorical interpretation of the Samaritan woman's five husbands, interpreting them as five different deities that had been worshiped in Samaria (since the same word would have been used for "husband" as for "lord," *baal*). This idea still shows up, especially in writers with a mystical slant; however, a literal interpretation of the woman's reference to her husband is far more likely.

2. See Brown, *Gospel according to John*, appendix 4, 533–38; and Ratzinger, *Jesus*, 345–55. Keener, *Gospel of John*, 1:620, writes that Jesus's precise words to the Samaritan woman in v. 26 are "quite close to the LXX of Isa 52:6, where God is speaking." ("LXX" is the usual symbol for the *Septuagint*, the Greek translation of the Old Testament, the Bible of Greek-speaking Jews in the New Testament era.)

3. The expression "God is spirit" (v. 24) simply shows Jesus affirming the basic biblical principle that God's nature is immaterial, spirit rather than flesh. Jesus does not wholly identify God with "the Spirit," since he later distinguishes the Spirit both from the Father and the Son (14:16, 26; 15:26). However, when Jesus speaks of worshiping "in Spirit and in truth" the worship John has in mind is worship inspired by God's Spirit, which Paul also intends in Phil 3:3. We may picture the worship of Johannine churches as visionary and ecstatic, resembling the worship in heaven described in Revelation, which opens with John identifying himself as "in the Spirit on the Lord's Day" (1:10). See Keener, *Gospel of John*, 1:616–19.

conventional sacrifices offered in the temple, which would accord with what we see in 2:16–17. To worship in Spirit and truth one must first drink of the living water God's Son gives.

An important thing we see in John's presentation of Jesus's conversation with the Samaritan woman is that Jesus employs the Greek word *proskyneō* when he speaks about worship (vv. 20–24). This word essentially means "to prostrate oneself." It describes the gesture of one who submits to a dominant figure—like a slave to a master, a subject to a ruler, or a devotee to a deity. It is the obeisance of the congregation in the Jerusalem temple at the most solemn moment of the service. The word describes a physical act, not an attitude. The point Jesus makes is that God wants people to worship him (i.e., be submitted to him) "in spirit and in truth." He says to the woman, "The hour is coming, and now is, when the true worshipers will worship the Father in spirit and truth, for such the Father seeks to worship him. God is spirit, and those who worship him must worship in spirit and truth" (4:24-25). It is one thing to prostrate oneself along with thousands of others before the Holy of Holies, but it is a qualitatively different thing *to be fully submitted in heart and soul to the rule of God*. God rejects merely superficial, external acts of devotion or submission. These can be a hypocritical pretense. God wants those who worship him to do so with sincere and true devotion—with hearts and minds yielded fully to him.

> **[4:19–26]** *¹⁹ The woman said to him, "Sir, I perceive that you are a prophet. ²⁰ Our fathers worshiped on this mountain; and you say that in Jerusalem is the place where men ought to worship." ²¹ Jesus said to her, "Woman, believe me, the hour is coming when neither on this mountain nor in Jerusalem will you worship the Father. ²² You worship what you do not know; we worship what we know, for salvation is from the Jews. ²³ But the hour is coming, and now is, when the true worshipers will worship the Father in spirit and truth, for such the Father seeks to worship him. ²⁴ God is spirit, and those who worship him must worship in spirit and truth." ²⁵ The woman said to him, "I know that Messiah is coming (he who is called Christ); when he comes, he will show us all things." ²⁶ Jesus said to her, "I who speak to you am he."*

RESPONSE. When Jesus tells the Samaritan woman about her marital status and her life, she discerns this Jew is surely no ordinary man; he must be a prophet. Therefore, she asks him the vital religious question of the moment, the one whose differing answers create the main cleavage between Samaritans and Jews: "Where should we worship? Here, or in Jerusalem?" (I need not remind you that differences about where, and when, and how we should worship are a primary source of division among the world's approximately 41,000 Christian denominations.) Jesus tells the woman that Jews know the One whom they worship and salvation comes from the Jews—a powerful acknowledgement for John's Gospel, in which Jesus's bitterest enemies seem to be labeled "the Jews." But, he adds, the time is coming when people will worship neither in Samaria on Mount Gerizim nor in Jerusalem on Mount Moriah. Indeed, the time has already come "when true worshipers will worship the Father in spirit and truth, for such the Father seeks to worship him. God is spirit, and those who worship him must worship in spirit and truth" (v. 24).

The woman is profoundly impressed by Jesus's words. He is clearly a prophet; no doubt about that. But, could he be more than a prophet? Thinking thus, she ventures to say, "I know that Messiah is coming (he who is called Christ); when he comes, he will show us all things" (v. 25)[4] Jesus replies using an expression which seems deliberately to allude to the sacred Name of God, an expression he will use again repeatedly in John: "I—who speak to you—am he." Jesus does unambiguously for the Samaritan woman something he does for no one else. He acknowledges himself to be the expected Messiah.

Health websites tell us many people in our country are in an early stage of dehydration and don't realize it. These people may live in lovely suburban homes and have spigots of filtered ice water built into their refrigerator doors, but they're not drinking as much water as they need. They also may not be addressing the far more serious thirst of the soul, which can only be satisfied by an encounter with God *in spirit and in truth.* Spirit and truth go together; they're indissolubly linked. To worship in spirit and truth is to respond to God's gift of new life in the Spirit by offering our new life back to God, making this offering of ourselves without any pretense, falseness, regret, or fear. When we worship in spirit and truth our focus is entirely on God rather than ourselves, on giving thanks for what we have been given and not asking for something different. When we drink from the spring of living water we enter a new life through the One who encounters us just as he encountered the Samaritan woman at the well. We put ourselves at his disposal. When we worship in spirit and truth, we're putting our lives in God's hands, whether we're worshiping with a multitude in a grand cathedral or all alone on a riverside. Such worship says, "Here I am, Lord. What would you have me do?"

Vv. 27–42. The woman witnesses to her neighbors, and many believe.

INTRODUCTION. The Samaritan woman becomes a witness whose testimony to Jesus leads to the conversion of the people of her village, and these converts will fulfill the prediction made in 3:16–17. The long dialogue between Jesus and the woman at the well is filled with metaphors and other Johannine literary devices, such as

4. See Keener, *Gospel of John*, 1:619–20. The Samaritans were expecting a special prophet like Moses (see Deut 18:15–20) to be sent from God in the last days, a figure known as the *Taheb* ("the restorer"). The *Taheb* would not be a king like the Jewish *Messiah* was expected to be, but John makes no effort to be precise about differences between Jewish and Samaritan beliefs; indeed, it serves his purposes to blend them and portray Jesus as being also the fulfillment of the Samaritans' expectations.

misunderstanding, double-meaning, and irony. The woman of Samaria is as important a figure in the Johannine theological scheme as the Good Samaritan is in the
Lukan portrayal of Jesus's teaching (see Luke 10:25–37).

The Greek expression used earlier in v. 4, translated "he had to pass through
Samaria," is not meant to identify geographic necessity in Jesus's journey, but rather
to describe his visit to Samaria as the mandate of God. That the Son should bear his
testimony to Samaritans is the Father's will. Thus, he "had to" go there. In this section
Jesus says, "My food is to do the will of him who sent me, and to accomplish his work.
Do you not say, 'There are yet four months, then comes the harvest'? I tell you, lift up
your eyes, and see how the fields are already white for harvest" (vv. 34–35). He speaks
of this episode in Samaria as submission to the Father's will, an act of obedience that
will yield a plentiful harvest.

John's account of Jesus's encounter with the woman of Samaria and her community appears to be evidence of the Samaritan mission's importance in the eyes of
Johannine Christians. Jesus's enemies' awareness of his early connection to Samaria
is conveyed by "the Jews'" later accusation (8:48), "Are we not right in saying that you
are a Samaritan and have a demon?" Those Jews in chapter 8 will want to stone Jesus;
but the Samaritans in chapter 4 believe in him.[5]

Some commentators make an effort to identify the "sower" and the "reaper"
mentioned in what is apparently a proverbial expression (vv. 30–37), but that exercise
is futile. The interchange between Jesus and the woman at the well and the townspeo-
ple whom she brings to meet him is a brilliant work of dramatic art, full of symbolic
richness. However, it is unlikely to be an allegory. The tense shift in v. 38 makes Jesus's
meaning obvious, "I sent you to reap that for which you did not labor; others have
labored, and you have entered into their labor."

[4:27–42] *27 Just then his disciples came. They marveled that he was talking with a woman, but none said, "What do you wish?" or, "Why are you
talking with her?" 28 So the woman left her water jar, and went away into
the city, and said to the people, 29 "Come, see a man who told me all that
I ever did. Can this be the Christ?" 30 They went out of the city and were
coming to him. 31 Meanwhile the disciples besought him, saying, "Rabbi,
eat." 32 But he said to them, "I have food to eat of which you do not know."
33 So the disciples said to one another, "Has any one brought him food?"
34 Jesus said to them, "My food is to do the will of him who sent me, and
to accomplish his work. 35 Do you not say, 'There are yet four months,
then comes the harvest'? I tell you, lift up your eyes, and see how the fields
are already white for harvest. 36 He who reaps receives wages, and gathers
fruit for eternal life, so that sower and reaper may rejoice together. 37 For
here the saying holds true, 'One sows and another reaps.' 38 I sent you to*

5. Acts indicates the importance of the witness to Christ in Samaria (Acts 1:8; 8:4–25; 9:31; 15:3).

reap that for which you did not labor; others have labored, and you have entered into their labor." [39] *Many Samaritans from that city believed in him because of the woman's testimony, "He told me all that I ever did."* [40] *So when the Samaritans came to him, they asked him to stay with them; and he stayed there two days.* [41] *And many more believed because of his word.* [42] *They said to the woman, "It is no longer because of your words that we believe, for we have heard for ourselves, and we know that this is indeed the Savior of the world."*

RESPONSE. The disciples, who left Jesus at the well when they went to look for food, find their Master talking with a local woman when they return. Conversation with strange women—not to mention Samaritan women—is strictly discouraged by the rabbis as improper behavior for any Jewish man and especially for a teacher. Nevertheless, the disciples politely refrain from making any comments. Instead, knowing Jesus must be famished, they encourage him to eat something, but he has no interest in the food they've brought. Jesus's hunger, both bodily and spiritual, is satisfied by doing exactly what his Father sent him to do. As soon as the disciples arrive, the Samaritan woman returns to the village to tell her neighbors about Jesus, leaving her water jug behind. (Perhaps John offers this as a sign that, just as doing the Father's will satisfies Jesus's hunger, so the living water Jesus supplies satisfies the woman's thirst). Jesus was convinced that God wanted him to go to Galilee by passing through forbidden Samaritan territory, and now that conviction is vindicated. The Father's plan is fulfilled. Here in Samaria among people who are not Jews, Jesus feels as if he and his disciples are walking through acres of grain standing ready for reapers. Those who are led by the Spirit, which "blows where it wills" (3:8), are sure to find themselves in challenging, yet always spiritually rewarding situations. This is true for all the characters that play a part in 4:5–42, Jesus, his disciples, the woman, and the Samaritan villagers.

In the story world of John's Gospel, the woman takes no time at all in giving her testimony about Jesus to the people in her village, and—regardless of whether she is a social outcast or not—her words evoke an immediate response. Even as Jesus is speaking to his disciples about the fields "white for harvest" (v. 35), the villagers are visible in the distance, walking towards the well, no doubt with the woman in the lead.

As he tells about the harvest of Samaritan believers, John wants his readers to recall Jesus's earlier dialogue with Nicodemus—and the commentary on it in 3:15–22. The Fourth Gospel tells us, "God so loved the world that he gave his only Son, that whoever believes in him should not perish but have eternal life. . . . God sent the Son into the world, not to condemn the world, but that the world might be saved through him" (3:16–17). The Samaritans are the first non-Jewish people, the first from "the world" to believe in Jesus. These non-Jews make a powerful and unique statement, "We have heard for ourselves, and we know that this is indeed the Savior of the world."

Jesus is not merely the Messiah of the Jews or the Taheb of the Samaritans; Jesus is *the Savior of the world.*

4:43–54. The second sign: Jesus heals the son of a royal official.

Vv. 43–54. A boy is healed because his father believes Jesus.

INTRODUCTION. Jesus, recognizing the truth of the proverb, "a prophet is not without honor except in his own country" (Mark 6:4; referred to in v. 44), spends two days in Samaria and then continues north to Galilee. The author of the Fourth Gospel, unlike the Synoptic writers, construes Jesus's "own country" as Judea, not Galilee, though he is aware that Jesus grew up in Galilee. The prologue tells us the incarnate Word "came to his own home," Judea, but "his own people received him not" (1:11). The Samaritans did receive him, however, and now Jesus goes back to Galilee where he grew up. His return is welcomed by Galileans who saw the signs (2:23;3:2) he did in Jerusalem at the Passover, signs that John mentions but does not describe. In Galilee, Jesus enacts his "second sign" (v. 54). Cana, the home town of Nathanael (21:2), a village not mentioned in any other gospel, is portrayed as the setting for the first two events John labels as signs.

A dignitary—whom we recognize as a royal official by his Greek title, *basilikos*—a member of the court of Herod Antipas, travels to Cana from his home in Capernaum to ask Jesus to come and heal his mortally ill son. Despite what some see as an apparent rebuff, "Unless you see signs and wonders you will not believe" (v. 48), this man perseveres and Jesus relents. He will not accompany the official to Capernaum, but tells him to return home, for his son will live. The man believes Jesus's word, and when he arrives at home and finds his child well, he and his whole household become believers. This is the first of only three healing miracles recounted in John. It seems to be a variant of the story of Jesus healing the centurion's servant at Capernaum, found in Matt 8:5–10 and Luke 7:2–10. Like the centurion in that version, the royal official could possibly have been a Gentile, not a Jew.

> [4:43–54] ⁴³ *After the two days he departed to Galilee.* ⁴⁴ *For Jesus himself testified that a prophet has no honor in his own country.* ⁴⁵ *So when he came to Galilee, the Galileans welcomed him, having seen all that he had done in Jerusalem at the feast, for they too had gone to the feast.* ⁴⁶ *So he came again to Cana in Galilee, where he had made the water wine. And at Caper'na-um there was an official whose son was ill.* ⁴⁷ *When he heard that Jesus had come from Judea to Galilee, he went and begged him to come down and heal his son, for he was at the point of death.* ⁴⁸ *Jesus therefore said to him, "Unless you see signs and wonders you will not believe."* ⁴⁹ *The official said to him, "Sir, come down before my child dies."* ⁵⁰ *Jesus said to him, "Go; your son will live." The man believed the word that Jesus spoke*

to him and went his way. ⁵¹ As he was going down, his servants met him and told him that his son was living. ⁵² So he asked them the hour when he began to mend, and they said to him, "Yesterday at the seventh hour the fever left him." ⁵³ The father knew that was the hour when Jesus had said to him, "Your son will live"; and he himself believed, and all his household. ⁵⁴ This was now the second sign that Jesus did when he had come from Judea to Galilee.

RESPONSE. Herod Antipas, the princeling whom the Romans set up to rule Galilee in 4 BCE, has a number of administrative officers attached to his court in Tiberias. These men of local power and political influence feather their nests from the royal coffers, as was the universal custom in that age, and they have enough clout to set poor Galilean villagers trembling. Antipas, like his father Herod the Great and other members of that ethnically mixed family, is only as Jewish as he needs to be in order to survive politically. "King" Herod Antipas is not especially devout, and most likely neither are his courtiers. The Fourth Gospel tells us here about one such Herodian who finds his way to Jesus, not because he's looking for the Messiah (far from it), but because he has a beloved son who is at death's door. Someone—a devout colleague or a soldier or a peasant, perhaps—has told this *basilikos* about a rabbi named Jesus who performed amazing feats in Jerusalem during Passover. Willing to do anything it takes to keep his boy alive, the man—accompanied, no doubt by the kind of retinue of flunkies favored by ancient officers of state—travels twenty-five miles uphill from his house in Capernaum to the insignificant village of Cana, looking for Jesus. The journey takes most of the daylight hours; John tells us that the official meets Jesus in the evening.[6]

The Fourth Gospel presents to its readers people who are drawn to Jesus for a variety of reasons, some selfish, others selfless. Our royal official falls in the latter category. He loves his son so much he will go to any length to find a cure for him. John's Gospel scorns those who follow Jesus around merely to applaud "signs and wonders" (v. 48) such as healing miracles or to fill their bellies (6:26–27)—not because the Son of Man is lacking in compassion for the sick or the hungry, but because he hopes people will learn to seek more from God than merely physical restoration or food. The Son of Man has come into the world to be what the Samaritans have already called him, the world's Savior. Jesus wants to give *salvation* to all who will receive it. Salvation means transformation—a new life as children of God—not just an improvement of their old life. Unless healed bodies or filled stomachs are understood as simply *signs*, a foretaste of something much better, something eternal, the recipients miss the point.

We wonder how this Herodian bigwig approaches Jesus. . . . Humbly? . . . Imperiously? . . . By himself? . . . With a squad of soldiers? Maybe he dresses in Pharisaical

---

6. Verse 52 says "at the seventh hour," which according to classical reckoning would be 7 p.m. See Edersheim, *Life*, I, 428.

style, complete with a prayer shawl, and tries to look as pious as possible. I assume he is humble, since John tells us the man "begged" Jesus to come down and heal his son (v. 47). He doesn't make a demand. Regardless of how the royal official presents himself, he communicates to Jesus that he has been told the good rabbi is a wonder-worker through whom the Almighty does great things. He earnestly desires the holy man to come with him to Capernaum and work a wonder for him: heal his dying child. A donkey is available to transport the rabbi down to the lakeside town. They can depart Cana at dawn.

The well-off *basilikos* knows better than to offer the rabbi a material reward for his prayers the way he would pay a physician for services rendered. Of course, if Jesus does request an honorarium the official will gladly oblige. Even so, the man assumes Jesus is like a doctor in at least this respect: he won't be able to do anything for the child without touching him, or at least seeing him. Unlike the parallel story in the Synoptics, Jesus does not immediately agree to the man's request (see Matt 8:7 and Luke 7:6). Instead, he says, "Unless you see signs and wonders you will not believe" (v. 48).

In John's Gospel, Jesus does not trust people drawn to him only because he can perform miracles. He isn't looking for an audience who'll say, "Wow! Isn't that awesome," and cheer, but for people who want to know him for who he is: the Son of God and Son of Man. Are we to take "Unless you see signs and wonders you will not believe," as a refusal to meet the official's request? This is open to doubt. The text says Jesus addresses his remark to "him," meaning the *basilikos*, but the "you" in Jesus's rebuke is plural. Therefore, it's possible the reprimand is really aimed at the curious bystanders who tag along behind the entourage of the royal official as his party makes its way into the village. Curious about what this elite visitor might want from Jesus, they linger in the street hoping to witness something memorable. The stern words may be directed to everyone in earshot. I don't read them as a brush-off from Jesus to this sincere father who has cast all his dignity aside and humbled himself to come and plead for Jesus's help.[7]

If we consider Jesus's rebuke as addressed more to the onlookers than to the *basilikos*, then the man's rejoinder, "Sir, come down before my child dies" (v. 49), may be understood as the man's way of saying to Jesus, "Ignore this bunch and please listen to me. I need your help right now. My boy is at death's door!" Jesus does not agree to go down with him to Capernaum, but he says, "Go home. Your son will live." The man takes Jesus's words as a promise and sets out at dawn to return to his home on the Sea of Galilee. En route, servants sent from his household intercept him to report his

---

7. In Mark 7:24–30 (and Matt 15:21–28) we read about Jesus being begged by a Gentile woman to cast a demon out of her daughter. At first he refuses, using an expression of rejection, and then agrees when the woman perseveres, demonstrating both sincerity and humility. He does not come in person to the child, but pronounces her healing from afar. Whether this episode in John illustrates the same point or a different one depends on the way we understand Jesus's remark in v. 48.

child's miraculous recovery. They say the boy began to get well at the very hour Jesus told his father, "Your son will live."

Because his son is restored to health exactly as Jesus promised, the royal administrator and his whole extended family are transformed. Like the child, they too have a new life—a life of trust in Jesus. Like the woman of Samaria, they will become witnesses to what God does through Jesus his Son.[8] John's account of the episode concludes with the narrator's observation, "This was now the second sign that Jesus did when he had come from Judea to Galilee" (v. 54). I wonder precisely *which* event John wants us to recognize as the sign. Is it the boy's restoration to health, achieved at long distance? That's what people generally assume.—But a more meaningful sign in terms of John's theology is that this *basilikos*, a Herodian whose religious bona fides are open to doubt, *believes Jesus's words*. For such a man to treat a word from Jesus as of equal power with the word of the Creator, whose pronouncement, "Let there be light" (Gen 1:3) caused light to be, is a sign of amazing confidence in the Word made flesh, the true Light that has come into the world to vanquish the darkness. This is the kind of belief that Jesus calls "blessed"—belief without seeing (20:29).

Doing Your Own Theology

Questions for reflection after reading John 4.

- John's Gospel chooses five women to illustrate different dimensions of what it means to believe in Jesus—his mother, the woman at the well in Samaria, Martha and Mary of Bethany, and Mary Magdalene. Jesus's mother, whom we meet in chapter 2, is not given a proper name in this gospel, but she is the first example of someone who displays unquestioning belief in his wisdom and power. With no idea of what Jesus will do, his mother orders the servants to do whatever he says. Now John introduces us to a second nameless woman, a Samaritan whom Jesus meets as he rests alone at noon beside a well to which the woman has come to draw water. Jesus boldly violates Jewish rules of propriety and asks her for a drink of water. Displaying wit and self-confidence, the Samaritan woman banters with him in a good-natured way before their conversation turns theological. Jesus tells her that if she knew who he really was, she would be asking *him* for water (v. 10). From its beginning John's Gospel makes clear that Jesus is God in our midst. What the Son does is his Father's work; what the Son speaks is his Father's

---

8. Luke's Gospel tells about Joanna the wife of Chuza, Herod Antipas' steward, who becomes a stalwart supporter of Jesus along with Mary Magdalene and Mary the mother of James. In Luke, she is one of the witnesses to the empty tomb (Luke 24:10). It would be a nice touch to be able to say that Chuza, her husband, was the royal official who came to Jesus in John 4:47. But there is no evidence to connect the two.

message.—*What attributes of his Father does Jesus disclose in his interaction with the woman at the well in Samaria? Are any of these qualities displayed in chapters 1–3?*

- The Samaritan woman discerns that Jesus is a prophet, so she asks him where people ought to worship. He replies "The hour is coming, and now is, when the true worshipers will worship the Father in spirit and truth, for such the Father seeks to worship him. God is spirit, and those who worship him must worship in spirit and truth" (vv. 23–24). When we discussed Jesus's prophetic demonstration in the temple, overturning the tables of money-changers and driving out the sellers of sacrificial animals (2:13–16), we proposed that Jesus might have been taking a stand against a familiar understanding of worship which presumes people can win God's favor by offering him sacrifices.—*If God has no needs of any kind, as we concluded in our earlier discussion, what does Jesus mean when he tells the Samaritan woman "true worshipers will worship the Father in spirit and truth, for such the Father seeks to worship him" (v. 23)? Why does the Father "seek" worshipers? If worship is offered to God, who is the beneficiary of that worship? What qualities make worship "in spirit and truth" different from other kinds of worship?*

- After John describes how a community of Samaritans comes to accept Jesus as "Savior of the world" (v. 42), he introduces a Herodian Jew, a royal official who comes to Jesus asking for a miracle—the healing of his sick child (vv. 46–54). Jesus refuses to cater to those who insist on seeing miracles before they will believe, but the royal official has not come to test the rabbi's ability to perform wonders. He is reaching out for his son's sake; he wants to save his child's life. When he makes that clear, Jesus declines to go with him to Capernaum, but tells him, "Go, your son will live" (v. 50). The man trusts Jesus's promise and goes home. Because his son is indeed healed, the royal official and his whole household believe (v. 53). The royal official departs for home, not knowing whether his boy will—in fact—be healed or not. He exemplifies the principle Jesus later enunciates to Thomas in 20:29, "Blessed are those who have not seen and yet believe."—*Have you ever taken a risk and acted in faith, trusting what you believed to be a promise made to you by God? What was the outcome? If you have never taken such a risky step, what do you think would ever motivate you to do so?*

Chapter Five

5:1–16. Jesus heals a paralyzed man on the Sabbath. The authorities begin to attack him.

Vv. 1–9. "Do you want to be healed?"

INTRODUCTION. Jesus makes a Sabbath-day journey to a double pool known as Bethesda or Bethzatha, just outside the Sheep Gate in the city wall.[1] An old tradition, whose origins are lost in the past, identifies the waters of one of the pools as having curative powers. At unpredictable intervals the water is visibly stirred, perhaps by erratic inflow from a hidden spring but presumably by an angel. Whether this occurs several times a day or only once in a great while is unknown. At these times the pool's therapeutic potency is regarded to be at its height. Consequently, the two pools are enclosed by five ornamental porticoes, where throngs of sick people sit or lie on pallets.

This place of healing is known to Gentiles as well as Jews. The name most English translations give for the double pool is Bethesda, though both the RSV and NRSV use the name Bethzatha. As early as the first century before Christ, a shrine to Asklepios, the Greek god of healing, is found near this pool complex. Before Herod Agrippa built a new wall in 44 CE, the pool was outside the Holy City, which made the presence of a pagan shrine at least endurable to Jews. Archaeologists excavated the site in the late nineteenth century, and it can be visited by tourists today. It is composed of two pools of unequal size with a colonnaded portico between them and similar structures on all four sides, creating the five porticoes mentioned in v. 2. A broad flight of stairs leads

---

1. Lindars, *Gospel of John*, 212–13, points out that the district where the pool lay, just outside the Jerusalem wall, was called Bethzatha ("House of Olives," because olive groves once grew there). The pool itself may have been called Bethesda ("House of Mercy," because of its healing properties). The exact name is uncertain since the Greek manuscripts of John are transliterating a Hebrew name. Most of the manuscripts use the name Bethsaida, which is almost certainly due to scribal confusion with the name of the town on the Sea of Galilee. Bethzatha and Bethesda are the other names given in the manuscripts.

down into one of the pools.[2] (See Fig. 9, p. 29.) In Jesus's day Bethesda is a pleasant venue, just northeast of the temple, and the sick crowd its shady porches, waiting for the water to bubble and swirl, each hoping to be the first to enter the pool and earn a healing. Those who are paralyzed or lame are at a disadvantage when it comes time to go down the steps into the water. They need assistance to get into the pool.

Most commentaries observe that major portions of chapters 5–7 seem to be out of logical order. Jesus's itinerary between Galilee and Jerusalem makes more sense if this material is substantially rearranged. Scholars offer various theories about how and why this apparent displacement occurred.[3] However, since the ancient manuscripts of John present the sequence we see in our modern Bibles, it seems obvious that if this gospel has an editor he wants readers to deal with the material in the order we have it now. The rationale for this arrangement is theological, not historical. We have to keep in mind that the events described in chapters 5–7 may have actually occurred in a sequence different from what we find in the text, which is also true for other events described in John, including the sequence of resurrection appearances in chapters 20–21 (see pp. 303–4 and 327–29, below).

Perhaps John places this story immediately after the account of Jesus's meeting with the woman at the well in Samaria and the healing of the royal official's son because the central character here, the frustrated lame man at the pool, responds to Jesus so differently from either of them. The insensitivity and ingratitude of this man whom Jesus restores to health is another illustration of his own people's inability to understand signs that point to God's presence in their midst. Although they claim to expect the Messiah, the Jews demonstrate they are unable to recognize him. Jesus will tell us they cannot identify the Son because they truly do not know the Father.

> **[5:1–9]** [1] *After this there was a feast of the Jews, and Jesus went up to Jerusalem.* [2] *Now there is in Jerusalem by the Sheep Gate a pool, in Hebrew called Beth-za'tha, which has five porticoes.* [3] *In these lay a multitude of invalids, blind, lame, paralyzed* [Other ancient authorities insert, wholly or in part, *waiting for the moving of the water;* [4] *for an angel of the Lord went down at certain seasons into the pool, and troubled the water; whoever stepped in first after the troubling of the water was healed of whatever disease he had.*] [5] *One man was there, who had been ill for thirty-eight years.* [6] *When Jesus saw him and knew that he had been lying there a long time, he said to him, "Do you want to be healed?"* [7] *The sick man answered him, "Sir, I have no man to put me into the pool when the water is troubled, and while I am going another steps down before me."* [8] *Jesus said to him, "Rise, take up your pallet, and walk."* [9] *And at once the man was healed, and he took up his pallet and walked. Now that day was the Sabbath.*

2. Von Wahlde, "Archaeology," 560–66.

3. See, e.g., Lindars, *Gospel of John*, 48–50.

RESPONSE. The Prophet Isaiah wrote, "Seek the Lord while he may be found, call upon him while he is near; let the wicked forsake his way, and the unrighteous man his thoughts; let him return to the Lord, that he may have mercy on him, and to our God, for he will abundantly pardon" (55:6–7). When I read the account of Jesus healing the crippled man at the pool, these words come to mind. The invalid at the pool is so fixated on getting his needs met by the quasi-magical healing waters that he thinks of nothing else, and the Jewish authorities are so obsessed with the minutiae of Sabbath regulations that they miss the work of God that has happened virtually before their eyes. Both fail to seek the Lord, even when he presents himself in their midst, ready to be found. The paralyzed man and the temple authorities represent two examples of the descendants of Abraham, to whom the Lord has now come, according to his promise. Their capacity to see, hear, and understand is very low. They're not prepared to recognize the One who has come. Jesus's healing of the lame man at the pool is a sign, though neither the man who is healed nor the Jewish leaders who learn of his healing can perceive it.—The question for twenty-first century readers is: do *we* have eyes that will see and ears that will hear?

Religious practices can open us to God; they can also blind us to unexpected divine visitations. Narrow, dogmatic, and purely ritualistic religion blocks seekers from God, who is portrayed as accessible only through proper channels. Often we see only what we expect to see. Anything different may as well be invisible, unless we are prepared for God to surprise us. In Luke's gospel Jesus offers a parable about servants who stay awake, watching for their master's return, even at an unexpected hour (12:35–40). The point of John's story about the healing of the lame man at the pool resembles Luke's parable. It appears that the author of the Fourth Gospel perceives the religion of Israel in his time as characterized by mechanical piety, obsessive legalism, and dead traditionalism. Jesus comes to the temple for a second time to disturb the religious routine.

A paralyzed man lies on a pallet as close to the pool as he can get. No able-bodied person appears to be with him to help him into the water. Jesus somehow knows that this unfortunate fellow has been coming to Bethesda for a long time. We can only guess about his personal circumstances. Perhaps kinsmen help him get here from his home in the morning, leave him lying on his pallet with a little food to eat, and then go to their work. The man has made friends with other invalids who are regulars at Bethesda. They lie or sit together near the water, keeping their eyes on its surface, and chatting with one another to pass the time.

Jesus looks down at the recumbent man and asks him, "Do you want to be healed?" Like other questions asked by Jesus in John's Gospel, this one invites readers to contemplate it as if addressed to them. There are two ways to hear the question, depending on the inflection with which we imagine it is asked. It can convey tenderness towards a lonely sufferer or it can express a hint of rebuke for a malingerer—which would mean, in the latter case, "Do you really *want* to be healed?" (v. 6). We can't discern which inflection Jesus uses for the man who cannot walk. Is he truly eager to be healed, or has he grown content to lie in the shade and visit with his friends? What about us: do we want God to come into our life and make us whole, or have we grown content with our chronic brokenness and our inability to walk the new paths where the Spirit would take us?

The man could conceivably answer Jesus's question by saying, "I *do* indeed want to be healed! Please, sir, would you be willing to sit with me and help me into the water when it stirs?" Instead he only voices self-pity, "I have no friend to help me into the pool at the right moment; when I'm trying to get myself down to the water, someone else steps down ahead of me" (paraphrase of v. 7). In other words, "My current situation is hopeless, isn't that obvious to you?"

With a tone of authority, Jesus says, "Stand up; pick up your mat; and walk around" (paraphrase of v. 8). At his words, the man feels sensation and strength return to his legs. He does what Jesus instructs. He climbs to his feet and starts to walk for the first time in thirty-eight years. A happy uproar ensues when this habitué of Bethesda suddenly stands up unaided and begins to walk. The pool has a reputation for cures, but they don't happen often, and this one is unique: the man is healed without getting in the pool! And he doesn't even walk with a limp. In his excitement, the long-time sufferer now made well forgets about the man who made him well. He doesn't run after the healer to thank him or even ask his name. Jesus, who in John's narrative never desires fame for his ability to work miracles, slips away through the high-spirited crowd that gathers around the man once lame, who now dances with glee while everyone else cheers.

Like the healed paralytic in the story, we accept God's mercies immediately, but often we're quite slow to express gratitude. Sometimes we fail even to consider that our apparent good fortune might best be understood as the work of God.

Vv. 10–18. The healed paralytic directs hostile priests and Pharisees to Jesus.

INTRODUCTION. After healing the paralyzed man, Jesus disappears into the crowd that fills the Bethesda arcades. The healed man makes his way into the nearby temple—still carrying his pallet as Jesus told him to do. After the return of the Jews from their Babylonian exile in the fifth century BCE, meticulous observance of the Sabbath becomes a primary obligation and social identifier of Jews. In the temple, the man encounters other Jews who criticize him for carrying his bedroll on the Sabbath. That is labor, and labor is forbidden. The former paralytic would like to escape their displeasure by passing the blame to the healer who told him to do this, but he doesn't even know Jesus's name. Later, Jesus encounters the healed man in the courts of the temple and tells him to "sin no more, that nothing worse befall you" (v. 14). The man goes immediately to find his accusers—almost certainly Pharisees—and he directs them to Jesus. Thereafter, the Pharisaical legal purists will begin to persecute Jesus. Jesus's warning that the man "sin no more" does not indicate that Jesus shares the popular idea that physical illness is punishment for sin.[4] He refers rather to the sin of turning away from the grace and love of God openly disclosed in God's Son. The ungrateful man healed at the pool represents those who have ample reason to love and believe in Jesus, but instead betray him. In John's Gospel, turning away from Jesus is to turn one's back on God, to choose death over life.

After this, Jesus will be subject to unceasing and ever-increasing enmity from the Jewish authorities. John usually labels Jesus's opponents simply "the Jews," though his actual critics in this instance are probably Jerusalem Pharisees.[5] Elsewhere this gospel will show Jesus confronted by representatives of the chief priests, and occasionally Pharisees and the chief priests will challenge him in tandem. Anger towards Jesus on this occasion is not as much for violating the Sabbath law (or encouraging someone else to do so) as for proposing that he possesses divine authority to permit what sacred tradition forbids (v. 18).

We imagine Jesus from 5:15 onward as being repeatedly "put on trial"—metaphorically-speaking—before a hostile Jewish law court.[6] That trial begins now, adjourns for a while, and then reconvenes. It adjourns again and proceeds to reconvene, then adjourn and reconvene several more times through John's Gospel. In these more-or-less judicial hearings before "the Jews," Jesus faces prosecutors or—more accurately—"persecutors" (v. 16), from the temple authorities and the Pharisees. He even faces accusation by some tentative "believers" (8:31). This protracted quasi-legal process will reach its culmination in a final, formal session, 18:28–19:16, when the chief priests, finally admitting that they have no king but Caesar (19:15), bring the true Messiah before the court of the Roman governor for final judgment. The whole, long business is laden with irony in John, because the man on trial is really the Judge of all.

> **[5:10–18]** [10] So the Jews said to the man who was cured, "It is the Sabbath, it is not lawful for you to carry your pallet." [11] But he answered them, "The man who healed me said to me, 'Take up your pallet, and walk.'" [12] They asked him, "Who is the man who said to you, 'Take up your pallet, and walk'?" [13] Now the man who had been healed did not know who it was, for Jesus had withdrawn, as there was a crowd in the place. [14] Afterward, Jesus found him in the temple, and said to him, "See, you are well! Sin no more, that nothing worse befall you." [15] The man went away and told the Jews that it was Jesus who had healed him. [16] And this was why the Jews persecuted Jesus, because he did this on the Sabbath. [17] But Jesus answered them, "My Father is working still, and I am working." [18] This was why the Jews sought all the more to kill him, because he not only broke the Sabbath but also called God his Father, making himself equal with God.

4. Jesus will correct that piece of folk wisdom in 9:2–3.

5. Kysar, *John*, 77. See Appendix Two pp. 357–58, below.

6. Kysar, *John*, 166.

RESPONSE. When scrupulous representatives of the Jewish authorities—probably Pharisees—accost the former invalid for carrying his pallet on the Sabbath, he defends himself by telling them he's obeying the instructions of the man who healed him. Shortly afterward, Jesus finds the man in the temple (where we hope he gave thanks for his healing) and warns him, "See, now you're well. So stop sinning, or else something a lot worse will happen to you" (paraphrase of v. 14). In John's Gospel, sin is not merely a transgression of the Law. *Sin* is failure to accept God's gift of a relationship with himself mediated through his Son, refusal of the new life God graciously offers. Jesus does not tell the ungrateful man to improve his morals or else he'll get sick again; he advises him to open himself to the much greater endowment the healer wants to give, for which his new physical mobility is merely a sign. If the former invalid rejects the greater gift, a consequence worse than physical impairment lies in store for him. His destiny will be a life cut off from God. For John, life separated from God is no life at all.

On one level, we might think of the paralytic's behavior as foreshadowing Judas's betrayal. One to whom Jesus gives loving favor and a new life betrays him into the hands of his enemies. Even though only the former invalid technically violated the Sabbath, the legal rigorists also accuse Jesus of breaking the Law by performing a non-urgent healing on the Sabbath. In addition, they want to hold him to account for telling the man to carry his pallet. In their determination to establish a proper definition of "work," the legalists abandon the Deuteronomic understanding of the Sabbath as a day of rest for people whose ancestors were forced to labor seven days a week as slaves in Egypt.[7] The Sabbath day celebrates Israel's God-given deliverance from the demands of alien taskmasters, yet these legal rigorists are taskmasters that enslave their own people with the minutiae of their traditions.

The rabbis of Jesus's time understand that although God rested on the seventh day from his six days' labor of creation, his work of giving life, ending life, and passing judgment (upholding the moral order of the universe) never ceases. The act of restoring a crippled man to full use of his body is obviously one of the life-giving works of God, performed through the merciful agency of his Son. There is no day of the week when such a work should be forbidden, including the Sabbath.[8]

When Jesus hears his accusers' challenge he replies, "My Father is working still, and I am working" (v. 17). Jesus's defense makes his situation even worse in the eyes of some of "the Jews," because now Jesus appears to claim divine authority to ignore a key commandment of the Law, a commandment that marks Jews as God's own people. Who does he think he is, to speak of God's work as his own work and of God as his own Father? As a consequence of healing the paralytic and then defending himself

7. See Deut 5:15.

8. Keener, *Gospel of John*, 1:646–47. The Pharisees would agree that the life-giving work of God went on without ceasing, including on the Sabbath. However, they would *not* agree with Jesus's assertion that he is God's Son and agent and therefore charged with doing his Father's work on the Sabbath.

boldly to his critics, Jesus becomes a target of persecution. John records in v. 18 Jesus's first explicit rejection by official representatives of his nation, but more rejection will soon follow. The Jewish leaders' hostility to him will grow bitter.

Enabling a paralyzed man to walk again is a life-giving act. John identifies the Son of God as, above all, the life-giver. The prologue says concerning the incarnate Word, "In him was life, and the life was the light of men" (1:4). *That is the great truth at the heart of John's Gospel.* Beginning with the prologue, John starts "putting down markers on a road of which Easter, not some 'going to heaven after death,' is the intended destination."[9] In words that probably formed the original conclusion to John, the author summarizes his purpose by saying that these things are "written that you may believe that Jesus is the Christ, the Son of God, and that believing you may have life in his name" (20:30). Furthermore, the life which the Son bestows is offered here and now to all who put their trust in the One whom the Father loves and sent into the world to be its Savior. The life he bestows is an eternal and limitless possession, not something to be deferred until after the general resurrection and final Judgment. When Jesus tells Martha, "I am the resurrection and the life" (11:25), he does not use "resurrection" merely as a metaphor for a present spiritual experience. It is indeed "a new life through which new possibilities are available in the present . . . [but also] the 'life of the age to come' brought forward into the present so that believers can enjoy it already and be assured that it will last through bodily death into God's future."[10]

5:19–47. Confronting "the Jews," Jesus claims authority as Son of God.

Vv. 19–47. "The Son can do . . . only what he sees the Father doing."

INTRODUCTION. The question is regularly raised, "Did Jesus actually claim to be God?" We find the question answered unambiguously in the affirmative only in the Fourth Gospel. John 5:19–47 reports the first occasion where Jesus describes his relationship with God and clearly portrays himself not only as God's Son but also his Father's personal representative on earth. Though he perceives the Son as subordinate to the Father (v. 19), not the Father's equal, the author of John clearly understands the incarnate *Logos* to be God, as written in the first verse of the prologue.

John presents vv. 19–47 as an extended address by Jesus on the subject of his authority as the agent of God. John locates this address within his narrative in a way which implies that Jesus delivers it to the Pharisees who caught the paralytic violating the Sabbath, though Jesus does not mention the specific issue of proper Sabbath observance. This is the first of a number of Jesus's monologues in the Fourth Gospel.[11]

---

9. Wright, *Resurrection*, 447.

10. Ibid.

11. O'Day, *Gospel of John*, 583. Some commentators connect vv. 17–19 with this address, but those

(Commentators call these monologues *discourses*.) Earlier we read similar but much shorter discourses of Jesus embedded within his dialogues with Nicodemus (3:3–15) and the Samaritan woman (4:7–26).

The Pharisees who confront Jesus believe in the resurrection of the dead—a resurrection of the wicked and the righteous alike, after which the wicked will be condemned and the righteous rewarded. John shows Jesus telling the temple authorities that his Father has empowered him to impart a dimension of resurrection life immediately—deliverance from the fear of judgment. He says, "He who hears my word and believes him who sent me, has eternal life; he does not come into judgment, but has passed from death to life" (v. 24). Those who believe will not face judgment at the general resurrection on the last day. John does not intend for his readers to understand this new life as a replacement of the future resurrection, but rather that the events taking place during Jesus's ministry—the reactions of people to Jesus, in belief or unbelief—are "true present signs of their future fate."[12]

[**5:19–47**] [19] *Jesus said to them, "Truly, truly, I say to you, the Son can do nothing of his own accord, but only what he sees the Father doing; for whatever he does, that the Son does likewise.* [20] *For the Father loves the Son, and shows him all that he himself is doing; and greater works than these will he show him, that you may marvel.* [21] *For as the Father raises the dead and gives them life, so also the Son gives life to whom he will.* [22] *The Father judges no one, but has given all judgment to the Son,* [23] *that all may honor the Son, even as they honor the Father. He who does not honor the Son does not honor the Father who sent him.* [24] *Truly, truly, I say to you, he who hears my word and believes him who sent me, has eternal life; he does not come into judgment, but has passed from death to life.*

[25] *"Truly, truly, I say to you, the hour is coming, and now is, when the dead will hear the voice of the Son of God, and those who hear will live.* [26] *For as the Father has life in himself, so he has granted the Son also to have life in himself,* [27] *and has given him authority to execute judgment, because he is the Son of man.* [28] *Do not marvel at this; for the hour is coming when all who are in the tombs will hear his voice* [29] *and come forth, those who have done good, to the resurrection of life, and those who have done evil, to the resurrection of judgment.*

[30] *"I can do nothing on my own authority; as I hear, I judge; and my judgment is just, because I seek not my own will but the will of him who sent me.* [31] *If I bear witness to myself, my testimony is not true;* [32] *there is another who bears witness to me, and I know that the testimony which he bears to*

---

verses fit better as a conclusion to the story of the healing at the Pool of Bethesda, allowing Jesus's announcement, "My Father is working still, and I am working," to serve as what Smith, *John*, 142–43, calls "the thematic key" to Jesus's discourse in vv. 19–47.

12. Wright, *Resurrection*, 442–43.

me is true. ³³ You sent to John, and he has borne witness to the truth. ³⁴ Not that the testimony which I receive is from man; but I say this that you may be saved. ³⁵ He was a burning and shining lamp, and you were willing to rejoice for a while in his light. ³⁶ But the testimony which I have is greater than that of John; for the works which the Father has granted me to accomplish, these very works which I am doing, bear me witness that the Father has sent me. ³⁷ And the Father who sent me has himself borne witness to me. His voice you have never heard, his form you have never seen; ³⁸ and you do not have his word abiding in you, for you do not believe him whom he has sent. ³⁹ You search the Scriptures, because you think that in them you have eternal life; and it is they that bear witness to me; ⁴⁰ yet you refuse to come to me that you may have life. ⁴¹ I do not receive glory from men. ⁴² But I know that you have not the love of God within you. ⁴³ I have come in my Father's name, and you do not receive me; if another comes in his own name, him you will receive. ⁴⁴ How can you believe, who receive glory from one another and do not seek the glory that comes from the only God? ⁴⁵ Do not think that I shall accuse you to the Father; it is Moses who accuses you, on whom you set your hope. ⁴⁶ If you believed Moses, you would believe me, for he wrote of me. ⁴⁷ But if you do not believe his writings, how will you believe my words?"

RESPONSE. John gives us Jesus's response to the accusation of violating the Sabbath, probably brought against him by scribes whose professional life is dedicated to interpreting the Law of Moses. In chapter 1 similar representatives of the Jewish establishment question John about his baptizing (1:19–22). They ask him, "Who are you? . . . Let us have an answer for those who sent us. What do you say about yourself?" Although the Fourth Gospel doesn't provide us with the questions the Pharisees ask Jesus in this instance, only his response, we assume their queries are much like those addressed earlier to the Baptizer. Perhaps Jesus's interrogators ask, "Why did you heal a sick man on the Sabbath and then tell him to break the Sabbath law? Who gave you authority to do this? What do you have to say for yourself?" In usual rabbinic practice, questioners expect the accused to offer a legal excuse or explanation for his behavior, supported by the judgments of rabbis in earlier generations. If he can cite sages of old who approved of doing as he has done, then the defendant will score valid debating points in the eyes of the Pharisees. But that is not Jesus's way. He does not appeal to the memory of what some great sage once said, but rather speaks on his own authority as the representative of his Father.

Since Jesus's time, his disciples have frequently been required to defend what they believe. Persistent judicial persecution of Jesus by the Jerusalem authorities set a precedent for his followers' arraignment before hostile judges, Jewish and otherwise, over the next three centuries.[13] The rhetorical genre now called Christian apologetics

---

13. Unfortunately, there is an even longer and sadder history of the church's persecution both of

found its first bold practitioner in Paul (see Acts 22:39–26:32). This eloquent apostle had many successors in the years when Christianity was establishing itself and again after the Enlightenment, when Christians in Europe began to feel ridiculed by "cultured despisers of religion."[14] In our own era we see Christianity assailed frequently by clever, media-savvy atheist polemicists.

If we are personally attacked by aggressive atheists or simply quizzed by neighbors who have no religion and cannot understand why anyone else should, we can take comfort from the knowledge that our Lord and his first disciples walked this road before us. Here John paints a picture of Jesus as a sharp-minded, able debater, unafraid of highly placed adversaries and willing to offend their theological sensibilities if that seems necessary.

I imagine 5:19–47 as Jesus's opening statement as his trial begins—his long-running quasi-judicial conflict with "the Jews." In the current instance, Jesus does not deny he told the healed man to carry his pallet; neither does he dispute whether he violated the rules by which the rabbis defined proper conduct on the Sabbath. Instead, Jesus offers a defense which enrages the prosecutors: he claims to be God's own Son, acting as the personal agent of his Father. He tells them, "My Father is working still, and I am working. . . . The Son can do nothing of his own accord, but only what he sees the Father doing; for whatever he does, that the Son does likewise" (vv. 17 and 19). The Father gives life, and the Son gives *new* life.

This section is full of elevated Johannine vocabulary about the person and work of Christ, offered as the words of Jesus himself, though the language seems obviously the product of lengthy post-Easter reflection by the author (or editor) of the gospel. We learn the Son does only what he sees the Father doing. His personal will is melded with the will of his Father. There exists both personal intimacy and functional unity between Father and Son, for the Son says, "I seek not my own will but the will of him who sent me" (v. 30).

For John, the single word "life" and the expression "eternal life" are interchangeable, and their meaning is the same. Jesus tells us, "Truly, truly, I say to you, he who hears my word and believes him who sent me, has eternal life; he does not come into judgment, but has passed from death to life" (5:24). It's challenging to try to explain to people of our day how it might feel to have eternal life as a present possession. John Wijngaards, a Roman Catholic priest and longtime missionary in India, describes the experience as "living in God's eternal today."[15] It starts now as a new and timeless quality of life, a life lived in intimacy with the Father, a life in which physical death no longer matters to the believer. The power of death and the fear of death are broken, and believers have no fear of the prospect of a future final Judgment at the end of his-

"unbelievers" and of Christians whose beliefs were judged as heretical.

14. The eighteenth-century German philosopher and theologian Friedrich Schleiermacher wrote a famous book in 1799 entitled *On Religion: Speeches to Its Cultured Despisers*.

15. Wijngaards, *Gospel of John and His Letters*, 219.

tory. Trust in the Father's love holds them and keeps them in peace. Although in vv. 26–29 John notes his expectation of a final Judgment, he asserts that the Father has installed his Son as the Judge. Those who know, love, and trust the Son of God in this life need have no fear of his consigning them to punishment on the last day.

Carrying forward the metaphor of a judicial proceeding, Jesus offers his prosecutors the testimony of four truthful witnesses who substantiate his rightful claim to exercise the Father's authority. The first witness is John (vv. 32–35); the second is the obvious works of the Father which he is doing, the most recent example of which is the healing at the pool for which he is being prosecuted (v. 36); the third is the Father himself, whose voice his enemies refuse to hear (vv. 37–38); and the fourth is Scripture, including the Torah (vv. 39, 46–47). Jesus says to his accusers, "You search the Scriptures, because you think that in them you have eternal life; and it is they that bear witness to me; yet you refuse to come to me that you may have life" (vv. 39–40). Four witnesses attest to the life-giving authority of the Son whom the Father has sent into the world, yet the Jerusalem authorities and the Pharisees will not heed them.

What if you or I were asked to produce witnesses whose testimony would prove that we are indeed disciples of Jesus Christ? Could we propose counterparts for at least the first three witnesses Jesus names to his critics? I suggest only the Lord's first three categories of witnesses, not his fourth, the testimony of Scripture. We should probably not try sifting through Scripture looking for proof-text illustrations that prove our discipleship. But might we not appeal, as Jesus once did, to the testimony of people who know us, works the Father has given us to do, and words the Father himself has spoken to us?

In Jesus's day the disciples of a great rabbi would seek to reproduce the life of their teacher. The rabbi was closer than a father to his disciples, and the disciples were his spiritual offspring.[16] At the Last Supper, after Jesus washes his disciples' feet, he says, "A new commandment I give to you, that you love one another; even as I have loved you, that you also love one another. By this will all men know that you are my disciples, if you love one another" (13:34–35). Since Jesus labels this commandment "new," he implies that the love he is asking from them goes beyond behavior expected from disciples of the scribes. We set ourselves up for humiliation if we try to recruit witnesses who will testify that we love one another the way Jesus loves us. None of us can bear comparison with our Lord. We're not worthy, and we know it. Nevertheless, Thomas à Kempis's classic, *The Imitation of Christ*, remains a best-seller after more than five centuries. Sincere disciples still want to imitate Jesus—recognizing that we

16. Contemporary Christians may be surprised to learn that the ideal of discipleship was modeled by the disciples of the Pharisaic scribes, beginning before the time of Christ. Disciples of prominent scribes were devoted, dedicated, and courageous in applying their teachers' interpretation of the Law. The Jewish public apparently extended to Jesus the honorific courtesies commonly given scribes— including the title "rabbi"—and the behavior of Jesus's disciples must have been expected to be as exemplary as that of the scribes' disciples. See Jeremias, *Jerusalem*, 242–44, for a description of the typical behavior of scribes' disciples.

will do so poorly or only occasionally. Accepting that our imitation of Christ will be imperfect, does anyone know us well enough to testify whether we're even making the effort? Are we bearing the sort of fruit Jesus expects from his disciples (15:8)?

Jesus tells his critics that John the Baptist testifies to his identity as Son of God. I spent my adult life as a pastor in different congregations. I hope there are people among whom I ministered over the years who remember times when I was at least somewhat Christlike in my love for them. Surely there were at least a few occasions when I put others' welfare ahead of my own, when in a small way I "laid down my life" for them. Perhaps these people could be for me what John the Baptist was for Jesus. Maybe there are some people who know me who would be willing to testify that my discipleship bore fruit.

Jesus told his accusers, "Truly, truly, I say to you, the Son can do nothing of his own accord, but only what he sees the Father doing; for whatever he does, that the Son does likewise" (v. 19). He named the miraculous works the Father did through him as the second great testimony to his identity as Son of God. In our own time, inexplicable, miraculous healings still happen, demonstrating the power of Christ at work through his disciples. One such occasion looms large in my own experience because I was the unexpected agent of the healing. It's a story worth recounting.

Late one afternoon a number of years ago I was called to a local hospital where an elderly parishioner was dying. Her name was Fran. The morning of the day before, I had sat in the surgery waiting room with her blind husband, Bill, while she underwent an operation for a serious abscess and peritoneal infection. After many hours, the surgeon—whom I knew—came out and told her husband and me that unexpected complications had presented themselves, and Fran's post-operative situation was grave. He had done all he could. Fran was going to the surgical ICU, but her condition was critical and her chances were slim. After sitting a bit longer with Bill and one of his adult children, I went home. Very late that afternoon, the surgeon asked the ICU nurse to call me. Fran was not likely to survive the night.

When I arrived, I learned Fran had not recovered consciousness after surgery. I stood by her bed, anointed her, and read the rite for the dying from the Book of Common Prayer. Bill and their children and older grandchildren were with me in the room, sobbing. After I had finished the ritual, I put my prayer book down and asked Fran's family to join hands with me and each another, forming a circle around her bed. Then I prayed in words like these, "Dear Lord, we are bold to ask for a miracle for Fran. Bill needs her help. Her family loves her and needs her too. Please leave Fran with us a while longer. The doctors have given up, but we haven't. We pray, heal her now in Jesus's name." After the prayer, I hugged Bill and his kids and told them to call me if they needed me. I left the room and went out to the desk, where I told the nurse, "It doesn't matter what time it is. If Fran dies during the night, please call me." No call came that night. The next morning I went back to the ICU. When I asked about Fran, the nurse on the desk said, "She's not here anymore."

I asked, "When did she die?"

The woman replied, "She didn't die. A little before midnight, her vital signs all returned to normal. Later she regained consciousness and wanted to sit up. She even wanted something to eat. The doctor moved her to a room in Transitional Care. I've never seen anything like this."

I found Fran's new room, and when I went in her happy family said, "It's a miracle! It's a miracle! That's what you prayed for, and it happened." Fran was awake and alert, and we had a short visit before I left so she could be alone with her family. Fran was about eighty years old then, and she was more than ninety when she finally left this life. I prayed for a miracle for her—quite literally—but in truth I had little expectation my prayer would be answered with an overnight complete medical turn-around. Despite my slender faith, Fran was healed. If anything was ever a testimony to the love and healing power of Christ, this was it. I spoke with her surgeon after I left her, and he agreed with my explanation. It could only be a miracle.

His Father's own voice is the third "witness" that Jesus says attests to his rightful claim to be the Son and earthly agent of God. Undoubtedly, Jesus has in mind some event in his life when the Father spoke to him, perhaps the heavenly voice at the time of his baptism described by the Synoptic gospels (see, e.g., Luke 3:22). I have experienced the quizzical looks and rolled eyes one can expect in our day when one says, "God spoke to me." Nevertheless, I admit to hearing the Lord speak to me with clarity half a dozen times. God's voice was never audible, but it was quite distinct in my mind. It touched my heart and changed my life. The first such occasion was at my ordination. I was kneeling in front of the bishop, aware of his hands on my head along with those of the attending presbyters. As the bishop was praying, the Lord spoke to me in these exact words: "Until now, you have done what you wanted to do. Hereafter, you shall do what I would have you do." Forty-four years ago I thought such episodes only happened to schizophrenics. I was a very sane rationalist, unlikely to hear the voice of God. Nevertheless, I did hear, and my life took a new direction immediately.

We are persuaded that Jesus is the Son of God and Savior of the World. If we commit ourselves to follow him as disciples, he will manifest himself in us and through us. We will, by God's grace, ultimately become *like* him. If we are "begotten from above by water and the Spirit" (3:5), as Jesus said to Nicodemus, our likeness to the Master will be the product, not of our own effort but of his Spirit at work within us. When Jesus proposes to his prosecutors four different witnesses on his behalf, those accusers reject his witnesses. The rabbinic legalists and the chief priests are Jesus's implacable adversaries in John's Gospel. Nevertheless, though the Jewish authorities did not believe Jesus or his witnesses, others did. Our own discipleship is built on their testimony. Neither your witnesses nor mine may convince twenty-first century "cultured despisers of religion." Nevertheless, some will hear our testimony and believe in the Lord we serve. When that happens, our own trust in Christ will grow.

Doing Your Own Theology

Questions for reflection after reading John 5.

- The paralytic man at the Bethesda Pool is a character type which appears nowhere else in the gospel tradition: a person Jesus miraculously heals, yet who displays neither belief in Jesus nor gratitude for his restoration to health. In fact, the man even betrays Jesus to those who will become his enemies. The paralytic's subsequent behavior compels us to recall the question Jesus asks him when he first encounters him at the pool, "Do you want to be healed?" Jesus finds him later in the temple, after the Pharisees have accused the man of violating the Sabbath, and tells him, "See, you are well! Sin no more, that nothing worse befall you" (v. 14). Rather than heed Jesus's warning, the paralytic goes directly to the Pharisees and identifies Jesus to them as the person that told him to break the Sabbath rules. As a character, the man compares unfavorably with the Samaritan woman and the royal official about whom we read in chapter 4 and he seems the precise opposite of the man born blind whom we will meet in chapter 9.—*Why do you think John tells us about the ungrateful paralyzed man? Does he represent a certain type of person, perhaps a type we might still encounter today?*

- Along with circumcision and special dietary laws, abstention from any form of work on the Sabbath still remains a key mark of identity which helps set observant Jews apart from other ethnic/religious groups. The Synoptic gospels present a total of five occasions when Jesus heals on the Sabbath; John tells about two others. He describes one here in chapter 5, the other in chapter 9.—*Do you think Jesus deliberately heals people on the Sabbath, knowing that it will provoke a reaction from the Pharisees, who are legal rigorists? Do you think Jesus wants to make a point about healing or a point about the Pharisees' rigidity concerning Sabbath observance in general? In what way might Jesus's point apply to twenty-first century Christians?*

- Jesus makes the Jewish authorities angry when he claims to be God's Son, acting in the world with his Father's authority. He offers his opponents four different "witnesses" who are able to testify to his identity as God's Son. He names [1] John the Baptist, regarded by the common people as a prophet sent from God (v. 33–35); [2] the miracles his Father performs through him (v. 36); [3] the voice of the Father himself (v. 37–38); and [4] the prophetic testimony of the Scriptures (vv. 39–40).—*If you consider yourself a disciple of Jesus, called to be like him—"to reproduce the life of your Master" in the world—what evidence would you offer to someone who disputes your claim to be Jesus's disciple?*

Chapter Six

6:1–15. Jesus feeds five thousand with five loaves and two fish.

Vv. 1–15. The crowd Jesus feeds wants to make him king.

INTRODUCTION. The events in chapter 5 are set in Jerusalem. This chapter, however, finds Jesus back in Galilee just prior to the second of three Passovers mentioned in John. As indicated in the introduction to 2:13–25, Passover is the setting for three pivotal moments in the Fourth Gospel. The first is the so-called "cleansing of the temple," when official hostility against Jesus begins (2:13–22). Here we come to the second, when after giving two signs—the multiplication of the loaves for the multitude and the theophany in the storm for the inner circle of disciples—Jesus, who is already misunderstood and regarded with suspicion by the temple authorities, is rejected by the crowds who have followed him and even by a member of his inner circle. The third and final Passover will be the setting for Jesus's passion and resurrection, and the account of it consumes the entire second half of the gospel (11:55–20:29).

Chapter 6 is John's longest as well as one of the most theologically dense. It details two of the seven signs scholars enumerate, leading up to Jesus's last week—though John makes it clear that belief in Jesus grounded exclusively on the seeing of signs can only be a partial faith. In the Fourth Gospel, seeing does not automatically lead to believing. The signs point to Jesus's true identity, but what he says about himself is the key that unlocks the significance of the signs. The heart of what Jesus teaches in this chapter is expressed near its climax, "It is the spirit that gives life, the flesh is of no avail; the words that I have spoken to you are spirit and life" (v. 63). This tells us that flesh and spirit belong together, and only when they are held together is real life possible.[1]

The feeding of the five thousand is the only miracle described in all four of the canonical gospels.[2] That Jesus presided over the feeding of a hungry throng near the

---

1. O'Day, *Gospel of John*, 612.

2. The Synoptic accounts of the feeding of the five thousand are Matt 14:13–21; Mark 6:32–44; and Luke 9:10–17. Both Matthew and Mark also describe a second miraculous feeding of a crowd that

shore of the Sea of Galilee is an indubitable fact. The precise details and exact location of that event are presented differently in each gospel, but the substance of all four accounts is the same: five thousand men plus unnumbered women and children are fed on the lakeside after Jesus gives thanks over five loaves of bread and two pieces of fish and distributes them to the crowd. (In the Synoptics he directs his followers to distribute them.) After everyone's hunger has been satisfied, the disciples gather twelve basketsful of bread fragments. The story of the feeding of the five thousand told by John is similar to the Synoptic versions, but the context in which John sets the event is sufficiently different from the other gospels to demonstrate a broader theological point.

We count the feeding of the five thousand as the fourth of John's signs. There is no doubt that the miracle of the loaves had symbolic significance for the early church on a variety of levels. Second century Roman catacomb frescoes sometimes show baskets of loaves alongside baskets of fish or pictures of five round loaves and two fish framing scenes that portray either the Last Supper, a Eucharist, an agape meal, or a funeral banquet.

> [6:1–15] *¹ After this Jesus went to the other side of the Sea of Galilee, which is the Sea of Tiber'i-as. ² And a multitude followed him, because they saw the signs which he did on those who were diseased. ³ Jesus went up on the mountain, and there sat down with his disciples. ⁴ Now the Passover, the feast of the Jews, was at hand. ⁵ Lifting up his eyes, then, and seeing that a multitude was coming to him, Jesus said to Philip, "How are we to buy bread, so that these people may eat?" ⁶ This he said to test him, for he himself knew what he would do. ⁷ Philip answered him, "Two hundred denarii would not buy enough bread for each of them to get a little." ⁸ One of his disciples, Andrew, Simon Peter's brother, said to him, ⁹ "There is a lad here who has five barley loaves and two fish; but what are they among so many?" ¹⁰ Jesus said, "Make the people sit down." Now there was much grass in the place; so the men sat down, in number about five thousand. ¹¹ Jesus then took the loaves, and when he had given thanks, he distributed them to those who were seated; so also the fish, as much as they wanted. ¹² And when they had eaten their fill, he told his disciples, "Gather up the fragments left over, that nothing may be lost." ¹³ So they gathered them up and filled twelve baskets with fragments from the five barley loaves, left by those who had eaten. ¹⁴ When the people saw the sign which he had done, they said, "This is indeed the prophet who is to come into the world." ¹⁵ Perceiving then that they were about to come and take him by force to make him king, Jesus withdrew again to the mountain by himself.*

---

numbers four thousand (Matt 15:29–38; Mark 7:31–37). Most commentators regard the two different miraculous multiplications of loaves as variant accounts of a single event.

RESPONSE. John tells us that a large number of people are following Jesus "because they saw the signs which he did on those who were diseased" (v. 2). Since John gives the details of only two healing miracles prior to this point (4:46–54 and 5:2–9), this serves as a reminder that Jesus also performed many other healing miracles. In addition to those who follow Jesus in order to be healed, even to the extent of following him to the western side of the lake, there seems to be a *second* crowd in John's story. This is the multitude Jesus sees coming to him (v. 5) after he has seated himself on the hillside with his disciples, in the traditional posture of a teacher ready to impart wisdom to his followers.[3] The second group may represent a category of people different from those who have followed Jesus across the lake.

Those who are following behind him have seen Jesus heal others who are sick, and they want cures for themselves. The group he sees coming to him could be those who are drawn to him for other reasons than his power to heal. For the first crowd, Jesus simply represents the means to a particular, practical, and personal end—physical healing. We can imagine the second multitude as being made up of those whose quest is spiritual, not physical. They are looking for the truth. But, as John will show in vv. 60–66, many of those who come to Jesus, for whatever reasons, will not persevere in following him. They will turn away because what he asks of them is more than they are willing to give.

The church in our generation tends to present Jesus mainly as a healer whose value consists in his ability to fix what's wrong with us—physically, psychologically, or spiritually—wise "Dr. Jesus." The Fourth Gospel wants us to understand that the Son of God comes not just to mend the brokenness of human bodies and minds, but to disclose the truth of God as our Father, a Father who intends all the rest of his children to bear the likeness of his First-Born.

I believe there's a deep hunger in people to know the truth. Competing voices try to drown out each other in an effort to persuade us of this or that, all claiming to offer some kind of truth. We find multiple 24/7 cable news channels featuring talking heads and catchy sound-bites, tens of thousands of online information websites (most of dubious merit), and countless numbers of newspapers, periodicals, and books. This information overload makes it nearly impossible for an ordinary person to sort out real truth from partial truth and untruth. It's easy for us to be convinced by one proposition or another propagated in the public media, only to discover later we've been deliberately misled. We've believed a lie.

---

3. Brown, *John I–XII*, 233, draws attention to the implication that there are two crowds involved in this story. John's language here recapitulates Jesus's own words in 4:35b, where—in the account of his ministry to the Samaritan woman at the well—Jesus tells his disciples "*lift up your eyes* and see how the fields are already white for harvest," referring to the Samaritan villagers who are visible in the distance, coming down the road. If John's setting for his story of the feeding of the five thousand is indeed on the western (Gentile) side of the lake, in distinction to the Synoptics, who place the event near Capernaum or else near Bethsaida, this may be an allusion to the Gentiles who by the time of the Fourth Gospel's publication are coming to understand Jesus's identity more quickly than Jews do.

In these first decades of the third Christian millennium, our sense of moral direction, of how to organize our thinking and make crucial decisions, is pulled one way then pushed another by propaganda from competing and conflicting interests—in politics, religion, economics, or the arts. So many options are presented that we can be almost paralyzed by the profusion of choices.

The supermarket symbolizes our era in history. You can't simply go to a supermarket and grab a loaf of bread, take it to the cashier, check out, and go home in five minutes the way you might have fifty years ago. If you're looking for whole wheat bread, you have to choose plain or stone ground, seven-grain or nine-grain, smooth-textured or wheat-berry, sliced or unsliced, with preservatives or without, or from any number of varieties of whole grain artisanal breads with fancy names which come in an array of shapes and weights—fat, round and heavy; oval, flat and medium; or long, skinny and light. And they're available in clear plastic bags, printed plastic bags, or paper bags. Your choice. The confusing enterprise of shopping for a simple loaf of bread is a metaphor for what life frequently feels like today.

People in our time need something credible that offers real hope for the future—not just entertaining distractions or transient thrills. We need resources for the journey of life. Popular culture mostly offers escapes and diversions or postmodern pseudo-truth. Feeding a spiritually famished soul such fare is like giving a starving refugee in Eritrea nothing but a doughnut and a cup of Kool-aid. She'll have high blood sugar for a few minutes, then afterwards she'll be even hungrier.—Children of God deserve a better diet than spiritual junk food.

John's account of Jesus feeding the five thousand leads us to think about the deepest hunger we can feel—and how God deals with that hunger. Start with the little boy in John's story, whose mother has packed him a lunch. When Jesus sees the throng coming toward him, he asks Philip, "How are we to buy bread, so that these people may eat?" (v. 5). That's a rhetorical question, meant to "test him" the same way the Hebrew Scriptures show God testing his prophets and people.[4] The disciples don't have any food, or at least not much, nor do they have enough money to buy supplies for a crowd so big. Andrew tells Jesus about a small boy among their group who has a picnic lunch of five barley rolls and two pieces of dried fish. Most likely he's the child of a disciple, maybe even one of the twelve. I picture the little boy hearing what Jesus says about feeding the crowd, then coming forward on his own volition, offering to share his lunch. This allows the Fourth Gospel to make a point similar to one made in Matt 18:3 (cf. Mark 10:15; Luke 18:17) where Jesus says, "Unless you turn and become like children, you will never enter the kingdom of heaven."

This little child is an example of discipleship for us. Jesus accepts his small barley loaves (the bread of poor people) and bits of fish, gives thanks to God for the life-sharing gift, then goes among the crowd, personally putting pieces of the shared bread into each person's hands. For Christians reading John today, it appears there's an

4. See, e.g., Gen 22:1; Exod 15:25; Jer. 17:10; 20:12.

obvious association between Holy Communion and Jesus's giving a portion of blessed bread to each of the hungry people on the lakeshore. A reference to the Eucharist may or may not have been intended by John; scholars disagree on the question.[5] However, the fact that John says Jesus "took the loaves, and when he had given thanks *[using a form of the Greek verb* eucharisteō*]*, he distributed them" (v. 11) seems to support the idea that eucharistic symbolism is deliberate.

Because Jesus will later tell these people "I am the bread of life" (v. 35), his personal act of distributing the bread underscores the reality that Jesus gives *himself* to everyone who comes to him. His relationship with those who receive him is intimate. Jesus puts himself in our hands: he loves us, feeds us, and satisfies our soul-deep hunger for the truth. He is our daily bread.

This chapter offers us a link between Word and Sacrament—since the bread of life has a clear connection both with the sacrament of Christ's presence, the Eucharist, and with his teaching of God's truth. The Fourth Gospel doesn't include an account of Jesus being tempted by Satan in the wilderness. Here it follows Jesus's feeding of the multitude with a teaching about the bread of life, which reminds us of what Jesus tells the tempter: "man does not live by bread alone, but by every word that proceeds from the mouth of God" (Matt 4:4, quoting Deut 8:3).

After the crowd eats its fill, they decide Jesus must surely be the prophet-greater-than-Moses their tradition tells them to expect (Deut 18:15–16). This inspires them to think about launching a movement to make him their king.[6] The crowd on the lakeside could have become the nucleus of a rebel army, intent on achieving this goal, had Jesus aspired to that kind of power. But when he realizes what they're discussing among themselves, he goes off into the hills to escape from them. He wants nothing to do with worldly kingship.

Once Constantine brought the church into league with the Roman state, Jesus's disciples ceased to treat their Master's disdain for worldly status and political power as deserving of their imitation. A Christian sitting on a throne creates a theological conundrum. How can a true disciple of Jesus of Nazareth exercise supreme governing authority? The problem has never been solved. One who commits to follow Christ is unable to wield absolute power without in some way betraying his Master. Nevertheless, history shows the seduction of power to be so great that Christians have for many generations chosen to ignore the obvious incompatibility between worldly power and faithfulness to Christ. Even in modern democracies, exercising vast power as an officer of government creates dilemmas for faithful disciples.

Later in John's Gospel we see Jesus being questioned by the Roman governor about his political aspirations (18:33–38). At one point in their dialogue Pilate asks, "So, you are a king?" And Jesus replies, "You say that I am a king"—meaning, *king*

---

5. See Kysar, *John*, 91–92.

6. It appears that some Jews expected not only that Elijah would return at Passover, but the Messiah himself would come at Passover time.

is your word for what I am—"For this I was born and for this I came into the world, to bear witness to the truth. Everyone who is of the truth hears my voice." Then the cynical politician asks Jesus the exact question the Beloved Disciple writes his gospel to answer, *"What is truth?"*

In 14:6 Jesus says, "I am the truth." Those who receive Christ receive truth. Our relational knowledge of Christ, our personal experience of Christ, is knowledge and experience of truth. Our life as followers of Christ is meant to be a *doing* of that truth. Jesus is the Word and wisdom of God made flesh, the bread of life, as he will later tell the crowd in the Capernaum synagogue (v. 35).[7] We understand this life both as a way of having community with brothers and sisters in this world and communion with God in eternity.

Our mission as Jesus's disciples is to live in a way that testifies to the One who incarnates truth. We're to feed a world that hungers for truth. Most churches take leadership roles in programs to feed the hungry, both in their own communities and far-away places. People who receive the groceries congregations donate to local food banks are hungry for breakfast cereal, fresh fruit and vegetables, loaves of bread, and cans of stew. I believe they, and all the rest of us, are even hungrier for truth. John tells us that Jesus is the true and living Bread which has been given us so that we can feed one another in this age of moral famine.

A little boy brings his lunch to the disciples to give to Jesus. Jesus thanks his Father for those few modest bites of food, then personally hands them out to the crowd—and, as he does so, more than five thousand souls are fed. In a spiritual sense, we're part of that five thousand on the lakeshore. Jesus is putting himself in our hands. He who is truth has entrusted himself to us, and because he has done so, we can become imitators of the small child who plays such a crucial role in this story. We are children of God, and he has given us living bread to share.

6: 16–21. A theophany: Jesus comes to his disciples, walking on the stormy sea.

Vv. 16–21. "It is I. Do not be afraid."

INTRODUCTION. After they describe Jesus's feeding of the five thousand, Matthew (14:22–33) and Mark (6:45–53) include stories similar to this one, but their versions are mainly dramatic nature miracles that emphasize Jesus's power to control the storm. John's description of the episode acknowledges the rough crossing of the lake at night

---

7. See Keener, *Gospel of John*, 1:679–80. As indicated in the introduction to 1:6–18 (see p. 7, above), the rabbis identified the *Logos* with the Torah, and they regarded the manna that fell in the wilderness as a symbol of Torah. This connection is explicit in Deut 8:3, "He humbled you and let you hunger and fed you with manna, which you did not know, nor did your fathers know; that he might make you know that man does not live by bread alone, but that man lives by everything that proceeds out of the mouth of the Lord."

and the disciples' fright at seeing Jesus walking to them on the stormy sea, but there is no mention of his calming the storm. His power over nature is evident in the Fourth Gospel's version, but its emphasis is on Jesus's words, "It is I; do not be afraid." The two Greek words translated "It is I," are the words "I AM," God's sacred name, which he revealed to Moses (Exod 3:13–14). Perhaps John intends his readers to understand no more from Jesus's words than, "You're seeing me, not a ghost; don't be scared." Since the Fourth Gospel, beginning with 4:26, shows Jesus using the same "I AM" expression as a divine self-reference, we are probably meant to see it the same way here, making this incident a theophany, a revelation of the presence of God.[8] John Wijngaards points out that the essence of the Hebrew sacred name, "I AM," particularly denotes God's *presence* as the One who saves his people. He writes,

> The 'I AM' of God is a 'being with others' or a 'being for others', [meaning] that God is able and prepared to act on behalf of the people whose God he wants to be . . . 'I AM' is a strong affirmation of God as the one who proves his divinity by what he does. He is a God who proves his worth by acting. The 'I AM' thus comes very close to the divine promise: 'I shall be with you' (Exod 3:12; Josh 1:5; 3:7; cf. Matt 28:20). This is the way it should be understood in John's Gospel. By saying 'I AM,' the Johannine Jesus asserts that the Father's saving work has become a reality in himself . . . Only those who recognize Jesus as 'God who saves' understand who he is.[9]

This theophany in the storm is the fifth of the seven signs described in John, leading up to the great, unique sign—Jesus's crucifixion and resurrection.

It is essential to remember that in the symbolic world of antiquity the sea was a fearsome place of mystery and chaos, for Jews and Greeks alike, and the same attitude applied to large bodies of water like the Galilean lake. Jonah 1:5–16 conveys this dread quite clearly as does Dan 7:2–7, where terrifying beasts rise out of the sea.[10] That's the reason why, in Revelation, John writes, "I saw a new heaven and a new earth, for the first heaven and the first earth had passed away, *and the sea was no more*" (21:1).

Those who went to sea on merchant or fishing vessels were always conscious of supernatural risks. Swimming was not a recreational activity, nor was mountain climbing. Like the sea, uninhabited wilderness beyond cities and villages with their adjacent farmlands and common pastures, was regarded in the New Testament era as inherently threatening and dangerous—potentially the habitat of evil spirits. Jesus's walking on the sea is a clear demonstration of God's power over the fearsome chaos which deep water stood for, a power alluded to in portions of the Hebrew Scriptures that were probably familiar to John's audience (e.g., Pss 29:3; 77:19; and Isa 51:9–16).

8. See Brown, *John I-XII*, "Appendix IV: *Egō eimi*—'I Am'", 533–38, for an exhaustive analysis of John's use of the "I Am" expression.

9. Wijngaards, *Gospel of John and His Letters*, 162, 163–64.

10. "The abyss" was the appropriate place for demons, as we can in Luke 8:31. See Malina and Rohrbaugh, *Social Science Commentary*, 128.

[6:16–21] *16 When evening came, his disciples went down to the sea, 17 got into a boat, and started across the sea to Caper'na-um. It was now dark, and Jesus had not yet come to them. 18 The sea rose because a strong wind was blowing. 19 When they had rowed about three or four miles, they saw Jesus walking on the sea and drawing near to the boat. They were frightened, 20 but he said to them, "It is I; do not be afraid." 21 Then they were glad to take him into the boat, and immediately the boat was at the land to which they were going.*

RESPONSE. Since we don't think of the sea as supernaturally threatening the way people once did long ago, the story of Jesus coming to his disciples, walking through the tempest on the waters of the lake, conveys a different message to us than it did to John's first audience. Though modern life may require us to sail in darkness directly into the teeth of a gale, the gales we must face head-on, unless we are sailors, are rarely the meteorological sort. But tempests of fear and doubt arise if we face the death of our spouse or child and when we approach our own life's end. In times of economic crisis we may be forced to deal with job loss or business failure and the possibility of losing everything we own. A few years ago I was part of a small group where at one meeting each of us named something that scared us. Nobody was foolish enough to brag, "I'm not afraid of anything," because we'd all have known that was a lie. Everybody is afraid of something. A few in our group had phobias. Some were afraid of failure. Others, shame and humiliation. Some, pain. Those whose jobs seemed at risk feared bankruptcy.

In addition to our private terrors, we sometimes also have acute feelings of anxiety when a human institution we've trusted proves itself to be surprisingly frail—when the boat in which we thought we could ride out the hurricane springs a serious leak. Christian art has long used a ship as the symbol of the church, the Lord's chosen instrument for the accomplishment of his work in the world. However, especially in America and Europe at the present time, one might judge that this ship—the institutional church, anyway—is taking on water and listing badly as it sails into the storm.

In addition to personal fears and shared anxieties about fragile human institutions, we also face the undeniable problem of *evil*. A century ago the romantic world of liberal idealism with its "scientific" confidence in the inevitability of human progress, dissolved in the unprecedented carnage of the Great War, the one people in 1914 hopefully labeled "the War to End War." Then another World War began scarcely two decades after the first one had ended, and the second reinforced our collective awareness of the grip that evil has on human society. The Holocaust extinguished the liberal illusion that western society is on the right path, and nothing that has happened since 1945 offers evidence that the power of evil is waning. Indeed, the present era of religious fanaticism, terror, and hatred suggests that the world's moral climate is degenerating, not improving. We must not deceive ourselves into supposing that the evil we face is somewhere "out there," beyond us, the way ancient people imagined frightening monsters or evil spirits rising from the sea. The evil we confront comes out of human beings. Evil is not embodied by fantastic creatures emerging from the ocean's depths, but is an emanation from the dark abyss of the human psyche. And because all of us are sinners, any of us is capable of manifesting evil.

What shall we do? How shall we live in a world so threatening? John offers an answer here in his little account of Jesus coming through the night, walking on the stormy waves of the Sea of Galilee to join his friends in their boat. This episode, the fifth of John's seven signs, is more important than it first appears. His disciples see Jesus coming towards them in the darkness, but until he speaks they are terrified. Are they seeing a specter from the deep, the ghost of a drowned fisherman, or perhaps a demon? Then he says to them, "It is I; do not be afraid" (v. 20).

Behind the Greek words, John would have us hear the Hebrew sacred Name of the Most High: "I Am." When Moses at the burning bush asks God how he wants to be known to his people, God answers, "I Am who I Am . . . Say to the people of Israel, 'I Am' has sent me to you" (Exod 3:14). It is important for us to know that the Hebrew phrase "I Am who I Am" may also be translated "I will be what I will be." Jesus tells his frightened disciples in their little boat and his twenty-first century disciples who are equally or even more afraid, "Have no fear. I Am. I *am* with you and I *will be* with you. I am all you need, no matter how great the evil you face, today or ever." We might say that in the context of John's Gospel, to *believe in* Jesus means to accept him as the visible saving presence of the Father.[11]

Jesus's words to his friends in the boat are this gospel's counterpart to what Matthew says are his final words to the disciples: "I am with you always, even to the close of the age" (Matt 28:20). This episode is a theophany, a revelation of the presence of God. John will show us in the second half of his gospel how God, in the person of his Son, confronts and defeats the power of evil. In the garden on the night of his betrayal, we see Jesus stand between his friends and the agents of darkness and ask the minions of evil, "Whom do you seek?" They reply, "Jesus of Nazareth." Then he tells them, using—as here—the Sacred Name, "I Am [he]. So, if you seek me, let these men go" (18:4–8). His friends will go free, and Jesus will be crucified. Concerning God's destroying the power of evil through his Son's willing self-offering, N. T. Wright says,

> The story of Gethsemane and of the cross itself present themselves in the New Testament as the strange, dark conclusion to the story of what God does about evil, of what happens to God's justice when it takes human flesh, when it gets its feet muddy in the garden and its hands bloody on the cross.[12]

When we sail in the dark through our personal tempests, when we confront our own sickening fears, when we come face to face with evil in one of its many guises, the crucified and risen Lord himself will be with us. No matter how long or perilous our voyage, no matter what storms we must endure, he always *is*. Our Savior is not simply

11. Wijngaards, *Gospel of John and His Letters*, 164.

12. Wright, "God, 9/11, the Tsunami, and the New Problem of Evil."

a figure from the distant past—a man who once was. Jesus is a living reality, and he will be with us to sustain us. As the next section of this chapter tells us, he is our bread for life's long journey.

6: 22–60. Jesus teaches about the Bread which comes down from Heaven.

Vv. 22–36. "I am the bread of life."

INTRODUCTION. Some members of the crowd whom Jesus fed the previous day remain in the same place on the eastern shore of the lake until the next morning. Then, after seeing Jesus's disciples depart without their master and noticing Jesus has not come back to the lakeside, some of them get into boats and row over to Capernaum, the town recognized as Jesus's home base. 6:22–24 provides a transition from the theophany on the stormy lake to Jesus's sermon to the synagogue crowd concerning the bread of God which has come down from heaven to give life to the world.

When he sees those who have just rowed across the lake, Jesus knows they are looking for him because they fail to understand the miracle of the loaves. Jesus attempts to correct their understanding and shift the focus from physical food to spiritual food, "the food which endures to eternal life" (v. 27), but these efforts lead nowhere. The people even ask him to perform a more obviously miraculous sign to show that he truly is the prophet-greater-than-Moses. They want more bread, but they don't want ordinary loaves, they want Jesus to supply them with new, distinctly supernatural bread—like the manna, which they imagine came down from heaven at Moses' request to feed the hungry Israelites in their wilderness wanderings. This is the only place in the canonical gospels where manna is mentioned. It is possible the people John describes are expecting manna because they *do* think Jesus is the Messiah, the prophet-greater-than-Moses. There is evidence in later Jewish literature of a belief that when the Messiah arrived, manna would again begin to fall.

In good rabbinical style, Jesus proceeds to interpret for his audience the story of God giving his people manna from heaven (Exod 16:4–32). He points out that it was his Father, not Moses, who gave their ancestors the manna. Furthermore, manna was not really the "true bread from heaven," but merely an antetype, bread that *prefigured* the "true bread which comes down from heaven and gives life to the world" (v. 33). The people tell Jesus they would like for him to provide them a lifetime supply of that true bread. This creates the context for his reply, found in vv. 35–40, which begins, "I am the bread of life; he who comes to me shall not hunger, and he who believes in me shall never thirst."[13]

In vv. 35–40 we hear echoes of Jesus's dialogue with the Samaritan woman to whom he offers "living water" (4:10–15). Whereas the Samaritan woman finally

13. Smith, *John*, 153–54.

understands him and believes, the Capernaum throng proves unable to grasp the meaning of Jesus's ironic response. They listen to him, but they will not believe. It is useful to notice the difference between what Jesus says about living water in chapter 4 and what he says about the bread of life here. He tells the woman at the well that he *gives* the living water, but here he tells the crowd that he *is* the bread of life. The people in the Capernaum synagogue show themselves to be as confused as Nicodemus when Jesus tries to explain to him about the need to be "born from above" (3:3–10). Simple metaphors seem wasted on all of them. This is a further elaboration of the prologue's seminal pronouncements, "the Word became flesh and dwelt among us, full of grace and truth" (1:14) and "he came to his own home, and his own people received him not" (1:11).

> **[6:22–36]** *²² On the next day the people who remained on the other side of the sea saw that there had been only one boat there, and that Jesus had not entered the boat with his disciples, but that his disciples had gone away alone. ²³ However, boats from Tiber'i-as came near the place where they ate the bread after the Lord had given thanks. ²⁴ So when the people saw that Jesus was not there, nor his disciples, they themselves got into the boats and went to Caper'na-um, seeking Jesus.*
>
> *²⁵ When they found him on the other side of the sea, they said to him, "Rabbi, when did you come here?" ²⁶ Jesus answered them, "Truly, truly, I say to you, you seek me, not because you saw signs, but because you ate your fill of the loaves. ²⁷ Do not labor for the food which perishes, but for the food which endures to eternal life, which the Son of man will give to you; for on him has God the Father set his seal." ²⁸ Then they said to him, "What must we do, to be doing the works of God?" ²⁹ Jesus answered them, "This is the work of God, that you believe in him whom he has sent." ³⁰ So they said to him, "Then what sign do you do, that we may see, and believe you? What work do you perform? ³¹ Our fathers ate the manna in the wilderness; as it is written, 'He gave them bread from heaven to eat.'"*
> *³² Jesus then said to them, "Truly, truly, I say to you, it was not Moses who gave you the bread from heaven; my Father gives you the true bread from heaven. ³³ For the bread of God is that which comes down from heaven, and gives life to the world." ³⁴ They said to him, "Lord, give us this bread always."*
>
> *³⁵ Jesus said to them, "I am the bread of life; he who comes to me shall not hunger, and he who believes in me shall never thirst. ³⁶ But I said to you that you have seen me and yet do not believe.*

RESPONSE. It is now the day after the miracle of the loaves. John resumes the story at the point where some of the people who were fed arrive in Capernaum looking for Jesus, but he does not mean to suggest that five thousand people get in boats and come swarming across the lake. The group is now obviously smaller, since it can assemble in the local synagogue to listen to Jesus. Nevertheless, this is a representative sample of the multitude who shared the miraculous meal. The first thing they do is ask Jesus a mundane question, "Rabbi, when did you come here?" (v. 25). Jesus ignores that query and addresses them with brusque candor. He knows precisely what they want from him: a more dramatic sign than the one they witnessed the previous day. The multiplication of the loaves and fish merely stimulated their appetite for signs. Many Jews believe that when the Messiah appears, he will provide super-abundant food for Israel—even manna from heaven, according to some. But, of course, the manna God gave Israel during their long-ago exodus wandering was perishable food. (See Exod 16:13–21.)

Jesus says to the hopeful crowd, "You rowed all the way over here, not because you understood my sign, but because you ate all you wanted yesterday. Stop working for perishable food! If you get it, you'll just eat and soon be hungry again. Instead, seek the kind of bread that lasts forever, the bread the Son of Man can give you" (paraphrase of vv. 26–27).

"*What are you seeking?*" That's what Jesus asks his first two disciples (1:38) and all who are reading this gospel. It's *the* crucial question of life, but we need someone to teach us what we should look for, what we truly need most. Jesus tells the crowd they should be looking for "living bread," but they don't understand him. Even though Moses in the Law speaks of God's Word as bread and thus "living bread" should be an obvious metaphor, Jesus's audience is mystified. John shows us again that the people to whom Jesus comes mistake his meaning because worldly assumptions dominate their minds. They want a political messiah who will bring liberation from Rome, not a spiritual messiah who will bring them freedom from sin and a new way of living.

Because they don't grasp his meaning, the people then say, "Very well. If we're not supposed to work for bread that doesn't last, then tell us what kind of works we should be doing in order to obey God's will." Jesus replies, "The only work the Father wants you to do is to trust in the One he has sent" (paraphrase of vv. 28–29). But they still can't understand. They are fixated on a very concrete expectation about how God and his Messiah should deal with Israel.

Although Jesus fed more than five thousand of them the day before, they absurdly ask him for another sign, reminding him of the manna Moses gave their ancestors during the exodus. Jesus answers, "First of all, it wasn't Moses who gave your ancestors bread from heaven; it's my Father who gives the true bread from heaven. And the true bread from heaven that gives life to world, which you say you want, is already here." He at least implies the sacred name in his self-identification: "*I am* that bread, the bread of life. Whoever comes to me will never be hungry again, and whoever believes in me will never be thirsty again. The only work the Father asks of you is to listen to me and believe in me" (paraphrase of vv. 33–35). Notice the change from past tense to present tense: through Moses, God *gave* the manna to their ancestors, but now God *gives* the true bread from heaven. Jesus is telling the crowd the manna they seek has already come down from heaven and is directly in front of them. He is that manna.[14]

The church must never forget that its mission is to give the world what the world truly needs, not what it fancies. In our business-oriented western culture, churches are tempted to be guided by market research that tells them what will sell to the general public. Our vocation as disciples, however, is not to be successful salesmen, but to be faithful followers of Jesus. Today—as when Jesus fed the multitude—what people need most is not necessarily what they're shopping for. Jesus tells them, "Look, I am here for you. I've come from God to be the bread you need—to give myself for you. I am the basic necessity of true life."

This is what Christians still proclaim to the world. Our work is not to give in to whatever craving prevails at the moment in our materialistic, entertainment-focused age, but to offer what every human being needs most: Jesus, the embodiment of truth, the bread of life. If people ask, "How do you know this is what we need," we can only answer, "I know because I'm a human being just like you, *and I have tasted the truth.*" Clearly, not everybody, even in our churches, will agree that Jesus is the basic necessity of life for every human soul. But that's the message John's Gospel gives us to proclaim.

Whatever food people might eat, whether a high-calorie diet in a rich country, or a semi-starvation diet in a poor, famine-stricken land, people eat in order to stay alive. If we eat nothing at all, we die. Those who eat a non-nutritious diet will suffer from deficiency diseases, while those who eat a nutritious diet will be healthy. By analogy, we say Jesus, the bread of life, is the perfect food for the soul. Nothing is better for us, nothing more satisfying, than the bread of eternal life. Jesus says, "I am the bread of life. He who comes to me shall not hunger, and he who believes in me shall never thirst" (v. 35). This is similar to what he tells the woman at the well in Samaria concerning the water she is drawing from Jacob's ancient well: "Everyone who drinks of this water will thirst again, but whoever drinks of the water that I shall give him will never thirst; the water that I shall give him will become in him a spring of water welling up to eternal life" (4:13–14). Jesus gives us living water; he himself is living bread. He embodies—and offers us—what every human soul needs.

The expression, "You are what you eat" is an applicable metaphor for us. We who feed upon Christ in Word and Sacrament are meant to *become* the "flesh" of Christ— in the sense that Jesus uses the word *flesh* in this teaching. If Christ is incorporated into us and we into him, then our lives in the world become manifestations of *his* life in the world. The practical challenge churches and individual Christians face is to turn this idea into tangible behavior. We are meant to become the Bread we eat. We can't be faithful to the gospel and treat this as simply a clever figure of speech. It's a mandate for action, to let the Word take flesh in us.

---

14. Kysar, *John*, 99–100. See also Marsh, *Saint John*, 296.

Vv. 37–60. "He who eats my flesh and drinks my blood has eternal life."

INTRODUCTION. It is interesting to observe how John blends Jesus's teaching about the resurrection with his proclamation of himself as the bread of life which has come down from heaven to give life to the world. (See, e.g., vv. 47–53.)

Although, unlike the Synoptics, the Fourth Gospel contains no description of the institution of the Eucharist at the Last Supper, the church reads chapter 6 as John's way of communicating to his readers the meaning of the sacrament. Eucharistic associations can be seen in this section, most vividly in vv. 50–58. Jesus's words about eating his flesh and drinking his blood shock the crowd. They are troubled by what he is teaching, and although they had been impressed by the miracle of the loaves, they decide that he has now gone too far. They say, "This is a hard saying, who can listen to it?" (v. 60).

We note that John's Gospel employs verbs for "seeing" in ways that indicate both eyesight and insight. However, in John as in other ancient writers, *seeing* (meaning true physical vision rather than metaphysical perception of truth) has primacy over *hearing*. In v. 45 Jesus tells the Capernaum crowd, "Everyone who has *heard* and learned from the Father comes to me." But this is modified immediately by v. 46, "Not that anyone has *seen* the Father except him who is from God; he has *seen* the Father." Marianne M. Thompson calls attention to the point that although John recognizes that all human beings are capable of hearing God, only Jesus, the divine Son, has *seen* God. There is a contrast, therefore, "between the way in which Jesus apprehends God and the way in which all others—including those who believe in Jesus—apprehend God."[15] Mortals may see "the glory of God" or perhaps even "the form of God," but Jesus is the only one who can truthfully claim to have *seen* the Father. He alone has had "direct access to and sight of God;" he is the sole "eyewitness of God." Therefore, only Jesus can rightly claim to know and have ability to reveal the Father to others.[16]

> [6:37–60] *37 All that the Father gives me will come to me; and him who comes to me I will not cast out. 38 For I have come down from heaven, not to do my own will, but the will of him who sent me; 39 and this is the will of him who sent me, that I should lose nothing of all that he has given me, but raise it up at the last day. 40 For this is the will of my Father, that every one who sees the Son and believes in him should have eternal life; and I will raise him up at the last day."*
>
> *41 The Jews then murmured at him, because he said, "I am the bread which came down from heaven." 42 They said, "Is not this Jesus, the son of Joseph, whose father and mother we know? How does he now say, 'I have come down from heaven'?" 43 Jesus answered them, "Do not murmur among yourselves. 44 No one can come to me unless the Father who sent*

15. Thompson, "Jesus: 'The One Who Sees God,'" 216–17.

16. Ibid., 217.

me draws him; and I will raise him up at the last day. ⁴⁵ It is written in the prophets, 'And they shall all be taught by God. ' Every one who has heard and learned from the Father comes to me. ⁴⁶ Not that any one has seen the Father except him who is from God; he has seen the Father. ⁴⁷ Truly, truly, I say to you, he who believes has eternal life. ⁴⁸ I am the bread of life. ⁴⁹ Your fathers ate the manna in the wilderness, and they died. ⁵⁰ This is the bread which comes down from heaven, that a man may eat of it and not die. ⁵¹ I am the living bread which came down from heaven; if any one eats of this bread, he will live for ever; and the bread which I shall give for the life of the world is my flesh."

⁵² The Jews then disputed among themselves, saying, "How can this man give us his flesh to eat?" ⁵³ So Jesus said to them, "Truly, truly, I say to you, unless you eat the flesh of the Son of man and drink his blood, you have no life in you; ⁵⁴ he who eats my flesh and drinks my blood has eternal life, and I will raise him up at the last day. ⁵⁵ For my flesh is food indeed, and my blood is drink indeed. ⁵⁶ He who eats my flesh and drinks my blood abides in me, and I in him. ⁵⁷ As the living Father sent me, and I live because of the Father, so he who eats me will live because of me. ⁵⁸ This is the bread which came down from heaven, not such as the fathers ate and died; he who eats this bread will live for ever." ⁵⁹ This he said in the synagogue, as he taught at Caper'na-um.

⁶⁰ Many of his disciples, when they heard it, said, "This is a hard saying; who can listen to it?"

RESPONSE. Even those in the Capernaum synagogue who might have considered themselves his disciples now demonstrate they do not understand Jesus's teaching about the true manna, the bread of life. Yesterday they said, "Jesus is the Messiah! Let us make him our king!" Now, because their minds are locked into worldly categories of thought and imprisoned by traditional assumptions about how God must deal with Israel, they are starting to turn from him.

Jesus tells the assembly it is the Father's will that everyone who sees and believes in him should have eternal life right now and be raised up by him on the last day. But these people appear to have no interest in eternal life. Instead, they go off on a different tangent because they're bewildered by his saying that he has "come down from heaven" (v. 38). When people in churches today hear something from the pulpit about eternal life they also often prefer to change the subject. Eternal life seems as incomprehensible to modern Christians as it was to those Jesus addressed in Capernaum on the day after he fed the five thousand. For a typical person in the pew, eternal life means "going to heaven when I die." The thought that eternal life might truly be a this-life experience, a life of intimacy with God today, not only a hope of heaven tomorrow, is slow to dawn in their minds.

The Capernaum crowd has a partial level of belief. They are like the disciples John shows us in Jerusalem back in chapter 2, who believe in Jesus when they see the signs he does, but to whom Jesus does not trust himself because he knows what is in their hearts (2:23–25). The Fourth Gospel shows that similar followers of Jesus, who respect him as a wonder-worker but fail to grasp his true identity, are also here among his countrymen in Galilee. Jesus says, "You have seen me and yet do not believe. All that the Father gives me will come to me; and him who comes to me I will not cast out" (vv. 36–37). It is the Father alone who draws people to know the Son. Those who regard the sign of the loaves as evidence that Jesus is a prophet will come no nearer to understanding. They fail to perceive his who Jesus truly is and appreciate what he offers them. Indeed, they will soon abandon him.

These Galileans make their limited point of view explicit, saying to one another, "This is Jesus, the son of Joseph, the builder. We know his father and mother. How can he say, 'I have come down from heaven'? We know he's not from heaven; he's just from Nazareth" (paraphrasing v. 42). They are expecting as God's Messiah someone they do not already know, someone obviously supernatural—a man literally from heaven, descending from the clouds, escorted by angels. But Jesus is a flesh-and-blood man, part of their own community, a carpenter, a builder. He could, perhaps, have built houses for some of them. Jesus has parents, brothers and sisters, and a personal history among them. These are rural people, and rural people make it their business to know all about their neighbors. The crowd in Capernaum are sure they know their countryman, Jesus from Nazareth. His earthly origins are deemed sufficient to explain him to them.[17] How can their neighbor have "come down from heaven"?

This is another example of the kind of irony John showed us in chapter 4. His fellow Galileans know the facts about Jesus's family history, but they emphatically do not know *him*. I imagine them laughing with one another, saying, "The carpenter who built our house now tells us he's 'the bread of life that has come down from heaven to give life to the world. '—Can you believe it? He's either joking or crazy." This attitude is true to life in our own day; people still behave this way. As it was with the lame man at the Pool of Bethesda, the Galileans' experience conflicts so much with their expectations that they are unable to recognize the moment of their visitation by God.

Does God still "come down from heaven" for people in the twenty-first century? Do we experience Christ entering our world to bring us eternal life? The experience of believers still demonstrates that God comes among us in the guise of an ordinary person, maybe someone we know, someone we meet every day. I have no doubt that God comes to us. The question is whether we recognize the reality of his presence, whether we perceive the moment of our visitation. The Bible shows God doing the unexpected, working through the least likely characters imaginable. Therefore, we should take care not to pass negative judgment on our neighbor's potential—or our own.

17. Smith, *John*, 155–56.

Jesus tells those in the Capernaum synagogue, "I am the living bread which came down from heaven; if any one eats of this bread, he will live forever; and the bread which I shall give for the life of the world is my flesh" (v. 51). In those days, people ate two meals a day, and the basic meal of the poor was mostly bread. They sometimes had a little cheese with a handful of olives and occasionally a piece of fish. But cheap bread was the principal ingredient of every meal for all except the upper class. Jesus compares himself to this sort of bread—because eternal life begins now. He is, thus, the bread of *ordinary* life as well as resurrection life.

The people to whom Jesus speaks ought to have no difficulty understanding his metaphors. They are familiar with the images and ideas found in the Wisdom books, which were among the most popular Hebrew literature of their time.[18] In these books, the Wisdom of God is personified, and she is described as feeding people with the "bread" of understanding (Sir 15:3). Lady Wisdom declares, "Those who eat me will hunger for more, and those who drink me will thirst for more; whoever obeys me will not be put to shame, and those who work with my help will not sin" (Sir 24:21–22). Rabbinical tradition also emphasized that Wisdom descended from heaven (Wis 9:10).[19] It seems clear that John sees Jesus as a masculine incarnation of the Wisdom of God, and for Jews (in distinction to Greeks) "wisdom" is always *practical*, shaping a life that will be lived in right relationship with God as well as with other people.

When Jesus tells his audience that the bread he is giving for the life of the world is his *flesh,* he is speaking not only about what the church comes later to call his sacramental body, but also his visible mortal life—his humanity, his observable way of being among us as one of us, embodying the Wisdom of God. Jesus comes into the world not only to reveal the truth of God to us, but to disclose to us the truth about ourselves. "Flesh and blood" was then, as now, simply a way of speaking about humanity, about a mortal human being. D. Moody Smith says "Jesus requires those who come to him desiring eternal life to consume his humanity; to them alone the promise of eternal life and resurrection is given."[20] We have been so catechized to think of the sacrament of the Eucharist as a "proclamation of the Lord's death" (1 Cor 11:26) that it is easy to miss the truth that this sacrament is also a concrete expression of our participation in the Lord's incarnation. In this text, the Fourth Gospel gives us material for meditation when we come to receive Holy Communion.

Jesus comes down from heaven to show human beings who God means for us to be for the sake of one another. We hunger to see God, and seeing God in Christ we catch a glimpse also of ourselves (see 1 John 3:2–3). Regardless of our human antecedents—family history, education, or profession—we are children of God, and we have more potential than we can begin to imagine. When we feed on Christ, incorporating

18. The Wisdom books in our Bible include Job, Psalms, Proverbs, Ecclesiastes, and the Song of Solomon, plus the Wisdom of Solomon and Sirach (Ecclesiasticus) in the Old Testament Apocrypha.

19. Keener, *Gospel of John*, 1:681.

20. Smith, *John*, 158.

him into ourselves, we can accomplish almost miraculous things. We become who we were destined to be in the providence of God.—If Jesus is showing us our true identity, who is he revealing us to be? And to what does recognition of our true identity call us?

The people who had received bread from Jesus's hands only the day before, who row over to Capernaum looking for more food, finally reject Jesus, not only because he refuses to provide precisely the sign they insist upon, but also because he won't tell them what they want to hear. Instead, he offers them mystical truth, "Just as the living Father sent me, and I live because of the Father, so whoever eats me will live because of me" (v. 57). They don't understand his meaning because they misconstrue wisdom metaphors that ought to be familiar to them. Instead, they complain that the words, "Eat my flesh . . . drink my blood," are intolerable.

6:61–71. "It is the spirit that gives life, the flesh is of no avail."

Vv. 61–71. "Do you also want to go away?"

INTRODUCTION. The thing that most sets John's Gospel apart from the Synoptics is that—unlike the others—the Fourth Gospel shows Jesus speaking frequently about himself, his identity, his relationship to the Father, and his mission. The claims that he makes for himself—particularly his claim to be God's Son—are shocking and offensive to Pharisees. But it seems that even some of the people who are drawn to Jesus—particularly those whose attraction comes exclusively from seeing miraculous signs—can be alienated by some of the things he says. Chapter 6 concludes with the departure of a cohort of one-time "disciples," some of whom had at one time wanted to make him their king. These followers go away from Jesus because they have not truly come to know him, and they take offense at sayings such as this one from his sermon in the synagogue at Capernaum, "As the living Father sent me, and I live because of the Father, so he who eats me will live because of me" (v. 57).

> **[6:61–71]** [61] *But Jesus, knowing in himself that his disciples murmured at it, said to them, "Do you take offense at this?* [62] *Then what if you were to see the Son of man ascending where he was before?* [63] *It is the spirit that gives life, the flesh is of no avail; the words that I have spoken to you are spirit and life.* [64] *But there are some of you that do not believe." For Jesus knew from the first who those were that did not believe, and who it was that would betray him.* [65] *And he said, "This is why I told you that no one can come to me unless it is granted him by the Father."*
>
> [66] *After this many of his disciples drew back and no longer went about with him.* [67] *Jesus said to the twelve, "Do you also wish to go away?"* [68] *Simon Peter answered him, "Lord, to whom shall we go? You have the words of eternal life;* [69] *and we have believed, and have come to know, that you are the Holy One of God."* [70] *Jesus answered them, "Did I not choose you,*

the twelve, and one of you is a devil?"[71] *He spoke of Judas the son of Simon Iscariot, for he, one of the twelve, was to betray him.*

RESPONSE. Trapped in worldly thinking, unable to understand Jesus's metaphors, the Capernaum audience reaches its limit. When Jesus says that if they want to have eternal life they must "eat his flesh and drink his blood"—which means that for them to have true life, they need to be filled with *his* life and become *like* him—they regard this teaching as "hard" and intolerable (v. 60). They will now abandon him. They will leave the light and go into the darkness. Why are they so thick-headed, these Galileans who have seen the signs and think of themselves as truth-seeking disciples? Why can they not grasp what Jesus means? They refuse to see that the true life of God is incarnate in their neighbor from Nazareth and that the path to eternal life lies in becoming one with him. They stay with Jesus only as long as he meets their physical needs and tells them what they want to hear. When he asks for their trust, for a deeper commitment, they turn away.

To the weak disciples who are leaving him Jesus calls out, "It is the spirit that gives life; the flesh is useless. The words I have spoken to you are both spirit and life."[21] This verse is the key to Jesus's teaching in this chapter. It's a shock for people today to hear Jesus say that "the flesh," which is what our world values most, really has nothing to offer. Does this mean that the material goods we work so hard to acquire and the physical life which gives us so much pleasure, count for nothing in God's eyes? John does not tell us that Jesus denigrates the significance of ordinary human life, life in the flesh. Rather, he teaches that for our flesh truly to *live*, even on this mortal plane, requires the animation of the spirit. Without the spirit, the flesh is dead.

There is a wistful moment for Jesus after everyone else in the Capernaum synagogue departs, leaving him alone with the twelve.[22] He turns to his closest friends and asks them, "Will you also now go away?" Peter answers for the group, "Lord, to whom shall we go? You have the words of eternal life; and we have believed and have come to know that you are the Holy One of God" (vv. 67–69). True belief leads to commitment—a way of life. It is essential to know what we believe and in whom we believe. Commitment is belief in action. Commitment to Jesus is the one great choice that will shape all our future choices.

---

21. Verse 63, as translated by Raymond E. Brown. Brown, *John I–XII*, 295.

22. I treat vv. 61–71 as set within the context of Jesus's discourse in the Capernaum synagogue following the feeding of the five thousand. However, the phrase "after this" in v. 66 may be understood as situating Jesus's dialogue with the twelve in vv. 67–71 considerably later in time.

Doing Your Own Theology

Questions for reflection after reading John 6.

- As John tells the story of the feeding of the five thousand, it appears there are two crowds of people involved—one that follows Jesus across the lake and another that comes to him after he has arrived on the other side. The first group knows of Jesus's power to heal the sick, and so they follow, seeking a cure for their ailments. (Part of this crowd may also trail after Jesus merely because they hope to see an amazing miracle.) The second group, those who come towards him once he and the disciples have arrived on the farther shore, seems to be made up of people seeking wisdom and truth, not miracles.—*Why do you think John tells readers about these two groups of people? Is there something you want Jesus to do for you? What's number one on your "want list," healing or provision for other physical needs for yourself or a loved one? . . . Or is something else more important to you, such as moral direction, wisdom, and the spiritual truth Jesus embodies? Do you think people whose quest is for spiritual truth are somehow superior to those whose needs are merely physical?*

- One of the interesting things about John's portrayal of the feeding of the five thousand—as compared with the way the other gospels tell the story—is that the episode John describes could be envisioned as "a miracle of sharing" rather than a strictly supernatural event. A child learns that people are hungry and want something to eat, and so he comes forward to share his simple meal of barley bread and pieces of fish This gesture of compassion and generosity from a mere child inspires adults in the throng to take out their own supplies and share them. So many people are willing to share that the needs of the vast crowd are more than met.—*What "bread" do you have that you might share? Are you sometimes reluctant to share your bread because you think it will be inadequate to meet the need? . . . or maybe it won't be good enough? What might help us learn to trust God to transform whatever we share—regardless of how poor or inadequate it seems— and make it life-giving for someone in need?*

- We might imagine a dramatization of the conclusion to chapter 6 this way: Jesus stands in the middle of the Capernaum synagogue alone with the twelve as he watches the crowd of fickle semi-disciples turn away from him and walk out. He calls to those who are leaving, "It is the spirit that gives life, the flesh is of no avail; the words that I have spoken to you are spirit and life" (v. 63). Many commentators understand this saying as the key to Jesus' teaching in chapter 6.—*What do you think Jesus means when he says, "the spirit gives life . . . the flesh is of no avail"? (Note that the word "spirit" here is not necessarily a reference to the Holy Spirit. In typical Johannine fashion, the word is ambiguous.) Write your own paraphrase of v. 63. What must a believer do in order to yield his or her "flesh" to be animated by the "spirit"?*

Chapter Seven

7:1–31. Jesus goes to the temple at Tabernacles. Conflict with "the Jews" grows.

Vv. 1–13. The people at the feast are divided in their opinion about Jesus.

INTRODUCTION. The Feast of Tabernacles or Booths, as most English translations name it, was one of three great holidays when all Jewish males within reasonable traveling-distance of Jerusalem were expected to come to the temple. The others were Passover and Pentecost. Of these, Tabernacles, celebrated between late September and late October, at the time of the olive, almond, and fruit harvest, was the most popular and festive. Tabernacles was an eight-day long agricultural celebration, but it also commemorated the forty years Israel spent wandering in the wilderness under Moses' leadership, living in temporary shelters (Lev 23:42–43). Throughout the celebration, the people of Israel would move out of their homes and live in huts. *Sukkot*, plural of the Hebrew word *sukkah*, "booth" or "hut," is the Hebrew name for the festival and is what Jews call it today. *Sukkot* were small improvised structures constructed of whatever raw material was at hand, roofed with palms or leafy branches, resembling what our nineteenth century forebears would have called brush arbors. Agricultural laborers during harvest season lived in such structures, erected out in the fields and orchards. During the feast, *sukkot* would even be constructed within the temple itself. It was a happy time, and the weather was usually pleasant. It's easy to imagine children being excited about camping out for a week.

As chapter 7 opens, Jesus is still in Galilee, where we left him at the end of chapter 6. John tells us that he has been staying away from Jerusalem "because the Jews sought to kill him" (v. 1). His brothers encourage him to leave home and go—presumably with them—to Judea for the feast, where "his disciples" might see him. He declines because, he says, "My time is not yet come" (v. 6a). However, after the brothers have gone, Jesus changes his mind and goes to Jerusalem alone, where people indeed are looking for him.

[**Vv. 1-13**] [1] *After this Jesus went about in Galilee; he would not go about in Judea, because the Jews sought to kill him.* [2] *Now the Jews' feast of Tabernacles was at hand.* [3] *So his brothers said to him, "Leave here and go to Judea, that your disciples may see the works you are doing.* [4] *For no man works in secret if he seeks to be known openly. If you do these things, show yourself to the world."* [5] *For even his brothers did not believe in him.* [6] *Jesus said to them, "My time has not yet come, but your time is always here.* [7] *The world cannot hate you, but it hates me because I testify of it that its works are evil.* [8] *Go to the feast yourselves; I am not going up to this feast, for my time has not yet fully come."* [9] *So saying, he remained in Galilee.* [10] *But after his brothers had gone up to the feast, then he also went up, not publicly but in private.* [11] *The Jews were looking for him at the feast, and saying, "Where is he?"* [12] *And there was much muttering about him among the people. While some said, "He is a good man," others said, "No, he is leading the people astray."* [13] *Yet for fear of the Jews no one spoke openly of him.*

RESPONSE. Six months after the feeding of the five thousand Jesus is still in Galilee. It's safer for him to stay in the province where he was brought up than to go south to Judea where "the Jews"—meaning the temple authorities and their Pharisee allies—are are plotting to get rid of him. Jesus is willing to face death; he even expects it, but he will expose himself to death only when he's certain his hour has come. He trusts the Father to make the approach of the hour known in due time. Until the Father guides him, Jesus will remain in relative seclusion at home, though he continues to do the kind of works his family members think he should want everyone to see. They tell him, "No man works in secret if he seeks to be known openly" (v. 4). However, the works of God often seem concealed from the perceptions of mortals, and when rendered visible they are regularly misunderstood by those who are not prepared to believe. In the synagogue at Capernaum Jesus told the disbelieving crowd who had witnessed the miracle of the loaves, "No one can come to me unless the Father who sent me draws him" (6:44*a*).

Jesus's brothers[1] do not believe in him, at least not yet; nor do they understand him. Jesus is not seeking "to be known openly" as they imagine he should. Of course, if Jesus were to become a person of renown in the capital, achieving respect from the authorities and trailed by throngs of devotees, the brothers would be happy to bask in his glory. But Jesus has no interest in creating a good impression or building a reputation for himself with awe-inspiring deeds of power. He only wants to do the will of the One who sent him and reveal the Father's glory; he seeks no glory for himself. His brothers are aware that some in Jerusalem and Judea admire Jesus, and they think of

1. "Brothers" is the Greek word used here. Whether these men are also sons of Mary, Joseph's children by an earlier marriage, or cousins of some degree is irrelevant for the Fourth Gospel's purposes.

such people as his disciples, though we already know enough about such so-called disciples to understand they're an untrustworthy, fickle lot. They believe Jesus is a miracle-worker, and they want to see him do something amazing, but they don't know his true identity or why he has come among them. They are unable to understand what he wants to teach them.

As in every age, the best work of witness for Christ is done today by men and women who have no concern for their personal reputations and are content to be anonymous servants of God, working behind the scenes, not looking for public adulation. When pastors, teachers, or missionaries are drawn into the world's game of self-promotion and career advancement—which does happen, as everyone in ordained ministry knows from experience—it shifts a Christian worker's focus from the glory of God to his own glory. Hunger for the spotlight is spiritually lethal.

Jesus declines to accompany his brothers to Jerusalem for the Feast of Tabernacles. Since they are living by the world's agenda and playing the world's game rather than seeking to do the Father's will, their "time is always here," as Jesus tells them (v. 6). They are prepared to compromise and adapt to any situation that could possibly be turned to their private advantage. Jesus will not do that. He will wait upon his Father's bidding and act only when he discerns the time is ripe—regardless of the personal cost.

Once his brothers go to Jerusalem with the rest of the family and people from their village, Jesus changes his mind and goes too—but he travels alone, in secret. John probably wants his readers to understand that Jesus is never guided by the advice and opinions of others, but exclusively by his perception of the Father's will.[2] He tarries at home in Galilee until he feels guided by the Father to make his way up to the temple, discerning that his hour is drawing near—the time of his passion, death, resurrection, and ascension—which will take place a few months later at Passover. He will not return to Galilee until he meets some of his disciples on the lakeshore after the resurrection (21:1–14).

Many are looking for Jesus at the feast, but the popular attitude is mixed. Some of the holiday throng feel warmly towards him and regard him as "a good man" (v. 12), though they're afraid to express their approval openly since he has clearly earned the hostility of the elite, whom John simply calls "the Jews" (v. 13). The virtually unanimous negativity of the chief priests and the Pharisees is shared by some of the ordinary people as well.

---

2. Was Jesus intentionally deceptive to his brothers in v. 8? Malina and Rohrbaugh offer a social psychology perspective on "lying" and "truth telling" in a collectivist culture like that of first-century Galilee. In such a culture there are "in-groups" and "outsiders." Only those who are members of one's "in-group" are *entitled* to know the truth. Truth must be concealed from outsiders. Jesus's brothers do not believe in him; they are outsiders, not members of his "in-group" and, thus, not entitled to know the truth. Malina and Rohrbaugh, *Social Science Commentary*, 143–46.

Vv. 14–29. Jesus teaches in the temple. "The Jews" immediately challenge him.

INTRODUCTION. Jesus's return to the temple sets the stage for what John will show us about the relationship between Jesus and the Jewish authorities, beginning here and continuing until he is laid in the tomb. "The Jews" will increasingly regard Jesus as a threat to the nation, a man who needs to be eliminated before he causes an irremediable disaster. These people have been suspicious of Jesus since his first visit to the temple. The motif of a quasi-judicial trial that convenes and adjourns over an extended period of time, introduced in 5:15, now resumes—with the chief priests and their Pharisaical allies treating Jesus as if he were on trial for a capital offense.[3] If we read carefully, however, we will see that in this extended "trial"—as well as in the hearing that will be held by the Roman governor (18:28–19:16)—the true Judge is the Son of God. John shows the humble preacher from Nazareth able to match wits with every adversary and meet any verbal challenge with a suitably sharp rejoinder.

As John tells Jesus's story, the desire to have him put to death was expressed long before the deed was actually carried out. Here at the Feast of Tabernacles, roughly six months before Jesus's crucifixion at the following Passover, the author shows us that Jesus is aware the authorities want to kill him (v. 19), although they deny it (v. 20). Even some Jerusalem observers are speaking of Jesus as "the man whom they seek to kill" (v. 25).

> [7:14–29] *14 About the middle of the feast Jesus went up into the temple and taught. 15 The Jews marveled at it, saying, "How is it that this man has learning, when he has never studied?" 16 So Jesus answered them, "My teaching is not mine, but his who sent me; 17 if any man's will is to do his will, he shall know whether the teaching is from God or whether I am speaking on my own authority. 18 He who speaks on his own authority seeks his own glory; but he who seeks the glory of him who sent him is true, and in him there is no falsehood. 19 Did not Moses give you the law? Yet none of you keeps the law. Why do you seek to kill me?" 20 The people answered, "You have a demon! Who is seeking to kill you?" 21 Jesus answered them, "I did one deed, and you all marvel at it. 22 Moses gave you circumcision (not that it is from Moses, but from the fathers), and you circumcise a man upon the Sabbath. 23 If on the Sabbath a man receives circumcision, so that the law of Moses may not be broken, are you angry with me because on the*

---

3. Personal experience with their hostility to followers of Jesus led John to ascribe to the Pharisees more political power than they actually possessed prior to the destruction of the temple and even to name them along with the chief priests as responsible for the arrest of Jesus (18:3), though Pharisees are not mentioned in the description of Jesus's trials and execution. The Jerusalem aristocracy included a number of wealthy Pharisees, some of whom, like the scribe Nicodemus, sat as members of the Great Sanhedrin, but until the destruction of the temple the great priestly families (only a few members of which were Pharisees) had a firm grip on power. See Keener, *Gospel of John*, 1:720; and Smith, *John*, 173.

Sabbath I made a man's whole body well? ²⁴ *Do not judge by appearances, but judge with right judgment."*

²⁵ *Some of the people of Jerusalem therefore said, "Is not this the man whom they seek to kill?* ²⁶ *And here he is, speaking openly, and they say nothing to him! Can it be that the authorities really know that this is the Christ?* ²⁷ *Yet we know where this man comes from; and when the Christ appears, no one will know where he comes from."* ²⁸ *So Jesus proclaimed, as he taught in the temple, "You know me, and you know where I come from? But I have not come of my own accord; he who sent me is true, and him you do not know.* ²⁹ *I know him, for I come from him, and he sent me."*

RESPONSE. When we review the earlier part of the Fourth Gospel, we see that every time Jesus appears in the temple, the leading Jews challenge his authority—beginning with their question about his setting free the animals being sold for sacrifice and upsetting the tables of the official money changers (2:18). The representatives of the high priest and the elders are the custodians of the Law. It is their prerogative to identify who has the proper credentials to be a teacher in the House of God. From what source does this rural tradesman-turned-prophet acquire authority to instruct anyone about the will of God, about what is right and what is wrong, or about the meaning of Torah? He has never "studied." That is to say, Jesus has never been the disciple of a sage, a rabbi, a scribe recognized and approved by the elders. Jesus never prefaces his teachings with the words, "As my master, Rabbi So-and-So once said . . ." or "According to the teachings of the elders . . ." Instead, he simply speaks on his own authority, without reference to anyone of higher status. When he speaks of himself he claims to be the agent of God, sent into the world to do his Father's will. This is shocking and blasphemous to pious Pharisees.

Are we very different from them? We twenty-first century Christians are deeply concerned about authority. Protestants generally assert the primacy of the Bible, claiming that authority resides in Scripture alone, but who decides which among many divergent interpretations of Scripture is the correct one? Which interpretation offers "the" Word of God for our time? Who has authority to interpret the Bible for us? Roman Catholic and Eastern Orthodox Christians say that the church itself makes that decision. They assign authority to sacred tradition and the ecclesiastical hierarchy, in much the same way as the Jews who challenge Jesus assign authority to the traditions of the scribes and elders who interpret the Law.

A story at the beginning of Mark's gospel casts some light on the encounter between Jesus and the temple authorities in John 7. Mark describes an occasion at the beginning of his ministry when Jesus, while teaching in the Capernaum synagogue, casts an unclean spirit out of a man in the presence of the village congregation. Then the people say to one another, "What is this? A new teaching! With authority he commands even the unclean spirits, and they obey him" (1:27). Jesus's authority comes from *the exercise of obvious power*, not from religious status or credentials, as he heals the sick and casts out unclean spirits. Mark says, "They were astonished at his teaching, for he taught them as one who had authority, and not as the scribes" (1:22). The scribes performed no miracles, but Jesus both performed miracles and spoke words of wisdom. Clearly, he had spiritual power. The only resort for his critics was to say that his spiritual power was demonic (v. 20).[4] In the Synoptics, the scribes and Pharisees assert that Jesus's power comes from Beelzebul and that "by the prince of demons he casts out the demons" (Mark 3:22; Matt 9:34; Luke 11:14–15).[5]

Jesus's focus is invariably *humane*. His interest is in the spiritual and physical wellbeing of his brothers and sisters, and his human compassion for them guides everything he does. John intends his readers to understand Jesus's words and deeds as the incarnation of God's loving care for his children. He doesn't reject the Law and the traditions of Israel, but bringing wholeness—giving abundant life—is more important to Jesus than is conformity to every rule of religious observance dictated by the traditions of the elders. This is particularly true in the present case, concerning what kind of labor is legally permitted on the Sabbath. His spiritual priorities are different from those of the chief priests and the Pharisees. Jesus honors the Sabbath, but he does so in the spirit of Deuteronomy, which directly connects the Third Commandment with the Israelites' deliverance from slavery in Egypt (see Deut 5:15). The Sabbath is meant to commemorate forever the freedom from bondage that God won for Israel at the exodus; it should, therefore, not become the occasion for a new slavery to legalism. In the work of Jesus, healing the sick on the Sabbath is a graphic display of God's power to liberate his people from oppression, in this case the oppression of disease. His enemies are angry and do not understand what he's doing. However, they prove incompetent to mount an effective attack. Jesus has an able response to every accusation.

The remarks of both the ordinary people and the elite indicate they're very sure about where Jesus comes from—Nazareth in Galilee. But they haven't failed to notice he claims to be sent into the world from God. In addition, they recognize he regularly speaks of God as his Father in a personal sense. His claim to be God's Son is part of what makes the priestly leaders and Pharisees so angry. The New Testament's assertion that Jesus was and is the Son of God remains a stumbling block to Jews as well as to Muslims (and other monotheists) in our own day. It's not the moral teaching of Christianity to which representatives of the other two so-called Abrahamic faiths object; it

---

4. When Jesus says, "I did one deed and you all marvel at it" (v. 21), he is referring to the healing of the paralyzed man at the Bethesda Pool (5:2–9) which led to an encounter with the authorities at the time of his last visit to the temple.

5. "Scribes and Pharisees" are often named together in the Synoptics, but *scribes* are only mentioned once in the Fourth Gospel, in 8:3, part of a story universally understood to be an interpolation, not originally part of the Gospel according to John). The scribes were a small but very influential class within the Jewish religious establishment, but John surprisingly chooses not to single them out and label them as a group. We might assume that a number of his references to "Pharisees," particularly in conjunction with the chief priests, are really references to Pharisee scribes.

is the scandal of particularity—the assertion that once, two thousand years ago, the One True God literally became a particular human being, a Jewish man named Jesus, the son of Mary and Joseph, a carpenter in the insignificant village of Nazareth in the backwater district of Galilee. If Christians are willing to treat the incarnation of God in Christ as merely a story rather than a historical event, or to agree that God may somehow become equally incarnate in every spiritually enlightened person, then the scandal of particularity will disappear—and, ultimately, so will Christianity.

7:30-52. Jesus uses the water-pouring ceremony to make a messianic claim.

Vv. 30-52. "If any one thirst, let him come to me and drink."

INTRODUCTION. The chief priests and Pharisees want to seize Jesus and dispose of him immediately, but their plans are frustrated for the time being. John tells us that the authorities' efforts fail "because his hour [has] not yet come" (v. 30); the time for his self-offering will not arrive until the next Passover. A historian would say that the arrest does not take place at Tabernacles because Jesus is surrounded by the crowd of pilgrims in the temple, a significant number of whom are impressed by his "works"— presumably the now widely-known healing of the paralyzed man at the Pool called Bethesda (5:2–9) as well as other miracles in Galilee. These sympathizers can't imagine that even the Messiah when he appears could do anything more wonderful (v. 31). Such popularity with the crowd protects Jesus for the moment, but it ultimately leads the high priest and his colleagues to take action when the opportunity to arrest him in secret finally presents itself on the night before the Passover.[6]

Zechariah (chapters 9–14) associates the Feast of Tabernacles with messianic expectation. This prophet who addressed the exiles returned from Babylon foretold that the messianic king would come to the temple riding on an ass at the festival of Tabernacles. Then the Lord would pour out a spirit of compassion and supplication on Jerusalem and living waters would flow out from the temple. By Jesus's time the solemn pouring out of water is a dramatic daily ritual during Tabernacles. A parade of priests and people goes down to the Pool of Siloam to fill a great golden pitcher with water while the Levite choir sings, "With joy you will draw water from the wells of salvation" (Isa 12:3). Then the pitcher is carried back up to the temple as the pilgrims and choir sing the *Hallel* (Pss 113–118). After marching around the great altar seven times on the last day of the feast, singing Ps 118:25, the priest bearing the pitcher ascends the altar and pours out the water while the high priest prays.[7] On the seventh day of the feast, right after this solemn water ceremony (with its explicit messianic connection), Jesus stands up in the midst of the worshipers and shouts to the crowd, "If any

---

6. Keener, *Gospel of John*, 1:718.

7. Brown, *John I–XII*, 326.

one thirst, let him come to me and drink. He who believes in me, as the Scripture has said, 'Out of his heart shall flow rivers of living water'" (vv. 37b–38). Many who hear this proclamation construe it as a vivid claim by Jesus to be the prophet-greater-than Moses or even the Messiah (vv. 40–41). This enflames the chief priests and Pharisees all the more.

> **[7:30–52]** *30 So they sought to arrest him; but no one laid hands on him, because his hour had not yet come. 31 Yet many of the people believed in him; they said, "When the Christ appears, will he do more signs than this man has done?"*
>
> *32 The Pharisees heard the crowd thus muttering about him, and the chief priests and Pharisees sent officers to arrest him. 33 Jesus then said, "I shall be with you a little longer, and then I go to him who sent me; 34 you will seek me and you will not find me; where I am you cannot come." 35 The Jews said to one another, "Where does this man intend to go that we shall not find him? Does he intend to go to the Dispersion among the Greeks and teach the Greeks? 36 What does he mean by saying, 'You will seek me and you will not find me,' and, 'Where I am you cannot come'?"*
>
> *37 On the last day of the feast, the great day, Jesus stood up and proclaimed, "If any one thirst, let him come to me and drink. 38 He who believes in me, as the Scripture has said, 'Out of his heart shall flow rivers of living water.'" 39 Now this he said about the Spirit, which those who believed in him were to receive; for as yet the Spirit had not been given, because Jesus was not yet glorified.*
>
> *40 When they heard these words, some of the people said, "This is really the prophet." 41 Others said, "This is the Christ." But some said, "Is the Christ to come from Galilee? 42 Has not the Scripture said that the Christ is descended from David, and comes from Bethlehem, the village where David was?" 43 So there was a division among the people over him. 44 Some of them wanted to arrest him, but no one laid hands on him.*
>
> *45 The officers then went back to the chief priests and Pharisees, who said to them, "Why did you not bring him?" 46 The officers answered, "No man ever spoke like this man!" 47 The Pharisees answered them, "Are you led astray, you also? 48 Have any of the authorities or of the Pharisees believed in him? 49 But this crowd, who do not know the law, are accursed." 50 Nicode'mus, who had gone to him before, and who was one of them, said to them, 51 "Does our law judge a man without first giving him a hearing and learning what he does?" 52 They replied, "Are you from Galilee too? Search and you will see that no prophet is to rise from Galilee."*

RESPONSE. John tells his readers that the Jewish leaders are unable to arrest Jesus, not because they lack the will or the resources, but because Jesus's "hour [has] not yet come" (v. 30). The Fourth Gospel—and, indeed, the whole New Testament—is characterized by confidence in the ultimate working out of God's wise plan. For the Beloved Disciple, human history is not a random sequence of meaningless and sometimes terrible events, a collection of merely coincidental phenomena, but rather a stage on which the loving, creative, and redemptive power of God is disclosed. Jesus summons his disciples to count on the ultimate fulfillment of his Father's will—which is broad enough to encompass even the wicked machinations of those who don't grasp the role they're playing in the divine scheme. This is difficult for people to accept in the twenty-first century. We struggle to understand how the working out of God's perfect will might somehow incorporate even hideous expressions of human sin, such as the Holocaust of the Jews or the virtual genocide of the indigenous peoples of the Americas after 1492. Nevertheless, faith in God's love, the energy that controls the universe, sustains us.

Jesus says to the Pharisees, "I shall be with you a little longer, and then I go to him who sent me; you will seek me and you will not find me; where I am you cannot come" (vv. 33–34). Naturally, the Pharisees don't get it. In order to make his theological points, John regularly uses incidents wherein people misunderstand Jesus. Jesus's enemies don't understand what he's talking about. They are unable to make the logical connections, even though the theme of seeking but not finding the Lord (or his Wisdom) recurs frequently in the Hebrew Scriptures. Concerning the leaders of both Israel and Judah the Prophet Hosea writes, "they shall go to seek the Lord, but they will not find him; he has withdrawn from them. They have dealt faithlessly with the Lord" (Hos 5:6–7a). The high priest and elders of the nation claim to know the Lord, but they are bereft of his Spirit. They declare that they seek him, but they look for him in all the wrong places. They refuse to see God's presence in his Son, who is doing his Father's works right before their eyes. Because they will not believe, they are unable to see. *Believing is seeing.*

Like Wisdom, whom Proverbs describes as standing in public places and crying out to passersby, begging them to pay attention and learn from her,[8] Jesus stands in the assembly of pilgrims in the temple and shouts, "If any one thirst, let him come to me and drink. He who believes in me, as the Scripture has said, 'Out of his heart shall flow rivers of living water'" (vv. 37–38).[9] Jesus tells the festal crowd essentially the same thing he said to the woman at the well in Samaria: that he gives living water to all who put their trust in him, living water that will become a continual fountain of refreshment for the thirsty soul (4:14). The Beloved Disciple says Jesus speaks "about the Spirit, which those who believed in him were to receive; for as yet the Spirit had

---

8. E.g., Prov 1:20–33; 8:1–36; 9:1–6.

9. Scholars cannot find any specific reference in either the Hebrew or Greek versions of the Old Testament Scriptures that might be the source of Jesus's quotation.

not been given, for Jesus was not yet glorified" (v. 39).[10] The imagery of v. 38 portrays the believer as an agent through whom the water of life, the life-giving Spirit, flows.

It surely upsets some of the people in the festal congregation—at least the Pharisees and priests—when at a solemn moment in the ceremony Jesus interrupts the service and shouts out his invitation. What Jesus does at the feast is as shocking to some worshipers in the temple as it might be to people in any church today if someone were to stand up during the distribution of Holy Communion and shout, "*I am the bread of life that came down from heaven, so come to *me* to get the true bread you need!*"

If we count the metaphors used for the Spirit of God in the New Testament, water is the one used most often. For instance, Paul writes, "by one Spirit we were all baptized into one body . . . and all were made to drink of one Spirit" (1 Cor 12:13). The people present in the temple on the day Jesus interrupts the solemn water-pouring ceremony can't fail to understand what he means. Jesus means that *he* is the answer to the high priest's ritual prayer. *He* is offering the "water" they truly need, not for their fields but for their souls—a direct connection to the life-giving power of God. John interprets this living water as the Holy Spirit, which in the future will flow out from Jesus and from the hearts of all who come to believe in him. If we take the Fourth Gospel's explanation seriously, we have to understand that the Holy Spirit streams out through us when we share our faith. We used to sing a song in church that included this refrain: "*There's a river of life flowing out through me. / It makes the lame to walk and the blind to see, / Opens prison doors, sets the captives free. / There's a river of life flowing out through me.*"

If we don't share it, our faith dies within us. I've lived most of my adult life in the American west and have flown many times across agricultural areas that depend on irrigation for viability. From the airplane we look down on the brown landscape and see broad circles where pivot irrigation has poured life-giving water on the dry land, creating green fields that produce food for animals and people. When we fly over Israel and Palestine, we can look down on the Jordan River Valley—the most productive part of that arid country. The Jordan starts in the north, near Lebanon, and flows south, creating the lake we call the Sea of Galilee. The countryside around that lake is the greenest, most productive land in the region. As we fly south we notice that the Jordan leaves the Sea of Galilee and continues to flow until it ends thirty or forty miles further in another lake, the Dead Sea. That sea is dead because water only flows into it, not out of it. When a lake traps all the water that comes into it and doesn't let any out, the mineral content of its water gradually grows so concentrated that no fish can live in it. The water becomes progressively more saline until the lake dies. That's what happens to believers if we don't discover some way to share our faith. We become like

---

10. In 19:30, when Jesus dies on the cross, the Greek of the text says he "hands over his spirit," and in 20:22, on the evening of the day of resurrection, Christ breathes on the assembled disciples and says, "Receive the Holy Spirit."

the Dead Sea. The water of life flows into us, but if it doesn't also flow *out from us*, it will ultimately become toxic, the water of death.

Most believers I know are very modest about the personal spiritual resources at their disposal. It's healthy for us to remain humble, but the testimony of the Fourth Gospel is that we who believe in Christ receive from him the life-giving Spirit of God. There is a stream of living water flowing into our souls, a gift from God. It's a stream that will keep on flowing, keep on re-filling us as long as we live, if we allow it to flow *through* us to others. There are many ways to do this. Sharing the water of life doesn't require that we become missionaries or itinerant evangelists or hand out tracts on street corners. If we're willing to share the water of life, the Holy Spirit will lead each of us to do so in a way harmonious with our personal temperament.

Jesus's invitation to the crowd of pilgrims in the temple, summoning them to drink the water of life he offers, makes an impression on some. They are convinced that he must be the Messiah or the prophet-greater-than Moses. But others doubt. Jesus doesn't have the credentials they are certain the Messiah or the prophet will have. His seemingly blasphemous public performance at the water-pouring ceremony makes the temple hierarchy ready to get rid of him immediately. They send agents to arrest him before he leaves the temple. But the Levite police disobey their orders. Jesus is so awe-inspiring to them that they can't bring themselves to seize him. Jesus also makes another positive impression on the elderly aristocrat and Sanhedrin member, Nicodemus, just as he had done much earlier when Nicodemus came to call on him (3:1–15). Nicodemus is a very influential man, and he protests against arresting Jesus without a formal hearing before the Sanhedrin. Though the Pharisees are scornful of Nicodemus, Jesus escapes arrest. His hour has not yet come.

Doing Your Own Theology

Questions for reflection after reading John 7.

- In 7:1–9 we learn that Jesus declines to accompany his brothers to Jerusalem for the Feast of Tabernacles "because the Jews sought to kill him" (v. 1). Jesus does not fear death, but he chooses to remain in Galilee because he knows his "time"—the hour for his sacrificial death—has not yet arrived. His unbelieving brothers try to convince him to go with them so his "disciples" in Judea might see the wonderful works he's doing. But Jesus stays behind for a few more days. Then he decides to go up to Jerusalem, but secretly, so no one will know that he's coming. His enemies are looking for him there, and so are other people—including both those who deem him "a good man" and others who are hostile to him (v. 12). Opinion about Jesus is divided. However, those who think well of him are afraid to speak about him openly, "for fear of the Jews" (v. 13; see also v. 43). This polarization of opinion somewhat resembles the situation in the USA in the opening decades of the twenty-first century. Christianity has numerous committed adherents, but has lost favor with a significant number of people in our society, particularly among public intellectuals and mainstream media opinion shapers. It can feel awkward, uncomfortable, or even risky for believers to speak about their relationship to Christ or their enthusiasm for the gospel, except in a securely Christian setting. They fear being mocked.—*Francis of Assisi famously said, "Preach the gospel at all times. When necessary, use words." Do you ever speak about your belief in Jesus to people you know are hostile or at least critical of Christianity? If so, how do you present your convictions? How do you discern when words are necessary and when talk should be avoided?*

- Jesus's enemies challenge his authority. By what authority does he tell someone to violate the accepted rules of Sabbath observance? (See vv. 15–24.) Contemporary Christians are deeply concerned about authority. Protestant Christians have historically asserted the authority of Scripture for determining doctrine and practice. But Scripture requires interpretation and application, and numerous differing opinions exist among Christians on that score. In the age of the Protestant Reformation, Catholics purportedly accused Protestants of espousing the maxim: "Every man his own pope." Whatever may have been the terms of the debate in the sixteenth century, it is manifestly true in the twenty-first century that believers decide for themselves where authority lies. A person can choose to submit to a traditional *magisterium* (i.e., an officially designated teaching authority, such as that held by the Pope), or the person can decide to acknowledge no authority beyond his or her private judgment.—*In seeking to understand Scripture, to what authority do you turn? Why? Do you have an open mind and listen carefully to views that challenge your existing opinions, or do you refuse to engage in dialogue with those who think differently? Is there someone whom you have come to regard as a person of both wisdom and spiritual power? From where do you think that person's wisdom and spiritual power comes?*

- Throughout John's Gospel, Jesus presents himself to Israel as God's Son and personal agent in the world. He speaks and acts with the authority of his Father. (See vv. 16–17 and 28–29.) Jesus's claim to be the Son of God gives great offense to the chief priests and Pharisees. The assertion that Jesus was and is the Son of God continues to be an obstacle for Jews as well as Muslims (and other monotheists) in our own day. It's not the moral teaching of Christianity to which other monotheists object; it is the scandal of particularity (see pp. 116–17, above). This scandalous understanding of the person of Jesus defines Christianity and makes it exceptional among the world's great religions. To argue for the unique status of Jesus as divine is categorically similar, in some ways, to arguing for the unique status of Earth as the only planet in the universe upon which intelligent life exists. There is no indisputable evidence available for either side in the argument.—*Have you ever been asked to explain the unique status of Jesus as God incarnate? What did you say? Why do you put your faith in Jesus and make him the cornerstone of your life, your faith, and your relationship with God?*

Chapter Eight

7:53–8:11. Jesus's enemies bring him a woman caught in adultery.

7:53–8:11. "Let him who is without sin among you be the first to throw a stone at her."

INTRODUCTION. The most ancient Greek manuscripts of the Fourth Gospel do not include the familiar account of Jesus and the woman taken in adultery, 7:53–8:11; the earliest ones pass directly from 7:52 to 8:12. On the basis of its inclusion by Jerome in the Latin Vulgate and some patristic references, Bible scholars regard the story as ancient and authentic, but most believe that it was not originally part of John, since its grammar and vocabulary fit better with Luke. Regardless of who first recorded it, however, this winsome account of a story illustrating Jesus's wisdom and compassion is vivid, meaningful, and familiar to Bible readers. Since the church treats it as inspired Scripture, the account appears in all modern translations of John.[1]

In John 7, Jesus's adversaries accuse him of violating the Sabbath and leading the people astray from the Law. Although they put him on the defensive, his astute responses make it difficult for them to discredit him. Even though it is an interpolation, the account of the woman taken in adultery fits well in this Johannine context and as a prelude to Jesus's discussion of sin, found in 8:21–38. The Law of Moses states that an adulterous woman and the man with whom she commits the act should be put to death (Lev 20:10). However, according to some accounts, it was at approximately this moment in history (ca. 30 CE) that the Romans take away the Great Sanhedrin's right to impose capital punishment. The scribes and Pharisees hope to compel Jesus into an untenable, compromised theological position. He either denies that the Law of Moses should be enforced or else he agrees that the woman should be stoned and, therefore, puts himself in the position of telling Jews they should disobey the Roman governor. The situation resembles that of Luke 20:20–25, where his enemies ask Jesus whether

---

1. Brown, *John I–XII*, 335–36, offers a concise survey of scholars' opinions concerning the origins of the story of the woman taken in adultery and why it ultimately is inserted at this point in the Gospel according to John.

it is right for Jews to pay tribute to Caesar. Both arguments are purely academic. No one who wished to remain alive and healthy would dare resist Caesar's tax collector. And, in practice, even though the death sentence had indeed been inflicted a few times in the preceding century, the traditions of the elders militated against the Great Sanhedrin actually imposing capital punishment for any offense, even though it was technically authorized by the Torah.[2]

> **[7:53–8:11]** *7:53 They went each to his own house, 8:1 but Jesus went to the Mount of Olives. 2 Early in the morning he came again to the temple; all the people came to him, and he sat down and taught them. 3 The scribes and the Pharisees brought a woman who had been caught in adultery, and placing her in the midst 4 they said to him, "Teacher, this woman has been caught in the act of adultery. 5 Now in the law Moses commanded us to stone such. What do you say about her?" 6 This they said to test him, that they might have some charge to bring against him. Jesus bent down and wrote with his finger on the ground. 7 And as they continued to ask him, he stood up and said to them, "Let him who is without sin among you be the first to throw a stone at her." 8 And once more he bent down and wrote with his finger on the ground. 9 But when they heard it, they went away, one by one, beginning with the eldest, and Jesus was left alone with the woman standing before him. 10 Jesus looked up and said to her, "Woman, where are they? Has no one condemned you?" 11 She said, "No one, Lord." And Jesus said, "Neither do I condemn you; go, and do not sin again."*

RESPONSE. Nowhere else in John's Gospel is there a mention of scribes, although we have already been introduced to one eminent member of this fraternity, Nicodemus (whom John never actually labels as a scribe; see 3:1–9). Throughout the Synoptic gospels, however, "the scribes and the Pharisees" show themselves Jesus's most ardent opponents. "Scribe" does not refer to someone who is mainly a calligrapher, a copier of scrolls, but rather to a scholar who has memorized the Torah and learned the opinions of the great commentators of earlier generations—a body of material known as "the oral Law" since it is not written down but rather passed from one generation to another by word of mouth.[3] These scribes are not all Pharisees, but the best known ones are, and the most eminent among that group sit in the Sanhedrin as expert interpreters of the Law, in much the same way that famous American jurists are appointed to the Supreme Court. For this reason, some modern English translations substitute the word "lawyer" for "scribe" in translating the name of their profession. Modern people would probably simply call them Scripture scholars or theologians. Jews in Jesus's day generally address prominent scribes as *rabbi*, an honorific title meaning

---

2. Elon, "Capital Punishment."

3. The opinions of the rabbis are not collected in written form until long after the time of Jesus.

something like "great one." It is not until after the New Testament era that the word rabbi comes to be employed as the common title of a teacher of Torah.

In this scene, Jesus is sitting in the temple, teaching, when a group of scribes and Pharisees—all male, naturally—arrive with a woman whom they compel to stand before him, in the midst of those gathered to listen. The accusers announce that the woman has been seized "in the very act" of committing adultery (v. 4). We aren't told how this arrest takes place, nor are we told why her partner was not also apprehended and brought to Jesus. The Law states that the adulterous man is as guilty as the adulterous woman and both should be put to death. The Law demands a minimum of two eyewitnesses in order to bring a charge of adultery. Eyewitnesses are only in a position to observe an amorous adulterous couple if they have been able to hide somewhere in advance of the couple's tryst in order to spy on them. In other words, her husband (or someone else) has probably set the woman up. And whoever set her up seems to be willing to let her male partner escape punishment. The scribes and Pharisees remind Jesus that Moses in the Law says that such a woman should be stoned—making no mention of her partner in the act—and they ask him what he would say about her.[4]

Since the Romans have withdrawn the right of the Sanhedrin to impose the death penalty, this is a clear effort to trap Jesus into advocating either disobedience to Moses or disobedience to Caesar. People are still sometimes stoned for adultery in Judea, but these are extra-judicial executions, acts we would compare to lynching. The Roman governor apparently takes no notice of them; but if a posse of prominent Pharisees arrives at his headquarters calling attention to a specific instance, that might force his hand.

As Jesus ponders how to reply, he is well aware that his answer could have consequences both for himself and for the unfortunate woman who—in this honor- and shame-driven culture—has now been deeply humiliated in front of an assembly of strangers. She could possibly be stoned, and so might he be. Or handed over to the Romans. Jesus bends down and writes with his finger "on the ground." (Since they were in the temple, he would be writing on the dusty, decorative marble pavement. There was no bare earth inside the temple enclosure.)[5] Does Jesus write out the text of the Law? Or a list of the sins of the accusers? Or, since the Greek word used here can as easily mean "draw" as "write," does he merely draw pictures, doodling, stalling for time while he thinks about how to answer?

If we keep in mind the Fourth Gospel context into which this non-Johannine story is inserted, Jesus knows that his hour has not yet come. To permit himself to be arrested now and packed off to Pilate for execution is not the Father's will. But

---

4. That is not exactly true, since Lev 20:10 only says that the adulterous couple should be put to death, not that they should be stoned, but death by stoning was the customary penalty.

5. Avraham, "Temple Mount Pavements." Recent archaeological research by the Temple Mount Sifting Project confirms that the entire temple enclosure as well as the enclosure of Herod's palace was paved with decorative, opus sectile marble.

he is not primarily oriented towards his personal security. The maxim from Mic 6:8 will guide him: "He has showed you, O man, what is good; and what does the Lord require of you but to do justice, and to love kindness, and to walk humbly with your God?" How does the incarnate Word do justice and practice loving-kindness in such a fraught situation? The woman must surely be guilty of adultery in the formal sense; but there are a number of other moral factors in play. Jesus must exercise careful discernment before he replies to the scribes and Pharisees.

Doing justice is rarely a simple, straightforward act. Quickly identifying that a misdeed has taken place and imposing a pre-assigned penalty on the apparently guilty party is not really "justice," not the doing of what is truly right in God's eyes. Jesus's predicament calls to mind that we, too, need the gift of discernment in situations when we are pressed to do whatever might be regarded as "the right thing" by our peers—to make a quick decision, assess blame, and assign punishment.

Jesus doodles or writes with his finger on the pavement, then stands up and says, "Let him who is without sin among you be the first to throw a stone at her" (v. 7). Here is wisdom. Here is mercy. And here, indeed, is justice. The Law requires that the eyewitnesses to the offense, the formal judicial accusers, participate in the stoning. In the present setting, everyone in the temple crowd observing this confrontation is likely to assume that the legal witnesses are standing there among the Pharisees and scribes. But since they have not brought the woman's male partner, obviously there has been some malfeasance on their part. Do the eyewitnesses wish to make themselves known to the crowd? Of course not. Doing so would open them to questions from the bystanders. The others who compose this little clutch of Pharisees want to pose as blameless before the Law, but they know they have connived with the eyewitnesses to create a situation which brings only the guilty woman "to justice" while permitting her male partner in sin to escape. In terms of Mic 6:8, what they contrive to do is patently neither just, nor kind, nor humble before God.

So, as Jesus stoops down to write once more in the dust, the party of self-righteous accusers departs without another word, beginning with the eldest, presumably the wisest. When Jesus stands up again, he and the woman are left alone together, encircled by the audience that watched the entire proceeding.

He asks her, "Woman, what happened to your accusers? Has anyone thrown a stone at you yet?" She replies, "No one, sir." Jesus then says, "Well, I'm not going to stone you either. Be on your way, then. And do not sin again" (paraphrase of vv. 10–11). Jesus has not come into the world to punish sinners, but to give them new life. As the Beloved Disciple put it in 3:17, "God sent the Son into the world, not to condemn the world, but that the world might be saved through him."

8:12–33. Jesus's confrontation with "the Jews" resumes.

Vv. 12–20. "I am the light of the world."

INTRODUCTION. The confrontation between Jesus and "the Jews," which is interrupted by the Fourth Gospel's interpolation of the story of the woman taken in adultery, now resumes with 8:12 and continues to the end of the chapter. The setting remains the temple precincts during the annual Feast of Tabernacles.

Some of what we read in this chapter recapitulates ideas the author presented earlier in the gospel. Just as Jesus's invitation to come to him and drink of living water resembles his invitation to the Samaritan woman in chapter 4, his proclamation of himself as the light of the world repeats a point made in the prologue and expanded upon in chapter 3. That Jesus is going away to a place where his enemies cannot find him is expressed in chapter 7, then reiterated in chapter 8. There are obvious elements of continuity between chapter 7 and chapter 8, since 8:12–59 deals with the working out of the controversy described in the preceding chapter, a controversy which, in turn, was generated by Jesus's healing of the paralyzed man at the Bethesda Pool in chapter 5. This illustrates John's circular style of writing; he makes particular theological points, then circles back to make some of these points again, but in a slightly different form. We will see this later in the Farewell Discourse (chapters 14–16).

On the first and perhaps also on the last night of the Feast of Tabernacles, four enormous lampstands are lit in the court of the women and some priests or Levites perform a sacred dance with torches. The light cast by these huge candelabra makes the whole temple area seem bright as day and even illuminates all the courtyards in Jerusalem.[6] This event provides the occasion for Jesus's proclamation that he is the light of the world, just as the water-pouring ceremony is the setting for his invitation to the crowd to come to him and drink from the river of living water (7:37–38). John's grand theme of Jesus as the life and light of the world leads us to the story of the healing of the man born blind in chapter 9, with its climactic evidence that the Pharisees are spiritually blind. This theme is invoked again in chapter 11 and chapter 12.

> **[8:12–20]** *¹² Again Jesus spoke to them, saying, "I am the light of the world; he who follows me will not walk in darkness, but will have the light of life." ¹³ The Pharisees then said to him, "You are bearing witness to yourself; your testimony is not true." ¹⁴ Jesus answered, "Even if I do bear witness to myself, my testimony is true, for I know whence I have come and whither I am going, but you do not know whence I come or whither I am going. ¹⁵ You judge according to the flesh, I judge no one. ¹⁶ Yet even if I do judge, my judgment is true, for it is not I alone that judge, but I and he who sent me. ¹⁷ In your law it is written that the testimony of two men is true; ¹⁸ I bear witness to myself, and the Father who sent me bears witness to*

---

6. O'Day, *Gospel of John*, 632.

me." ¹⁹ *They said to him therefore, "Where is your Father?" Jesus answered, "You know neither me nor my Father; if you knew me, you would know my Father also." ²⁰ These words he spoke in the treasury, as he taught in the temple; but no one arrested him, because his hour had not yet come.*

RESPONSE. In the context of the Tabernacles festival, with its water-pouring ceremony and its lighting of monumental candelabra, Jesus identifies himself with both water and light. Aware that light from these huge lampstands could be seen everywhere in Jerusalem, Jesus claims even wider power of illumination for himself. He says, "I am the light of the world; he who follows me will not walk in darkness, but will have the light of life" (v. 12). This resonates with the prologue, where John tells us, "In him was life, and the life was the light of men. The light shines in the darkness, and the darkness has not overcome it" (1:4–5). In Matthew's gospel Jesus says to his disciples, "*You* are the light of the world." Both things are true, and he quite likely said both things, but in different contexts. A disciple is meant to reproduce the life of his Master, and if Jesus is the light of the world, his disciples must shine with that same light. The disciples' light is reflected from their Master—but even though the reflected light is not as brilliant as the Master's, it is the same light as his, coming from the same source.

"He who follows me will not walk in darkness, but will have the light of life." Disciples have the light of life; that's what we're meant to reflect. For theological reasons, John's narrative is full of stark, dualistic contrasts. It describes a world where only light and dark exist, with nothing in between. When there is plenty of light, human beings can do everything our life calls for: work, play, study, eat, and take care of one another. When there is absolutely no light—as in a mine when there is a cave-in and all artificial light is lost—the people involved can scarcely move without hurting one another. They can only sit still and pray for rescue.

We understand the gospel writer's theological rationale for contrasting light and dark, day and night. But the truth is that none of us lives in a world where there are only two possible situations: either plenty of light or no light whatsoever. No one except a person who is completely blind or else trapped in a mine cave-in is obliged to cope with *total* darkness. Most of us, however, must manage from time to time with inadequate illumination—*some* light, but not enough. For those of us whose eyesight is not as good as it once was, the more light we have, the easier it is to read or drive the car or appreciate the paintings in a museum. In dim light, we can perceive that there is something or someone there, but we can't tell who or what. In dim light, we can see that there is printing on a page, but we can't make out what it says. Without enough light, we grow frustrated, even angry. We can't understand the world around us. We can't connect with our neighbors. We can't live a full life. If we live in semi-gloom, we have only a diminished life, not a full and happy one. *Jesus is the light of the world.* When we live as Jesus's disciples, walking in the brilliance of his light, we're able to see things as they really are—we can perceive situations clearly, appreciate things fully, and flourish in a way that is not possible for those who must endure a life in perpetual shadows. If "believing is seeing," as the title of this book asserts, then believing in the light of the world yields a sharpness of vision, of insight, attainable in no other way.

Jesus's opponents, the Pharisees, being petty-minded, choose to quibble: "You are bearing witness to yourself; your testimony is not true" (v. 13). It is correct that two other witnesses are required for a person's explanation about himself to be accepted in a Jewish religious court; but that does not make the individual's personal testimony *untrue*. It simply means that it is uncorroborated until there are two others who testify. But Jesus is speaking of mysteries known only to God. No one else is competent to address the question under discussion. No mortal could possibly know what Jesus knows or confirm the truth of his attestation. He knows the Father, and the Father knows the Son. Therefore, Jesus simply makes the assertion—obviously unacceptable to the Pharisees—that the only conceivable witnesses to his true identity are his Father and himself. The traditions that govern admissibility of evidence in a Jewish religious court do not provide for the possibility of first-hand testimony from the mouth of God.

Vv. 21–33. "You will know the truth, and the truth will make you free."

INTRODUCTION. Jesus continues to offend the chief priests and leading Pharisees by the ways he describes himself and speaks about his intimate relationship with God. When they hear him say, "You are from below, I am from above; you are of this world, I am not of this world" (v. 23), we can imagine how greatly his words shock and offend these aristocratic, educated, important men of the Sanhedrin. What can this rustic from Nazareth mean by telling them that *he* is "from above" while *they* are "from below"? They have researched his family history; they know the identity of his parents and the inconsequential Galilean village where he grew to manhood.

Yet, even as he deepens the rift between himself and the Jewish rulers, Jesus continues to attract ordinary people to "believe in him" (v. 30). Nevertheless, the expression "believe in him" is laden with ambiguity. John makes it clear that though a number of "believers" are attracted to Jesus for a variety of reasons—many are not truly *devoted* to him. They are not true disciples yet, at least not the sort of disciples Jesus has in mind in vv. 31–32.

> [8:21–33] [21] *Again he said to them, "I go away, and you will seek me and die in your sin; where I am going, you cannot come."* [22] *Then said the Jews, "Will he kill himself, since he says, 'Where I am going, you cannot come'?"* [23] *He said to them, "You are from below, I am from above; you are of this world, I am not of this world.* [24] *I told you that you would die in your sins, for you will die in your sins unless you believe that I am he."* [25] *They said to him, "Who are you?" Jesus said to them, "Even what I have told you*

from the beginning. ²⁶ I have much to say about you and much to judge; but he who sent me is true, and I declare to the world what I have heard from him." ²⁷ They did not understand that he spoke to them of the Father. ²⁸ So Jesus said, "When you have lifted up the Son of man, then you will know that I am he, and that I do nothing on my own authority but speak thus as the Father taught me. ²⁹ And he who sent me is with me; he has not left me alone, for I always do what is pleasing to him." ³⁰ As he spoke thus, many believed in him.

³¹ Jesus then said to the Jews who had believed in him, "If you continue in my word, you are truly my disciples, ³² and you will know the truth, and the truth will make you free." ³³ They answered him, "We are descendants of Abraham, and have never been in bondage to any one. How is it that you say, 'You will be made free'?"

RESPONSE. "Who are you?" That's the question put to Jesus in various ways in all the Gospels. Sometimes it's worded differently, as when the questioners turn to one another and ask, "Who is this?" John's theological purpose is to answer that question as clearly and completely as possible. The Fourth Gospel is explicit where the Synoptics are merely allusive or indirect. John pulls no punches. We may read Matthew, Mark, and Luke and still wonder, "Even though this gospel writer is sure Jesus is the Messiah, does he also think of Jesus as divine, or does he not?" Such uncertainty is not present when we look at John. Readers of John must conclude that Jesus, a very ordinary working man from Nazareth, is God-with-us. Jesus is not only the long-anticipated Messiah and prophet-greater-than Moses; he is the divine *Logos* in human guise, the only Son of the Father, God's personal representative, the earthly agent of the Almighty, and the incarnation of the Wisdom of God.

For Jesus to articulate these claims, even obliquely, in a confrontation with the highest authorities in Judaism is to invite immediate condemnation. In the minds of the chief priests and Pharisees, for a mere mortal to pretend to be God in human flesh is the worst of all possible blasphemies, a sin calling for the severest punishment. Therefore, Jesus is never unambiguously explicit in announcing his true identity to "the Jews." However, he's quite daring in what he does tell them, as we see here in chapter 8: "Where I am going you cannot come" (v. 21); "You are from below, I am from above; you are of this world, I am not of this world" (v. 23); "You will die in your sins unless you believe that I AM [he]" (v. 24); and "When you have lifted up the Son of man, then you will know that I AM [he]" (v. 28).[7]

John tells us that some of those who hear Jesus "believe in him" (v. 30). But what does that mean? The word *believe* is used in a variety of ways in the Fourth Gospel. In what sense do any members of his audience in the temple at the Feast of Tabernacles

---

7. "I Am [he]" in vv. 24 and 28 is literally the Greek expression *egō eimi*, the Divine Name, "I AM." Our RSV translation of both verses inserts the pronoun "he," but no such pronoun appears in the Greek text.

believe in Jesus? Clearly, since the hearers' belief in him is going to turn sour very quickly, they must neither believe in him as God in human flesh, nor as the earthly agent of the Almighty. The most we can gather from the Fourth Gospel is that these hearers' opinion is—at least for the moment—swayed in Jesus's favor by his charismatic personality and the forcefulness of his speech, keeping in mind they already have heard that he works miracles. Crowds are fickle. We observe this in modern audiences—whether in politics, religion, education, or the performing arts. Many preachers, politicians, and performers can affect a group and earn its enthusiastic approval in the early afternoon, then offend them by a word or gesture and be flatly rejected before the day is over. In Matthew's gospel, Jesus even speaks of his closest disciples as men with "little faith."[8] Belief waxes and wanes—among those who populate John's Gospel and those who read that gospel today.

"Jesus then said to the Jews who had believed in him, 'If you continue in my word, you are truly my disciples, and you will know the truth, and the truth will make you free'" (vv. 31–32).[9] One clause of this famous saying of Jesus, "the truth will make you free," has become popular all over what was once called Christendom. Usually expressed in Latin or Greek, it is the official motto of numerous orders and organizations, colleges and universities, both religious and secular. *Ye shall know the truth and the truth shall make you free* is even carved in stone in the entrance to the Original Headquarters Building of the Central Intelligence Agency. Those who chose to inscribe it there were oblivious to the irony involved in such an act. Raymond Brown writes, "The hackneyed use of this phrase in political oratory in appealing for national or personal liberty is a distortion of the purely religious value of both truth and freedom in this passage."[10]

The opening words of the sentence are the operative ones for readers to consider, "*If you continue in my word*, you are truly my disciples, and you will know the truth." The "truth" referred to here is God's self-revelation in the person of his Son, as we see in v. 36, which tells us that it is the Son who makes us free. To "continue" in Jesus's "word" is to *abide in his message*, which is the same as abiding in Jesus himself. The person and the message of God's Son, are one. He is God's "Word made flesh." Those who live in union with him—who reproduce his life in the way faithful disciples are meant to do—will be free indeed. To be free in this context means to be delivered from bondage to sin in the same way that the Hebrews were set free at the exodus from bondage to Pharaoh, free from slavery to behaviors, habits, or desires that cut mortals

8. See, e.g., Matt 6:30; 8:26; 14:31; and 16:8. In Mark 9:23–24, Jesus says to the man who brought his epileptic son to be healed, "All things are possible to him who believes." And the man responds, passionately, "I believe; help my unbelief!" None of the gospels portrays faith/belief as flawless in any of the disciples. Only the faith of Jesus himself—faith in his Father and in the Father's providence—is absolute and without defect.

9. "The Jews" as used here refers merely to people of Judea and Jerusalem, not the hostile Jewish authorities.

10. Brown, *John I–XII*, 355.

off from God. The logic of this argument is intended to be circular: to abide in the Son is the very substance of liberty. To be set free by the Son is to be delivered from even the possibility of becoming a slave to sin.

As is typical of the thick-headed opponents of Jesus we meet in John's Gospel—including those to whom he spoke at Capernaum in chapter 6—some of them now make an obviously foolish reply. They say, "What do you mean by telling us we will be 'set free'? We're the descendants of Abraham, and we've never been anybody's slaves" (paraphrase of v. 33). John's rhetorical irony is heavy, for since coming into the Promised Land under Joshua, the descendants of Abraham have been ruled in turn by Philistines, Assyrians, Babylonians, Persians, Greeks, and now by Romans. Children of Abraham have been taken away as slaves by a series of alien conquerors. A bloody war will be fought with Rome in a futile effort to win their freedom in 66–73. During that conflict, Herod's new temple will be destroyed, never to be rebuilt, and tens of thousands of Jews will be sold into slavery. Jesus's audience is quite wrong. As a nation, the descendants of Abraham are most assuredly not free, and they will not be free again until 1948.—But Jesus is not speaking of political or even personal freedom. A slave laboring in a tin mine or a wheat field can enjoy a freedom no human captor can take away, the freedom of the soul.

As I read John's Gospel in the twenty-first century I must ask myself: How *free* am I? What forms do my personal bondages take, the habits from which I can only be liberated by the truth of Christ? To what temptations do I most quickly fall? What fears control my reflexes? What master do I serve? If we are seeking a glorious propositional truth, a single, shining, intellectual concept, like the cosmologists' elusive "theory of everything," a truth we can encapsulate in words or a formula, we will never find it. We will learn interesting things, of course, valuable things. And we will devise clever, memorable ways to express them. We may rightly call these discoveries of science, mathematics, or philosophical logic "truths of a lesser sort"—propositions that have facticity. But none of them are the *truth* of which Jesus speaks to those who hear him teaching in the temple during the Feast of Tabernacles in the year 32 CE. The truth that sets a human being free cannot be captured in language or expressed mathematically. It is manifested only in a *life*—lived by the Son of God, and by extension lived by the children of God.

8: 34–59. Jesus's argument with "the Jews" grows bitter, and they try to stone him.

Vv. 34–59. Jesus's enemies ask, "Have you seen Abraham? . . . Who do you claim to be?"

INTRODUCTION. This important section describes Jesus's divisive argument with "the Jews" concerning their status as children of Abraham. He makes clear in v. 37

that he is speaking of their paternity only metaphorically. All Jews literally descend from Abraham according to the flesh, but Jesus denies that his opponents are truly the great patriarch's spiritual heirs. Instead, Jesus says the Devil is really the spiritual father of these men who cannot even bear to hear the word he speaks to them from God. The Fourth Gospel displays some congruence with Pauline theology, though no direct dependence on any of Paul's letters. However, it appears from this section that John either does not know or does not accept Paul's ideas concerning justification by faith. Nowhere does he echo Paul's teaching about the faith of Abraham (as outlined in Gal 3:6–9).

This section of dialogues with "the Jews" which began in 7:14 ends with their attempt to stone Jesus in 8:59. They will ultimately succeed in putting him to death, but only after he has fulfilled all that the Father sent him to do. His hour is approaching, but it has not yet struck.

[8:34–59] [34] *Jesus answered them, "Truly, truly, I say to you, every one who commits sin is a slave to sin.* [35] *The slave does not continue in the house for ever; the son continues for ever.* [36] *So if the Son makes you free, you will be free indeed.* [37] *I know that you are descendants of Abraham; yet you seek to kill me, because my word finds no place in you.* [38] *I speak of what I have seen with my Father, and you do what you have heard from your father."*

[39] *They answered him, "Abraham is our father." Jesus said to them, "If you were Abraham's children, you would do what Abraham did,* [40] *but now you seek to kill me, a man who has told you the truth which I heard from God; this is not what Abraham did.* [41] *You do what your father did." They said to him, "We were not born of fornication; we have one Father, even God."* [42] *Jesus said to them, "If God were your Father, you would love me, for I proceeded and came forth from God; I came not of my own accord, but he sent me.* [43] *Why do you not understand what I say? It is because you cannot bear to hear my word.* [44] *You are of your father the devil, and your will is to do your father's desires. He was a murderer from the beginning, and has nothing to do with the truth, because there is no truth in him. When he lies, he speaks according to his own nature, for he is a liar and the father of lies.* [45] *But, because I tell the truth, you do not believe me.* [46] *Which of you convicts me of sin? If I tell the truth, why do you not believe me?* [47] *He who is of God hears the words of God; the reason why you do not hear them is that you are not of God."*

[48] *The Jews answered him, "Are we not right in saying that you are a Samaritan and have a demon?"* [49] *Jesus answered, "I have not a demon; but I honor my Father, and you dishonor me.* [50] *Yet I do not seek my own glory; there is One who seeks it and he will be the judge.* [51] *Truly, truly, I say to you, if any one keeps my word, he will never see death."* [52] *The Jews said to him, "Now we know that you have a demon. Abraham died, as did the prophets; and you say, 'If any one keeps my word, he will never taste death.'* [53] *Are you greater than our father Abraham, who died? And the prophets died! Who do you claim to be?"* [54] *Jesus answered,*

"If I glorify myself, my glory is nothing; it is my Father who glorifies me, of whom you say that he is your God. [55] But you have not known him; I know him. If I said, I do not know him, I should be a liar like you; but I do know him and I keep his word. [56] Your father Abraham rejoiced that he was to see my day; he saw it and was glad." [57] The Jews then said to him, "You are not yet fifty years old, and have you seen Abraham?" [58] Jesus said to them, "Truly, truly, I say to you, before Abraham was, I am." [59] So they took up stones to throw at him; but Jesus hid himself, and went out of the temple.

RESPONSE. In this section it's difficult to distinguish between what represents the opinion of the people in the temple who are witnessing the confrontation between Jesus and his enemies and what represents the attitude of the hostile priests and Pharisees themselves. Perhaps John wants us to see that the crowd of common people, in its own capricious way, is just as obstinate as the Pharisees in their refusal to understand what Jesus is trying to say. If John's recollection of the episode approaches being historically accurate, Jesus's opponents have already decided that the Nazarene is a threat to the nation, someone they need to eliminate—if not because of his blasphemous claim to be the Son of God, then because he abuses the Sabbath, misleads the people, and threatens the chief priests' and Pharisees' role as the rightful religious leaders of Israel.

Although Jesus concedes that his adversaries are literally descended from Abraham, he tells them their real father is the Devil, the father of lies. A simple reading of the third chapter of Genesis shows that the Serpent—Satan—beguiles Eve and Adam in the Garden of Eden with falsehoods and half-truths. The Serpent leads them into lying to God and hiding from God—practices that constitute an apt description of sin. The ultimate result of this sin is their death.

The intent of this portion of the Fourth Gospel seems evident. John wants readers to recognize that the group he labels ironically as "the Jews"—meaning primarily the Pharisees who have driven followers of Jesus out of some synagogues—are themselves the deceivers of Israel. Their father is the Devil, although they claim to be children of God. Jesus says, "Why do you not understand what I say? It is because you cannot bear to hear my word" (v. 43). We may rephrase Jesus's words this way, "Because you don't accept who I am, you can't understand what I'm talking about."[11] That is a fundamental point in Jesus's message, both to the Pharisees and chief priests and to all who read the Fourth Gospel. Until we believe in who Jesus is—the timeless truth of God made manifest in a single human life—we will not be able to make sense of what he is telling us. *Believing is seeing.*

---

11. Smith, *John*, 186, says, "Jesus makes a play on words that is difficult to capture (v. 43): 'What I say' translates *lalia* (speech, what is uttered), while 'word' renders *logos* (communication and, according to 1:1–18, what Jesus is). It is not too much to say that because they do not accept Jesus they do not really know what he is talking about."

For Jesus's challengers, trapped in a literalism that blocks them from understanding him, the breaking point comes when Jesus tells them, "Your father Abraham rejoiced that he was to see my day; he saw it and was glad." The stupefied Pharisees and their priestly allies reply, "How can you say that you've seen Abraham? You are not even fifty years old" (paraphrase of v. 57). Jesus then proposes a claim to pre-existence and identification with God that enrages them: "Truly, truly, I say to you, before Abraham was, I AM" (v. 58). This use of the Sacred Name repeats what Jesus said to his disciples at the theophany during the storm on the Galilean lake (see 6:20). It inspires his opponents—and maybe some bystanders—to take up pieces of construction rubble and try to stone him for blasphemy. But Jesus's hour has not yet come. In the melee, he hides from the angry mob, then makes his way safely out of the temple, bringing an end to this particular set of mutually hostile dialogues with "the Jews."

Doing Your Own Theology

Questions for reflection after reading John 8.

- Doing justice is rarely a simple, straightforward act. Quickly identifying that a misdeed has taken place and imposing a pre-assigned penalty on the apparently guilty party is not really "justice," not the doing of what is right in God's eyes. In the story of the woman taken in adultery (vv. 1–11), Jesus's predicament reminds us of times when we have been pressed to "do the right thing" by our peers—particularly to make a quick decision, assess blame, and assign a predetermined harsh punishment. Jesus's opponents among the scribes and Pharisees want to trap him into incriminating himself, which would create a situation in which someone in the crowd could shout that Jesus should be stoned (as later happened to Stephen; see Acts 8:54–58). Yet Jesus appears more interested in securing mercy and authentic justice for the accused woman than in protecting himself from his enemies.—*Have you ever felt pressured to side with legalists and call for harsh treatment of an accused offender, even though you were privately not convinced of the person's guilt? What did you do? If forced to choose between the letter of the law and extending mercy, how are you more likely to choose? On what grounds might you refuse to impose a penalty on someone who seems to be legally guilty of an offense?*

- One of the most familiar of Jesus's sayings in John's Gospel is, "I am the light of the world; he who follows me will not walk in darkness, but will have the light of life" (v. 12). John often employs the rhetoric of dualism, exemplified in this contrast between light and darkness. But neither Jesus, nor John, nor anyone who reads John's Gospel imagines that all moral crises in human life can be characterized as choices between black or white, good or evil, right or wrong. No one lives in a binary moral universe. At times a decision can be made between obvious right and obvious wrong, but more often we are compelled to choose from among an array of morally imperfect options. Believers pray for the kind of discernment that Jesus manifests in the case of the woman taken in adultery.—*In view of the reality of life in a moral universe that requires not only black and white choices, but decisions among many shades of gray in between, how do you understand Jesus's statement, "He who follows me will not walk in darkness, but will have the light of life"? Can you recall a hazy moral situation in which you truly needed to ask for the light of Christ in order to know what to do? What light enabled you to make a decision?*

- A famous and oft-quoted statement of Jesus is found in v. 32, "You will know the truth, and the truth will make you free." Many who quote this saying habitually neglect to include the words of Jesus which precede and modify it (v. 31), "If you continue in my word, you are truly my disciples and you will know the truth . . ." etc. The "truth" that is referred to here is God's self-revelation in the person of his Son, as we see in v. 36, which tells us it is the Son who makes us free. To "continue" in Jesus's "word" means to *abide* in his message, which is the same as abiding in Jesus himself, since his message is identical with his person.—*In what different ways do you personally employ the word "truth"? How do you understand the meaning of truth in the context of John's Gospel? Can you identify a single specific truth you have learned from your personal experience of abiding in Jesus' word? Can you describe how this truth has made you feel free?*

Chapter Nine

9:1–34. Jesus gives sight to a man blind from birth.

Vv. 1–34. "As long as I am in the world, I am the light of the world."

INTRODUCTION. The story of Jesus giving sight to the man born blind in chapter 9 is a contrasting counterpart to the story of the healing of the lame man at the Bethesda Pool in chapter 5.[1] In both instances, Jesus takes the initiative to heal a sufferer who has not asked for his aid. The two men respond in opposite ways to their healings. The paralyzed man points out Jesus to the temple authorities as a Sabbath-breaker. The man born blind, who is also healed on a Sabbath, clings steadfastly to his conviction that Jesus is sent by God, which leads the Pharisees to revile him as "born in utter sin" and cast him out of their presence (v. 34).

This story of Jesus giving sight to the man born blind is an artistically constructed, dramatic narrative. It is related to the foregoing and following material only loosely, although it seems to be set in the vicinity of the temple, the scene for chapters 7 and 8. Jesus anoints the blind man's eyes with mud, sends him to the Pool of Siloam to wash, and he comes back seeing. This may be a thinly veiled allusion to baptism and new creation; it was certainly regarded as such by the early church.[2] The washing relates to the water from Siloam that plays a symbolic role in the temple ceremonies during the Tabernacles festival as well as Jesus's invitation to the crowd to come to him and drink (7:37–38). The reference to Jesus as the light of the world (v. 5) connects with 8:12 as well as with 3:19–21, where the author of the gospel tells us, "This is the judgment, that the light has come into the world, and men loved darkness rather than light, because their deeds were evil." John Newton's well-known hymn, "Amazing Grace," found its inspiration in the words of the man born blind, "One thing I know, that though I was blind, now I see" (v. 25).

---

1. A helpful parallel comparison of the elements of the two healing stories is provided in Culpepper, *Anatomy*, 139.

2. Brown, *John I–XII*, 380–81.

For John's intended audience, the man born blind is an example of those who are expelled from their local synagogue after their eyes have been opened to the truth of Christ.[3] Those who "cast them out" (v. 34) are people who choose blindness (vv. 39–41). There has been much debate concerning the issue of whether any followers of Jesus were ever expelled from a synagogue—especially during Jesus's ministry. Despite what is said in v. 22, it was not a violation of the Law or of rabbinical tradition to regard any particular person as the Messiah. It was, however, a shocking blasphemy to treat a mere man as Son of God. There were undoubtedly sectarian divisions within many synagogues, both in Judea and in the diaspora, which resulted in particular members being ejected by local leaders.[4] What Paul writes in Gal 1:13–23 about his own former zeal as a persecutor of the followers of Jesus offers substantiation to the charge that Jews who named Jesus as Messiah were sometimes expelled from their usual synagogues. But evidence suggests that Jewish followers of Jesus were still participating in the life of some synagogues after the Bar Kokhba Revolt (132–5 CE) and even later in some cases. Recent research shows that Christians were worshiping in synagogues in Syria, for example, even in the late fourth century.[5] The separation of Christianity from Judaism was a protracted and very complex process, not an event to which a single date may be attached. (See Appendix Two, pp. 358–59, below.)

[9:1–34] [1] *As he passed by, he saw a man blind from his birth.* [2] *And his disciples asked him, "Rabbi, who sinned, this man or his parents, that he was born blind?"* [3] *Jesus answered, "It was not that this man sinned, or his parents, but that the works of God might be made manifest in him.* [4] *We must work the works of him who sent me, while it is day; night comes, when no one can work.* [5] *As long as I am in the world, I am the light of the world."*

[6] *As he said this, he spat on the ground and made clay of the spittle and anointed the man's eyes with the clay,* [7] *saying to him, "Go, wash in the pool of Siloam" (which means Sent). So he went and washed and came back seeing.*

[8] *The neighbors and those who had seen him before as a beggar, said, "Is not this the man who used to sit and beg?"* [9] *Some said, "It is he"; others said, "No, but he is like him." He said, "I am the man."* [10] *They said to him, "Then how were your eyes opened?"* [11] *He answered, "The man called Jesus made clay and anointed my eyes and said to me, 'Go to Siloam and wash'; so I went and washed and received my sight."* [12] *They said to him, "Where is he?" He said, "I do not know."*

3. See Brown, *Community*, 71–73.

4. Cirafesi, "Johannine Community," 350–52, disputing the thesis of J. L. Martyn and its supporters, argues the historical likelihood that some followers of Jesus were expelled from their local synagogues during Jesus's lifetime. See also Robinson, *Redating*, 272–75.

5. See Lieu, "Synagogue," and McLaren, "From Jewish Movement." See also Stark, *Rise*, 49–71.

[13] *They brought to the Pharisees" the man who had formerly been blind. [14] Now it was a Sabbath day when Jesus made the clay and opened his eyes. [15] The Pharisees again asked him how he had received his sight. And he said to them, "He put clay on my eyes, and I washed, and I see." [16] Some of the Pharisees said, "This man is not from God, for he does not keep the Sabbath." But others said, "How can a man who is a sinner do such signs?" There was a division among them. [17] So they again said to the blind man, "What do you say about him, since he has opened your eyes?" He said, "He is a prophet."*

[18] The Jews did not believe that he had been blind and had received his sight, until they called the parents of the man who had received his sight, [19] and asked them, "Is this your son, who you say was born blind? How then does he now see?" [20] His parents answered, "We know that this is our son, and that he was born blind; [21] but how he now sees we do not know, nor do we know who opened his eyes. Ask him; he is of age, he will speak for himself." [22] His parents said this because they feared the Jews, for the Jews had already agreed that if any one should confess him to be Christ, he was to be put out of the synagogue. [23] Therefore his parents said, "He is of age, ask him."

[24] So for the second time they called the man who had been blind, and said to him, "Give God the praise; we know that this man is a sinner." [25] He answered, "Whether he is a sinner, I do not know; one thing I know, that though I was blind, now I see." [26] They said to him, "What did he do to you? How did he open your eyes?" [27] He answered them, "I have told you already, and you would not listen. Why do you want to hear it again? Do you too want to become his disciples?" [28] And they reviled him, saying, "You are his disciple, but we are disciples of Moses. [29] We know that God has spoken to Moses, but as for this man, we do not know where he comes from." [30] The man answered, "Why, this is a marvel! You do not know where he comes from, and yet he opened my eyes. [31] We know that God does not listen to sinners, but if any one is a worshiper of God and does his will, God listens to him. [32] Never since the world began has it been heard that any one opened the eyes of a man born blind. [33] If this man were not from God, he could do nothing." [34] They answered him, "You were born in utter sin, and would you teach us?" And they cast him out.

RESPONSE. At the opening of this section, John presents his readers with an old and troubling question, *"Why do the innocent suffer?"* Jesus's disciples propose a traditional Jewish answer: the innocent suffer for the sins of their parents (see Exod 20:5). Or perhaps they suffer—somehow—for their own sins, which means they only *appear* to be innocent.[6] There are people in our day who regard the question, "why do the innocent suffer," as essentially meaningless. They recognize no "why" to suffering beyond the biological consequences of disease or the results of bad choices, made either by the sufferer or others. Concerning the man born blind, Jesus tells his disciples, "It was not that this man sinned, or his parents, but that the works of God might be made manifest in him" (v. 3). That is to say, Jesus intuits meaning, even divine purpose, in the man's lifelong blindness. His lack of sight strikes Jesus as a gift, since it provides an occasion for the work of God to be revealed. The only thing that can make undeserved suffering tolerable to the human spirit is "what God makes of it when he does his work upon it."[7]

My wife's eldest son died of a brain tumor at age 48. Bill was a brilliant, kind, successful, and spiritually mature man, who faced his impending death with profound wisdom. He knew long before any of the rest of the family that his life was going to end much sooner than he wished. Once during his illness, as we were having a telephone conversation about spiritual things, Bill told me, "I believe everything in life is a gift of God. Everything. Including the things that don't look much like gifts."

It's conventional wisdom that a person should try to make the best of an unfortunate situation. However, only God-given insight allows a person to identify the knowledge that he will probably die within a year as a gift, to say nothing of perceiving that his untimely and unwanted death might—somehow—fit within the larger purposes of God. When Jesus and his disciples encounter the man born blind begging for alms from people who are coming to the temple, the disciples treat the blind man merely as a worthy subject for theological discussion. Seeing him, they ask their Teacher, "Who sinned? This man, or his parents, that he was born blind?" (v. 2). Jesus sees the man quite differently, as a gift from God, and recognizes his blindness from birth as a portent of divine grace.

People who walk in the light of God recognize and accept both their limitations and their strengths and live in peace with God and others. They know what they can do and what they cannot do; they are aware of what they know, and what they do not know. This kind of enlightenment is a work of divine grace.

See is a potent word in the Fourth Gospel. For the Beloved Disciple, to *see* betokens more than the exercise of one's natural eyesight. There are two types of people in this story about Jesus and the man born blind: those who *can* see and those who *cannot*. Jesus can see. The man born blind ultimately can see, too, although at the beginning of the story his eyes are sightless. All the other characters in the story are also

---

6. Apparently a few rabbis taught that prenatal sin was possible. (See Brown, *John I–XII*, 371.) People who believe in reincarnation and accept some version of the Indian idea of *karma* say that people suffer as a punishment for evil they have done in a previous life—which is a way of saying that apparently innocent sufferers are actually not innocent at all.

7. Marsh, *Saint John*, 376.

blind, at least to some degree, despite the fact that their physical eyes are functioning normally.

Sometimes darkness can be frightening to us who spend our days in the light with eyes that operate properly. But the man born blind has always lived in the dark. He knows no other reality, so he isn't afraid of the darkness. He is a poor beggar, barely a "man"—maybe just a year or two past the legal maturity age of 13.[8] He goes tap-tap-tapping his way with a stick in hand through the crowded, crooked streets of Jerusalem every day, invariably following the same familiar path until he comes to his favorite spot, probably near the near the stairs leading up from the city to the temple. There, he sits down on his cloak, stretches up his hands to passers-by, and begs. "Alms for a poor blind man? . . . Thank you, and may Heaven bless you. Peace be with you. . . . Alms? Alms?" I'm sure that when Jesus comes along, trailed by his disciples, the man reaches up and asks, "Alms, kind sir? . . . Alms for a poor blind man?"

Because the beggar is blind, his hearing is acute, as are his senses of touch and smell. These senses inform him when people are stopping beside him and they tell him about what else is going on—the sounds and scents that accompany the set hours of sacrifice and incense offering, the noisy rumble of the crowd going in and out of the temple. If he follows his usual route to and from home and sits in his familiar spot by the steps, he is secure. The man born blind knows his limitations, and he knows his strengths. He is an innocent.

The Pharisees do not perceive their limitations, and they over-rate their strengths. Confident they are the chosen of the Lord and righteous in God's eyes, the Pharisees are certain of their ability to grasp the significance of events and interpret the ways of God to others. They proudly know the letter of the Law by heart, and it is their infallible guide. They do debate with each other about its interpretation, but the Law of Moses is supreme. They are confident of their knowledge and of their capacity to pass judgment on sinners.

Here is something we can observe as a fact in our own time just as it was in the time of Christ: Those who presume to see everything by the lamp of legalism tend to view the world in black and white. They read the Holy Book as a law code and interpret the significance of everything in terms of law-keeping or law-breaking. That was true when Jesus healed the man born blind and it's true even in the third Christian millennium, as the continuing fragmentation and judgmental sectarianism among Christians demonstrates. Demand for certainty, coupled with intolerance of ambiguity and a need always to be right, impels otherwise decent people to point fingers at one another and shout, "Sinner! Lawbreaker! Heretic! God is going to punish you, just wait and see. The Bible says so. *We* possess the truth; *you* have no truth at all. We can't have fellowship with such as you until you repent and become like us. Anything else would be an abomination before God." Even the disciples of Jesus look at this poor young blind man from a legalistic,

---

8. Ibid., 383; and Keener, *Gospel of John*, 1:788. A man was legally "of age" at 13.

black-and-white point of view. The beggar has always been blind. He has never seen a sunset, or a rose in bloom, or the smiling face of his beloved. But the disciples' first thoughts about him are not of pity or sympathy, but only of sin and judgment. They take it for granted that his blindness is punishment from God, and their single question to Jesus concerning the man is whether he is being punished for his own or his parents' sin. We must allow that in this story John offers us the disciples' hard-heartedness as a foil to the compassion of their Master.

Jesus answers his narrow-minded friends by saying, "This man didn't sin, and neither did his parents. This happened so that the works of God might be revealed in him. We must be about the business of doing the works of him who sent me while it is still day. Night is coming, and then no one can work. As long as I'm in the world, I am the light of the world" (paraphrase of vv. 3–5). Then he spits on the dusty marble pavement, makes a pinch of muddy paste, and puts it on the blind man's closed eyelids. (I wonder what the blind beggar thought when he felt Jesus gently smearing something on his face.) There is a quality of authority in Jesus's voice, and everyone who hears him notices it. No one has ever spoken as this man does (see 7:45–46). When he tells the beggar to go to the Pool of Siloam and wash, the man goes obediently, probably led by the hand of one of Jesus's disciples.

Jesus takes the initiative. The blind beggar doesn't ask for healing, and he exhibits no knowledge of who this stranger might be. He only wants alms, maybe a coin or two. Jesus surprises this innocent soul with a gift more valuable than any quantity of money, something the man has no idea anyone could offer.—Is that not often God's way of dealing with us? He encounters us during an ordinary day, touches us in an unexpected way, and leaves us with an unanticipated, scarcely believable blessing.

Why did Jesus not heal the man born blind instantly? Why the business of spitting on the dust and making a muddy ointment? Why the washing in the Pool of Siloam? Augustine of Hippo answered this question long ago in a sermon. He told his congregation that John means to show us this innocent man as a representative of the whole human race: all of us are blind from birth. The anointing of his eyes with mud is a fresh, new act of creation, carried out by the same One through whom all things had come into being.[9] When Jesus says, "I am the light of the world," we are told that this is more than a miracle involving eyesight; it's about new creation. It is not so much about eyesight as *in*sight, and how even you and I may come to "see" the truth. Such enlightenment is always a surprising work of God's grace—a gift. In our blindness and ignorance we know nothing except that our soul is empty, barren, wanting. We don't know what we need to fill our emptiness, we can only pray for mercy. The beggar asks only for alms, but Jesus gives him a new life, a life in the light.

---

9. Augustine of Hippo, *Homilies*, XLIV, 1–2. Augustine also told his congregation, in the same sermon, that "unbelief is blindness" and "faith is enlightenment." (*Si enim caecitas est infidelitas, et illuminatio fides; quem fidelem quando venit Christus invenit?* "For if unbelief is blindness, and faith enlightenment, whom did Christ find a believer at his coming?")

Without Jesus, we who pride ourselves on our wisdom and claim to understand the laws of nature and God are blind. We overrate our strengths and are oblivious to our limitations. We need a good dose of what philosophers call "epistemological modesty." Such modesty requires us to confess that there is much we do not know and cannot explain. We don't have all the answers, especially to the great question, *Why?* John's Gospel tells us that without Jesus humankind will stumble blindly through history, accidentally crushing beautiful things, falling into the traps of evil, wounding ourselves, and threatening all that live around us. We need the light of the world. We need to see the world (and ourselves) in his light.

The story of Jesus and the man born blind confirms something we understand intuitively: there's a knowledge that comes only from first-hand experience. No amount of speculative reasoning, logic, or wishful thinking can substitute for *the solid assurance that comes when we have an experience of grace.* The Pharisees in their legalistic blindness want to trap the naïve, once-blind, young beggar. First, they doubt he has really been blind from birth. So they haul his terrified parents into the official hearing and demand that they tell their boy's story. The parents confirm that their son has been blind from his mother's womb, but they will say no more. They are afraid of what might happen to them if this blind child of theirs is found to be consorting with a man deemed dangerous by the powers-that-be. Ignorance is their refuge. This is not epistemological modesty; it is shameful cowardice.

The story as John tells it spells out the increasing knowledge of the man born blind as first his sightlessness and then his ignorance of Jesus are gradually replaced by gifts of understanding and insight once he has washed in Siloam. At the same time, the Pharisees—who claim far greater knowledge than they actually possess—are shown to be both blind and uncomprehending. The Pharisees order the man born blind to explain exactly how his sight has been restored, in hopes he might explain away the healing or at least reject the healer. When he tells them Jesus kneaded clay and put it on his eyes, the Pharisees crow, "Aha! Just as we thought, this so-called healer is a Sabbath-breaking sinner! Making clay on the Sabbath is forbidden." But the beggar is a simple man, and he has the simple assurance that can only arise from a powerful personal experience. When confronted by the Pharisees' ruling that Jesus is a sinner, he replies: "I don't know whether he's a sinner or not. But I *do* know this: I used to be blind but now I see" (paraphrase of v. 25). There's no arguing with this kind of experience, this kind of knowledge. He *knows* the man who opened his eyes is the agent of God. It's obvious. Who else could do anything like this?—The proud custodians of the Law respond with disdain at the beggar's simple credulity and "cast him out" (v. 34).

Vv. 35–41. The man born blind believes in Jesus and worships him.

INTRODUCTION. Just as Jesus explicitly identifies himself as the long-awaited Messiah to a humble Samaritan village woman (4:26), so now he identifies himself to a similarly humble Jerusalem beggar as the apocalyptic Son of Man (v. 37), to whom, according to Daniel, the Almighty will give universal dominion (Dan 7:13–14). John's message is clear: the Son of God chooses to make himself more clearly known to the meek and lowly than to the high and mighty. When the beggar learns who Jesus is, he not only says "Lord, I believe" (v. 38), but prostrates himself in adoration, worshiping Jesus just as Thomas will do later (20:28).

> [**Vv. 35-40**] *35 Jesus heard that they had cast him out, and having found him he said, "Do you believe in the Son of man?" 36 He answered, "And who is he, sir, that I may believe in him?" 37 Jesus said to him, "You have seen him, and it is he who speaks to you." 38 He said, "Lord, I believe"; and he worshiped him. 39 Jesus said, "For judgment I came into this world, that those who do not see may see, and that those who see may become blind."*
>
> *40 Some of the Pharisees near him heard this, and they said to him, "Are we also blind?" 41 Jesus said to them, "If you were blind, you would have no guilt; but now that you say, 'We see,' your guilt remains.*

RESPONSE. These last verses are the spiritual heart of this story of the man born blind. The learned Pharisees reject the beggar after the poor, badgered man gives his testimony to them a second time, angrily expelling him from their gathering and perhaps from the synagogue community, reviling him as "born in utter sin" (v. 34). When Jesus discovers the way the Pharisees dealt with the innocent man he healed, the good shepherd—as he will call himself in 10:11—goes looking for him. When he finds the man born blind, Jesus asks him, "Do you believe in the Son of Man?" (v. 35).[10] Jesus identifies himself with the "son of man" in Daniel to whom the Almighty gives "dominion and glory and kingdom, that all peoples, nations, and languages should serve him . . . an everlasting dominion, which shall not pass away" (Dan 7:14)—a universal, supreme authority to which Roman emperors jealously pretended.

The man born blind asks Jesus, "Who is he, sir, that I may believe in him?" (v. 36). Jesus replies, "You have seen him, and it is he who speaks to you."—Could it be that the apocalyptic Son of Man is a simple Galilean, dressed in a humble workman's clothes, not in costly robes, standing there beside him in the busy Jerusalem street? Indeed so.—The man whose eyes he opened says, "Lord, I believe," and worships him (v. 37). He prostrates himself before Jesus the way the whole congregation of Israel does at the most solemn moment of the temple service. In John's Gospel, this innocent beggar whose eyes have been opened by the Son of Man, is the first person truly to believe, to come to total faith, and to do instinctively what truly believing inspires, which is *to worship*. One who is encountered by God must worship. We will see precisely this in Thomas' response, when the risen One comes seeking him after the resurrection, holding out his wounded hands to his disciple, saying, "Do not be

10. "Son of Man" is Jesus's favorite title for himself in all four canonical gospels.

faithless, but believing (20:27). Thomas puts words to the once-blind beggar's earlier actions. He exclaims, "My Lord, and my God!"—*Believing is seeing!*

As you read the story of the man born blind you may ponder your own experiences of encounter with God. A few of you may be the beneficiaries of miracles. Others have seen friends or family members touched, transformed, and made new by Jesus. If you know no such people personally, you most likely have read credible stories about them. And those stories don't all fit a single pattern, because no law restricts how Christ may do his work of giving light and life to the human soul. There is but a single constant principle that applies in every case: *Jesus can give new sight only to those who recognize and admit their blindness.* We may close our eyes and refuse to see. We may choose blindness. Some choose to be blind to any beauty that is more than a pleasant feeling; some choose to be blind to any truth that is more than a mathematical computation; some choose to be blind to any goodness that is not the same as usefulness.—And some choose to be blind to the glory of God that always shines from the face of Christ.

Jesus is the light of the world. He desires that all should see, all be made new, and no one remain in darkness.—So, where are our (perhaps chosen) "blind spots"? In what ways are you and I who read the testimony of the Beloved Disciple still in darkness, or at least in shadows? Are we ruled by the past, or by habits that are so much a part of us that we can't imagine living without them? Or are we, like the Pharisees, so sure we know all the answers and have black-and-white certainty on our side that we're unable even to imagine that *we* could possibly have a blind spot?

Might we choose to be blind to ourselves? Indeed. We can be so self-confident that we call a mirror cracked and its image distorted if it shows us something we don't want to see—such as our own smug self-confidence, narcissism, and pride. But when faith opens our eyes, the Light of Christ illuminates our image in the mirror and allows us to see ourselves as we really are. With limitations, sins and failures, yes—but also strengths and gifts. With a cloudy past, yes—but also a bright future. With ignorance about many things in heaven and on earth, yes—but also assured knowledge of one great thing: we are God's own children, sisters and brothers of the Christ.

There's an old English proverb that goes back to the mid-sixteenth century: "None are as blind as those who will not see." The question John's Gospel now invites us to ponder is this: By what light do we see our way forward in this world?

———————————

Chapter Nine

Doing Your Own Theology

Questions for reflection after reading John 9.

- Concerning the man born blind, Jesus tells his disciples, "It was not that this man sinned, or his parents, but that the works of God might be made manifest in him" (v. 3). That is to say, Jesus intuits meaning, even divine purpose, in the man's lifelong blindness. His lack of sight strikes Jesus as a gift, since it provides an occasion for the work of God to be revealed. People often ask, "How can a loving God allow the innocent to suffer?" This is the classic question of theodicy.—*Does Jesus's answer to the disciples help you answer this question? Why or why not? Have you been able to look at some of the most painful experiences in your own life and see them in any sense as blessings in disguise?*

- The story of Jesus and the man born blind confirms something we understand intuitively: that there's a kind of knowledge that comes only from first-hand experience. No amount of speculative reasoning, logic, or wishful thinking can substitute for the solid assurance that comes when we have an experience of grace. The once-blind beggar is a simple man, and he has the simple assurance that can only arise from a powerful personal experience. When confronted by the Pharisees' ruling that Jesus is a sinner, he replies: "I don't know whether he's a sinner or not. But I *do* know this: I used to be blind but now I see" (paraphrase of v. 25). There's no arguing with this kind of experience, this kind of knowledge. He *knows* that the man who opened his eyes is the agent of God. It's obvious. Who else could do anything like this? The title of this book, *Believing is Seeing*, derives from the premise that believing in Christ is itself a kind of "seeing" (a form of insight into the truth).—*What part does believing play in your personal ability to "see" God? In your own words describe how you now understand God and the work of Jesus Christ in your life?*

- When he discovered the Pharisees had cast the man born blind out of their synagogue, Jesus went looking for him. When he found him, Jesus asked, "'Do you believe in the Son of man?' He answered, 'And who is he, sir, that I may believe in him?' Jesus said to him, 'You have seen him, and it is he who speaks to you.' He said, 'Lord, I believe', and he worshiped him" (vv. 35–38). In John's Gospel, this innocent beggar whose eyes have been opened by the Son of Man, is the first person truly to believe, to come to total faith, and to do instinctively what truly believing inspires in us, which is *to worship*. One who is encountered by God must worship.—*Understanding worship in this case as a spontaneous act of adoration rather than participation in a liturgical act, can you describe an experience in your life which led you to respond immediately with worship? What was the experience and what was your "worshipful" response?*

Chapter Ten

John 10:1–21. Jesus tells the hostile
Pharisees he is the good shepherd.

Vv. 1–21. Jesus describes the ways he serves as shepherd of God's flock.

INTRODUCTION. There were no chapter divisions in the Bible until the thirteenth century and no verse divisions until three hundred years after that. The beginning of a new chapter in our English-language Bible does not mean there's a change of scene in John's narrative. In the portion of John now labeled 10:1–21, Jesus is continuing to speak to the Pharisees we met in the previous chapter, men who dealt spitefully with a poor blind beggar to whom Jesus gave the ability to see for the first time.

As he talks to these hostile Pharisees in vv. 1–21, Jesus uses metaphoric images of a shepherd and his sheep to describe his relationship with the people of God. The Fourth Gospel never presents Jesus as using parables such as those we find in the Synoptic Gospels, but here it does show him using parable-like language—a way of speaking that John calls "a figure" (v. 6). Jesus uses figurative language like this only once more in the Fourth Gospel, when he chooses the metaphor of a vine and its branches to describe his relationship with his disciples (15:1–6).[1]

There is an emphasis throughout John, and especially here, on the importance of hearing Jesus and heeding his words. Sheep in a domestic flock know the voice of their shepherd and follow him because they trust him; therefore, those who are truly God's people will recognize Jesus's voice as the voice of their true shepherd and will follow wherever he leads them. Those who refuse to heed his voice, such as the Pharisees who cast out of their synagogue the man born blind, demonstrate by their behavior that they are not members of God's flock.

This presentation—presumably addressed to the Pharisees and the leading priests—may be divided into two segments, vv. 1–10 and vv. 11–21. Jesus mixes his shepherding metaphors in an effort to make himself understood. In the first segment

1. Köstenberger, *Encountering John*, 109.

148

he tells his audience "I am the door of the sheep" (v. 8), though he obviously also means for them to identify him with the shepherd who leads the flock in and out of the door. (Mixed metaphors are not unusual in the gospel tradition.) Those who do not come into the sheepfold through the door cannot be trusted. If they come into the sheepfold by some other way than through Jesus "the door," they are clearly *not* Jesus's disciples, not really shepherds, but rather thieves and robbers. We can feel confident in picturing the Pharisees and chief priests as "thieves and robbers."

In the second segment Jesus tells his hearers, "I am the good shepherd" (v. 11), and he emphasizes the self-sacrificial role of the good shepherd who gives his life for his sheep. The "hireling," however, cares nothing for the sheep. When the wolf comes he flees and leaves the flock unprotected. The hireling does this because the sheep are not his own; the hireling doesn't know the sheep and they don't know him. There is no bond between them. However, the connection between Jesus and his flock is as close as the relationship between Jesus and his Father: "I know my own and my own know me, as the Father knows me and I know the Father" (vv. 14–15). The good shepherd loves his sheep and dies to save them. This illustrates how John wants his readers to understand the meaning of Jesus's impending death. Jesus is not going to be a victim of his enemies; he is going to lay down his life. He is also going to take it up again, by the power of his Father. John's Gospel is more explicit than the Synoptics in making this point. For John, Jesus's death and resurrection are the two correlative dimensions of a single great salvific event, the event which demonstrates the unity of power and will that exists between the Father and the Son.

Vv. 19–21 make it clear that "the Jews" are at this point still divided in their feelings about Jesus. Some think him mad, and perhaps demon-possessed, but others are not so sure. Nevertheless, even those who think that God may have used him to give sight to the blind are still far from faith.

> **[10:1–21]** *¹ "Truly, truly, I say to you, he who does not enter the sheepfold by the door but climbs in by another way, that man is a thief and a robber; ² but he who enters by the door is the shepherd of the sheep. ³ To him the gatekeeper opens; the sheep hear his voice, and he calls his own sheep by name and leads them out. ⁴ When he has brought out all his own, he goes before them, and the sheep follow him, for they know his voice. ⁵ A stranger they will not follow, but they will flee from him, for they do not know the voice of strangers," ⁶ This figure Jesus used with them, but they did not understand what he was saying to them. ⁷ So Jesus again said to them, "Truly, truly, I say to you, I am the door of the sheep. ⁸ All who came before me are thieves and robbers; but the sheep did not heed them. ⁹ I am the door; if any one enters by me, he will be saved, and will go in and out and find pasture. ¹⁰ The thief comes only to steal and kill and destroy; I came that they may have life, and have it abundantly.*

¹¹ I am the good shepherd. The good shepherd lays down his life for the sheep. ¹² He who is a hireling and not a shepherd, whose own the sheep are not, sees the wolf coming and leaves the sheep and flees; and the wolf snatches them and scatters them. ¹³ He flees because he is a hireling and cares nothing for the sheep. ¹⁴ I am the good shepherd; I know my own and my own know me, ¹⁵ as the Father knows me and I know the Father; and I lay down my life for the sheep. ¹⁶ And I have other sheep, that are not of this fold; I must bring them also, and they will heed my voice. So there shall be one flock, one shepherd. ¹⁷ For this reason the Father loves me, because I lay down my life, that I may take it again. ¹⁸ No one takes it from me, but I lay it down of my own accord. I have power to lay it down, and I have power to take it again; this charge I have received from my Father." ¹⁹ There was again a division among the Jews because of these words. ²⁰ Many of them said, "He has a demon, and he is mad; why listen to him?" ²¹ Others said, "These are not the sayings of one who has a demon. Can a demon open the eyes of the blind?"

RESPONSE. It might help to start this response with a question: What *need* do you perceive in your daily life that you meet through prayerful meditation on Scripture? Every reader could answer differently, and the same person might give different answers at different times. Answering the question myself, I would reply that reflection on what I encounter in Scripture meets a need I have to understand myself, recognize my place in the world, and deepen my relationship with God. Human beings instinctively search for personal meaning and understanding. Our capacity to discover meaning is facilitated when someone provides us with metaphors and analogies that make sense to us within the context of our own life situation. The Bible is a treasury of images, stories, and concepts that allow us to understand and describe how we fit into the grand scheme of things, our relationship to God, and our spiritual connection with other people.

The illustrations from shepherding that Jesus uses when he speaks to the Pharisees are instantly significant to them, just as they would be to anyone else living in the mostly rural, pastoral society of the first century Mediterranean world. Twenty-first century urbanized Americans do not, however, immediately understand them; we need help in order to make personal connections with Jesus's comments about shepherds and sheep. First, we need to be alert to the fact that God is frequently portrayed in the Hebrew Scriptures as a shepherd, with Israel as his flock. For example, here are a few references drawn exclusively from the Psalms: 77:20, "Thou didst lead thy people like a flock by the hand of Moses and Aaron;" 78:52, "He led forth his people like sheep, and guided them in the wilderness like a flock;" 80:1, "Give ear, O Shepherd of Israel, thou who leadest Joseph like a flock;" and 95:7, "He is our God and we are the people of his pasture, the sheep of his hand." God's shepherding care, not only for Israel as a whole but for the individual, is celebrated in our best-loved psalm, Ps 23: "The Lord is my shepherd, I shall not want . . ." Six hundred years before Jesus, the

Prophet Ezekiel had criticized "the shepherds of Israel"—most likely referring to the regal and priestly establishment of the time—for feeding themselves rather than feeding the sheep (Ez 34:1–3). Ezekiel prophesied that the time was coming when God would set up over his people "one shepherd, my servant David, and he shall feed them and be their shepherd . . . I, the Lord, will be their God, and my servant David shall be prince among them" (Ez 34:23–24).

We grasp the pastoral role of a shepherd, but modern readers are so far removed in time from those who wrote the Hebrew Scriptures that we don't readily perceive the connection the ancients saw between a king (or a king's officials) and shepherds. In antiquity, people in pastoral societies regarded the shepherd not only as the nurturer and caretaker of the sheep, but also as the "ruler" of the sheep. The picture of the shepherd with his flock is one of the key images the gospel writers use to portray believers' relationship with Christ and one another. The faithful are God's flock, and Jesus is their rightful Shepherd King. Although, by the first century, when the Gospels are being written, it has been many centuries since Israel lived as a society of shepherding people, cultural memory of their early historic existence as a community of wandering herdsmen is still present. The figure of David still looms large in the imagination of every first-century Jew. Everyone knows that David, the "man after God's own heart," was merely a shepherd boy tending his father's sheep when God told Samuel to anoint him as king of Israel in place of Saul. When he writes his gospel, John has no need to spell out the obvious messianic association of Jesus with David. Like David the shepherd boy, the Messiah Jesus becomes the good shepherd of his Father's flock.

Contemporary believers have learned to understand that we, too, are God's flock. But how easily do urban people identify with sheep? I live in a university town in southwestern Montana, a state where sheep are raised commercially. But I haven't had any personal experience with sheep except to call on a parish family that raises them. The number of Americans who have first-hand experience with sheep is relatively small. Even if we grow up in Australia or in a sheep-ranching area in the USA, the way sheep are raised today—as a commodity—has a limited similarity to the way sheep-raising was conducted in Jesus's day. John's first readers know about large flocks managed as commercial operations by owners that draw their livelihood exclusively from raising sheep. These large flocks are cared for primarily by hired hands, although in some cases there is involvement by the owner's family. Such a commercial sheep-raising operation seems to be what Jesus has in mind when he speaks of sheep who are looked after by "a hireling, and not a shepherd, whose own the sheep are not" (v. 12).

To connect with the shepherding images Jesus uses here, we need to know that many rural households in Judea and Galilee whose livelihood comes from some different pursuit will also have a little domestic flock of sheep, maintained to provide the family with wool, milk, and occasionally meat. (For such households, their few sheep are too valuable to be slaughtered and eaten except on very rare occasions.)The shepherd of such a domestic flock will typically be one of the owner's sons.[2] This is probably the situation Jesus is thinking about when he tells the Pharisees that he is the good shepherd. Sheep in a little flock like this are treated by their young shepherd as part of his family. He gives each one a name, and they learn to come when he calls them. Each sheep in a domestic flock of fewer than twenty animals will be relatively much more valuable to its owner than one sheep in a big, commercial flock of many hundreds or even thousands. The gospel writer's own church was small, and the number of Jews who believed in Jesus as Messiah and Son of God was small relative to the total number of Jews. This is a fact to keep in mind as we reflect on John's Gospel in the twenty-first century, when Christians number about two billion and megachurch congregations in our country can range from 10,000 to 40,000 members.

It is worth noting that in Luke 12:32 Jesus tells the disciples, "Fear not, *little flock*, for it is your father's good pleasure to give you the kingdom." His comments about the "hirelings" in vv. 12–13 relate to big commercial sheep-raising operations and are aimed at the Pharisees and chief priests. All of Jesus's other shepherd-and-sheep illustrations apply to a small, domestic flock whose usual sheepfold is the courtyard of the family home—with stone walls on three sides (including a gate), and the house itself forming the fourth. When weather permits, the shepherd takes his flock to pasture in the hills and stands guard over them at night, either in a temporary sheepfold constructed from briars and brushwood or in a permanent fieldstone fold they share with the neighbors' domestic flocks. Because the sheep all know their respective shepherds, it's easy for each shepherd to call his own flock out in the morning and lead them to graze.

Jesus as a boy may well have looked after a little domestic flock in Nazareth. Understanding the way such a little flock was tended in Jesus's time helps us appreciate the imagery he uses to portray the intimacy between the flock and its shepherd. We can begin to envision ourselves as part of Jesus's little flock. Our shepherd knows us and perceives that each of us is unique. He prizes us and will protect us at all costs. He is concerned for our nurture, our safety, and our future. It's not an overstatement to say the shepherd *loves* his flock, and his sheep respond to his attention by listening to his voice and following him wherever he wishes to take them, though they will run away from strangers and refuse to follow them. When the flock is on the move, the shepherd walks slowly ahead, playing a flute some of the time, but mostly calling out often to his sheep, talking to them, letting them hear his voice. Though the animals are looking down at the grass to graze, they're always listening to their shepherd, and following the sound of his voice. The fact that the sheep *heed the voice* of their shepherd is one of the elements that makes the shepherd metaphor so significant in the Fourth Gospel.

---

2. 1 Sam 16:11 says David, the youngest of Jesse's eight sons, was absent "keeping the sheep" on the occasion when the Prophet Samuel came to Bethlehem to anoint a new king to take the place of Saul.

John tells us that we are God's little flock, and Jesus is our shepherd. He is our guide, our leader, and our king. In frightening times, he will always be near, offering words of comfort, peace, and healing. Each of us is precious to him, and no one is lost in the crowd. Jesus reminds us that he has other sheep than us. They also know his voice and follow him. These others may have a different sheepfold, at least for the time being, but we and they are members together in the good shepherd's own flock. This is a gospel word of support for Christian unity and is as powerful as what we will read later in Jesus' High Priestly Prayer (17:20–23).

If we're the sheep and Jesus is our good shepherd, where and how do we encounter the good shepherd today? Where do we hear his voice? Where do we feel his touch?—Of course, we hear him in his own words in John and in the other gospels. We also hear him speaking to us in the quiet of our hearts when we practice the discipline of listening prayer. We sometimes hear him or see him in the voices and behavior of people around us, including many who probably don't realize they're speaking and acting on behalf of the good shepherd.

Jesus says, "The good shepherd lays down his life for the sheep" (v. 11). No doubt there are exceptions to the rule, but I think most of us, particularly in times of crisis, uncertainty, and fear, yearn for a protector, someone wiser and stronger than we are, who will watch over us, take care of us, comfort us, and shield us from harm. Loving parents lay down their lives, metaphorically and practically, for their young children. They pay whatever personal price it takes to keep their children safe and provide for their well-being. Children in such families instinctively trust mom and dad, and this trust is well-placed. Their parents are laying down their lives for them because they want their offspring to have the best possible future and experience the joy and fullness of life. Such parents want their children to experience their selfless love in a way that empowers the children to pass along that same love to the next generation. This is what Jesus does. The good shepherd lays down his life for us in the expectation that we will imitate his example and share that same self-offering love with each other. That's the point he makes in 13:34 when he gives his disciples the new commandment, "love one another as I have loved you." In the same way that compassionate parents' lives are bound up with their children, the good shepherd's life is bound up with the life of his flock.

These verses in John provide images and ideas that help us in the quest to understand and describe our relationship with God and the world around us. John invites us to see ourselves as members of the good shepherd's flock—each of us known and loved by him and deemed precious to him. He calls us by name and leads us, if we will heed his voice. We're part of a community that God intends should enjoy a happy and fulfilling quality of life, an "eternal life." The Lord himself came among us to open the gate to that life—a life that's available right now, not only in a future Paradise. The shepherd's sacrificial love empowers us to put aside our selfish ways and love one another as the good shepherd loves us.

John 10:22–42. The climax of Jesus's public ministry. Again "the Jews" try to stone him.

Vv. 22–42. "The Jews" tell Jesus, "We stone you for blasphemy."

INTRODUCTION. We arrive now at the climax of Jesus's public ministry as John describes it. In a sense, this is the pivotal moment in the Fourth Gospel. 10:22–39 ends the account of Jesus's quasi-judicial interrogations by "the Jews," a sequence of conflict stories that begins with 5:16. Despite the issue of Sabbath-breaking and other matters, Jesus's clash with "the Jews" focuses on a single theological question: Is Jesus, or is he not the Son of God, sent by his Father into the world for its salvation?[3]

10:1–21 is set in the same context as the healing of the man born blind, the streets of Jerusalem at the time of the Feast of Tabernacles. With v. 22, the scene shifts. Three months have gone by and it is now the Feast of the Dedication (the Jewish festival called *Hanukkah*), which falls in early December. Cold winds are blowing. Jesus is walking in the Portico of Solomon on the eastern side of the temple enclosure, sheltered from the wind by its outside wall. Like Tabernacles, the Feast of the Dedication is a happy time, a "feast of lights" commemorating an event that took place in 165 BCE, when Judas Maccabeus rebuilt and rededicated the great altar which the Seleucid king Antiochus Epiphanes had desecrated by setting up an idol on it.

"The Jews"—which means Jesus's antagonists among the Jerusalem Pharisees and chief priests—surround him and demand that he speak plainly to them about his claims. Does he, or does he not assert that he is the Messiah? Those who read John's Gospel know Jesus has been trying to explain his identity to these critics in various ways for a long time (see 5:31–47; 8:28–29, 38), but they are unable to accept what he says. The purpose of John's Gospel is to proclaim Jesus's identity and describe his saving work. From it, readers learn that he is the Son of God, the Son of Man, and indeed, the Messiah. The figure of the shepherd and his sheep that Jesus uses in 10:1–15 is a familiar Old Testament metaphor for the rule of God. Its connection with David, the shepherd boy, is obvious and its messianic implication is unmistakable. But his antagonists cannot agree with what he is telling them. Jesus is nothing like the princely Messiah they hope for, and they refuse to concede that the works he does in his Father's name confirm his identity as God's Son.

Jesus's enemies are men of authority and power in the Jewish religious community, but in the figurative language Jesus uses these elders are not truly members of God's flock. Because they aren't among the sheep the Father has put in his Son's hands, they are not able to understand his voice and come to him (v. 29; see also 6:37, "All that the Father gives me will come to me"). When Jesus tells them, "I and the Father are one" (v. 30), his opponents again take up stones to throw at him, just as they had done at Tabernacles when he told them, "Before Abraham was, I Am" (8:59).

---

3. Marsh, *Saint John*, 405.

Jesus's enemies want to stone him for blasphemy, "because you, being a man, make yourself God" (v. 33). For the first time, blasphemy is explicitly named as the charge against Jesus, though it is presumed in 8:59. There is profound irony here: Jesus is not a mere man who is "making himself God," but rather God has made himself a man—this particular man, the son of Mary from Nazareth. In vv. 34–38 Jesus uses a sound rabbinical argument based on Ps 82:6 to respond to their anger at his claim to be the Son of God, but his opponents will not be persuaded, even though he uses their own rhetorical techniques to explain himself. They try again to arrest him, and once more he escapes their clutches. His hour has not yet arrived, but it is approaching.

In v. 40 Jesus departs from Jerusalem and returns to the Jordan Valley, to the place where John baptized him, a spot not far from where Moses' chosen successor, Joshua once led the twelve tribes of Israel into the Promised Land. Raymond E. Brown postulates that at one point in the development of the Fourth Gospel 13:1 followed 10:42; chapters 11–12 were an editorial insertion.[4] Whether that theory is correct or not, John's story of Jesus's ministry now comes full circle. The Son of God will not return to the Holy City until he arrives at Passover to lay down his life, to fulfill the Baptizer's testimony that he is the Lamb of God who takes away the sin of the world. After v. 38, Jesus does not argue again with his adversaries among "the Jews." From now on—except at his hearing before Annas and his conversation with Pilate on the day the Passover lambs are sacrificed—Jesus speaks only to the crowd and to his "sheep." (Chapter 11 tells us Jesus comes back from beyond the Jordan to Bethany in response to the death of Lazarus, but after Lazarus is raised he returns to the edge of the wilderness without entering Jerusalem.)

> **[10:22–42]** *²² It was the feast of the Dedication at Jerusalem; ²³ it was winter, and Jesus was walking in the temple, in the portico of Solomon. ²⁴ So the Jews gathered round him and said to him, "How long will you keep us in suspense? If you are the Christ, tell us plainly." ²⁵ Jesus answered them, "I told you, and you do not believe. The works that I do in my Father's name, they bear witness to me; ²⁶ but you do not believe, because you do not belong to my sheep. ²⁷ My sheep hear my voice, and I know them, and they follow me; ²⁸ and I give them eternal life, and they shall never perish, and no one shall snatch them out of my hand. ²⁹ My Father, who has given them to me, is greater than all, and no one is able to snatch them out of the Father's hand. ³⁰ I and the Father are one."*
>
> *³¹ The Jews took up stones again to stone him. ³² Jesus answered them, "I have shown you many good works from the Father; for which of these do you stone me?" ³³ The Jews answered him, "It is not for a good work that we stone you but for blasphemy; because you, being a man, make yourself God." ³⁴ Jesus answered them, "Is it not written in your law, 'I said,*

---

4. Brown, *John I–XII*, 414–15.

you are gods'? ³⁵ If he called them gods to whom the word of God came (and Scripture cannot be broken), ³⁶ do you say of him whom the Father consecrated and sent into the world, 'You are blaspheming,' because I said, 'I am the Son of God'? ³⁷ If I am not doing the works of my Father, then do not believe me; ³⁸ but if I do them, even though you do not believe me, believe the works, that you may know and understand that the Father is in me and I am in the Father." ³⁹ Again they tried to arrest him, but he escaped from their hands.

⁴⁰ He went away again across the Jordan to the place where John at first baptized, and there he remained. ⁴¹ And many came to him; and they said, "John did no sign, but everything that John said about this man was true." ⁴² And many believed in him there.

RESPONSE. When third millennium Christians read John's Gospel, it's possible for us to miss a great deal of its meaning unless we keep in mind—despite his frequent hostile references to "the Jews"—that John is writing his gospel for Jewish followers of Jesus who are now living far from their homeland. They are deeply versed in what we call the Old Testament; it is their Bible. They observe the Jewish holy days and seasons in the same way they have done all their lives and as their parents and ancestors did before them. True, they are disciples of Jesus the Messiah and Son of God, and a historian would say that they are *becoming* "the church;" but they understand themselves simply as Jews (joined perhaps by a few God-fearing Gentiles) who rejoice that the long-promised Messiah has come. Ideas and symbols associated with Passover, Pentecost, Tabernacles, and the Feast of the Dedication resonate with them. Because the Romans demolished it twenty years before, only the older members of their community recollect seeing Herod's great temple in all its grandeur. However, stories about the temple and the significance of its festivals continue to be current among them.

When John's community reads about what Jesus says and does during the Feast of Tabernacles (chapters 7–9), they immediately understand the symbolic connections he wants to make through his claim to be the true source of living water and the light of the world. Now, as they read about what he says at the Feast of the Dedication, they quickly grasp that God has consecrated Jesus and sent him into the world (v. 36) to be the new focus of human communion with God. We observe how John employs this theme of replacement a number of times in the first half of his gospel. Jesus is sent to fulfill and replace the rituals of the old Law, which John demonstrates by means of Jesus's first sign: changing the water of Jewish purificatory washing into wine for a wedding celebration in Cana at the beginning of his ministry (2:1–11). He is the source of living water, the light of the world, and in his own person Jesus is the new Tabernacle (see 1:14), the new temple (see 2:21), the new link between earth and heaven (see 1:51).

As we reflect on this conclusion to Jesus's public disputes with "the Jews," we note how much depends on the way his fellow Jews decide to think about him. He is clearly much more than a simple Galilean village tradesman. The sages in Jerusalem did not train him, but he speaks with an assurance that exceeds the authority of any scribe they've ever heard. Some people claim that Jesus healed them and others say they witnessed those healings.—Could this man be a prophet, as the common people believe John the Baptist was? Is this Galilean, indeed, the Messiah? Or is Jesus a deluded and dangerous radical—perhaps a magician in league with demons—flouting Israel's sacred traditions, violating the Sabbath, speaking of the holy temple as if it were unnecessary, and claiming to represent God in a way no mortal ever possibly could?[5]

With vv. 37–38 we come to the crisis point of the gospel. Human decision for or against Jesus is the crucial issue.[6] In v. 39 the leaders of the nation render their verdict. They recognize that Jesus is claiming equality with God, which means to them that the Nazarene is a blasphemer, a deceiver of the people, and perhaps even a demonized madman. Whether he healed the lame or gave sight to the blind is irrelevant to most of them (see vv. 19–21). They are not sheep of his flock, and they cannot recognize that he and the Father are united. From this point forward, the single-minded intent of those who reject Jesus as Son of God and Messiah is to arrest him and see that he is put to death.

10:22–42 is John's transition to chapters 11 and 12, which in turn compose the introduction to the Beloved Disciple's description of Jesus's crucifixion and resurrection. The recital of events in vv. 22–42—Jesus's final disputation with his adversaries, their flat rejection of his claims, their subsequent effort to kill him, and his escape back to the Jordan where he started his ministry nearly three years before—begins to set the stage for the arrival of Jesus's hour and the fulfillment of his mission as the Lamb of God who takes away the sin of the world.

These verses focus us sharply on *the* decisive issue of John's Gospel: the nature of Jesus's relationship to God. Most people in our age frame the question this way: *"Is Jesus divine, or is he not?"* The answer each reader of John gives to that question is crucial, because it defines the spiritual stance of our life. It reveals whether we are members of the good shepherd's flock or not. That's the challenge presented by the Fourth Gospel.

In John, Jesus does nothing without a purpose. Every act and every word has meaning for those who are following him because they want to know him. I wonder about what symbolism Jesus might have intended by returning to the Jordan River after his decisive rejection by the "disciples of Moses" (9:28)—going back to the place

---

5. Welch contends that an "underlying and commonly shared fear . . . associated with magic or the supernatural may have played a much more instrumental role" both in the Sanhedrin's hostility to Jesus and in Pilate's willingness to acquiesce in the chief priests' insistence that Jesus be put to death. Welch, "Miracles," 349.

6. Smith, *John*, 211.

where the Beloved Disciple and his companion first began following him, back to the place of his baptism, to the spot where John the Baptist had proclaimed to all who would listen, "Behold, the Lamb of God, who takes away the sin of the world! This is he of whom I said, 'After me comes a man who ranks before me, for he was before me.' I myself did not know him; but for this I came baptizing with water, that he might be revealed to Israel." And John added, "I saw the Spirit descend as a dove from heaven, and it remained on him. I myself did not know him; but he who sent me to baptize with water said to me, 'He on whom you see the Spirit descend and remain, this is he who baptizes with the Holy Spirit.' And I have seen and have borne witness that this is the Son of God" (1:29–34).

John's prologue tells us, "The Law was given through Moses; grace and truth came through Jesus Christ" (1:17). The earliest Jewish audience for this gospel, even though they are hearing it in Greek, know that in Greek as well as in Hebrew Jesus's name is that of Joshua (*Yeshua* or *Yehoshua*), the man God told Moses to set apart to take his place as the shepherd of Israel, the flock of God, to lead them into the Promised Land (see Num 27:12–23). Might Jesus by his return to the east side of the Jordan have meant to show himself as the prophetic replacer of Moses (see Deut 18:18), a new and greater Joshua? He now will cross the Jordan River as Joshua did, leading his own little flock of twelve disciples (representing the twelve patriarchs of Israel) up to Jerusalem, the city David the shepherd king conquered and made his own. Once Jesus enters the Holy City with his followers, he will be prepared for his "hour," the hour of his death as the Lamb of God, his victory, and his glory.

As we reach this point in the gospel, when Jesus concludes his public ministry after his rejection by the disciples of Moses, it's good to contemplate what it might mean for modern Christians to think of ourselves as being like the man born blind—women and men whose faith has given us eyes to see Jesus as the Son of God and, therefore, to worship him. We might think about the events, the circumstances, and the people who helped shape our decision to worship this Jewish teacher, a man whose own people rejected him. How we identify Jesus's relationship to God and his singular role in the working out of God's purposes is the crux and stumbling block of the Christian faith. It is the dividing line between Jews and Christians, the source of Christians' distinctive religious identity in the dialogue with other religions, the so-called scandal of particularity.[7] If Jesus is not unique in the way we believe he is, if Jesus is not the Son of God and Savior of the world, crucified on a dark Friday and raised from death on the following Sunday morning, then we who follow him may be "of all people most to be pitied" (1 Cor 15:19).

Though it seems odd to me, there are people who self-identify as Christian, including even some who serve as pastors and seminary teachers, who nevertheless also describe themselves as "beliefless."[8] Some of them are people who regard religion

7. O'Day, *Gospel of John*, 678.
8. Schuck, "I'm a Presbyterian Minister."

as having social value, but do not believe in God. Others *do* believe in God, but feel comfortable saying, "Jesus is not divine. Jesus is not God." They read the Fourth Gospel, as we are doing, but they are not persuaded—just as the scribes and chief priests in Jerusalem are not persuaded. Naturally, since they are scholars, they examine relevant biblical texts before making up their minds, and they have plausible, learned rationales for their thinking. They will affirm Jesus's unique sense of mission, but assert that he was not divine and did not think of himself as divine. For them, Jesus is *not* the Savior of the world. Neither did he rise from the dead, except metaphorically. They comfortably think of Jesus in the past tense because, though he was an authentic figure of world history, he is still merely a famous dead man to them—no different from Lincoln or Aristotle. He is dead but his words live on, just like the words of Lincoln and Aristotle.

It would make us less odious in the eyes of many of our anti-religious contemporaries if, instead of worshiping Jesus as divine, we simply adopted the viewpoint of these pastors and teachers. We could join the ranks of the Deists who regard Jesus as a great prophetic advocate for social justice, but not as the Son of God, not as the human face of God—not divine.[9] It would be simple, maybe even sensible in the eyes of the secular world, to describe Jesus as a visionary Jewish teacher and holy man, maybe a kind of shaman who convinced himself that God was speaking to him. We would then be free from the taint associated with the scandal of particularity.

However, demoting Jesus to the rank of a delusional prophet raises new problems. If we agree with the Pharisees who rejected Jesus in his own day, if we decide that he was not "one with the Father," not sent into the world to do God's will, as John tells us he claimed to be (10:30), what authority can we say lies behind the profound things he said and the unusual things he did?—Simple human perceptivity? Why should anything about Jesus be taken seriously if he was merely a deranged provincial holy man who thought he was the Son of God, sent from heaven to save the world? Perhaps Jesus had a personality disorder; perhaps he was a megalomaniac. But, if so, then how do we understand what John calls his "signs"? And how do we explain the courage of those who ultimately went to their deaths asserting that they had seen Jesus alive again after he was crucified? We would have no choice but to do what Thomas Jefferson did and take scissors to our Bibles, snipping out parts that don't fit our assumptions. As wise and well-meaning as the Pharisees who rejected Jesus might have been, as brilliant as Deists like Voltaire, Jefferson, Edison, and Planck were, if we take a view of Jesus contrary to what John tells us was Jesus's view of himself, problems multiply.

I engage in these ruminations in order to make one point: If Jesus is *not* the incarnate Son of God, the enfleshment of God's love, sent into the world as his Father's personal representative, "the image of the invisible God" (as Paul calls him in Col 1:15), then nothing else about Jesus matters very much. He is reduced to the status of merely an interesting character in ancient history, the founder of a faith community

9. Dunn, *Did the First Christians Worship Jesus*, 122.

that played a significant role in western civilization. However, "we have believed and have come to know," as did Peter and the others who composed the good shepherd's little flock, that Jesus is "the Holy One of God" (6:68–69).

God is infinitely beyond our capacity to describe or to know, except to the degree that God chooses to disclose Godself. Our limited minds cannot encompass God; all we can do is prostrate ourselves in silent awe before the divine mystery. But John's Gospel tells us that for our sake God chose to reveal himself in Jesus. The man from Nazareth is the human face of God; he is in the Father and the Father is in him. He both shows us who God is, and who we are as God's children. Because we believe the testimony of the Beloved Disciple, we entrust ourselves to Jesus. We understand our destiny as essentially linked to his. As I reflect on the Pharisees' and priests' rejection of Jesus's claims, I remind myself that how I choose to think about Jesus is the most important decision I can ever make.

Doing Your Own Theology

Questions for reflection after reading John 10.

- Understanding the way such a small domestic flock of sheep was tended in Jesus's time helps us appreciate the imagery he uses in chapter 10 to portray the intimacy between the flock and its shepherd. We can begin to envision ourselves as part of Jesus's little flock. Our shepherd knows his sheep and perceives that each of us is unique. He prizes us and will protect us at all costs. He is concerned for our nurture, our safety, and our future. It's not an overstatement to say that the shepherd *loves* his flock, and his sheep respond to his attention by listening to his voice and following him wherever he wishes to take them, though they will run away from strangers and refuse to follow them. The good shepherd lays down his life for us in the expectation that we will imitate his example and share that same self-offering love with each other.—*Who embodies for you the shepherding care of Jesus, serving as his agents? . . . Your pastor? . . . Your parents? . . . Your Christian friends? In what practical ways has the good shepherd taken care of you through these agents—comforting, healing, and protecting you? Do you ever take a shepherding role yourself, as an agent of the good shepherd? If not, why not?*

- With vv. 37–38 we come to the crisis point of the gospel: "If I am not doing the works of my Father, then do not believe me; but if I do them, even though you do not believe me, believe the works, that you may know and understand that the Father is in me and I am in the Father." These verses focus us sharply on the decisive issue of John's Gospel: the nature of Jesus's relationship to God. Most people in our age frame the question this way: "Is Jesus divine, or is he not?" The answer each reader of John gives to that question is crucial, because it defines the spiritual stance of our life. It reveals whether we are members of the good shepherd's flock. That's the challenge presented by the Fourth Gospel.—*We rarely examine the constellation of meanings that can apply to the name "God" (or the word "god"). Has what you have read in these first ten chapters of John influenced your answer to the question, "Is Jesus divine or not?" Without trying to use technical theological language, what would it mean—in your own words—to say that Jesus is divine? What challenges might you face if you publicly acknowledge that Jesus is divine?*

- How we identify Jesus's relationship to God and his singular role in the working out of God's purposes is the crux and stumbling block of the Christian faith. It is *the* dividing line between Jews and Christians, the source of Christians' distinctive religious identity in the dialogue with other religions, the so-called "scandal of particularity." If Jesus is not unique in the way we believe he is, if Jesus is not the Son of God and Savior of the world, crucified on a dark Friday and raised from death on the following Sunday morning, then perhaps we who follow him may be "of all people most to be pitied" (1 Cor 15:19).—*When you consider your own personal history, what would you identify as the pivotal experiences that led to your belief in Jesus? Have there been occasions when you played a role in helping bring someone else to believe in him? Keeping in mind the crucial role that John's Gospel gives to witnesses, under what circumstances are you able to be, in any sense, a witness for Christ?*

Chapter Eleven

John 11:1–44. Jesus's last and greatest sign: the raising of Lazarus.

Vv. 1–44. "Did I not tell you that if you would believe you would see the glory of God?"

INTRODUCTION. It appears that John sometimes rearranges the chronological sequence of episodes in the life of Jesus in order to make theological points. The account of the raising of Lazarus is probably such an event.[1] At the end of chapter 10 Jesus leaves Jerusalem and goes to Bethany beyond the Jordan, where he had been baptized (see, 1:28). Then, in chapter 11, responding to a message from his dear friends, Mary and Martha, concerning their brother Lazarus's illness, he returns to the vicinity of Jerusalem, to their home in a different Bethany located on the Mount of Olives. At the end of chapter 11, after raising Lazarus, Jesus goes away again, this time to Ephraim on the edge of the Judean wilderness. However, when chapter 12 opens, he comes back to the home of his friends in Bethany near Jerusalem.

How do we explain this awkward back-and-forth? It would vanish and Jesus's journey to Jerusalem in John would match what Mark and Matthew describe if 13:1 were to follow immediately after 10:42. John seems to have placed chapter 11 and chapter 12 where we find them because the Beloved Disciple (or, more likely, his editor) wants the raising of Lazarus to stand as the crown and climax of Jesus's signs, the first of which was given at a wedding (2:1–11). Now the last is offered at a funeral.

The restoration of Lazarus to life fulfills what Jesus promises in 5:25, "Truly, truly, I say to you, the hour is coming, and now is, when the dead will hear the voice of the Son of God, and those who hear will live." In chapter 9 Jesus gives vision to one born sightless, showing himself to be the light of the world. Now in chapter 11 the voice of the Son of God summons a lifeless man out of his tomb, still wrapped in his shroud, demonstrating that Jesus gives life to the dead. This final dramatic sign provokes the Sanhedrin to decide on his judicial execution at the same moment Jerusalem crowds

---

1. Brown, *John I–XII*, 412, 427–29.

are welcoming him with palms and singing. John underscores for us the paradox that brings Jesus to his *hour*. His last and greatest miracle, giving life to a dead man, leads directly to the life-giver himself being killed.[2]

The Fourth Gospel identifies Bethany for its readers as "the village of Mary and her sister Martha" (v. 1), clearly assuming the two women will be recognized by readers familiar with traditions about Jesus and his friends. Other than John's second reference to them in 12:1–8, the two are otherwise named only in Luke 10:38–42, where their home is described as being Martha's and no mention is made of a brother. These sparse references lead us to think of the little family in Bethany as intimate friends, with whom Jesus and his disciples sometimes stay while visiting Jerusalem. They are the only individuals John describes as "loved" by Jesus (v. 5). Without other evidence, we might speculate that Martha is a well-to-do unmarried woman, a childless widow whose younger siblings Mary and Lazarus share her home. Given the customs concerning inheritance in first century Judea, it would be logical to picture Martha as a wealthy widow and Lazarus as her much younger, unmarried, dependent brother— otherwise, the house would be described as his, not Martha's.[3]

As in his explanation to the disciples concerning the man born blind, that the man's blindness occurred "so that the works of God might be made manifest in him" (9:3), so here Jesus explains to the disciples that the illness of their friend Lazarus "is not unto death; it is for the glory of God, so that the Son of Man may be glorified because of it" (v. 4). John uses the word glory in two ways here. The glorification of the Son of Man is the praise due to the Son because he performs the Father's work. The glory of God is the revelation of God's presence and life-giving purposes in the work of his Son, a work that will soon be consummated on the day of resurrection. We understand Jesus's apparently pointless delay in leaving for Bethany simply as a dimension of what circumstances require in order for God's glory to be revealed. His disciples remind Jesus in v. 8 that returning to Bethany in Judea to give life to Lazarus puts his own life in jeopardy. The Fourth Gospel contains no parallel to the command Jesus gives to his disciples in the Synoptics to take up the cross and follow him (Mark 8:34; Matt 10:38; Luke 14:27). However, Thomas' response here, "Let us also go, that we may die with him" (v. 16), is an affirmation that John, like the Synoptic writers, understands that Jesus's faithful disciples must be prepared to pay for their faithfulness with their lives. (See 15:12–13.)

2. Ibid., 429. See also Marsh, *Saint John*, 416–17.

3. See Malina and Rohrbaugh, *Social Science Commentary*, 193–95. Capper, "Essene Community Houses," 496–502, proposes a theory that the name Bethany (which means "house of the poor" or "house of affliction" in Aramaic) for "the village of Martha and her sister Mary," derives from the fact that the village is the site of a poorhouse-hostel similar to others operated in the Jerusalem area and in many villages of Judea (but not Galilee) by celibate Essene monks. He postulates that Martha and Mary are wealthy women from Jerusalem who are patrons of this poorhouse-hostel, a place where Jesus and his disciples often stay as guests. This explains why, later in 12:4–5, bystanders might question Mary's extravagant "wasting" of costly ointment on Jesus, since it could have been sold in order to help support the poorhouse and its Essene community. (See also Capper, "Holy Community," 114–18.)

In the Fourth Gospel every act of Jesus to which the Beloved Disciple bears witness is described with a single goal in mind: that those who receive his testimony might believe in Jesus and have eternal life (see 20:31). Therefore, before they depart for Judea Jesus tells the disciples very plainly that he is glad Lazarus has already died, "so that you may believe" (v. 15). Even the faith of those who are his dearest friends— Martha, Mary, and the disciples—is still inadequate, but this last and greatest sign will nurture its growth. When Martha goes out to welcome Jesus on his arrival, she addresses him respectfully as "Lord," but ruefully tells him, "if you had been here, my brother would not have died," then adds a whisper of hope in the face of discouragement, "Even now I know that whatever you ask from God, God will give you" (vv. 21–22). Jesus assures her that Lazarus will rise again, but Martha answers with only a conventional sentiment, "I know that he will rise again in the resurrection at the last day" (v. 24).

This provides the occasion for Jesus's final, ringing "I Am" pronouncement: "I Am the resurrection and the life; he who believes in me, though he die, yet shall he live, and whoever lives and believes in me shall never die" (v. 26). The Son of God is telling his dear friend Martha that the resurrection will not be deferred to the last day; she is speaking to the One who embodies the resurrection, who gives life to the dead! Yet even this dramatic proclamation does not bring Martha's faith to the level Jesus seeks. That will not happen until he demands that the stone sealing her brother's tomb be taken away. Martha, a polite and proper lady, demurs. After four days Lazarus's body has begun to decompose and the stench of death will overwhelm the fragrance of his burial ointments. Responding to her protest, Jesus declares, "Did I not tell you that if you would believe you would see the glory of God?" (v. 40).[4] With that promise, the tomb is opened, and Jesus cries, "Lazarus, come out!" (v. 43). Suddenly the dead man shuffles out, still in his grave clothes, alive again. Jesus manifests his love for Lazarus by giving his friend life. This permits John's readers to understand that Jesus manifests his love for us by giving us new life.

> [11:1–44] *¹ Now a certain man was ill, Lazʹarus of Bethany, the village of Mary and her sister Martha. ² It was Mary who anointed the Lord with ointment and wiped his feet with her hair, whose brother Lazʹarus was ill. ³ So the sisters sent to him, saying, "Lord, he whom you love is ill." ⁴ But when Jesus heard it he said, "This illness is not unto death; it is for the glory of God, so that the Son of God may be glorified by means of it."*
>
> *⁵ Now Jesus loved Martha and her sister and Lazʹarus. ⁶ So when he heard that he was ill, he stayed two days longer in the place where he was. ⁷ Then after this he said to the disciples, "Let us go into Judea again." ⁸ The disciples said to him, "Rabbi, the Jews were but now seeking to stone you,*

---

4. Jesus's reply to Martha in v. 40 provides the title for this book: "Did I not tell you that *if you would believe you would see* the glory of God?"

and are you going there again?" ⁹ Jesus answered, "Are there not twelve hours in the day? If any one walks in the day, he does not stumble, because he sees the light of this world. ¹⁰ But if any one walks in the night, he stumbles, because the light is not in him." ¹¹ Thus he spoke, and then he said to them, "Our friend Laz'arus has fallen asleep, but I go to awake him out of sleep." ¹² The disciples said to him, "Lord, if he has fallen asleep, he will recover." ¹³ Now Jesus had spoken of his death, but they thought that he meant taking rest in sleep. ¹⁴ Then Jesus told them plainly, "Laz'arus is dead; ¹⁵ and for your sake I am glad that I was not there, so that you may believe. But let us go to him." ¹⁶ Thomas, called the Twin, said to his fellow disciples, "Let us also go, that we may die with him."

¹⁷ Now when Jesus came, he found that Laz'arus had already been in the tomb four days. ¹⁸ Bethany was near Jerusalem, about two miles off, ¹⁹ and many of the Jews had come to Martha and Mary to console them concerning their brother. ²⁰ When Martha heard that Jesus was coming, she went and met him, while Mary sat in the house. ²¹ Martha said to Jesus, "Lord, if you had been here, my brother would not have died. ²² And even now I know that whatever you ask from God, God will give you." ²³ Jesus said to her, "Your brother will rise again." ²⁴ Martha said to him, "I know that he will rise again in the resurrection at the last day." ²⁵ Jesus said to her, "I am the resurrection and the life; he who believes in me, though he die, yet shall he live, ²⁶ and whoever lives and believes in me shall never die. Do you believe this?" ²⁷ She said to him, "Yes, Lord; I believe that you are the Christ, the Son of God, he who is coming into the world."

²⁸ When she had said this, she went and called her sister Mary, saying quietly, "The Teacher is here and is calling for you." ²⁹ And when she heard it, she rose quickly and went to him. ³⁰ Now Jesus had not yet come to the village, but was still in the place where Martha had met him. ³¹ When the Jews who were with her in the house, consoling her, saw Mary rise quickly and go out, they followed her, supposing that she was going to the tomb to weep there. ³² Then Mary, when she came where Jesus was and saw him, fell at his feet, saying to him, "Lord, if you had been here, my brother would not have died." ³³ When Jesus saw her weeping, and the Jews who came with her also weeping, he was deeply moved in spirit and troubled; ³⁴ and he said, "Where have you laid him?" They said to him, "Lord, come and see." ³⁵ Jesus wept. ³⁶ So the Jews said, "See how he loved him!" ³⁷ But some of them said, "Could not he who opened the eyes of the blind man have kept this man from dying?"

³⁸ Then Jesus, deeply moved again, came to the tomb; it was a cave, and a stone lay upon it. ³⁹ Jesus said, "Take away the stone." Martha, the sister of the dead man, said to him, "Lord, by this time there will be an

odor, for he has been dead four days." ⁴⁰ Jesus said to her, "Did I not tell you that if you would believe you would see the glory of God?" ⁴¹ So they took away the stone. And Jesus lifted up his eyes and said, "Father, I thank thee that thou hast heard me. ⁴² I knew that thou hearest me always, but I have said this on account of the people standing by, that they may believe that thou didst send me." ⁴³ When he had said this, he cried with a loud voice, "Lazarus, come out." ⁴⁴ The dead man came out, his hands and feet bound with bandages, and his face wrapped with a cloth. Jesus said to them, "Unbind him, and let him go."

RESPONSE. Forty-some years ago, when I was a graduate student in London, I took off from my research for two weeks in April and went around Europe visiting historic places. Since I was a medieval historian, I investigated many ancient churches. One was the Romanesque cathedral of Saint-Lazare in Autun, France, dedicated to the Lazarus whom John tells us Jesus raised from the dead. It was a damp, chilly, overcast afternoon when I went there, and the vast church was fairly empty of visitors. The only light was what came through the stained glass windows. I made my way up to the choir of the cathedral and stood for a long time looking at a reliquary that looked to me like a glass aquarium enclosed in gothic stonework. Inside the case I could see what appeared to be human bones, supposedly those of the young man Jesus had called out of his first tomb nearly twenty centuries earlier.

Jesus touched thousands of people and had scores of disciples, but he also had close, personal friends. Among these were a matronly but childless widow named Martha, her younger sister, Mary, and their much-younger brother, Lazarus. As the Fourth Gospel tells the story, they live in a village called Bethany, located on the Mount of Olives just under two miles from the walls of Jerusalem. When Lazarus falls seriously ill, his sisters send a messenger down to the Jordan, to another place called Bethany, to find Jesus and tell him, "Lord, the one whom you love is sick" (v. 3). The message to Jesus is not, "Lazarus has been diagnosed with an incurable cancer." Or "Lazarus has had a stroke. Come at once." They don't have to add such details, because in first century Judea, nobody sends a messenger a day's journey just to say, "Your old friend has a terrible cough." If his sisters want Jesus to know that Lazarus is ill, this means they think the situation is dire. Jesus knows that, but he remains where he is; he does not head directly to Lazarus's bedside. Instead, Jesus deliberately stays two more days on the far side of the Jordan, allowing time for Lazarus to die.

Observe how Jesus chooses to inform his disciples about Lazarus's death. He tells them "Lazarus has *fallen asleep,* but I go to awake him out of sleep" (v. 11). Jesus means that Lazarus is dead, though his disciples behave as though they don't understand until he tells them flatly, "Lazarus is dead" (v. 14). "Falling asleep" was a common ancient euphemism for dying, but that John portrays Jesus as using it is theologically important. We must make note of it.

In one sense, modern Christians might think of Mary and Martha as true believers who must face the crisis of unanswered prayer. They're Jesus's friends, not random strangers hoping for help. They have a plausible claim to special treatment—to a miracle—but they don't get it. At least they don't get the treatment they want. And it's not because Jesus doesn't get their message that they fail to receive the attention they expect, or because Jesus is busy with more important things. The Lord doesn't come up speedily to Bethany to lay hands on their brother and heal him because Jesus fully intends that Lazarus should die—or, rather, that he should "fall asleep."

Unanswered prayer always raises questions for true believers. But one inescapable point is this: no matter how close we feel to God, no matter how long we pray, simply delivering us from suffering, or even dying, is not necessarily the best thing God can do for us. One of the most poignant verses in the Bible comes from the Letter to the Hebrews, "It was fitting that he, for whom and by whom all things exist, in bringing many sons to glory, should make the pioneer of their salvation perfect through suffering" (2:10). A fundamental message of the New Testament is, *God loves us*. But God's love for us doesn't require him to shield us from pain. God knows—and we know, too—there are some things we can't learn except through pain, or distress, or failure.

When Jesus finally arrives, Martha probably wants to hiss, "Where were you? What kept you? Don't you care about us anymore?" But Martha controls herself and only says, very respectfully, "Lord, if you had been here, my brother would not have died. And even now I know that whatever you ask from God, God will give you." Then Jesus answers her by saying something that sounds like what we say in the Creed: "Your brother will rise again" (v. 23).

Imagine adult children who've been with their beloved brother as he breathes his last in a little ICU cubicle in the local hospital. When they finally leave the ICU, they run into their pastor, arriving—too late!—to be with them and offer comfort at the end. In tears, they say: "Bud is gone, Father Joe. He's gone. He died ten minutes ago." They don't need to hear Father Joe say, "Cheer up. You'll see him again in heaven." That may be what they believe, but it's not what they want to hear right then. They want Bud back, if only for another day, or even another hour. They want to hear him crack a joke; they want to share a hamburger and a beer with him. They want something real, something familiar. Something *right now*. Promise of reunion in the sweet by-and-by is unsatisfying at a time like this.

Martha suppresses her negative feelings, the way the people coming out of the ICU would suppress theirs, and gives Jesus a polite and proper reply, "Yes, I know he's going to rise again on the last day" (paraphrase of v. 24).—On the last day, sure, but not now. He's dead right now. Dead. *Gone!*

Instead of saying "Your brother will rise again," Jesus could have said, "Don't cry, Martha, and don't be afraid. Look, I'm really sorry I didn't make it in time, but I'm here now and just trust me. I'm going to bring Lazarus back to you." But he doesn't say that either. Instead, he says something that seems even stranger: "I am the resurrection and the life; he who believes in me, though he die, yet shall he live, and whoever lives and believes in me shall never die.—Do you believe this?" (v. 26).

"I am the resurrection and the life? . . . Everyone who lives and believes in me will never die?" What does Jesus mean by *"live"*? What does he mean by *"die"*? And what does he mean when he says that he *is* the resurrection? When in the Fourth Gospel Jesus makes an "I am" statement that has a predicate, like "I am the good shepherd" or "I am the light of the world," the predicates describe what Jesus *is* in relation to us. We should apply those predicates quite personally as we ponder our relationship with Christ.[5]

What's the main thing you and I believe about Jesus? Do we really believe he's the life-giver? Do we believe he truly is *God* with us? Do we believe that to trust in him with all our heart places us beyond the power of death?—Or do we, like many other people who would describe themselves as (somehow) "Christians," hold to the shallow perception of Christ as simply a "superb moral example"?

Twenty years ago Robert Capon wrote, "We are in a war between dullness and astonishment." He said the most critical issue facing Christians isn't abortion, pornography, or economic justice. He said "the critical issue for Christians in our era is *dullness*. In the church, we've lost our astonishment. The gospel isn't Good News anymore; it's just 'okay' news. Christianity is no longer assumed to be life-*changing*, but merely life-*enhancing*."[6] It's an optional extra to the standard life package. We don't expect Jesus to turn us into fanatic believers, in fact most of us would probably be nervous if that started happening. What we want is a Christ who will make us into socially-acceptable, fully contemporary, "spiritual-but-not-religious" people.

Martha can't answer Jesus's question, "Do you believe this?"—Does she believe that Jesus is the resurrection and the life and that anyone who believes in him, though they die, yet they will live, and whoever lives and believes in him will never die?—She can't answer that question because everything seems *un*believable to her at the moment. So she answers a slightly different question, one Jesus has not asked. She tells him who she thinks he is in a very formal, theological sense. She says, "Yes, Lord; I believe that you are the Christ, the Son of God, he who is coming into the world" (v. 27). She does not grasp that Jesus is talking, not about an event that will occur in the distant future, but *something that is happening in the present moment*. "The resurrection and the life" are here for her right now. Modern readers must take note that, for Jesus's contemporaries, the prospect of resurrection as a possibility for any single mortal before the last day is an utterly novel proposition.

Jesus leaves Martha and encounters Mary, who until now has been sitting on the floor of their house, weeping, putting handfuls of dust in her hair, as mourning Jewish women traditionally do. She talks with Jesus, then the two of them walk out to the

---

5. Brown, *John I–XII*, 434.

6. Capon, *Astonished*, 120.

tomb. When they arrive there, Jesus weeps. He doesn't wail, in the theatrical sense that professional mourners did at funerals in that culture. He sheds real tears.—*But why?*

I think Jesus weeps because two people whom he knows well and loves very much have failed to understand that for all who put their trust in the Son of God, the death of the body is no more to be regretted than falling asleep. He weeps because these good women are treating the physical death of their beloved little brother as if it were the end of his existence, rather than simply a phase as natural as sleep. In addition, we might also construe that Jesus weeps because Lazarus is merely a child. The suffering and death of an innocent child inevitably evokes tears of pity from a sympathetic adult.

After drying his tears, Jesus says something shocking. He says, "Take away the stone" (v. 39). Practical, well-mannered Martha, who expects to see her brother again only on the last day, says "Oh, no, Lord. No. He's been in the tomb four days. The smell will be disgusting" (paraphrase of v. 39). Jesus answers her with words I think should be inscribed over the front doors of every church building: *"Did I not tell you that if you would believe, you would see the glory of God?"* Believing is seeing. If we believe, we will see the glory of God—the evidence of God's presence and the manifestation of God's providence. Here's the way it works for you and me in our personal lives: The Lord comes to us when our hope has died. He comes to us when the stench of our loss has become the only reality we're able to perceive and then—contrary to our logical expectations—he gives new life. *"If you believe, you will see the glory of God!"*

Ignoring Martha's resistance, the bystanders open the tomb. After a prayer to the Father, Jesus speaks to the lifeless ears of his young friend who has been stone cold dead four days and says to him, *"Lazarus, come out!"* (v. 43). All the mourners who have come from Jerusalem to console the sisters hold their breath. Then they hear sounds from within the shadowed tomb and then Lazarus comes shuffling out, still wrapped in his grave clothes. Jesus says, "Unbind him, and let him go!" (v. 44).

The story of Lazarus is for those of us today who're spiritually bound up in the grave clothes of a tepid, diluted Christianity, people whose Jesus is a great moral teacher, but not the Lord of Life, and whose faith is little more than an unfocused, hopeful lack of certainty. The Lazarus story calls us to a new relationship with God. It calls us to have the faith Jesus sought from Mary and Martha—not a belief that there's a way to get whatever we want from God whenever we ask, just because we're Christians. And not a shallow confidence that there's a way to escape pain and heartbreak, but a faith that in God's providence for us who believe in Jesus the death of our body is no more to be feared than falling asleep. God is Lord of Life. And this means he is the giver of a new life right now. Lazarus did not rise from his tomb never to die again. He was raised to the life he had before; but I am sure it felt new to him. And it *was* new. It was a life in which death held no terror, a life that would bear more fruit than he could ever before have imagined. Lazarus is a symbol to us of the new "resurrection life" possible for us right now, if we are willing to die to our old status quo.[7]

The faith to which Jesus summons us is a confidence that no matter how bad life stinks, no matter how many times we've been beaten down by economic misfortune, disease, prejudice or other circumstances, the Life-giver is still here. He raises the dead—and I mean *dead* in every way we use the word, whether metaphorically or otherwise. Jesus calls forth new life in circumstances where our instincts make us want to shout, "Don't open the tomb! There'll be a stench."

Jesus is the resurrection and the life. Believe it. And if you do, you will see the glory of God.

John 11:45–57. The raising of Lazarus leads the Sanhedrin to condemn Jesus to death.

Vv. 45–57. Caiaphas says, "It is expedient for you that one man should die for the people."

INTRODUCTION. A feature of chapter 11 that sets it apart from chapters 5–10 is that here the expression "the Jews" is used exclusively in the generic sense, referring to the people of Judea and Jerusalem, and not as a shorthand designation for Jesus's enemies. However, some of the Jerusalem residents who witness the raising of Lazarus go and make a report about it to those enemies.

The seventy-one member Sanhedrin at this time is composed of very senior priests (most of whom are Sadducees, though some of very high rank are Pharisees); elders (wealthy, prominent, influential citizens, mostly belonging to no sect); and scribes (highly respected experts in Jewish law, almost all of whom are Pharisees).[8] The chief priests constitute the majority, and they are very rich, powerful aristocrats whose families keep their privileges by collaborating with the Romans. A number of the most influential aristocratic priests are members of the bet Hanan family.[9] The largely apolitical, mostly Pharisee scribes, whose concern is exclusively for meticulous observance of the Law, are a minority in the Sanhedrin. However, the scribes are disproportionately influential because ordinary Jews esteem them as holy men and hold them in much higher regard than the chief priests, whom the common people consider to be mostly venal and corrupt. Vv. 47–53 reveal that the Sanhedrin's decision to seek the death of Jesus is motivated by the priestly Sadducees' political unease, not the Pharisees' theological

7. Culpepper, *Anatomy*, 141.

8. For the presence of Pharisees among the chief priests, see Kruger, *Gospel*, 96–100. The *Sagan*, the second-highest-ranking priest (just beneath the high priest), was usually a Pharisee.

9. Acts 4:5. The Hebrew name *Hanan* is expressed with different spellings in Greek—Annas, Ananus, or Ananias. For names of the members of the bet Hanan family who held the office of high priest, see *Wikipedia.com*, s.v. "Annas." See also Edersheim, *Life*, I, 263–64; Josephus, *Antiquities*, XVIII.ii.2, 377.

issues. The chief priests' concern about Jesus is fear of what his increasing popularity might lead the Romans to do, while the Pharisees' are shocked by what they regard as Jesus's blasphemy (see, 10:31–33). Caiaphas, the ruling high priest, advises the Sanhedrin that Jesus should be put to death for political reasons, in order to prevent a catastrophic Roman reaction, arguing that "it is expedient for you that one man should die for the people, and that the whole nation should not perish" (v. 50).

No reader can miss what John Marsh calls "the most forceful example of Johannine irony. Words spoken in opposition to Jesus, and in an attempt to destroy him in order to save the temple and the Jewish nation, actually turn out in one sense to be true prophecy: Jesus will indeed die for the people, and not only for the Jewish people, but for all the people of God whom he will gather together."[10] Furthermore, although the Sanhedrin manages to arrange the execution of Jesus, the Romans still will ultimately visit ruin on both temple and nation.

> **[11:45–57]** *45 Many of the Jews therefore, who had come with Mary and had seen what he did, believed in him; 46 but some of them went to the Pharisees and told them what Jesus had done. 47 So the chief priests and the Pharisees gathered the council, and said, "What are we to do? For this man performs many signs. 48 If we let him go on thus, every one will believe in him, and the Romans will come and destroy both our holy place and our nation." 49 But one of them, Ca'iaphas, who was High Priest that year, said to them, "You know nothing at all; 50 you do not understand that it is expedient for you that one man should die for the people, and that the whole nation should not perish." 51 He did not say this of his own accord, but being High Priest that year he prophesied that Jesus should die for the nation, 52 and not for the nation only, but to gather into one the children of God who are scattered abroad. 53 So from that day on they took counsel how to put him to death.*
>
> *54 Jesus therefore no longer went about openly among the Jews, but went from there to the country near the wilderness, to a town called E'phraim; and there he stayed with the disciples. 55 Now the Passover of the Jews was at hand, and many went up from the country to Jerusalem before the Passover, to purify themselves. 56 They were looking for Jesus and saying to one another as they stood in the temple, "What do you think? That he will not come to the feast?" 57 Now the chief priests and the Pharisees had given orders that if any one knew where he was, he should let them know, so that they might arrest him.*

RESPONSE. The Jewish hierarchy—the chief priests and leading scribes—are implacable in their hostility to Jesus. From what we can discern in John, the Pharisees oppose Jesus (1) because he does not show what they regard as due respect for the

---

10. Marsh, *Saint John*, 442.

temple and its sacred, eternal function as God's chosen place for encounter with his people; (2) because he does not keep the Sabbath with the rigor with which they think it should be kept; and, most of all, (3) because he claims to be God's Son and agent on earth, speaking for God and supplanting all other authorities including them. They have told Jesus they want to stone him "because you, a man, make yourself God" (10:33). The priestly Sadducees concur fully with the Pharisees' complaints and, in addition, fear that large numbers of the common people might rally behind Jesus against the Roman overlords. Ordinary folk might be inspired to armed rebellion because of Jesus's evident willingness to tolerate being called "Messiah" by some of his followers, and by his own self-designation as "Son of Man." The Son of Man is the one to whom, according to the Prophet Daniel, God will give "dominion and glory and kingdom, that all peoples, nations, and languages should serve him . . . an everlasting dominion that shall not pass away" (7:14).

The Sadducees themselves deny the authority of the prophetic books, but they know ordinary Jews take the prophets seriously, and the status of Daniel's Son of Man sounds like that claimed for himself by the Roman emperor. Of course, Jesus is making no move to lead a rebellion and never presents himself as a warlike figure. They may even be aware that he once ran away and hid rather than let the Galileans proclaim him king (see 6:15). Yet the chief priests wonder, "What if . . . ?" They ask themselves, "What if Jesus does decide to put on a crown and lead a mob against the Romans?" He is reported to have raised a man in Bethany from the dead. Everyone is talking about it. Even if this did not really happen, he could possibly assure gullible followers that if they fall in battle against the Romans he will raise them from the dead, just as he did the fellow in Bethany. This could encourage thousands of men to fight for him, imagining themselves to be immortal.

Such a scenario sounds like Greek mythological nonsense to the chief priests. Sadducees believe in neither miracles nor resurrection of the dead. They're worldly, pragmatic, and realistic; and they are aware that the consequences of a Jewish rebellion against Rome will be devastating for themselves, their families, their class, and the nation. Roman reaction to a rebellion will result in a loss of the eminent priestly families' wealth and political power, because Rome will hold them responsible for having allowed the crisis to develop.[11] Caiaphas has reached a meeting of minds with the Roman prefect. The current situation is not ideal, but it is tolerable from the priestly hierarchy's point of view. The governor maintains the high priest's role as supreme authority among the Jews, and the chief priests do their part to see that potential revolutionaries are dealt with as quickly as possible. Nothing must be permitted to disturb this status quo.

The Sanhedrin recognizes that the recent episode in Bethany, "the purported raising of Lazarus from the dead," as the elders and prominent priests would no doubt have put it, has stirred up the common people—Jews whom their leaders regard as sinners,

11. O'Day, *Gospel of John*, 697.

ignorant of the Law. No question about it, Jesus's so-called signs are having an effect, and the powers-that-be know that if these signs continue, "everyone will believe in him" (v. 48*a*). If the people believe that Jesus raised Lazarus from the dead, they will construe this demonstration of divine power as evidence that all Jesus's claims to be Son of God are true. Therefore, it's time to put a stop to the signs before disaster strikes.

From a purely political point of view, Caiaphas's plan to eliminate Jesus rather than risk war with Rome is objectively reasonable. History tells us about countless carefully chosen, politically expedient murders; indeed, they happen today. But even the wisest and most politically astute rulers sometimes misread the signs of the times and miscalculate the consequences of their actions. Caiaphas is politically shrewd, but spiritually dead. His misunderstanding and misreading of Jesus is total. But his warning to his colleagues, "that it is expedient for you that one man should die for the people, and that the whole nation should not perish," is eerily prescient, precisely as the Fourth Gospel tells us. Jesus will indeed die "not for the nation only, but to gather into one the children of God who are scattered abroad" (vv. 50–52). John draws our attention to the inscrutable mystery of God, who uses even the wickedness of men like Caiaphas for his own redeeming purposes. "God so loved the world that he gave his only Son" (3:16).

Doing Your Own Theology

Questions for reflection after reading John 11.

- Martha and Mary send a message to Jesus, telling him about their brother's illness. Jesus does not respond to their message in the way they had hoped he would. (See vv. 1–6, 21.) Modern Christians might think of Mary and Martha as true believers who have to face the crisis of unanswered prayer. They're Jesus's friends, not random strangers hoping for help. They have a plausible claim to special treatment—to a miracle. They ask for one, in effect, but don't get it. At least they don't get the treatment they want. Unanswered prayer often raises questions for believers.—*How do you deal with your own apparently unanswered prayers? Have there been times when unanswered prayer led to a crisis of faith for you? Have there been times when God taught you something important through an apparently unanswered prayer? Do you believe that God uses everything in the life of a person of faith to their benefit? (See Rom 8:28.)*

- Observe how Jesus chooses to inform his disciples about Lazarus's death. He tells them "Lazarus has *fallen asleep*, but I go to awake him out of sleep" (v. 11). Jesus means that Lazarus is dead, although his disciples behave as if they don't understand him until he tells them flatly, "Lazarus is dead" (v. 14). "Falling asleep" was a familiar ancient euphemism for dying. That John portrays Jesus as using it may be theologically significant for readers of his gospel.—*What might be Jesus's implied theological message concerning physical death when he tells his disciples, "Lazarus has fallen asleep"? How do you, as a believer, think about death?*

- When Martha objects to Jesus's demand that the stone sealing Lazarus's tomb be removed, he answers her with the words, "Did I not tell you that if you would believe, you would see the glory of God?" (v. 40). The premise that underlies John's Gospel and which gives this book its title is: *Believing is seeing.* If we believe, we will see the glory of God, the evidence of God's presence and the manifestation of God's providence.—*Describe some things that you have "seen" on your spiritual journey but which an unbeliever would have missed.*

Chapter Twelve

John 12:1–11. Mary bathes Jesus's feet with ointment and wipes them with her hair.

Vv. 1–11. Mary of Bethany honors Jesus with a bold, yet humble gesture of love.

INTRODUCTION. As we approach Jesus's "hour of death and glory,"[1] the pace of John's Gospel slows. Chapters 12–20, more than one-third of the book, cover only a single week. Chapter 12 introduces this week of Jesus's passion with three scenes: (1) his being anointed by Mary of Bethany in preparation for burial (vv. 1–11); (2) his triumphal entry into Jerusalem (vv. 12–19); and (3) the arrival of his hour (vv. 20–36). Following these three scenes, the concluding portion of the chapter, vv. 37–43, offers a theological explanation for Jesus's rejection by "the Jews." The Book of Signs then ends with a declaration by Jesus that summarizes his teaching up to this point (vv. 44–50).[2] Each of these four sections of chapter 12 is sufficiently significant in John's story to be given separate treatment.

All four gospels include a story of Jesus being anointed by a woman. The others are Mark 14:3–9, which is repeated verbatim in Matt 26:6–13, and Luke 7:36–38. There are similarities and differences among the three accounts, and biblical commentators discuss whether they describe a single event or two different ones. Without trying to resolve that question, I wish to draw attention to the interesting correspondences between John's story of Jesus's anointing by Mary at a meal in Bethany and the story of Jesus's visit to the Bethany home of Martha and Mary for a meal found in Luke 10:38–42. In both stories, Martha serves at table; in Luke, Mary sits at Jesus's feet and listens as he teaches, while in John Mary anoints Jesus's feet. In both stories, Jesus defends Mary against criticism of her inappropriate behavior. This is one of a number

---

1. Brown, *John I–XII*, 417.

2. Keener, *Gospel of John*, 2:886–87.

of instances where Luke and John appear to share a common body of traditions about Jesus.

John's account of Mary's bathing Jesus's feet with costly ointment and drying them with her hair anticipates Jesus's washing of his disciples' feet in chapter 13.[3] The connection is intentional, otherwise why would Mary be described as drying Jesus's anointed feet? One does not dry or wipe off perfume. John wants readers to understand that Mary is not only anointing Jesus, but washing Jesus's feet—using precious balm rather than water.

Judas offers an objection to Mary's extravagant act of love and service (vv. 4–5). He judges that the ointment is worth at least 300 denarii, three hundred days' wages for an ordinary laborer, and opines that the ointment should have been sold and the proceeds "given to the poor" (v. 5). Leaving aside for the moment the gospel writer's interjection that Judas only offered his complaint because he was in the habit of pilfering from the disciples' common purse, Judas' objection lends plausibility to Brian J. Capper's theory that the house in Bethany was not Martha's and Mary's personal residence, but rather an Essene "house of the poor," of which the two wealthy Jerusalem women are patrons.[4] If the sisters are typically generous in their financial support of this Essene establishment for the poor, observers like Judas might regard Mary's "wasteful" substitution of costly ointment for water in the washing of Jesus's feet as a thoughtless and inappropriate gesture. If we construe Jesus's rejoinder, "the poor you always have with you, but you do not always have me" (v. 8), as spoken in the context of an episode that occurs in an Essene poor house, it becomes more easily understandable. Charity to the poor is indeed a righteous act, and poor people will always be coming to that house seeking help. But this is the last time Jesus will be there.

It is worth noting that the Greek sentence is obscure here, and the RSV translation of v. 7, ". . . Let her keep it for the day of my burial," makes no logical sense in this situation. Ointment that has already been poured out cannot at the same time be kept for a later occasion. A variant reading found in different manuscripts is more logical: "*She has kept it* for the day of my burial." The point of Jesus's remark is that Mary should be allowed to do what she has done because she has unknowingly prepared his body for burial.[5]

John tells us that once they learn Jesus has returned from his place of retreat, "a great crowd of the Jews" (v. 9), simply meaning in this case people from Jerusalem, come out to Bethany to see both him and Lazarus, whom he raised from the dead. Word about the miracle has spread through the city, and this makes the chief priests plan to kill Lazarus, too—since he is now a focus of public attention, inspiring "many of the Jews" to "go away" and believe in Jesus (v. 11). "Going away and believing in Jesus" suggests conversion from rabbinical Judaism to what at this very early stage

3. O'Day, *Gospel of John*, 703.

4. Capper, "Essene Community Houses," 471.

5. Kysar, *John*, 189.

we might call the Jesus Movement in Judaism, i.e., to the sect which will one day be known as "the church." Readers of John learn from Lazarus's example that those who follow Jesus must expect to find their lives threatened, for the world will hate them (15:18).[6]

> **[12:1–11]** [1] *Six days before the Passover, Jesus came to Bethany, where Lazarus was, whom Jesus had raised from the dead.* [2] *There they made him a supper; Martha served, and Lazarus was one of those at table with him.* [3] *Mary took a pound of costly ointment of pure nard and anointed the feet of Jesus and wiped his feet with her hair; and the house was filled with the fragrance of the ointment.* [4] *But Judas Iscariot, one of his disciples (he who was to betray him), said,* [5] *"Why was this ointment not sold for three hundred denarii and given to the poor?"* [6] *This he said, not that he cared for the poor but because he was a thief, and as he had the money box he used to take what was put into it.* [7] *Jesus said, "Let her alone, let her keep it for the day of my burial.* [8] *The poor you always have with you, but you do not always have me."*
>
> [9] *When the great crowd of the Jews learned that he was there, they came, not only on account of Jesus but also to see Lazarus, whom he had raised from the dead.* [10] *So the chief priests planned to put Lazarus also to death,* [11] *because on account of him many of the Jews were going away and believing in Jesus.*

RESPONSE. John's Gospel, like that of Luke, makes note of Jesus's relationships with significant women, beginning with his mother (2:1–5; 19:25–27) and continuing with the Samaritan woman (4:7–42), Martha and Mary (11:1–40), the women at the cross (19:25), and Mary Magdalene, who has the dignity of being the first to whom the risen Christ reveals himself (20:1–2, 11–18). We may surely apply to Mary, the sister of Martha and Lazarus, the pledge that Mark's gospel tells us Jesus makes after an unnamed woman anoints him in the home of "Simon the Leper" in Bethany: "Truly, I say to you, wherever the gospel is preached in the whole world, what she has done will be told in memory of her" (Mark 14:9).

The usual understanding of the story in vv. 1–8 is that Jesus is being entertained as the honored guest at a dinner party in the home of Martha, Mary, and Lazarus, in gratitude for what he has recently dramatically done for them by raising Lazarus from death to life.[7] Mary's shocking and unprecedented gesture of pouring a large vessel of costly spikenard on Jesus's feet as he reclines at table, then drying them with her hair is an unforgettable portrayal of one woman's extravagant display of thankfulness, selfless love, respect, and humble service. It anticipates the unique gesture of love that Jesus

---

6. Keener, *Gospel of John*, 2:866.

7. Capper's theory concerning the Essene "house of the poor" has not yet become sufficiently well-known to feature in many commentators' analyses.

will perform for his disciples later in the week as he washes their feet at the Supper (see 13:3–10). The bathing of Jesus's feet with expensive perfumed ointment is by itself a bold act; using her hair to dry Jesus's feet is not only bold but potentially outrageous, since custom in her culture dictates that adult women should keep their hair veiled in mixed company. This episode (as well as the story in Luke 10:38–42) portrays Mary as a brave and self-confident young woman who refuses to be deterred by the possibility that she might be scolded for her behavior, either by her elder sister or by men in her community. The familiar cliché could apply to Mary; she "marches to the sound of a different drummer." However, those who understand how God works in the human heart would describe Mary as one who is led by the Spirit.

We can't know whether John intends us to think of the anointing as planned in advance or spontaneous. The fact that Jesus chooses to defend Mary's gesture by interpreting it as an unwitting preparation of his body for burial does not imply that Mary actually anticipates Jesus's death as near. We can only speculate about what Mary might be feeling at the moment other than love and gratitude for Jesus's restoring her brother to life. The container of spikenard may be the most valuable thing she possesses, perhaps an heirloom or part of her trousseau. Yet she chooses to "waste it on Jesus," as Judas Iscariot might put it, in an exceptional gesture of sincere devotion.

If I were asked whether I have ever been moved to even a vaguely similar act of unconventional love and respect in order to honor Christ, I would be forced to answer that I have not been. Like most Christians in our age, I have usually been habitually careful in my religious behavior—guided by local customs and sensitive to possible criticism from those who might be watching. After all, I am an Episcopalian, and ours is a traditionally reserved and mannerly community of believers, not often given to emotional displays. Perhaps the twenty-first century will see us change.

Does Jesus's reply to Judas's criticism of Mary, "the poor you always have with you, but you do not always have me" (v. 8), excuse twenty-first century disciples from hoping that *we* might one day have the opportunity to honor our Lord in a uniquely personal and extravagant (even shocking) fashion, just as Mary did? Are we to understand that now the *only* way we may give ourselves unreservedly to Christ can be through acts of mercy to the poor? If we have occasion to embrace a leper as Francis of Assisi did or undertake sacrificial service in a Third World environment, we can be confident that, according to Jesus's words in Matt 25:40, "as you did it to one of the least of these my brethren, you did it to me." But I'm convinced there is also a place—and even a need—for our private acts of deep, seemingly irrational devotion to the person of our Lord. John says the house in Bethany is filled with the fragrance of the perfume Mary pours on Jesus's feet. Likewise, our own homes—and our churches, too—are filled with an aroma of holiness by the humble acts of piety and contemplation whereby Jesus's faithful disciples honor the One who is unseen, yet ever near.

John 12:12–19. Jesus enters Jerusalem.
A crowd comes out to welcome him with palms.

Vv. 12–19. Passover pilgrims greet Jesus as King of Israel.

INTRODUCTION. Just as the four canonical gospels each contains a story about Jesus being anointed, so each also contains a description of his triumphal entry into Jerusalem some days before the crucifixion (Matt 21:1–11; Mark 11:1–11; Luke 19:28–40). Of the four, John's account is the shortest and only John suggests that Jesus entered the city on a Sunday (v. 12). It is also unique in another respect. It tells us there was a great crowd of people who came out from the city to welcome Jesus (vv. 12–13), but implies that there was another group who accompanied him as he came down the Mount of Olives from Bethany (vv. 16–17).[8] Those who come out from the city to welcome him are probably Passover pilgrims, while those who arrive with him are his disciples and other witnesses to the raising of Lazarus. John shows his readers that the act of Jesus which drives the authorities finally to apprehend him and have him crucified is his last and greatest "sign," the giving of life to a dead man.

Two aspects of John's story deserve our particular attention:

First: The crowd that comes out to greet Jesus, crying "Hosanna! Blessed is he who comes in the name of the Lord, even the King of Israel" (v. 13)[9] is waving branches of palm. Palm branches (which are mentioned only in John) are associated with the welcome accorded a conqueror. Such a display has both nationalistic and messianic overtones, and the implication is that this crowd sees Jesus as the Messiah who will free the Jews from their Gentile overlords. The people of Jerusalem once welcomed Simon Maccabeus, the militant high priest and first prince of the Hasmonean dynasty, with palm branches and singing after he won the freedom of Jerusalem, when "the yoke of the Gentiles was removed from Israel" in 142 BCE (1 Macc 13:41–51).[10]

Second: Hearing this messianic acclamation by the palm-waving crowd, Jesus finds the colt of an ass and sits on it to ride the rest of the way into the city. John tells us that Jesus does this because "it is written, 'Fear not, daughter of Zion; behold, your king is coming, sitting on an ass's colt!'" (v. 15)[11] The prophetic symbolism here is obscure to us, and even Jesus's disciples did not understand it until after the resurrection (v. 16). The point of the gesture is this: a conquering, messianic king rides in a chariot, but a king who comes in peace, like the one referred to in Zech 9:9, rides an ass. Choosing to mount the colt of an ass is Jesus's way of emphasizing that he is a king of peace, not a warrior Messiah who will lead a war against Rome. The prophet

---

8. The two crowds John describes at the time of the triumphal entry are parallel to the two crowds described at the time of the feeding of the five thousand—one of which is following Jesus while the other comes to him after he has taken his seat on the hillside to teach. (See 6:1–5.)

9. Ps 118:26, with the reference to the king inserted.

10. Reicke, *New Testament Era*, 63–66.

11. Phrases from Zeph 3:16 and Zech 9:9.

Zechariah describes the Messiah as saying, "I will cut off the chariot from Ephraim and the war horse from Jerusalem; and the battle bow shall be cut off, and he shall command peace to the nations" (Zech 9:10a). John emphasizes the non-threatening, non-militaristic character of Jesus's messiahship.

John shows Jesus as Messiah, but the future of his kingdom lies beyond the boundaries of this-worldly life, as Jesus later tells Pilate (18:36). Jesus sees that the way of humility, peace, and self-oblation is the only path by which to lead the people of God into the kingdom the Father has in store for them.[12]

> [12:12–19] *[12] The next day a great crowd who had come to the feast heard that Jesus was coming to Jerusalem. [13] So they took branches of palm trees and went out to meet him, crying, "Hosanna! Blessed is he who comes in the name of the Lord, even the King of Israel!" [14] And Jesus found a young ass and sat upon it; as it is written,*
>
> *[15] "Fear not, daughter of Zion; behold, your king is coming, sitting on an ass's colt!"*
>
> *[16] His disciples did not understand this at first; but when Jesus was glorified, then they remembered that this had been written of him and had been done to him. [17] The crowd that had been with him when he called Laz'arus out of the tomb and raised him from the dead bore witness. [18] The reason why the crowd went to meet him was that they heard he had done this sign. [19] The Pharisees then said to one another, "You see that you can do nothing; look, the world has gone after him."*

RESPONSE. Jerusalem is packed with people on the fifth day before Passover, and new pilgrims are arriving continuously—often traveling together in sizeable groups from the Judean hinterland, Galilee, Syria, and beyond. Therefore, roads to the city and especially routes to the temple are clogged with noisy, happy people singing and shouting greetings to one another.

When a band of pilgrims from a particular town or district comes through the gates, fellow-countrymen who have been expecting them will come out to greet the new arrivals. John and the Synoptic writers all focus their attention on Jesus and his companions, but as we modern people attempt to imagine the scene we should envision the crowd that comes out to receive Jesus and the crowd that accompanies him down from Bethany as being enveloped by a significantly much larger throng, the majority of whom probably take no notice of either Jesus and his friends or their reception committee of Galilean compatriots. To put it simply, the arrival of Jesus of Nazareth in Jerusalem for Passover might be a very important moment for a segment of the multitude, but it is probably not the center of attention for everyone. It is not as remarkable and amazing an event as we traditionally surmise.

12. Marsh, *Saint John*, 460.

Nevertheless, a significant portion of the Passover pilgrim horde knows something about Jesus, and what they know—or think they know—is that he is the Messiah. He is the King of Israel. He is the one who will deliver God's chosen people from bondage to the heathen Romans. He has shown signs of power; he has even raised the dead. Those who march with Jesus will have a joyful future in a new Israel. These enthusiasts greet him ecstatically, chanting the *Hallel*, saying "Hosanna! Blessed is he who comes in the name of the Lord, even the King of Israel!" (v. 13). It's possible that these are some of the very people from whom Jesus fled a year ago in Galilee when they wanted to take him by force and make him king after he fed them on the lakeside. They do not understand him. They do not understand what the Father sent him into the world to accomplish. So, Jesus tries to divert them by mounting the colt of an ass and riding it through the mass of people on foot, hoping that at least some of these fervent Messiah-seekers will remember the significant prophecy of Zechariah that describes the coming King as a humble man of peace. Alas, the gesture is too subtle. Even his disciples miss its meaning and don't realize its symbolism until long afterward. The Pharisees despair that "the world has gone after him" (v. 19, another bit of Johannine irony), and the chief priests are confirmed in their conviction that Jesus will bring down the wrath of the Romans upon them. They are about to devise a plan to arrest him and have him killed.

John's account of the triumphal entry invites contemporary readers to ask ourselves some serious questions. Do we who sing glorious, martial hymns in our churches on Palm Sunday celebrating "the victory of the cross" truly grasp what Jesus means when he enters the city of Jerusalem riding on a donkey that Sunday morning before his death? Or are we caught up in the same kind of triumphalist enthusiasm exhibited by the militants who welcome him by waving palm branches and shouting the traditional conqueror's psalm? Perhaps Christians have been marching for too many centuries in glorious parades behind tall, gold processional crosses, waving our swords—either literally or figuratively. The symbolism of the crusade still has a grip on our emotions. But the cross of Jesus is really not a "triumphant sign" for his disciples, save in the most ironic sense.

That's what the gospel of John, that master of irony, will soon show us. In five days King Jesus will arrive at the summit of his triumph and glory on a hill named Golgotha. He will wear his crown as he climbs that hill, but it will be a diadem of thorns. He will take his place on a throne, but that throne will be a wooden cross, and men who despise him will nail him to it. Jesus is indeed our King, but his kingdom, and the kingdom he promises his disciples (cf. Luke 12:32), is very clearly "not of this world" (18:36).

John 12:20–36. Jesus's long-awaited hour arrives.

Vv. 20–36. Greeks come, wanting to see Jesus.

INTRODUCTION. In the Synoptic gospels, Jesus goes directly to the temple after the triumphal entry and expels the animal sellers and overturns the tables of the money-changers. Matthew, Mark, and Luke treat this act as the last straw, the final provocation that impels the high priest and his colleagues to seek Jesus's death. John, however, places his own description of this event—usually labeled "the cleansing of the temple"—at the very outset of Jesus's public ministry, during the first of the three Passovers the Fourth Gospel describes (2:13–25). For John, it is the raising of Lazarus, Jesus's giving of new life to a friend, *not* the cleansing of the temple, which is the ultimate aggravation to the Sanhedrin. The scene in 12:20–37, which John places immediately after the triumphal entry, probably takes place in the outer court of the temple.

If the "Greeks" who are in Jerusalem to worship during the feast are Gentiles, as most commentators believe, rather than Greek-speaking Jews from the diaspora, they cannot enter the sacred precincts, but must remain in the ritually unclean outer court. John, neither here nor in his own account of Jesus overturning the tables of the money changers and driving out the sellers of sacrificial animals (2:13–19), makes use of the verse from Isa 56:7 that Mark's gospel attributes to him on that occasion, "My house shall be called a house of prayer for all the nations" (Mark 11:17). However, since John sees the risen body of Jesus becoming the ultimate replacement of the temple as the meeting place of all people with God, Isa 56:7 is a prophecy the Beloved Disciple may have in mind as he describes the Greeks who desire to see Jesus.[13] John identifies the mission of God's Son as universal in 3:16–17; the Samaritans label Jesus "Savior of the world" in 4:42; Jesus himself announces that anyone who comes to him "will never be cast out" in 6:37; and at last even the Pharisees say in v. 19, "The whole world has gone after him."

Among Jesus's disciples, Philip and Andrew have Greek names. It was not unusual for Jews living in ethnically mixed areas like Galilee to have a Greek name as well as a Hebrew name. However, the fact that these Gentile inquirers express to a disciple with a Greek name their desire to "see Jesus," and this Greek-named disciple then shares their request with a second Greek-named disciple, subtly manifests our gospel writer's interest in the Gentile mission—and particularly so if we understand the verb *see* in a metaphoric sense. The Greek word used here for *see*, a word John employs to indicate not only seeing with the eyes but understanding with the heart, is the exact word Jesus uses when he replies to Andrew and his anonymous companion at the beginning of the gospel after the two ask where he dwells. Jesus tells them, "Come and *see*" (1:39). This is an example of the tight literary unity we find in the Fourth Gospel.

---

13. Ibid., 462.

The arrival of Gentiles who want to see him precipitates Jesus's proclamation that the long-awaited hour of his glorification has come (v. 23). John wants readers to understand that the glory of the Son of God, revealed in his death and resurrection, is for the world, not only for the descendants of Abraham. Jesus says, "Now is the judgment of this world, now shall the ruler of this world be cast out; and I, when I am lifted up from the earth, will draw all men to myself" (vv. 31–32). The double entendre expressed in the idiomatic expression, "to be lifted up," is common in Mediterranean society of the first century. Dependent on context, hearers recognize it as meaning either elevation in status—as in the enthronement of a ruler—or execution by crucifixion or hanging.[14] In the case of Jesus, his being lifted up on the cross is the moment of his exaltation. Ironically, the Roman *titulus* or tablet nailed to his cross will make Jesus's regal status clear in three languages: "Jesus of Nazareth, the King of the Jews" (18:19).

Unlike the Synoptics, John's Gospel does not describe Jesus as experiencing a traumatic time of agonized wrestling with whether to accept "the cup of suffering" the Father has for him. Vv. 27–28 offer the Fourth Gospel's perspective on Jesus's emotional state. John tones down the intensity of Jesus's agony, making mention of it only here—not in the garden scene. His "soul is troubled" (v. 27, reflecting Ps 42:6), but his commitment to do the Father's will is calm and certain.

> [12:20–36] *20 Now among those who went up to worship at the feast were some Greeks. 21 So these came to Philip, who was from Beth-sa'ida in Galilee, and said to him, "Sir, we wish to see Jesus." 22 Philip went and told Andrew; Andrew went with Philip and they told Jesus. 23 And Jesus answered them, "The hour has come for the Son of man to be glorified. 24 Truly, truly, I say to you, unless a grain of wheat falls into the earth and dies, it remains alone; but if it dies, it bears much fruit. 25 He who loves his life loses it, and he who hates his life in this world will keep it for eternal life. 26 If any one serves me, he must follow me; and where I am, there shall my servant be also; if any one serves me, the Father will honor him.*
>
> *27 "Now is my soul troubled. And what shall I say? 'Father, save me from this hour'? No, for this purpose I have come to this hour. 28 Father, glorify thy name." Then a voice came from heaven, "I have glorified it, and I will glorify it again." 29 The crowd standing by heard it and said that it had thundered. Others said, "An angel has spoken to him." 30 Jesus answered, "This voice has come for your sake, not for mine. 31 Now is the judgment*

---

14. Keener, *Gospel of John*, 2:873. When the Roman soldiers crucified a victim, typically he was first laid supine on the ground and nailed through the wrists to the cross-beam, the *patibulum*. Then the executioners literally lifted him up by means of this cross-beam and slotted it into place atop the vertical member, the *stipes*, which was left permanently in place at the site designated for crucifixions. (See pp. 286–87 and Fig. 12, p. 255, below.) Keener calls attention to the use of the expression at the beginning of the fourth Servant Song, Isa 52:13.

of this world, now shall the ruler of this world be cast out; ³² and I, when I am lifted up from the earth, will draw all men to myself." ³³ He said this to show by what death he was to die. ³⁴ The crowd answered him, "We have heard from the law that the Christ remains for ever. How can you say that the Son of man must be lifted up? Who is this Son of man?" ³⁵ Jesus said to them, "The light is with you for a little longer. Walk while you have the light, lest the darkness overtake you; he who walks in the darkness does not know where he goes. ³⁶ While you have the light, believe in the light, that you may become sons of light."

When Jesus had said this, he departed and hid himself from them.

RESPONSE. This chapter of John has a singular message for modern readers, a word about "the real Jesus," an indication of what constitutes true glory for Jesus and for his disciples. When Jesus enters the city of Jerusalem on the Sunday morning before he goes to the cross, he does so as a man we'd describe as well on his way to becoming famous. Many in the Passover throng have his name on their lips. They're on the lookout for him.

He has the attention of a segment of them who choose to recognize him as the long-awaited Messiah, the true King of Israel who will expel the Romans and restore the glory and pride of the nation. These people are waving palm branches as he arrives. All Jesus has to do is act the part, ride into the city on a horse, not a little donkey, and yell, "Down with the Romans! Down with the high priest and his collaborator cronies!—Come on, let's go! Are you with me?" Hundreds, probably thousands of men would be ready to fight for him. Some are already carrying swords.

On this very day some God-fearing Gentiles approach a Galilean disciple of Jesus and say, "Please, sir, we'd like to see Jesus" (v. 21). From what John tells us about this incident, we can assume the episode involves more than some curious Gentiles simply hoping to meet the Man of the Hour (and, if it happened in our day, take a selfie with him). To convert all of this into our contemporary idiom, let's imagine that John is telling us, "Here are a couple of foreigners—Gentiles, just like you. They're not involved in Jerusalem politics. They don't know anything about what's been happening between the Sanhedrin and Jesus. They don't understand Jewish nationalism. But they've heard about Jesus and they see a chance to get close to him." Choosing for their go-between an apparent friend of Jesus who speaks Greek and dresses like they do, *these foreigners try to make a personal connection with Jesus.* They aren't just hoping for a fresh angle on the Jesus whose image is being peddled to the public in a hostile way by his enemies or in a political way by Zealots who hope to use Jesus in their battle against the Romans. Here the Beloved Disciple tells twenty-first century readers of his gospel, "If you want to know 'the real Jesus,' pay close attention to what I'm about to show you."

When he learns about the foreigners' interest, Jesus says, "The hour has come for the Son of Man to be glorified." The anti-Roman crowd would agree whole-heartedly with that observation. They're ready for Jesus to be "glorified" too. But they have a typical worldly idea of *glory*—a victory parade led by the conquering hero dressed in an impressive uniform, wearing a crown, and riding in a golden chariot, with his defeated enemies trudging behind him in chains. A segment of the emotionally wound-up Passover mob is ready to respond as we do when we're sure our own moment of national glory has arrived: "*Sound the trumpet! Raise the battle cry! Take up your weapons!*"

Yes, the zealous, partisan crowd agrees a hundred percent that Jesus's moment of glory has arrived. But Jesus's understanding of the *glory* that the Father is about to reveal in the eyes of the world has nothing in common with the popular imagination. Not in the first century and not today. The Son of Man's vision of glory is quite different. He has come, not to defeat his enemies, not to destroy them, but to *save* them. (See 3:17)

Do you and I really want to *see* Jesus? . . . Or do we just want to *use* Jesus? We can go to church all our lives and never truly see him, never come to know him. Think about this question. If you were to decide to make yourself rich and famous by inventing a new religion, what symbol will you choose to represent your god or goddess? You'll probably want something beautiful, impressive, and dignified—something that will immediately identify the desirable, magnetic, made-for-television qualities of your new deity. If you have enough cash, you'll hire a high-end Hollywood ad agency to come up with a very simple graphic device, a logo that will suggest the means by which your new deity will provide peace of mind, material prosperity, vigorous health, and an endless life of pleasure to his or her devotees.

Nobody hoping for success with a new "start-up" religion will choose as a primary logo the picture of a beaten-up, bleeding man, dying while nailed to a cross. That's the image of a loser, a victim. There's not anything glorious or attractive about a poor man dying a terrible, public death.—That is, there's nothing attractive unless we're willing to learn from that poor, dying man to have a totally new, absolutely countercultural understanding of "glory."

Do we want to "see Jesus"? Do we want to learn hard lessons from him? Jesus says: "The hour has come for the Son of Man to be glorified. Very truly, I tell you, until a grain of wheat falls into the ground and dies, it remains just one single grain. But if it dies, it yields a great harvest. Those who are in love with the life they have in this world will lose their life. But those who turn their backs on the life of this evil age will have eternal life in the kingdom of God that is coming" (paraphrase of vv. 23–25). A grain of wheat, a seed, has to "die" (as it appeared to ancient people), to be buried in the ground, if it is to produce a harvest. That's the powerful, paradoxical truth of the cross. That's the glory of the cross.

I've preached for over forty years, mostly in comfortable suburban American churches. It's difficult to get prosperous, contented people—people who want to get church over with so they can go play golf—to understand that the need to let go of this life is an essential truth borne out in Jesus's words and in his life. The spiritual truth is that we need to unclench our fists and not keep clinging so tightly to the world's beguiling promises of security, success, or power. We must stop hugging to ourselves the swiftly-passing "glories" the world offers.

Jesus lets his enemies have their way. He doesn't fight back; he doesn't play the role of an embattled, mythic hero who wrestles against enemies who are able to take him down only because they outnumber him twenty to one. Letting his enemies have their way does not proceed from any weakness on Jesus's part. Indeed, the opposite is true: he is far stronger than they imagine. Obeying the Father, Jesus is passive. He permits the powers of evil take his life, so all humankind might see that the power to kill is nothing in comparison to the Father's power to give new life. Jesus's "passivity in his passion" is, in fact, a display of strength.

Do you and I really want to "see Jesus"? Do we want to let him change us? Jesus lets go of this life and the potential for being the kind of King-Messiah the Jerusalem zealots think they want. Instead, he chooses to be a king who comes to die—but not *only* to die. Jesus dies in order to live anew and give his new life to us. He becomes the seed that must be buried before it can produce a harvest, a harvest of disciples who will go on to plant their own seeds by letting go of their old lives, their old pretenses, and their false selves so as to be formed in the likeness of their Master. John shows us that, trusting what he knows is his mission from God, and aware of what his resurrection will mean, Jesus chooses to accept the cross and become a man who, to most of his contemporaries, appears to be only one more pathetic, well-intentioned failure.—Not the kind of deliverer they're looking for. Not a man they want to imitate.

His contemporaries are wrong. They refuse to "see" Jesus. Do *we* want to see him, to understand him and the mission to which he calls his disciples? The words John says Jesus speaks on that Palm Sunday when the Greeks come hoping to see him are full of prophetic vision which still holds true: "Now is the judgment of this world. Now the dark ruler of this world is being driven out. And I, when I am lifted up from the earth, will draw all people to myself" (paraphrase of vv. 31–32).

When we renounce the way of power and domination and choose the path of self-sacrifice in its place, we join our Lord in pronouncing judgment on the powers of this world. We see the arrogant vanity that dominates our age for the fraud that it is because of the light of glory streaming from the face of the Crucified—who still cries out, *"When I am lifted up from the earth, I will draw all people to myself."*

John 12:37–50. Jesus's message summarized in his own words.

Vv. 37–50. "He who believes in me, believes not in me but in him who sent me."

INTRODUCTION. John tells us that Jesus concludes his last public discourse with a warning that the Jews should believe in him while they still have the opportunity to do so. He says, "While you have the light, believe in the light, that you may become sons of light" (v. 36*a*). After these words, he goes away and hides himself from the Passover throng (v. 36*b*). The remainder of chapter 12 functions as a meditative coda to the first half of John's Gospel, which I have—following the guidance of Raymond E. Brown—labeled "the Book of Signs." In her commentary on John's Gospel, Gail R. O'Day offers a helpful description of this coda. She writes,

> It is helpful to envision this section along the analogy of the theater. With Jesus's exit at 12:36, the curtain has come down on his public ministry. In vv. 37–43, the Evangelist, the 'playwright,' reveals himself directly to the audience and comments on the dilemma with which the first 'act' ends: Why do Jesus's own reject him? After he completes his speech, he, too, disappears behind the curtain, and the stage is completely empty and dark. The voice of Jesus is then heard (vv. 44–50), crying out to the darkened theater from the wings, his own voice providing the final commentary on the drama that has played itself out before the audience. When Jesus finishes speaking, the audience is once again alone in the darkness, with Jesus's offer of salvation ringing in their ears.[15]

The key question Jesus's disciples are going to be required to answer, beginning from the earliest years of the church's mission, is "Why did his own people reject him?" This is a particularly serious difficulty for Gentiles, because they can see clearly that the Jewish Messiah is rejected by most Jews. The answer that the Fourth Gospel proposes is the same one Paul offers in Rom 9–11: the Messiah's rejection is foretold by the prophets.

Commentators point out that the Fourth Gospel makes frequent use of the Prophet Isaiah, drawing from Isaiah the idea that Jesus is the revelation of the glory of God.[16] Some even think that Jesus (whose name in Hebrew is almost the same as Isaiah's) saw himself in Isaiah's four Servant Songs.[17] The Fourth Servant Song portrays the Servant as "despised and rejected by men; a man of sorrows, and acquainted with grief; and as one from whom men hide their faces he was despised, and we esteemed him not" (Isa 53:3). In v. 40, John quotes Isa 6:10, in which the Lord says to Isaiah, who has offered himself to be sent as a servant of the Lord, to be his spokesman to

---

15 O'Day, *Gospel of John*, 718.

16. Smith, *John*, 243.

17. See, e.g., Barker, "Isaiah," 489–542. The four Songs of the Servant of the Lord are Isa 42:1–4; 49:1–6; 50:4; and 52:13—53:12.

Israel: "Make the heart of this people fat, and their ears heavy, and shut their eyes; lest they see with their eyes, and hear with their ears, and understand with their hearts, and turn and be healed." This explanation from prophecy is difficult for twenty-first century readers because it may be read as implying that the Jews were predestined to disbelieve. We better understand John as seeing that the Jews' rejection of Jesus is no different from their longstanding refusal to believe the prophets, except now they are rejecting and planning to put to death God's Son. Nevertheless, not even unbelief can thwart God's plan of salvation; it will be disclosed in the fullness of time. Jesus has not come to condemn the world, but to save it (v. 47)

> [12:37–50] *37* *Though he had done so many signs before them, yet they did not believe in him;* *38* *it was that the word spoken by the prophet Isaiah might be fulfilled:*
>
> *"Lord, who has believed our report, and to whom has the arm of the Lord been revealed?"*
>
> *39* *Therefore they could not believe. For Isaiah again said,*
>
> *40* *"He has blinded their eyes and hardened their heart, lest they should see with their eyes and perceive with their heart, and turn for me to heal them."*
>
> *41* *Isaiah said this because he saw his glory and spoke of him.* *42* *Nevertheless many even of the authorities believed in him, but for fear of the Pharisees they did not confess it, lest they should be put out of the synagogue:* *43* *for they loved the praise of men more than the praise of God.*
>
> *44* *And Jesus cried out and said, "He who believes in me, believes not in me but in him who sent me.* *45* *And he who sees me sees him who sent me.* *46* *I have come as light into the world, that whoever believes in me may not remain in darkness.* *47* *If any one hears my sayings and does not keep them, I do not judge him; for I did not come to judge the world but to save the world.* *48* *He who rejects me and does not receive my sayings has a judge; the word that I have spoken will be his judge on the last day.* *49* *For I have not spoken on my own authority; the Father who sent me has himself given me commandment what to say and what to speak.* *50* *And I know that his commandment is eternal life. What I say, therefore, I say as the Father has bidden me."*

RESPONSE. True faith, in the end, demands that we put our trust in the love and providence of God our Father. Although it may seem to us, as it did to the author of First John, that "the whole world is in the power of the Evil One" (1 John 5:19), the broad testimony of Scripture is that God uses for his saving purposes even circumstances that appear to be self-evidently unredeemable. (See Rom 8:28). In the prologue to his gospel—before his readers have the opportunity to learn about Jesus's signs, before they hear Jesus's testimony, before they see how the leaders of the Jews react to him and the way his neighbors misunderstand him—John tells them, "The true light that enlightens every man was coming into the world. He was in the world, and the world was made through him, yet the world knew him not. He came to his own home, and his own people received him not. But to all who received him, who believed in his name, he gave power to become children of God; who were born, not of blood nor of the will of the flesh nor of the will of man, but of God" (1:9–13).

The divine Son came to the world, "and the world knew him not." He came to his own people, and they "received him not" (1:10–11). But the world's ignorance and his own people's obstinacy cannot prevent the Son from fulfilling his Father's will—at the cost of his own life. The cross is a price the Son is glad to pay in order for his Father's will to be accomplished. And the Father's plan is for nothing less than the redemption of all his children, the gathering together of his scattered flock under one shepherd (see 10:15*b*–16).

During times when the world's darkness appears ready to overwhelm us, when truth seems always on the scaffold while wrong sits on throne,[18] when our bright hopes have been crushed by dismal circumstances and our good intentions count for nothing, the Fourth Gospel yields the wisdom we need and the consolation we crave. John reminds the little flock of Christ that though our journey could prove long and perilous, the good shepherd always leads his sheep safely home. When our life situation seems predestined to result in one disappointment after another, he assures us that—as Jesus told Martha, standing at the tomb of Lazarus—"if only you will believe, you will see the glory of God" (paraphrase of 11:40).

As he stitches the pieces of the Beloved Disciple's great gospel together near the end of the first century, John's editor wants those who read it to understand how the Beloved Disciple thought about Jesus, all the way to the end of his long life: "In him was life, and the life was the light of men. The light shines in the darkness, and the darkness has not overcome it" (1:4–5). This is recapitulated by the way he concludes the "Book of Signs." Now that Jesus's dark hour has come, we watch as the Light starts to overcome the Darkness.

Doing Your Own Theology

Questions for reflection after reading John 12.

- Mary's act of bathing Jesus's feet with costly ointment and then wiping them with her hair is a bold and potentially scandalous gesture. It is behavior that marks her as a member of Jesus's circle of followers whose love for their Master overrides any purely personal considerations, even for her reputation.—*What do you*

18. Lowell, "Present Crisis."

imagine moved Mary so deeply? Has there ever been a time in your life when you were thus moved by your own feelings for Christ? To what sort of behavior were you inspired by those feelings? If you were criticized for your behavior at the time, how did you deal with the criticism?

- Jesus's decision to enter the city of Jerusalem riding on the colt of an ass seems a deliberate attempt to identify himself with the Messiah as King of Peace, as portrayed by the Prophet Zechariah. This symbolic act was a sign to the zealots in the Passover crowd that Jesus would refuse to lead them in a war against the Romans. Despite the explicitly peaceful symbolism of Jesus's triumphal entry, history shows us that Christians have long been attracted to heroic, martial imagery in describing the mission of Christ and his church. For example, most of us have sung hymns such as, "Lead on, O King eternal, the day of march has come;" "The Son of God goes forth to war, a kingly crown to gain;" "Onward, Christian soldiers, marching as to war;" and "Lift high the cross . . . led on their way by this triumphant sign, the hosts of God in conquering ranks combine."—*What do you think accounts for the popular appeal of militaristic imagery in portraying the mission of the church? In what other ways does "King Jesus" continue to be misunderstood down to this day, both by believers and non-believers? What aspects of his identity and his kingdom are the hardest for you to grasp and accept?*

- On the day of his entry into Jerusalem, some God-fearing Gentiles approach a Galilean disciple of Jesus in the outer court of the temple, and say to him, "Please, sir, we'd like to see Jesus" (paraphrase of v. 21). When he learns about these foreigners' interest, Jesus says, "The hour has come for the Son of Man to be glorified" (v. 23). His long-awaited hour has arrived, the hour of his glory and his sacrifice. Jesus's understanding of the *glory* that the Father is about to reveal in the eyes of the world has nothing in common with the popular imagination, either in the first century or today. The Son of Man's vision of glory is very different. He has come, not to defeat his enemies, not to destroy them, but to save them. (See, 3:17.) A crucial question for us is this, "Do we really want to *see* Jesus?"—*What do you believe constitutes "glory" in God's eyes? How does that differ from our ordinary definition of glory? Could seeing Jesus afresh through John's Gospel change your life? Do you really want to "see" Jesus, or do you stop short, afraid of the demands he might place on you?*

A General Introduction to John 13:1–20:30.
"The Book of Glory" Begins.

The purpose of the first half of John's Gospel, the Book of Signs (as Raymond E. Brown labels it), is to proclaim the identity of Jesus as Son of God, Messiah, and Savior, and detail how he is ultimately rejected by his own people (1:11). The second half of the gospel, which I imitate Brown in calling the Book of Glory, begins here. Between 13:1 and 20:23 it covers only four days, but they are the momentous days which reveal the fullness of Jesus's glory—the days of his passion and resurrection—beginning with the Last Supper and ending with his appearance to the disciples on the Sunday evening of the resurrection. 20:24–29 recounts Jesus's appearance to the disciples plus Thomas one week after the resurrection. 20:30–31 marks the original conclusion to the gospel, before an editor added the epilogue (chapter 21) and prologue (1:1–18).

In the Book of Glory, the focus of our attention shifts away from Jesus's "own people," the Jews, who "received him not" (1:11), despite his having exhibited signs that would confirm his true identity. Now our focus moves to his disciples, to those "who received Jesus, who believed in his name" (1:12). They are truly "his own" (v. 1), his "sheep" (10:26–28), his "friends" (15:14), his "chosen" (15:16), whom he will send into the world to be his witnesses (17:18), guided by "another Counselor" (14:16), the "Spirit of truth" (16:13). These disciples will reproduce their Master's life, including his suffering and rejection by the world (15:18–20). The Fourth Gospel rarely labels them as "the twelve"[1] and never as "apostles." John deliberately avoids such terms, thus permitting his audience more easily to envision themselves as members of Jesus's faithful community of friends to whom the Book of Glory is addressed. Chapters 13–17 describe how Jesus spends his last night with his friends, loving them, teaching them, consoling them, and preparing them for his departure from the world.

Many New Testament commentators label a large section of the Book of Glory as Jesus's "Last" or "Farewell Discourse."[2] This discourse forms a single, somewhat repetitious literary unit. John constructs it in order to help readers grasp the significance of the events that are about to take place: Jesus's death and resurrection and the sending of the Spirit (chapters 18–20). The goal of the Farewell Discourse in terms of the Fourth Gospel's narrative is to prepare Jesus's disciples for the life they are going

---

1. Only in 6:67–71 and 20:24.

2. A number of commentators describe the Farewell Discourse as beginning with 13:1 and ending with 18:1, when Jesus and the disciples leave the city and walk across the Kidron Valley to a garden on the slopes of the Mount of Olives. I choose to begin the Farewell Discourse with 14:1 and end it with 16:33, since with 17:1 Jesus stops speaking to his friends and begins praying to his Father.

to have after the Son has returned to the Father. They are not to be afraid, for they will not be left all alone. They will be guided by "another Counselor," the Spirit, whom Jesus will send to be with them and in them (14:14–17), as their constant companion.

Chapter Thirteen

John 13:1–30. At the Last Supper, Jesus washes his disciples' feet.

Vv. 1–11. Having loved his own who were in the world, Jesus loves them to the end.

INTRODUCTION. Chapter 13 depicts Jesus's Last Supper with his disciples. John's portrayal of the event is in most respects decidedly unlike the picture given in the Synoptic gospels.[1] Rather than telling about the bread and wine and recording Jesus's so-called "words of institution" of the Eucharist, John describes Jesus as washing the disciples' feet and giving them the new commandment of love (vv. 34–35), obedience to which will identify them to the world as his disciples.

In addition, the Fourth Gospel implies that this last meal of Jesus with his disciples is not a Passover meal (v. 1); instead, it occurs on the evening of the day of preparation of the Passover.[2] Modern readers must keep in mind that the Jews counted days from sunset to sunset, from evening to evening. Thus, a meal taken after sunset would be the first meal of the day. Thus, a supper on Thursday (as we count the days) would by Jewish reckoning be a Friday meal. John's chronology places Jesus's death on the cross at the precise time on Friday, the day of preparation, when priests in the temple are beginning to slay the Passover lambs. Experts have differing opinions about John's Passover chronology. Some regard John as more trustworthy than the Synoptics on this score, while others believe John changes the chronology in order to fit events to

---

1. Cook, "Last Supper and Passover," proposes that the Last Supper was an ordinary meal, but Mark chose "to portray it as a Passover observance by fashioning and inserting a single paragraph between (what we identify as) 14:11 and 17. The proposed insertion revised the time-line of the surrounding original tradition that Jesus was to be arrested before Passover ('not during the feast')."

2. According to the Jewish lunar calendar each new day begins at sunset; therefore, John describes the Last Supper as taking place at the beginning of the day of preparation of the Passover. By our modern reckoning the Supper is on Thursday evening, but by the Jewish calendar Friday had begun. (See 13:30.) Reicke, *New Testament Era*, 180, asserts that the Johannine chronology is historically more likely to be correct than the Synoptic chronology, and that Jesus's Last Supper with his disciples is not the Passover meal.

his understanding of Jesus as the Lamb of God who takes away the sin of the world.[3] There is evidence of banquet-style meals being held on the eve of holy days and weekly on the eve of the Sabbath by pious—usually Pharisee—religious groups known as *chaburah* (from the Hebrew word for "friend"). Some suggest that Jesus and his disciples could have constituted such a *chaburah,* and their supper on the eve of Passover (i.e., Thursday evening) would, therefore, have been a *chaburah* meal.[4] The earliest recorded description of the Last Supper in the New Testament is in 1 Cor 11:23–32, and it makes no mention of the Supper being a Passover. However, in 1 Cor 5:7 Paul writes, "Christ our paschal lamb has been sacrificed," using a metaphor used in John, but not in the Synoptics.[5]

Nevertheless, the question of whether the Last Supper should be seen as a Passover meal cannot be completely resolved. Despite v. 1 indicating that the supper is "before the Feast of the Passover," there are ambiguities in John's description which make his setting for the occasion seem like that of a Passover meal. For example, participants are reclining, which was done by Jews at Passover and formal banquets (including *chaburah* meals), but not at ordinary meals; and Jesus dips a morsel of bread and gives it to Judas, as a host might do with the paste of bitter herbs served at Passover. Some experts propose that Jesus and his followers made use of an older calendar and observed the Passover on an earlier day than most Jews.[6]

Jesus's act of washing the disciples' feet—including those of the traitor, Judas—is the dramatic centerpiece of the Last Supper in John's account. Customarily, a host's servant would wash the feet of guests as an act of hospitality upon their arrival, or they would be provided water to wash their own feet. For the host to perform this servile act in person—and to do so while the guests are reclining at the feast—is extraordinary and unprecedented.[7] Jesus renders a profoundly humble service to his disciples, one they would probably be unwilling to perform for him. This imbues Jesus's washing of his followers' feet with moral power. Disciples would routinely function in most ways as their teacher's servants, gladly doing anything he asks of them. However, that cheerful service typically does not extend to the removing of sandals and washing

---

3. See Brown, *John XIII–XXI,* 555–56; Lindars, *Gospel of John,* 444–46; Smith, *John,* 250. Köstenberger, *Encountering John,* 133, says nothing in John precludes that Jesus's Last Supper with his disciples was a Passover and asserts that in the year of Jesus's crucifixion (which he regards as 33 CE) Passover ran from Thursday evening to Friday evening.

4. Dix, *Shape,* 50–52.

5. Tabor, "Mark," although disputing the historicity of John's portrayal of Jesus, asserts that the Johannine chronology of Jesus's last days has independent authority, granting that the Last Supper was probably not a Passover seder.

6. Humphreys, "Mystery," indicates that a some Jewish sects followed different calendars. According to one of them, Passover was on Wednesday in the year 33 CE. If Jesus and his disciples followed this calendar (and if Jesus died in 33, which is questionable), his Last Supper with the twelve could have been a Wednesday night Passover. John's description of Jesus being crucified on Passover would also be correct, because according to the prevailing calendar, the Passover in 33 was on Friday.

7. Keener, *Gospel of John,* 2:901–4; O'Day, *Gospel of John,* 722.

of feet, and no rabbi would insult a disciple by requesting such menial service from him.[8] According to the Law, not even a Jewish slave could be required to wash his master's feet—a Gentile slave, yes. But a Jewish slave, no.[9]

> **[13:1–11]** *¹ Now before the feast of the Passover, when Jesus knew that his hour had come to depart out of this world to the Father, having loved his own who were in the world, he loved them to the end. ² And during supper, when the devil had already put it into the heart of Judas Iscariot, Simon's son, to betray him, ³ Jesus, knowing that the Father had given all things into his hands, and that he had come from God and was going to God, ⁴ rose from supper, laid aside his garments, and girded himself with a towel. ⁵ Then he poured water into a basin, and began to wash the disciples' feet, and to wipe them with the towel with which he was girded. ⁶ He came to Simon Peter; and Peter said to him, "Lord, do you wash my feet?" ⁷ Jesus answered him, "What I am doing you do not know now, but afterward you will understand." ⁸ Peter said to him, "You shall never wash my feet." Jesus answered him, "If I do not wash you, you have no part in me." ⁹ Simon Peter said to him, "Lord, not my feet only but also my hands and my head!" ¹⁰ Jesus said to him, "He who has bathed does not need to wash, except for his feet, but he is clean all over; and you are clean, but not every one of you." ¹¹ For he knew who was to betray him; that was why he said, "You are not all clean."*

RESPONSE. The words with which John introduces this story are serious and deserve our attention. The Beloved Disciple writes, "Now before the feast of the Passover, when Jesus knew that his hour had come to depart out of this world to the Father, *having loved his own who were in the world, he loved them to the end*" (v. 1).

We must be clear about the meaning of the word "love" used in John's Gospel, a meaning which is always the same, no matter which of two different Greek words the author uses to name it.[10] Our psychology-focused age reflexively understands love as an *emotion*, something we feel in response to the behavior, beauty, or desirable qualities we find in others. However, the Bible portrays God's love as an act of the divine will, a gift. Such love is God's *choice*, not God's response to anyone or anything.

---

8. See Morris, *Gospel according to John*, 141; Köstenberger, *Encountering John*, 242. There is evidence that, on occasion, a disciple would offer to wash his rabbi's feet as a gesture of respect, but that would only be a voluntary, unexpected act.

9. Smith, *John*, 252.

10. The Greek word most frequently used in the New Testament to name God's love for human beings as well as our love for God and one another in Christ is the verb *agapaō* (and the cognate noun, *agapē*). The verb *phileō* (and the corresponding noun, *philia*), which in more formal Greek implied affection and friendship, is occasionally used, but experts suggest that we would be wrong to read distinctions into the meaning of the two words as used in the New Testament. They are more or less semantically interchangeable. See Keener, *Gospel of John*, 2:1004n159.

The Hebrew Scriptures say that God chooses Israel. Neither God's decision to reveal himself to Abraham, nor his love for the children of Abraham, is a response to loveable qualities they display. Indeed, the people of Israel are consistently pictured in the Old Testament as stubborn, rebellious, willful, and disobedient, yet God chooses—for God's own reasons—to show them favor, to care tenderly for them and—as we might put it—to deliberately befriend them.

God's love for his people is expressed in covenant faithfulness (i.e., unshakable loyalty), steadfast kindness, compassion, justice, mercy, and patience. The New Testament shows these also as characteristics of the love of Christ for his disciples—a love grounded in obedience to his Father, who entrusted this little flock to him. Jesus says about them, "My sheep hear my voice, and I know them. They follow me; and I give them eternal life. They shall never perish, and no one shall snatch them out of my hand" (10:27). Now that his hour has come, the good shepherd is going to share a last supper with the disciples the Father has given him. He will use every available means on this final evening together to help them understand that what is about to happen on the following day is really an expression of his love for them—and is essential to the Father's plan, not just for their future, but the future of the world he came to save. The opening verse of this section colors everything Jesus says and does from this point until the moment when, on the cross, he utters the words, "It is finished," bows his head and gives up his spirit.[11]—"Having loved his own who were in the world, he loved them to the end" (v. 1).

Most Americans in our time don't readily comprehend what life was like in the stratified, slave-owning, first century social order. It's difficult to picture ourselves, or anyone else, as a menial person of no status—technically a "living tool" according to Roman Law—a chattel servant utterly at the owner's disposal, expected to labor from before dawn until after dark at dirty and difficult tasks with no compensation. For most of us, nothing in our personal experience equips us to connect with such a life. We can scarcely imagine being required to sleep every night on the hard floor of a corridor outside our owner's bedroom so that we'll be able to respond instantly if summoned, or being subjected to a brutal whipping when the master is not pleased with us. Slaves in a Roman household spent their lives in trembling awareness that they could be crucified at their master's pleasure. Even if we are aware of those facts of ancient history, they don't ordinarily enter our minds when we read John's familiar story of Jesus washing his disciples' dirty feet—assuming the role of the lowest-ranking servant in a Jewish household. As the eyewitness who describes these things sees it, the self-sacrifice of the Lamb of God begins right here.[12] "All we like sheep have gone astray; we have turned every one to his own way; and the Lord has laid on him the iniquity of us all" (Isa 53:6).

---

11. Gibson, "Johannine Footwashing," 4.

12. Lindars, *Gospel of John*, 449.

This moment is the turning point in the Fourth Gospel's grand narrative of the world's redemption: "Jesus, knowing that the Father had given all things into his hands, and that he had come from God and was going to God, rose from supper, laid aside his garments, and girded himself with a towel. Then he poured water into a basin, and began to wash the disciples' feet, and to wipe them with the towel with which he was girded" (vv. 3–5). Unlike the Synoptics, John does not depict Jesus going down into the Jordan to be baptized along with the repentant multitudes. But the footwashing scene has the same significance; it portrays the divine Son as choosing to identify with sinners.[13] He gives himself to them. This is his mission; he has been sent into the world for their sake.

The men reclining, Greco-Roman-style, side-by-side on dining couches surrounding three sides of a square dining table know very well who is supposed to do the washing of feet, even in a modest Jewish household. Footwashing is always done by the lowest-ranking person, a female Gentile slave if one is available. When there are no menials on hand to serve them, the host provides water and guests wash their own feet. It's no exaggeration to say that Jesus's disciples are stunned by his behavior. There's probably nothing else he could do that would shock them more. We may imagine them lying in paralyzed silence as their Master kneels at each one's feet, removes each man's sandals, and begins this degrading servile task. Theirs is a very traditional and structured, hierarchical society. Jesus's behavior violates everything they have been taught about what is correct and what is improper. The disciples are aware that if long-standing rules of social propriety are to be abrogated in such a way, it is clearly *they* who should be washing their Master's feet, not the other way around. And let us not overlook the fact that although in John's story world Jesus knows precisely what Judas Iscariot is going to do, he treats the traitor the same way he treats everyone else at the table. He renders him a humble and tender personal service.

No one seems to know how to respond or what to say. That is left to Peter, the most outspoken of the disciples. Even after watching Jesus go around the table, he still acts befuddled. He doesn't grasp what's happening. The Greek text makes Peter's emphatic pronouns clear, "Do *you* wash *my* feet?" Jesus replies, "You don't understand this right now, but the time is coming when it will all make sense to you" (paraphrase of v. 7).

Peter's refusal is adamant, "No. Never in a million years will I let *you* wash my feet!" Then Jesus tells him, "If I don't wash you this way, then you will have no share in me" (paraphrase of vv. 7–8). Now the meaning becomes clear. This humble act is one by which Jesus links his followers' lives to his own. It is his gift to them. It makes a point related to the one he made in Capernaum at the previous Passover: "Unless you

---

13. It's worth noting that John the Baptist speaks of Jesus as one "the thong of whose sandals I am not worthy to untie" (Luke 4:16a). This might be regarded as the hint of a connection between John's footwashing story and the Synoptics' account of Jesus being baptized. Presumably, in 13:4 we should presume that Jesus unties the sandals of all the disciples before he washes their feet.

eat the flesh of the Son of Man and drink his blood, you have no life in you" (6:53). His disciples must accept Jesus's serving them in this way, just as they must ultimately come to embrace the gift of his death for them. They do not deserve either gift, of course. They have no claim on such treatment. Yet, it is God's choice. God's grace. God's love. God's glory.

Such a love must be understood and owned. The recipient must welcome and receive the gift, or it becomes null and void. Judas Iscariot, like the others, is washed. Like the others, he will receive the bread and the cup. But Judas is not cleansed (see vv. 10*b*–11). His life is not united with his Master's. He will have no share in him.

Vv. 12–30. Jesus's humble service to his disciples is an example for them.

INTRODUCTION. Jesus, his disciples' teacher and Lord, chooses to humble himself and serve his followers in the lowliest and most unthinkable of all ways, by stooping to wash their feet. John shows that this gesture of Jesus is much more than simply an example of humble service for his disciples to imitate (vv. 12–15). Our gospel writer means for it to prefigure the self-oblation of Jesus, the Suffering Servant, which is to follow on the morrow, about which the apostle Paul had written to the Christians in Philippi some thirty years earlier: "Christ Jesus . . . though he was in the form of God, did not count equality with God a thing to be grasped, but emptied himself, taking the form of a servant, being born in the likeness of men. And being found in human form, he humbled himself and became obedient unto death, even death on a cross" (Phil 2:5–8).

Verse 20, "Truly, truly, I say to you, he who receives any one whom I send receives me; and he who receives me receives him who sent me," anticipates what the risen Lord will say to these disciples—minus Thomas—when they gather behind locked doors on the evening of the day of resurrection: "As the Father has sent me, even so I send you" (20:21). The Father sent his Son into the world to be his unique agent, to reveal him, proclaim his words, and accomplish his life-giving work. In the same way, after the resurrection the Son will send his disciples to be his own agents, to reveal him (and, in revealing him, to make known the Father also), to speak for him, and to do even "greater works" than he himself has done (14:12).[14]

In v. 23 John names for the first time the "disciple whom Jesus loved," and indicates that he is reclining at Jesus's right on the dining couch, "close to the breast of Jesus." This position permits the Beloved Disciple to lean to his left, putting his head against Jesus's chest, to whisper Peter's question about his betrayer's identity. It also appears that the person reclining on Jesus's left, the place of honor on such formal occasions, is none other than the betrayer himself, Judas Iscariot—since only a person in that position would be near enough for Jesus to pass him a morsel (v. 26). The irony

14. Lockwood, "Spiritual Fatherhood," 98.

of Judas being in the seat of honor is easily missed by most of us, since only specialists in the subject are familiar with the seating hierarchy applied on such occasions.

[13:12–30] *¹² When he had washed their feet, and taken his garments, and resumed his place, he said to them, "Do you know what I have done to you? ¹³ You call me Teacher and Lord; and you are right, for so I am. ¹⁴ If I then, your Lord and Teacher, have washed your feet, you also ought to wash one another's feet. ¹⁵ For I have given you an example, that you also should do as I have done to you. ¹⁶ Truly, truly, I say to you, a servant is not greater than his master; nor is he who is sent greater than he who sent him. ¹⁷ If you know these things, blessed are you if you do them. ¹⁸ I am not speaking of you all; I know whom I have chosen; it is that the Scripture may be fulfilled, 'He who ate my bread has lifted his heel against me.' ¹⁹ I tell you this now, before it takes place, that when it does take place you may believe that I am he. ²⁰ Truly, truly, I say to you, he who receives any one whom I send receives me; and he who receives me receives him who sent me."*

²¹ When Jesus had thus spoken, he was troubled in spirit, and testified, "Truly, truly, I say to you, one of you will betray me." ²² The disciples looked at one another, uncertain of whom he spoke. ²³ One of his disciples, whom Jesus loved, was lying close to the breast of Jesus; ²⁴ so Simon Peter beckoned to him and said, "Tell us who it is of whom he speaks." ²⁵ So lying thus, close to the breast of Jesus, he said to him, "Lord, who is it?" ²⁶ Jesus answered, "It is he to whom I shall give this morsel when I have dipped it." So when he had dipped the morsel, he gave it to Judas, the son of Simon Iscariot. ²⁷ Then after the morsel, Satan entered into him. Jesus said to him, "What you are going to do, do quickly." ²⁸ Now no one at the table knew why he said this to him. ²⁹ Some thought that, because Judas had the money box, Jesus was telling him, "Buy what we need for the feast"; or, that he should give something to the poor. ³⁰ So, after receiving the morsel, he immediately went out; and it was night.

RESPONSE. John's imagery in vv. 4–12 is full of paradox. When Jesus removes his outer garment, wraps a towel around his waist, and kneels to wash each one's feet (vv. 4–5), the reality of God's glory is disclosed to the disciples at the supper. This is a theophany parallel in many ways to the Synoptic portrayal of the transfiguration. But here in John's Gospel, the glory of God is disclosed in servant love—not dazzling light. When Jesus completes his labor, lays aside the towel, puts his robe back on and resumes his place at the table, the moment of "transfiguration" has passed. The disciples now see only Jesus's usual appearance: a traditional Jewish teacher in the company of his faithful disciples at a fellowship meal. They don't comprehend that what they just witnessed is in truth a divine revelation, though in due time the Spirit will lead them to remember and understand.

The message of all four gospels is that the way of the Lord and the way of his disciples must be the same.[15] The disciple must reproduce the life of the Master. Jesus asks those who are at table with him, "Do you know what I have done to you? You call me Teacher and Lord; and you are right, for so I am. If I then, your Lord and Teacher, have washed your feet, you also ought to wash one another's feet. For I have given you an example, that you also should do as I have done to you. Truly, truly, I say to you, a servant is not greater than his master; nor is he who is sent greater than he who sent him" (vv. 12b–16).

Many churches practice the washing of feet as a ritual on the evening of Thursday in Holy Week, just before Good Friday. This is an emotional experience, as many of us can personally testify. The ceremony is all the more precious when it inspires us to discover new ways of humbly serving one another in our ordinary lives.

Church history shows that striving for status, prestige, and primacy over other Christians is an endemic affliction of the church, one that goes all the way back to the inner circle of Jesus's followers. Luke records that, even at the Last Supper, the disciples dispute about which one of them should be deemed "the greatest" (Luke 22:24). Yet, Jesus teaches them that "the servant is not greater than his master." Ideally, all pastors, whether their place on the ecclesiastical organizational chart is low or high, endeavor to embody in their ministries the descriptive title ironically claimed since the Dark Ages by the Bishops of Rome: "servant of the servants of God." Blessed are such servants (v. 17).

Verse 18 is challenging to understand. The language is ambiguous, perhaps intentionally: "I know whom I have chosen." Does John mean that Jesus called Judas to be a disciple, knowing that in spite of being chosen, Judas would betray him? Or does he mean that Jesus has not really chosen Judas in the same way he chose the others, and so Judas will betray him?[16] Either reading is possible. I understand it this way: Judas is a man Jesus himself called. Just like the others, he was chosen. Now Judas makes his own choice to betray the Master who trusted and honored him (v. 18). John can only explain such unfaithfulness as the work of Satan—the fallen angel, the enemy of God.

What kind of impulse, what sort of need, would drive a friend to betray a dear friend? Such an act could only happen if the betrayer loves himself more than he loves his friend. Inordinate self-love permits us to use those who love us in order to get what we want. Satisfying our own dark desires becomes more important than anything else.

At the supper, Jesus knows what Judas is going to do, and he doesn't move to stop him. He only says, "What you have to do, do quickly." But what about the others who were there at the table? Do we ever think about them, about what they could have done? At the supper table Jesus tells the Beloved Disciple (and we assume he tells Peter) that Judas is going to betray him. Why don't the Beloved Disciple and Peter do

---

15. Marsh, *Saint John*, 485.

16. Ibid., 491.

something to stop him? Could it be that Jesus is waiting to see what they will do, once they know?

Why is it that none of the friends of Jesus there at the table can see that Jesus's own patient, selfless love calls for the active expression of *their* love in order to exercise its power? Is it possible that Jesus went to the cross because the others at the table that night were unable to take the risk of loving the potential betrayer enough to intervene? That makes them accomplices in the betrayal, does it not?

In our contemporary context, each of us has an opportunity to betray the Lord. Maybe we would never be as treacherous as Judas. But we might be like the Beloved Disciple or Peter, accomplices in someone else's act of betrayal—too weak or too afraid or too timid to reach out to stop a fellow believer who is walking away from the light into the darkness.

John regularly shows Jesus possessing miraculous insight, perceiving the secrets of other hearts. Though he is aware of the role Judas is playing, he makes no move to block him from his treacherous deed. Instead, he says, "What you are going to do, do quickly" (v. 27). Jesus knows what's going on, and he intends to drink the cup that the Father gives him (see 18:11).—The Lord sees the secret intentions of our hearts.— What does he see in us?

John 13:31–38. The betrayer goes out. Jesus gives his disciples a new commandment.

Vv. 31–38. "By this all men will know that you are my disciples, if you have love for one another."

INTRODUCTION. The betrayer goes out into the darkness to set in motion the political machinery that will take Jesus to the cross. Once Judas exits the room, Jesus announces to his disciples, "Now is the Son of Man glorified, and in him God is glorified" (v. 31). The glory of the Father and the Son is about to be made visible in the Son's laying down of his life for the flock the Father has given him—and for the world, the object of God's love. His washing of the disciples' feet a few minutes earlier was an anticipation of the greater self-offering which will take place tomorrow. (In similar fashion, the transfiguration event portrayed in the Synoptics is a revelation of the glory of Jesus's resurrection.)

The disciples cannot go where Jesus is going now because they don't yet understand the gift of his life laid down in love. They are not ready to pass this gift along by laying down their own lives. Not yet. But afterwards, when Jesus is raised from the dead, he will send the Spirit-Paraclete to teach them and help them understand how to follow where the good shepherd has led the way. Jesus gives them his new commandment in this context, before the Passion Narrative, because for the disciples to love one another as he has loved them demands readiness to die for one another.[17] Peter, grasping the gravity of the moment, imagines himself ready to follow Jesus to death immediately (as Thomas had said a week earlier, 11:16), but Peter and his companions have no idea of what an ordeal the next hours will bring.

Some commentators treat Jesus's Farewell Discourse as starting with v. 31, after Judas has departed, since there is a shift of mood at this point, as Jesus begins to speak to them about his going away (v. 33). Other commentators begin his final discourse with 14:1, because what Jesus says in 14:1–16:33 is spoken to all the disciples (using the second person plural), whereas vv. 36–38 compose a private dialogue with Peter, in which Jesus addresses the lack of realism in Peter's bold claim of willingness to die for his Master. Such formal literary divisions are obviously artificial. For the sake of simplicity in organizing the material, I regard the contents of chapters 14–16 as constituting Jesus's Farewell Discourse.[18]

> [13:31–38] [31] *When he had gone out, Jesus said, "Now is the Son of man glorified, and in him God is glorified;* [32] *if God is glorified in him, God will also glorify him in himself, and glorify him at once.* [33] *Little children, yet a little while I am with you. You will seek me; and as I said to the Jews so now I say to you, 'Where I am going you cannot come.'* [34] *A new commandment I give to you, that you love one another; even as I have loved you, that you also love one another.* [35] *By this all men will know that you are my disciples, if you have love for one another."*
>
> [36] *Simon Peter said to him, "Lord, where are you going?" Jesus answered, "Where I am going you cannot follow me now; but you shall follow afterward."* [37] *Peter said to him, "Lord, why cannot I follow you now? I will lay down my life for you."* [38] *Jesus answered, "Will you lay down your life for me? Truly, truly, I say to you, the cock will not crow, till you have denied me three times."*

RESPONSE. That which Jesus demonstrates by his footwashing manifestation of self-denying love, he now commands his disciples to continue. Paradoxically, by assuming the task of a slave Jesus refuses the status-based, false glory of this world and discloses the glory of God to those who believe in him.[19] In time, his followers' obedience to the Lord's new commandment will draw them into sharing their Master's role. Their love for one another will reveal the glory of God to the world, just as God's glory is revealed through Jesus's love for them. After Judas departs, Jesus tells his disciples they should "keep his commandments" (14:15, 21; 15:10); however, a review of John's Gospel shows that nowhere does he specifically identify other commandments. The Beloved Disciple describes only one: "love one another; even as I have loved you" (v. 34).

17. Keener, *Gospel of John*, 2:923.
18. O'Day, *Gospel of John*, 735.
19. Smith, *John*, 259.

By itself, the commandment to love isn't new for Jews (see Lev 19:18). They are taught that love of neighbor is, at least in principle, a foundation of community life. But there is no definitive model for the shape such love should take. What's truly new about Jesus's commandment is that it provides a standard, an example worthy of imitation: "love one another; *even as I have loved you.*" By laying down his life for others, Jesus demonstrates that he loves his disciples more than he loves his own life. In teaching right behavior, Jewish sages had long taught that God's people were to imitate the character of God as revealed in the Torah. Now, for followers of Jesus, imitation of God is perfectly modeled by the servant Christ, especially by his self-sacrifice.[20] In another example of the occasional overlap between Paul's thinking and that of the Fourth Gospel, we see this standard expressly identified in the Letter to the Ephesians, "Be imitators of God, as beloved children. And walk in love, as Christ loved us and gave himself up for us, a fragrant offering and sacrifice to God" (Eph 5:1–2).

Commentators on John point out that the community for which the gospel seems to be written places its emphasis on love for one another *within* the community, the church.[21] First John, a very useful lens through which to understand the Fourth Gospel, stresses the vocation of disciples to practice love for the brethren—obviously implying the members of their Christian community. However, it is fair to say that neither John's Gospel nor First John cautions *against* practicing love for those who are outside the church. John tells his readers that God loves "the world" (3:16), and the love practiced by Jesus's followers is intended to identify them in the eyes of "all men" (v. 35). I am convinced that Jesus never meant his disciples' love to be restricted exclusively to one another within the boundaries of a closed fellowship, but rather that the practice of indiscriminate compassionate charity towards all should be forever known as *the* defining characteristic of his followers.

History attests that this is precisely what would soon come to pass. Late second century documents show that Christians—still a small minority—routinely translated Jesus's precept of love for one another into a practice of community social service. During the plagues and epidemics that often ravaged their cities, Christians would make it a rule to nurse and care for all church members and often extended the same loving attention to their sick and dying non-Christian friends. Nursing of plague victims was virtually unknown in the ancient world; pagans commonly abandoned even their nearest and dearest, leaving them to die unattended in the streets. Christians' methodical practice of love and mercy for one another and even for people outside their own religious community *as aspects of an obligation to God* was unprecedented in the ancient world. The very idea that a deity might care whether mortals loved one another was unknown in antiquity, *except* within Judaism. Pagan plague victims who

---

20. Keener, *Gospel of John*, 2:924.
21. See, e.g., Brown, *John XIII–XXI*, 613–14; Kysar, *John*, 217–18; Smith, *John*, 260.

owed their survival to the care they received from Christian friends would obviously be inclined to join their friends' community.[22]

I like the way John Marsh in his commentary on John describes the love of Jesus for his disciples, the love he here commands them to imitate:

> In a word, it is to be love of the kind that will 'reverse the roles,' and bring the leader to serve as a slave, and the innocent to serve as the guilty, in the love that will bring peace to the world by its sacrificial quality. It will be love that, like Christ's love for his own, does not ask questions about worthiness, but simply gives itself in humble service. It is much like the love sometimes crudely demanded in a fairy story, where a kiss is demanded for some loathsome creature. For such has been the love of God for men, and the love of Jesus for his own.[23]

As long as the love of Christ is manifested by his disciples in the world, the world is still encountering Jesus.

Doing Your Own Theology

Questions for reflection after reading John 13.

- The words with which John introduces his story of Jesus's washing his disciples' feet at the Last Supper are serious and deserve our attention. He writes, "Now before the feast of the Passover, when Jesus knew that his hour had come to depart out of this world to the Father, having loved his own who were in the world, he loved them to the end" (v. 1). Our psychology-focused age reflexively understands love as an emotion, something we *feel* in response to the behavior, beauty, or desirable qualities we see in others. However, the Bible portrays God's love as an act of the divine will, a gift. Such love is God's *choice*, not God's response to anyone or anything.—*In modeling God's love for people, how do you choose to love others? To what extent do you choose to love others to whom you are not close, by whom you are challenged, and whom you dislike? If you choose to love them in spite of your feelings towards them, does your relationship with them change? Jesus expresses his love for his Father through obedience and expresses his love for his disciples through the actions that obedience demands. Can you describe ways you express your love for God through obedience and your love for others through obedient action?*

22. Stark, *Rise*, 76–94.
23. Marsh, *Saint John*, 496.

- The Beloved Disciple remembers every detail of Jesus' Last Supper with his friends, and what he recalls most vividly is not the sharing of the food, but Jesus's act of self-disclosure in servant love. Their Master assumes the role of the humblest servant in a household: he washes the dirty feet of every guest. This virtually unprecedented behavior stuns the disciples. Jesus knows Judas is going to betray him—which the others do not know—yet he washes Judas's feet just as he does the feet of the others. He even puts Judas in the place of honor at the table.—*Why do you think the footwashing made such a profound impression on John? What do the details of this story tell you about Jesus's love? Can you remember a time when God called you to cross social boundaries or violate community norms in obedience to him, to manifest his love for the world?*

- In western culture, Judas has become the archetypal traitorous friend. What kind of impulse, what sort of need, would drive a friend to betray a dear friend? Such an act could only happen if the betrayer loves himself more than he loves his friend. Inordinate self-love permits us to use those who love us in order to get what we want. Satisfying our own dark desires becomes more important than anything else. Judas is a man Jesus himself called. Just like the others, he was chosen. Now Judas is making his own choice to betray the Master who trusted and honored him (v. 18). John can only explain this unfaithfulness as the work of Satan—the fallen angel, the enemy of God. At the supper table Jesus tells the Beloved Disciple (and we assume he tells Peter) that Judas is going to betray him.—*Why do the Beloved Disciple and Peter fail to stop Judas, once Jesus has told them what their friend is about to do? Does their remaining inert make them morally complicit in Judas's betrayal? Why do you think John tells us this little "story within the story"?*

A General Introduction to Chapters 14–16.
The Farewell Discourse

There is not a sharp division between what Jesus says to his disciples, gathered around the table after he has washed their feet, and the so-called Farewell Discourse. However, a shift in *mood* does take place at 13:31, after Judas the betrayer leaves the room. Except for Jesus's dialogue with Peter, vv. 36–38, warning him not to be so confident about his readiness to sacrifice himself for his Master, the gospel writer constructs his narrative to the end of chapter 16 as Jesus's formal farewell, ostensibly spoken to his friends on the night before he was crucified. Although some commentators include chapter 17 in the Farewell Discourse since it is set within the same context, I choose to treat chapter 17 as unique, mainly because Jesus's words in this chapter are not addressed to his disciples. Instead, they constitute a prayer addressed aloud to his Father, presumably uttered in the hearing of his friends. At the end of the prayer, traditionally labeled Jesus's "High Priestly Prayer," Jesus and the disciples leave the walled city, cross the brook Kidron, and go up to the garden on the Mount of Olives (which is named *Gethsemane* only in Mark and Matthew).

The farewell or last testament is a common genre in ancient literature. There are a number of examples in the Old Testament, including the entire book of Deuteronomy, which is presented in the Pentateuch as Moses' farewell address to the Hebrew people.[1] Jesus's Farewell Discourse tells his disciples to anticipate the coming of the Paraclete, identifying the Holy Spirit by a Greek title usually given to one who functions as advocate or intercessor for someone else—a noun found in no New Testament Book except John's Gospel and First John.[2] The RSV usually translates this term as "Counselor," and identifies the Counselor as the "Spirit of truth" whom Jesus says "the Father will send in my name" (v. 26).[3] One of the principal works of the Spirit-Paraclete, the Counselor, when he comes, will be to "teach you all things and bring to your remembrance all that I have said to you" (v. 27). Many modern commentators agree that the discourse itself must be understood as a product of reflection, remembrance, and inspiration imparted to the Beloved Disciple—and his editor—by "the Counselor,

1. Examples of this genre in the Old Testament and other ancient literature are described in Brown, *John XIII–XXI*, 597–601, and O'Day, *Gospel of John*, 737–39.

2. The word *paraklētos* is found, outside of the Fourth Gospel, only in 1 John 2:1 in the NT, where it is translated as "advocate" in the RSV: "If anyone does sin, we have an advocate with the Father, Jesus Christ the righteous." The related verb, *parakaleō* (meaning "call to one's side" or "appeal to"), however, occurs 109 times in the NT.

3. The word can also be translated as "advocate" (see 1 John 2:1), "mediator," or "helper," even perhaps "interpreter." "Comforter," the translation used in the King James Version, is less satisfactory.

the Spirit of truth" (vv. 16–17). In the years following the resurrection, the promised Spirit-Paraclete comes to be recognized by Jesus's followers as the Spirit of the risen One himself, abiding with them and continuing to teach them.[4]

The frequent questions asked of Jesus and comments made by his disciples during this Farewell Discourse call attention to their relatively dim perception and failure to grasp the cosmic objective of Jesus's mission and the deep truth of his identity, though they do love him and have sincerely committed themselves to him. At several points in the discourse Jesus draws a specific contrast between how they understand things now and how they will understand later. There is a great deal yet for them to be shown, and much for them to learn from the Spirit-Paraclete, but there is a sharp difference between their authentic trust in Jesus and the skeptical unbelief of the crowds who do not know what to make of him.[5]

As we read the Farewell Discourse, we discern that portions of it could easily have been words spoken by the historical Jesus after the Last Supper, although much of it has a timeless quality—as if uttered by the risen and ascended Lord, addressing his disciples from the perspective of eternity. For example, in the very last words of this discourse, portrayed as spoken on the eve of the crucifixion, Jesus tells his friends, "In the world you have tribulation; but be of good cheer, I have overcome the world" (16:33). This triumphant affirmation at the end of the Thursday night discourse describes "the world"—meaning in this case the power of Satan, sin, and death that pervades all human society—as *already* defeated, even though readers of the gospel know that, chronologically, the cross and resurrection by which the Savior's victory will be won, are yet to come. The resurrection is three days in the future.

This way of thinking should not surprise us, however, because it is consistent with what we have already encountered in John, whose post-Easter theological perspective is plain to see, beginning with the gospel's prologue. Gail R. O'Day writes that the Beloved Disciple, in constructing for his gospel's earliest readers a Farewell Discourse of Jesus, "which glides without notice from past, to present, to future, shows how God's new age is already shaping his disciples' lives . . . The future for which they wait is already underway, because Jesus's 'future' victory is in fact [their] present reality."[6]

Readers will notice a great deal of circularity and repetition in the Farewell Discourse, which some commentators explain by attributing it to an editor who chooses to weave together two alternative versions of a single account, just as the editors of Genesis combined two creation narratives.[7] Repetition is a common rhetorical

---

4. This is elaborated in Burge, *Anointed Community*, 137–43. In Rom 8:9–10, Paul identifies the Spirit with Christ, writing, "You are not in the flesh, you are in the Spirit, if the Spirit of God really dwells in you. Anyone who does not have the Spirit of Christ does not belong to him."

5. Hurtado, "Remembering and Revelation," 199–200.

6. O'Day, *Gospel of John*, 738.

7. Kysar, *John*, 219–20.

technique in ancient literature, however, and John's Farewell Discourse—although obviously repetitious—exhibits both literary unity and a clear progression of thought.

Chapter Fourteen

John 14:1–31. The Farewell Discourse begins. Jesus prepares his disciples for his departure.

Vv. 1–11. "I am the way, and the truth, and the life."

INTRODUCTION. The Farewell Discourse is going to reveal to us the depth of Jesus's empathy and emotional sensitivity to his disciples. A compassionate tone is evident in chapter 14 and will be sustained throughout the extended farewell. Points Jesus makes in this section are going to be reiterated and elaborated upon in chapters 15 and 16.

In 13:33 Jesus tells his disciples, "Yet a little while I am with you. You will seek me; and as I said to the Jews so now I say to you, 'Where I am going you cannot come.'" This announcement creates a context both for Jesus's dialogue with Peter (13:36–38), who quickly asserts his readiness to follow him anywhere, even to the death, and for the opening section of chapter 14. In 14:1–3 Jesus counsels his friends not to be troubled (or "terrified") by these words about his imminent departure, but to trust that he is going away "to prepare a place" for them in his Father's "house," using a Greek word we could also translate as his Father's "household." "Household" offers a more nuanced image than "house," implying more about intimacy of community and essential connectedness with the Father than merely a place of residence.

The Greek word translated "place" in v. 2, is found nowhere else in the New Testament except in v. 23 of this same chapter, where the RSV translates it as "home." In that verse Jesus tells his disciples that in the future both he and the Father will come and "make our home" with anyone who loves Jesus and keeps his word. We have observed that the use of words or expressions which allow a variety of possible meanings is typical of the Fourth Gospel. The Farewell Discourse can be interpreted as speaking both of the disciples' future entrance into God's heavenly home after this earthly life has ended—a traditional Jewish expectation—and also of their coming to enjoy, in the midst of this mortal life, a new and amazing degree of intimacy with God, a genuine mutual indwelling. The latter is an entirely novel idea, growing out of Jesus's own unity with the Father. Since the Greek word in question is formed from a verb that means "to abide" or "remain," a verb used often in John, the thought behind both v. 2 and v. 23 surely has more to do with an enduring relationship than only with a place.[1] In any case, both of these future states of being depend on Jesus's "going away" from the disciples right now.

It is interesting that nothing in this part of the Farewell Discourse explicitly states that Jesus's departure is going to be through death, especially an agonized and shameful death by crucifixion. Of course, he already has fled an attempt by the temple authorities to stone him for blasphemy (10:31–39), and Peter's expression of willingness to lay down his life for Jesus (13:37) implies that the disciples know their Master's life is in danger. Still, Jesus's friends might logically assume he is speaking of going away from Judea for safety's sake, traveling in a way they would be unlikely to share, perhaps a sea voyage. However, we must keep in mind that the gospel writer's intended audience for this Farewell Discourse is—in fact—not really the little band of disciples at the supper table that Thursday night, but the early community of believers, a body of people who already know the details of the story.

Verse 6, "I am the way, and the truth, and the life; no one comes to the Father, but by me," is one of the seminal theological statements of John's Gospel. It is another of Jesus's revelatory "I Am" pronouncements, and offers readers a profound subject for reflection. It calls attention again to the revelation of God's nature which depends on the single individual, Jesus of Nazareth. This is an exclusive claim, another incidence of the so-called scandal of particularity.[2] One can say that John sees Jesus as "*the* way" to the Father because, as the Beloved Disciple has told us from the very beginning of his gospel (e.g., 1:4, 14, and 17), Jesus is "the truth" and "the life."[3] He is "all that humans need in order to find release from the realm of darkness and misunderstanding."[4]

It is important that contemporary readers of John not treat v. 6 as a proud claim that Christians can assert against Jews, Muslims, Buddhists or any other religious community. John is writing from the perspective of first century Judaism, addressing his book to fellow members of a small and beleaguered sect of Jews who have been inspired to worship Jesus as the Son of God. Christians in our age misread the gospel if we treat v. 6 as a proclamation Christ intended to be employed two thousand years later in a contest between rival monotheistic world religions, competing with one another for the souls of the masses. It is also essential to note that Jesus does not say no one "comes *to God*" except through him. What he says is, "No one comes *to the Father* but by me." The crucial and unique claim of Christians is our vision of Jesus as the way to a personal relationship with God *as Father*. Only Christianity explicitly invites all

1. Kysar, *John*, 221.
2. See Keener, *Gospel of John*, 2:941–42.
3. Brown, *John XIII–XXI*, 621.
4. Kysar, *John*, 223.

people to see God as their Father, and Jesus's own way of speaking about God, evident in all four gospels, demonstrates his consciousness of an intimate, filial connection with God.[5]

Philip, who in 1:45 proclaims his early confidence that Jesus is the one "of whom Moses in the law and also the prophets wrote," now shows that—despite three years as a disciple—his belief in Jesus is still not yet all it could be. He asks Jesus to "show us the Father" (v. 9), and Jesus replies, "Do you not believe that I am in the Father and the Father in me?" (v. 10). He invites Philip to believe more deeply, another affirmation that—for John—*believing is seeing.*

> **[14:1–11]** [1] *"Let not your hearts be troubled; believe in God, believe also in me.* [2] *In my Father's house are many rooms; if it were not so, would I have told you that I go to prepare a place for you?* [3] *And when I go and prepare a place for you, I will come again and will take you to myself, that where I am you may be also.* [4] *And you know the way where I am going."* [5] *Thomas said to him, "Lord, we do not know where you are going; how can we know the way?"* [6] *Jesus said to him, "I am the way, and the truth, and the life; no one comes to the Father, but by me.* [7] *If you had known me, you would have known my Father also; henceforth you know him and have seen him."*
>
> [8] *Philip said to him, "Lord, show us the Father, and we shall be satisfied."* [9] *Jesus said to him, "Have I been with you so long, and yet you do not know me, Philip? He who has seen me has seen the Father; how can you say, 'Show us the Father'?* [10] *Do you not believe that I am in the Father and the Father in me? The words that I say to you I do not speak on my own authority; but the Father who dwells in me does his works.* [11] *Believe me that I am in the Father and the Father in me; or else believe me for the sake of the works themselves.*

RESPONSE. I have preached so many sermons at funerals using John 14:1–6 as my text that I am able to recite much of it from memory. This is magnificent language: "Let not your hearts be troubled; believe in God, believe also in me. In my Father's house are many rooms; if it were not so, would I have told you that I go to prepare a place for you? And when I go and prepare a place for you, I will come again and will take you to myself, that where I am you may be also" (vv. 1–3).

Nothing is more comforting to a grieving community of Christian friends and family members than this assurance from the lips of Jesus that the parent, spouse, or friend they love and for whom they mourn has now taken Jesus's hand and gone with him to a new, eternal abiding place in his heavenly Father's house, a home that our departed loved one will share with Christ himself—and one day also with us. This is

---

5. McNab, *Finding the Way*, 46; O'Day, *Gospel of John*, 744. In Mark 14:36 Jesus addresses God as *Abba*, the intimate name by which a Jewish child addressed his father. Paul asserts, in Gal 4:6, that "God has sent the Spirit of his Son into our hearts, crying, '*Abba!* Father!'"

not a novel way of understanding the promise of these words of Jesus to his disciples after their last supper together. The interpretation dates at least back to Irenaeus in the second century, and may be much older.[6] It is particularly apt if we think of Jesus as having his own imminent death in mind when he talks to his friends and bids them farewell on Thursday night before he goes to the cross. This way of reading the material is sentimental, but sentiment is appropriate under these circumstances. When we deal with our sorrow at the death of someone we love, trying to cope with the prospect of a lifetime without the companionship of a dear parent, spouse, or friend, Christ's promise of a future reunion in his presence gives us hope and solace.

If we assume that the disciples are conscious that this is their last evening with Jesus, the last of the many *chaburah* fellowship meals they have shared during the three years they've been together, then it's logical to assume that Jesus's friends are feeling sad and beginning to grieve. Such an emotion-laden context is not explicit in these first verses of chapter 14, but it's alluded to later in the Farewell Discourse, when Jesus says, "Because I have said these things to you, sorrow has filled your hearts" (16:6). Their "hearts are troubled" as ours would be if we were grappling with the prospect of our best friend being executed by his enemies tomorrow. The gospel writer is clearly in touch with the realities of human emotional states. Even though he usually portrays Jesus as amazingly serene and peaceful, he has already described three recent occasions when Jesus himself feels thus "troubled."[7]

Recognizing their grief and feeling empathy for them, Jesus exhorts his friends to trust him in the same way they trust God. Jews know that God is ever-faithful to his people, and Jesus, God's Son, pledges to prove similarly faithful to them. God chose Abraham and fulfilled his promise to give him and his descendants an everlasting inheritance, a land of their own. God sustained the descendants of Abraham throughout their tumultuous history, repeatedly delivering them from bondage to their enemies and bringing them back to the promised land. The disciples can have the same confidence in Jesus which they've always had in the providence of God.

When we take this view of vv. 1–6, we see Jesus as consoling his sad friends with the promise that, although he is about to die and leave them behind in the world, he is going ahead of them to prepare an eternal abiding place for them with the Father, and at their deaths he will come and take each of them to be with him, "that where I am, you *(plural)* may be also" (v. 3). This passage from John is often linked at funerals to excerpts from Paul, such as "For we know that if the earthly tent we live in is destroyed, we have a building from God, a house not made with hands, eternal in the

---

6. Keener, *Gospel of John*, 2:937. The idea of a heavenly dwelling place for the righteous was also common in Judaism. (See Keener, *Gospel of John*, 2:934–35.)

7. 11:33, when he sees Mary's grief at the death of her brother Lazarus; 12:27, when he speaks of the inevitability of his own death; and 13:21, when he has to face the fact that one of his chosen disciples will betray him.

heavens" (2 Cor 5:1).[8] However, there is another, equally attractive and plausible way of interpreting what Jesus says here, a way that doesn't contradict the promise of life together in eternity, but which regards that prospect from a different perspective. This alternative understanding sees life in union with Jesus and the Father *as an experience believers will share on this side of death*, not only in a postmortem heavenly realm. It will be a continuation and deepening of the personal intimacy they have shared with their Lord all along. His "coming again" to them, promised in v. 3, can legitimately also be understood as the presence of the risen One in the person of the Spirit. (This will be explained in vv. 18–24.)

The pivotal moment arrives when Jesus adds, "And you know the way where I am going." This provokes Thomas to reply, "Lord, we do not know where you are going; how can we know the way?" (vv. 4–5). If we think of Jesus as describing his own circumstances here, then the "way" (meaning the route) he is going is the way of the cross. His is the way of a life laid down in love, which was foreshadowed for the disciples when he stooped to wash their feet earlier that evening. But with v. 6 there is a shift, and it becomes his followers' way which is under consideration. Jesus presents the disciples with himself—meaning the life he has shared with them in the world as well as his coming death and resurrection—as their route to intimacy with the Father. And it's a route they will be able to avail themselves of immediately *because* he is going to the Father. Replying to Thomas' query, "How can we know the way?" Jesus tells them, "I am the way, and the truth, and the life; no one comes to the Father except through me. If you men really knew me, then you would recognize my Father, too. From now on, you do know him and have seen him" (vv. 6–7, as translated by Raymond Brown).[9]

Again and again, John has shown us that Jesus's disciples are slow to grasp the full significance of their Master's words. Now—at the very end of their time with him—they still don't seem to get it. We can go back through John's Gospel and count the many times Jesus tries to demonstrate to them who he is and what the Father sent him into the world to do, but they never grasp the point he's trying to make. We can draw comfort from reading about how difficult it is for our Savior's closest friends to recognize what is right before their eyes, since—like them—we struggle to understand and believe, until the "aha!" moment finally comes and the Lord gives us insight.

We first meet the man named Philip back in chapter 1. He is the third of Jesus's disciples, and the first specifically chosen and invited by Christ himself to follow him (1:43). In 6:8, Philip, who has been Jesus's companion from the beginning, says to his Master, "Show us the Father, and we shall be satisfied" (v. 8). He has been with him day after day for three years; nevertheless, he still requires Jesus to explain, "He who has seen me has seen the Father" (v. 9). Philip demonstrates a lack of understanding and—more—a lack of faith. Jesus has to press him, saying, "Do you not believe that I

8. See Brown, *John XIII–XXI*, 626.
9. Ibid., 617.

am in the Father and the Father in me?" (v. 10). *Believing requires a decision, a choice, and a commitment.* We twenty-first century believers have this in common with Philip and the other disciples: coming truly to believe in Jesus as the unique Son of God is a process, sometimes a protracted one.

There is a difference between Father and Son, but no separation. Jesus has already said that the Son does only what he sees the Father doing (5:19) and speaks only what the Father gives him to say (12:49–50). We imagine Jesus saying, in exasperation, "Philip, you've been with me from Day One. Don't you really believe in me yet? If you want to see the Father, look at me! If you want to hear the Father, listen to me" (paraphrase of vv. 9–10). John's Gospel depicts our increasing perception that God is in Christ as a mystical process by which believers begin to see, to acquire spiritual insight. (See 9:17, 30–40).[10]

Believing is seeing. The disciples won't come to the fullness of faith, they won't be able to see clearly, and they won't be able to assemble the complicated jigsaw puzzle of all they have experienced with Jesus until *after* their Lord has been raised from the dead and the Spirit-Paraclete has come to help them understand the meaning of what their Master said and what he did when he was with them. Then, at last, they will grasp that Jesus is "the way" because he is the perfect revelation of the Father. He is not simply a prophet God sent into the world to direct people to the path that leads to heaven. After the resurrection, the disciples will ultimately perceive that when they saw Jesus with them on the roads of Galilee they were seeing the Father, and in knowing Jesus as their teacher, friend, and companion they were knowing the Father. Jesus's life among them was not simply *pointing to* the truth; his human life was and is for all people in all times and all places the *enactment* of Truth, with a capital "T," the transcendent object of human desire.

The message of the Farewell Discourse, the comforting promise of Jesus to his slow-witted disciples concerning the future, repeats in different language the same claim that he announces to "the Jews" when he debates with them in the temple at the Feast of the Dedication. On that occasion Jesus tells the Pharisees and their priestly colleagues, "My sheep hear my voice, and I know them, and they follow me. I give them eternal life, and they shall never perish, and no one shall snatch them out of my hand. My Father, who has given them to me, is greater than all, and no one is able to snatch them out of the Father's hand. I and the Father are one" (10:27–30).

The "place" which Jesus's death, resurrection, and sending of the Spirit prepares for us who love him, is the one intended for God's children from the beginning of time. It's not a spatial place, like a hotel room in heaven; it is a state of mutual indwelling, a timeless communion with the Father and the Son. It is God making God's own home in our hearts and welcoming us to rest in that presence, now and forever.

---

10. Lockwood, "Spiritual Fatherhood," 90.

Vv. 12–31. "I will not leave you desolate; I will come to you."

INTRODUCTION. The Farewell Discourse is meant to prepare Jesus's followers for the changed circumstances they soon will face. Their future and the future of the church will depend upon his disciples believing what Jesus has told them about himself and the Father, and trusting in what Jesus promises. His friends' relationship with one another and with God will be mediated through Jesus. In their coming mission to the world the disciples will do "greater works" than their Master, not meaning that they will perform more dramatic miracles than his (because, as we have observed, John has no interest in sensationalism), but that they will have a wider scope for their work of evangelization. Their ministry will extend far beyond Judea, Galilee, and Samaria, addressing Gentiles as well as Jews. It will be grounded in what Jesus is going to accomplish through his death and resurrection.

Here Jesus tells them, "If you love me, you will keep my commandments" (v. 15). In the disciples' relationship with Jesus, as in the relationship of Israel with the God of Abraham, true *obedience* is the indisputable evidence of love. The same standard applies to the Son's relationship with the Father. In v. 31, Jesus says, "I do as the Father has commanded me so that the world may know that I love the Father." John's Gospel names only one commandment that Jesus gives his friends: "love one another as I have loved you" (13:34). However, in view of v. 23, "If a man loves me he will keep my word, and my Father will love him," we can logically treat "commandments" and "word" (*logos,* meaning "message") as synonyms.

Jesus will ask the Father to send his friends "another Counselor" (v. 16), who will be with them forever—one whom they can understand as a successor to Jesus, their original Counselor.[11] The Counselor whose arrival is anticipated is called the "Spirit of truth" (v. 17). Because we know that Jesus himself is "the truth" (v. 6), we understand that experience of the Spirit-Paraclete as Counselor is another way for the disciples to know the perpetual, indwelling presence of the Lord Jesus himself. This is what is meant by the words "you know him, for he dwells *with* you, and will be *in* you" (v. 17). During the three-year ministry Jesus was "with" his disciples; in the future, after the resurrection and coming of the Spirit, he will be "in" them. The Spirit-Paraclete / Counselor will continue to teach them, just as Jesus has done, and will help them to understand many things they were not able fully to comprehend when the Lord was with them in the flesh. We might say that the Spirit bears to Jesus the same relationship that Jesus bears to the Father. That is, just as one sees the Father in Jesus (v. 9) so also one experiences Jesus in the Spirit (vv. 15–17, 26). Jesus says and does only what he sees and hears the Father doing (8:28; 5:19–20). The Spirit will say only what he hears from Jesus (16:13)[12] We are probably correct to assume that the Beloved Disciple

---

11. Keener, *Gospel of John*, 2:966–69. "Counselor" is how the RSV translates the Greek word *paraklētos.*

12. Burge, *Anointed Community*, 140.

compiled or constructed the Farewell Discourse (and perhaps much of his gospel) under the prophetic inspiration of the Spirit (see v. 26 and also 16:13–16).

Recall that at the beginning of his ministry, immediately after Jesus is baptized by John, two of John's disciples leave their teacher and begin to follow Jesus. One is Andrew and tradition tells us the other—who is unnamed—is the Beloved Disciple. When Jesus notices them walking behind him, he turns and asks, "What are you looking for?" And they reply, "Where do you live?" (Or, "Where do you abide?") He answers, "Come and see" (paraphrase of 1:38–39a). Three years later, on his last night with those disciples and their comrades, Jesus gives the final answer to their question, "Where do you live?" He tells them, "If a man loves me, he will keep my word, and my Father will love him, and we will come to him and make our home with him" (v. 23). That is to say, in the future God will come to live within those who love and obey the Son. *Everyone who is seeking God will meet God in Jesus's disciples.*[13]

This section—like the entire Farewell Discourse—affirms repeatedly and in different ways the mystical communion with Jesus and the Father that is to be the heart of believers' common life.[14] Although their Master will be "going away" from them through death, he will "come again" to them and they will "see" him (vv. 18–19). Not only will they see him with their physical eyes in his resurrection appearances; they will always "see" him in the metaphysical sense that identifies seeing with *knowing.* Jesus will manifest himself to those who love and believe in him; however, those who reject him and do not believe in him will never see him. The Lord's parting gift to his friends is a peace unlike anything the world can offer (v. 15). It is almost a synonym for eternal life, and it will sustain them through frightening times in their fight against "the ruler of this world."[15]

Logically, v. 31, "Arise, let us be going," might indicate that chapter 14 once constituted the entire Farewell Discourse. If one eliminates chapters 15–17 and reads chapter 18 next, the transition is seamless. Nevertheless, all ancient manuscripts of the Fourth Gospel are organized in exactly the same way as our modern Bibles. This tells us that the final editor of John deliberately allowed the seemingly out-of-place sentence at the end of v. 31 to remain as it is.[16] Perhaps that editor construed these words of Jesus differently from the way we usually do. It's possible to paraphrase v. 31 in contemporary speech as, "Come on, let's get going." Rather than a signal that the time has come to leave the supper table, these words might be Jesus's invitation to his

13. This is John's way of expressing what Paul means when he tells the Corinthians "you are the body of Christ" (1 Cor 12:27).

14. There is congruence between the way John portrays the presence of Christ indwelling the community of believers and the way Paul describes the identification of believers with Christ in, e.g., Col 3:1–4.

15. Kysar, *John*, 233.

16. O'Day, *Gospel of John*, 752–53.

friends to join him in the struggle against the "ruler of this world," a combat for which he is fully prepared, now that his hour has come.

> **[14:12–31]** [12] *"Truly, truly, I say to you, he who believes in me will also do the works that I do; and greater works than these will he do, because I go to the Father. [13] Whatever you ask in my name, I will do it, that the Father may be glorified in the Son; [14] if you ask anything in my name, I will do it.*
>
> [15] *"If you love me, you will keep my commandments. [16] And I will pray the Father, and he will give you another Counselor, to be with you for ever, [17] even the Spirit of truth, whom the world cannot receive, because it neither sees him nor knows him; you know him, for he dwells with you, and will be in you.*
>
> [18] *"I will not leave you desolate; I will come to you. [19] Yet a little while, and the world will see me no more, but you will see me; because I live, you will live also. [20] In that day you will know that I am in my Father, and you in me, and I in you. [21] He who has my commandments and keeps them, he it is who loves me; and he who loves me will be loved by my Father, and I will love him and manifest myself to him." [22] Judas (not Iscariot) said to him, "Lord, how is it that you will manifest yourself to us, and not to the world?" [23] Jesus answered him, "If a man loves me, he will keep my word, and my Father will love him, and we will come to him and make our home with him. [24] He who does not love me does not keep my words; and the word which you hear is not mine but the Father's who sent me.*
>
> [25] *"These things I have spoken to you, while I am still with you. [26] But the Counselor, the Holy Spirit, whom the Father will send in my name, he will teach you all things, and bring to your remembrance all that I have said to you. [27] Peace I leave with you; my peace I give to you; not as the world gives do I give to you. Let not your hearts be troubled, neither let them be afraid. [28] You heard me say to you, 'I go away, and I will come to you.' If you loved me, you would have rejoiced, because I go to the Father; for the Father is greater than I. [29] And now I have told you before it takes place, so that when it does take place, you may believe. [30] I will no longer talk much with you, for the ruler of this world is coming. He has no power over me; [31] but I do as the Father has commanded me, so that the world may know that I love the Father. Rise, let us go hence.*

RESPONSE. The portion of the Farewell Discourse we read in chapter 14 both begins and ends with Jesus exhorting his friends at the supper table not to be troubled or afraid (vv. 1 and 27). He doesn't tell them explicitly that he is about to be arrested and put to death, but he has already made clear he is "going away"—to a place they can't go with him, at least not now (see 13:31, 36). Jesus understands the sorrow, grief, confusion, and uncertainty his friends will feel after his death. As John portrays the scene of the Farewell Discourse, the disciples know Jesus is in danger but are unaware that it is only hours until he will be taken from them by death. Everyone in Jerusalem knows a mob tried to stone Jesus not many months before, and word on the street is that the chief priests are preparing a plot against him. The band of disciples knows Jesus's life is at risk—in the same way that family and friends of a soldier serving in a theater of war are aware the soldier's life is on the line every day. But they don't realize the critical moment will arrive that very night.

Jesus, facing death himself, endeavors to comfort his friends. He seems more concerned about their feelings than about his own, although John has already told us Jesus felt troubled, too, acknowledging his very human apprehension about what is soon to ensue (see 12:27; 13:21). It's worth remembering that Mark's portrayal of the scene on Golgotha, which occurs fewer than twenty-four hours later, reports Jesus saying only one thing from the cross: "My God, my God, why hast thou forsaken me?" (Mark 15:34). This so-called cry of dereliction from the crucified Christ is a quotation of Ps 22:1, but it's also the wail of a very human victim, feeling the stark loneliness of dying. The Father does not forsake his Son, but in that dark hour the Crucified One *feels* alone and abandoned in his solitary torment. As he talks to his friends after the supper, trying to prepare them for what is about to happen, Jesus anticipates the loneliness and fear which will pervade his disciples after his death—the very emotions he will experience himself the following afternoon.

Circumstances often force us to deal with the loss of someone upon whom we have long relied as our guide and mainstay through the perils and chances of life— perhaps a dear parent, older sibling, teacher, or friend. When that person dies, the emotion of loss overwhelms us and we don't know how we'll find our way forward. Sometimes we feel as if our own life has ended. If such feelings are typical for ordinary people like us, we can only guess the depth of bereavement Jesus's friends experience when he is taken away from them and brutally put to death.

True, the gospel accounts tell us it is scarcely three days before Jesus is raised from death to life. But we may be confident that it takes much longer than three days for his disciples to move beyond the shock, pain, and disorientation caused by their Master's death—even though they have the wonderful sign of his resurrection to give them hope. The Jesus they once knew is still *gone*. Life is not the same anymore. Life will never again be as it was during the years they were merely apprentices gathered around their Master. That's essentially what the risen One means when he tells Mary Magdalene outside the tomb on Easter morning, "Don't hang on to me" (paraphrase of 20:17).

After Jesus's death and resurrection, his disciples' daily life will be utterly changed. They will not have their friend and teacher, the tradesman-rabbi from Nazareth, to sit with them by the campfire, answer their questions, laugh at their stories, pray with them, and speak to them the words of life. In critical situations where Jesus took action and they were simply bystanders, now *they* will be required to act. In circumstances where the hostility of the authorities was directed at Jesus, that hostility will now turn on them. Their Master will no longer be there in the flesh to speak or to act; that responsibility will fall to them.

That responsibility will fall to them! The work of a disciple is to reproduce the life of his Master. Jesus's disciples' period of apprenticeship is ending, and their life's work is about to begin. This is the primary underlying message of the Farewell Discourse. After Jesus is crucified and raised from the dead, his disciples will become his agents, sent to carry on his saving work. They will speak for him. They will act as he directs. And he says they will do even greater works than he has done in their presence (v. 12). When the risen One appears to them as they huddle behind locked doors on the evening of the day of resurrection, he is going to tell them, "As the Father has sent me, even so I send you" (20:21).

Jesus's farewell to his friends, as John offers it here and in the following two chapters, is meant to prepare these friends so they will understand *how* they are to overcome their loss and fear and carry on their Master's work after he is no longer with them in the flesh. Put simply, Jesus is telling them not to be afraid, because just as the Father has been with *him*, so Jesus will always be with *them*: "I will not leave you orphaned; I will come to you" (v. 18, NRSV). Although he will not be with them in the flesh, he will be with them through the Spirit: "the Counselor, the Holy Spirit whom the Father will send in my name . . . will teach you all things and bring to your remembrance all that I have said to you" (v. 26). The Father and the Son will make their home together in the hearts of those who love and obey Jesus. Because the disciples of Jesus will experience the presence of God, truly "within them" rather than "out there" somewhere beyond the skies, disciples will be able to invite those who are seeking God to come and find God through fellowship with them. (This is the essence of 1 John 1:3.)

The gospel writer intends Jesus's parting words to be read as a message to the young church in the first generation of its witness. As we begin the third millennium of the church's mission we still need to read them the same way. If we love Jesus and treasure his words, if we have received the gift of his indwelling Spirit, we can trust that he lives in us and we live in him. He will give us his own words to speak in moments of crisis. He will teach us what we need to learn. The "ruler of this world" will threaten, and the struggle against evil is going to be long. People around us may be afraid, but Jesus gives those who belong to him a peace that the world cannot give (see v. 27). Because he lives in us, we have a life worth living and a cause worth serving.

Doing Your Own Theology

Questions for reflection after reading John 14.

- The opening words of chapter 14 are frequently read at funerals: "Let not your hearts be troubled; believe in God, believe also in me. In my Father's house are many rooms; if it were not so, would I have told you that I go to prepare a place for you? And when I go and prepare a place for you, I will come again and will take you to myself, that where I am you may be also" (vv. 1–3). These words provide believers the simple assurance that, when we die, Jesus will come and take us to be with him "in my Father's house."—*Jesus tells his disciples, "I go to prepare a place for you." How do you think about death and life after death? What is your mental picture of the place Jesus might prepare for you? Do you imagine the life to come as shared in intimate community with others, or do you imagine it some other way?*

- After he says, "I am the way, and the truth, and the life," Jesus adds, "No one comes to the Father, but by me" (v. 6). Later he says, "He who has seen me has seen the Father . . . I am in the Father and the Father is in me" (vv. 9–10).—*What do you think Jesus means when he says, "No one comes to the Father, but by me"? How do you understand the difference between the Son and the Father? When you pray, do you think of yourself as addressing the Father or the Son?*

- The only commandment Jesus gives his followers in John's Gospel is for them to love one another as he has loved them (13:34–35). This provides background for what we read in vv. 15–16, "If you love me, you will keep my commandments. And I will pray the Father, and he will give you another Counselor, to be with you forever, even the Spirit of truth" (vv. 15–16). Because we know that Jesus himself is "the truth" (v. 6), we understand that experience of the Spirit as Counselor is another way for the disciples to know the perpetual, indwelling presence of the Lord Jesus himself.—*Here Jesus seems to be saying that his sending of the Spirit to his disciples will be conditioned upon their loving him and keeping his commandment to love one another. How would you describe your personal experience of the Spirit? Do you discern any connection between your willingness to show love to others and your experience of the presence of the Spirit?*

Chapter Fifteen

John 15:1–31. The Farewell Discourse continues:
The disciples are Jesus's friends, intimately united to him.

Vv. 1–17. "I am the vine, you are the branches."

INTRODUCTION. The Synoptic gospels show Jesus teaching primarily through stories, pithy metaphors, and figures of speech—collectively categorized as parables. As we have observed in our reading of the Fourth Gospel, the Johannine Jesus teaches differently. Although he makes frequent use of simple metaphors, in the Fourth Gospel Jesus mostly delivers lengthy monologues, this Farewell Discourse, for example. Or he engages in running dialogues, such as his extended debate with "the Jews" in chapters 7, 8, and 9. Only twice in John does Jesus use a parable-like way of speaking. The first instance is the extended metaphor of the shepherd and the sheep in 10:1–16, and the second is the portrayal of the vine and its branches here in 15:1–7. Both of these are sometimes called allegories, though that label applies more accurately here than to the material in chapter 10. There, Jesus says "I Am the door of the sheep" and "I Am the good shepherd" (10:7, 11), though the reader is left to guess who the other characters might represent. In 15:1–7, all the characters are explicitly identified: the vine is Jesus (the final "I Am" saying in the gospel), the vinedresser is his Father, and the branches are the disciples.

Various Old Testament books employ the figure of a vine or vineyard to symbolize Israel (e.g., Ps 80:8–16; Isa 5:1–7; Jer 2:21). The Synoptic gospels show Jesus using the same image (e.g., Mark 12:1–9). Jesus's portrayal of himself here as "the true vine" and his disciples as its branches (vv. 1–2), identifies the Messiah and his followers as the new People of God, the new Israel.[1] It would have been logical and consistent with Old Testament imagery for Jesus to say to his disciples, "*We* are the true vine." That he applies to himself a figure that has always been used for the community, saying "I Am

---

1. Smith, *John*, 280. Köstenberger points out that Jesus is the replacement of Israel in much the same way as he is "the replacement of the temple and the fulfillment of the symbolism of various Jewish festivals." Köstenberger, *Encountering John*, 149.

the true vine," is a very significant expression of the theology of the Fourth Gospel: the union between Christ and his people is intimate and personal. Just as the Father and Son are one, so the Son and his disciples are one, he in them and they in him (v. 5).[2] The "fruit" of the vine is one element in the allegory that is not specifically identified. An obvious possibility is mutual love, manifested in a variety of ways. Other possibilities include Christian witness, moral behavior, or virtues such as those Paul names as fruit of the Spirit in Gal 5:22–23.[3]

Since the fruit of any plant reproduces the life of that plant, we can grasp that the fruit of the true vine in this allegory reproduces the life of Christ himself. The Father is the vinedresser (literally, "farmer"), and he makes sure the branches of the true vine bear as much fruit as possible. That vine is precious to him. Caring for a vineyard is more labor intensive than any other form of ancient agriculture. Vines must be tied to trellises or other supports to raise them from the ground. The soil around them requires special care, and the vines themselves demand constant attention—particularly pruning. By calling his Father the vinedresser, Jesus communicates the high degree of love and concern God has for the little community of Jesus's disciples. They are essential to his work in the world.

The Father ensures his precious vine's fruitfulness by the exercise of thorough pruning—the Greek word for which also means "cleansing." Branches that prove to be fruitless are lopped off, and those that do bear fruit are pruned so they will bear even more (v. 2). This cleansing/pruning activity can never cease because the vine never stops producing fruit. Jesus says, "By this my Father is glorified, that you bear much fruit, and so prove to be my disciples" (v. 8).[4] This can be read as an allusion to 13:35, "By this all men will know that you are my disciples, if you have love for one another." It is also consistent with understanding that the mission of a disciple is to reproduce the life of his Master. The life of their Master is characterized by his love for them (see 13:34), a love which they just now experienced in a unique way when he served them by washing their feet, and which they will experience even more powerfully in his dying for them. The gift of his life laid down in love for them is anticipated in v. 13, "Greater love has no man than this, that he lay down his life for his friends."

The allegory's verisimilitude appears to break down when Jesus describes the need for branches to "abide in the vine" (v. 4), since branches of a grapevine cannot move from one vine to another. However, if we compare this image with Paul's metaphor of branches grafted into an olive tree (Rom 11:17–24), then we can see the command to "abide in the vine" as a warning to disciples not to become apostate. They must persevere as Jesus's disciples, "abide in the vine," and not depart from the

2. Marsh, *Saint John*, 519.

3. Keener, *Gospel of John*, 2:997–98.

4. We might wonder whether the emphasis on the disciples' fruit-bearing is a Johannine counterpart to the amazing harvest that comes from "the seed that fell on good soil" in the Synoptic parable of the seed and the soils (see Mark 4:3–8).

fellowship of Christ's followers (i.e., the church) to return to the community of Jews who reject Jesus as Son of God and Savior. The fate of such apostates is to be "thrown into the fire and burned" (v. 6). The reference to branches that do not abide in the vine might also apply particularly to Judas, the traitor, since in John's narrative this allegory is offered by Jesus while his disciples are still gathered around the supper table after Judas departs from them into the darkness.

Vv. 7–12 convey and develop the same message John has already communicated in 13:34–35 and 14:13–14, 21–24. Those who wish to learn from a particular rabbi seek him out and ask to become his disciples. If he accepts them, they act as his servants, albeit of a special kind. Unlike other Jewish teachers of his era, Jesus chooses his disciples and invites them to follow him (v. 16). Now he tells them that he will no longer call them his servants, but rather his friends (vv. 14–15). The ancient ideal of true friendship emphasizes faithfulness and loyalty of the sort exemplified in the relationship between David and Jonathan in the Old Testament (1 Sam 18:1–4). Friends open their hearts to one another; they trust one another with their plans and secrets. The Old Testament describes both Abraham and Moses as "friends of God" (2 Chr 20:7; Isa 41:8; Exod 33:11). To be friends of Jesus, just as Abraham and Moses were friends of God, means to be invited into a relationship of special intimacy with the Son of God, through whom they come to the Father.

This section concludes with an allusion to the mission that the disciples will have, after their Lord is raised and after the Spirit-Paraclete comes. Jesus says to them, "You did not choose me, but I chose you and appointed you that you should go and bear fruit and that your fruit should abide" (v. 16*a*). The disciples are to "*go and bear fruit.*" He uses the same word that he used earlier when he said that he was "going" to the Father (14:28). He is going to the Father, and they are going into the world as his witnesses (v. 27). As his witnesses, they will "bear fruit that abides"—that is to say, they will make disciples for their Lord, disciples who will persevere in faith, despite the adversities that are sure to come.

> **[15:1–17]** [1] *"I am the true vine, and my Father is the vinedresser.* [2] *Every branch of mine that bears no fruit, he takes away, and every branch that does bear fruit he prunes, that it may bear more fruit.* [3] *You are already made clean by the word which I have spoken to you.* [4] *Abide in me, and I in you. As the branch cannot bear fruit by itself, unless it abides in the vine, neither can you, unless you abide in me.* [5] *I am the vine, you are the branches. He who abides in me, and I in him, he it is that bears much fruit, for apart from me you can do nothing.* [6] *If a man does not abide in me, he is cast forth as a branch and withers; and the branches are gathered, thrown into the fire and burned.* [7] *If you abide in me, and my words abide in you, ask whatever you will, and it shall be done for you.* [8] *By this my Father is glorified, that you bear much fruit, and so prove to be my disciples.*

*⁹ As the Father has loved me, so have I loved you; abide in my love.
¹⁰ If you keep my commandments, you will abide in my love, just as I have
kept my Father's commandments and abide in his love. ¹¹ These things I
have spoken to you, that my joy may be in you, and that your joy may
be full. ¹² "This is my commandment, that you love one another as I have
loved you. ¹³ Greater love has no man than this, that a man lay down his
life for his friends. ¹⁴ You are my friends if you do what I command you.
¹⁵ No longer do I call you servants, for the servant does not know what
his master is doing; but I have called you friends, for all that I have heard
from my Father I have made known to you. ¹⁶ You did not choose me, but
I chose you and appointed you that you should go and bear fruit and that
your fruit should abide; so that whatever you ask the Father in my name,
he may give it to you. ¹⁷ This I command you, to love one another.*

RESPONSE. As John tells the story, once Jesus finishes his Farewell Discourse (chapters 14–16) and prays to the Father for his friends (chapter 17), they will leave the walled city and go out together to a garden on the lower slopes of the Mount of Olives. Even though it's now past sunset, their little group can look back toward the city and notice the last rays of sunlight glinting from the huge gold grapevine adorning the temple façade.[5] A grapevine is the primary biblical symbol of Israel.

Jesus tells his disciples he is the "true vine," and they are the branches. We can apply his words to ourselves. Christ is the vine, and we, too, are his branches. Cut off a branch of the vine and the branch dies. The vine produces the branch; the branch does not generate itself. We may boast of being self-made men or women, but there are no "self-made branches." Every branch exists only because of the vine and its only life is given by the vine.

The prophets taught that Israel, the Lord's chosen vine, was planted to bear "the fruit of righteousness" (Isa 5:7). Holy men of old knew that if the people of God were to produce the fruit of righteousness, it would only happen if they lived in such an intimate relationship with God that the Lord's own character became visible in their common life. God's' character made manifest in his people is "godliness."

The prophets grieved over Israel's failure to bear the godly fruit of righteousness. Isaiah wrote that God came to his vineyard looking for good grapes and only found sour grapes. God came seeking righteousness from his people and instead found violence and bloodshed (Isa 5:1–7). In essence, Jesus tells his friends in this part of the Farewell Discourse, "Israel has failed to produce the fruit of godliness. But *I* am the true vine. I am the fulfillment of what the gold grapevine on the temple represents. If I am that vine, then *you* are my branches. Stay connected to me, and you will bear the fruit my Father seeks. If you remain united to me, in time you will become like me. Without me, you can do nothing. But with me, you can do anything." Jesus again states

5. Josephus, *Antiquities*, XV.xi.3, 335.

the basic fact of the disciple's life, true then and true now. It's all about "you in me, and I in you." Our lives are barren unless we are in intimate communion with Jesus.

What do you think is the fruit God wants from the branches of his vine? Consider the biological function of fruit, whether it's grapes, or apples, or plums, or even acorns. Fruit *reproduces the life* of the parent plant. The fruit of our union with Christ is the reproduction of Christ's life in us and among those to whom the Father sends us. This process of reproduction operates on two levels: personal (the transformation of our own character) and evangelistic (the making of new disciples).

Jesus tells the disciples that his Father is the vinedresser, the master gardener, the owner and guardian of the vineyard. The master gardener comes to his precious vine looking for fruit, and he cuts off any branches that aren't producing. Those bearing at least some grapes don't get removed, but they do get docked. Pruning stimulates them to produce better grapes.

People who are merely domestic gardeners know that a severe cutting back is called for if their lilacs are to look beautiful or their cherry trees are to bear edible cherries. The best gardeners know how to prune—what to cut, where to cut, and when to cut. Think about your own shrubs and trees, if you have any. . . . Are there overgrown lilac bushes, twenty feet tall? . . . Leggy forsythias? . . . Old cherry trees that have almost reverted to wild? Do you imagine that if your shrubs and trees could talk, they'd tell you, "Oh, I'd *love* a good pruning"? Of course not. If they could talk, they'd shriek, "Don't come near me with that saw! Put away those shears! Please. I *need* all my little twigs and branches and leaves. I love all these suckers on my trunk. Don't they make a pretty pattern? If you cut me back, I'll be miserable. I might even die!"—But you tell the frightened tree, "You won't die. In time, you'll be better than ever."

Do you think *you'd* ever agree to be pruned? Whack—off goes that job you thought was your passport to a comfortable retirement. Buzz—off go your children to live far away. Chop—off goes your big investment in Kodak, or Lehman Brothers, or some other once-great but now failed corporation. This kind of cutting back also happens to congregations. God takes away some people, takes away some money, and takes away pieces of our beloved "old time religion." Then we wail, "How will we ever get along without those wonderful members, that dependable income, or our sacred traditions?" But the master gardener says, "Be quiet! You won't die. Just keep abiding in the vine. You'll be more fruitful in a few years, and you'll have more life in the Spirit than you ever thought possible."

We have an old shrub rose in our garden that had to be cut down almost to the ground. It grew back and is now beautiful. Believing in Jesus means trusting that the master gardener knows how, when, and precisely where to prune us. However, we are settled and comfortable just as we are. We don't like the idea of having our lifestyle altered. Few of us are likely to volunteer for more than a haircut. Yet, abiding in Christ entails sharing the Master's confidence in his Father's infinite wisdom. So when the master gardener comes along with his saw and shears, we will cooperate. We can't live "wild" and still be united to the true vine, and that union is what we need. Christ in us, and us in him.—Without him, we can do nothing. With him, we can do anything.

The Farewell Discourse is preparing Jesus's disciples to deal with a drastic change, a change they will not welcome. Their Master will be taken from them. He's not about to take a sea voyage to a far-off land; he is going to die. He will be put to death by his enemies in less than twenty-four hours. Paradoxically, the cross will be a kind of "pruning," not for Jesus but for his disciples. They will be required hereafter to live and bear fruit as branches of the vine after the true vine himself has been cut off from them in the flesh.

The only way his bereft followers will be able to bear fruit in years to come is if they learn from what Jesus is trying to teach them in these last moments of serenity together. What he is telling them is hard to grasp. But the Spirit-Paraclete will come, and when he comes he will remind them of the words the Lord speaks to them on this night after the supper. The Spirit will help them, and in time they will understand. Because he lives, they will live.

Jesus wants his disciples to realize the depth of his love for them and how vital it is for them to love one another as much as he loves them. He tells them they are no longer merely his apprentices, his servants. They are his *friends*. Their bond with him is deep and will become even deeper. He will always be loyal to them, and they must be equally dedicated to one another, for that is how friends behave. Tonight Jesus has given them one example to imitate: he has washed their feet. Tomorrow he will give them another: "Greater love has no man than this, that a man lay down his life for his friends" (v. 13). He will die for them.

Most American Christians today are unlikely ever to be called upon to die for our brothers and sisters, or for our faith. No doubt, some will. But most will not. A former missionary who was once threatened with execution by a hostile government told me that he thought he could have gone out and faced the firing squad if he had known for sure that his last words would be heard around the world and that someday a monument would be put up to honor him. He could have faced the guns, if he'd known he'd be a martyred hero.

The challenge for us is not whether to accept heroic martyrdom. Instead, the test presented daily to husbands and wives, parents, partners, pastors, and friends, is whether we will choose to "lay down our life" for those we love in ways no one else will ever see, in ways that will earn us no reward, recognition, or praise. The real challenge for each disciple of Christ is to put aside our personal agenda, pleasures, profits, and dreams—again and again—in order to serve and care for those who need us the most.

Vv. 18–31. "I chose you out of the world;
therefore, the world hates you."

INTRODUCTION. The concluding section of chapter 15 conveys Jesus's warning to his disciples concerning what they can expect to face when the time comes for them to go and bear fruit for him in the world.[6] Their lives are knit together with his; he abides in them and they in him. Therefore, the people who rejected Jesus are also going to reject them and those who listened to Jesus will listen to them. The Lord identifies with his disciples, with his church. This is echoed in Acts, where Luke tells us that Saul of Tarsus hears the voice of Jesus on the road to Damascus saying to him, "Saul, Saul, why do you persecute *me*" (Acts 9:4). Saul is not persecuting Jesus personally, but rather his church. However, the Lord is present in his people; the two are one.

Other than Jesus's bestowal of the Spirit on the disciples in 20:21–22, this section of the Farewell Discourse is as close as John's Gospel comes to a commissioning or sending-out of the disciples for their mission in the world. There is nothing in John as broadly stated as in Matt 10, a chapter devoted entirely to the mission of the disciples in the world and the adversities they will face. Nevertheless, what Jesus says here in vv. 18–20 sounds a lot like Matt 10:24–25, "A disciple is not above his teacher, nor a servant above his master; it is enough for the disciple to be like his teacher, and the servant like his master. If they have called the master of the house Beelzebul, how much more will they malign those of his household." And vv. 26–27 seem to state the promise of Jesus also found in Matt 10:19–20, "When they deliver you up, do not be anxious how you are to speak or what you are to say; for what you are to say will be given to you in that hour; for it is not you who speak, but the Spirit of your Father speaking through you."[7]

Jesus's references to the hostility of the world in this section is confusing to modern readers, especially those of us who learned to sing "This is My Father's World" in Sunday School sixty-plus years ago.[8] It is obvious that "the world," in this context, means everyone who opposes the Johannine understanding of Jesus's identity and mission. It is difficult to see this as other than a radically sectarian assessment. For John, sin is not moral failure but rather *theological error*. "'Sin' is defined by whether one believes that God is present in Jesus, that Jesus is the incarnate Son of God."[9] Earlier in his gospel, John tells us that the Baptizer describes Jesus as "the Lamb of God who takes away the sin of the world" (1:29). Jesus takes away the sin of the world by embodying the truth of God *in* the world. Later in his narrative John writes, "God so loved the world that he gave his only Son, that whoever believes in him should not

---

6. Most commentators agree that this theme continues through 16:4, but since this book is organized around the chapter structure of the gospel, the continuation of the thematic material in 16:1–4 will be treated in the next chapter.

7. See Burge, *Anointed Community*, 205–8.

8. Babcock, "This Is My Father's World."

9. O'Day, *Gospel of John*, 764.

perish but have eternal life. For God sent his Son into the world, not to condemn the world, but that the world might be saved through him" (3:16–17).

How does the earlier description of God's love for the world and Jesus's mission to "take away the sin of the world" and "save" the world square with this portrayal of the world as *hating* both Jesus and his friends? John does not see the world as inherently evil, since it came into being through the agency of the *Logos* himself (1:2–3). The world belongs to God; nevertheless, it is the zone of conflict, the battlefield whereupon the cosmic struggle between God and Satan, righteousness and sin, light and dark, life and death, will be consummated.

It appears to the gospel writer and his community—as it will sometimes seem to other Christians in later years—that the power of sin and death is winning and "the whole world is in the power of the evil one" (1 John 5:19). In such a situation, those who belong to Christ feel like a tiny, embattled expeditionary force sent from God to face a countless host of worldly warriors of the Evil One. Yet, we will see that the last word of the Farewell Discourse is written to give hope to the weary soldiers of Christ: "In the world, you have tribulation; but be of good cheer, I have overcome the world" (16:33*b*). When Jesus is laid in the tomb the next afternoon, his friends may fear that death and evil have won the battle. But when Sunday dawns, their Lord's surprising defeat of death will become obvious. The risen One will send the Spirit-Paraclete to bear witness to the truth of his victory, and that Spirit will empower the testimony of Jesus's disciples as they go into the world believing in their Lord.[10]

Here Jesus tells his friends that the world's hatred of them is not personal; it is not because of anything they have done. Instead, it is because of him. Because he chose them "out of the world" (v. 19) and made them his own, this makes them the target of the world's hate exactly as he is the target of that hate. Although the world may hate them, they are never counseled to hate the world. The Lord's mandate to his disciples is always love.

> **[15:18–27]** [18] *"If the world hates you, know that it has hated me before it hated you.* [19] *If you were of the world, the world would love its own; but because you are not of the world, but I chose you out of the world, therefore the world hates you.* [20] *Remember the word that I said to you, 'A servant is not greater than his master.' If they persecuted me, they will persecute you; if they kept my word, they will keep yours also.* [21] *But all this they will do to you on my account, because they do not know him who sent me.* [22] *If I had not come and spoken to them, they would not have sin; but now they have no excuse for their sin.* [23] *He who hates me hates my Father also.*
>
> [24] *If I had not done among them the works which no one else did, they would not have sin; but now they have seen and hated both me and my Father.* [25] *It is to fulfil the word that is written in their law, 'They hated me*

---

10. Marsh, *Saint John*, 527–30.

*without a cause.' ²⁶ But when the Counselor comes, whom I shall send to
you from the Father, even the Spirit of truth, who proceeds from the Father,
he will bear witness to me; ²⁷ and you also are witnesses, because you have
been with me from the beginning.*

RESPONSE. Jesus tells his friends, "If the world hates you, know that it has hated me
before it hated you" (v. 18). This warning fits the circumstances of the Johannine believers at the time John's Gospel begins to circulate, the last decade of the first century
of the Christian era. During the years Jesus's disciples spend in his company, they have
occasion to witness the anger directed at their Master by the chief priests and many of
the Pharisees. Their hostility is focused on Jesus, however, not his disciples. This soon
will change. After Jesus is crucified, those who arranged for his execution will turn
their angry attention to his most prominent followers—the company to whom the
Farewell Discourse is addressed.

Today American Christians live in a society that continues to pay at least polite
respect to their faith. Though this may be a post-Christian age, particularly in comparison with the first half of the twentieth century, typical church members rarely
come face-to-face with hatred. However, hostility to religion in general and Christianity in particular is more evident now than any time we can remember. The rhetoric of
militant atheists, whose anti-Christian vitriol is posted widely on the internet, often
feels a lot like hatred. Is there guidance for us in this portion of Jesus's Farewell Discourse? The Johannine community is an embattled sectarian minority, on the defensive against a "world" that seems to stand in hateful opposition to all that community
esteems as good and true. Should we modern believers in Christ isolate ourselves in a
cultural ghetto, walled off from the sinful and threatening world? Should we protect
our children by enrolling them in safe Christian schools and colleges to keep them
from being tainted by the sin that pervades "the world"? Should we only do business
with companies that display a Christian fish symbol on their signboards or advertise
on our congregation's website? Should we restrict our entertainment options to explicitly Christian films and concerts and only read books we can find in LifeWay or
Family Christian Stores?

In twenty-first century America there are already a large number of Christians
"who live in a cocoon that enables them to go through life almost completely insu-
lated, without ever having to deal with non-Christians."[11] If we look at church history,
it's clear this behavior is not new. It is visible in the ascetic movement that begins in
the third century in Egypt and Syria, and afterward spreads through the Mediterranean Christian sphere. Thousands of men and women flee from the worldly cities
of their age and live as hermits in the desert or else in communities of monks and
nuns in monasteries remote from everyone else. A similar attitude characterizes later
Protestant groups, such as the Amish and the Hutterites, and even the Puritans who

11. Köstenberger, *Encountering John*, 153.

cross the Atlantic to establish their "godly commonwealth" in the Massachusetts Bay colony. The Latter Day Saints' trek to the valley of the Great Salt Lake in the nineteenth century is a comparable phenomenon.

The Farewell Discourse at this point resembles the exhortation of a general to his troops on the eve of a battle in which they will be vastly outnumbered by a powerful and terrifying foe. Jesus warns his disciples of the dangers they will face. He wants them to be prepared. They know how harshly the world dealt with their Master, and now they must anticipate the same treatment. Disciples of Jesus are to expect the worst: that they will be hated by the world. Nevertheless, Jesus sends them *into* that world! He tells them to go into that unsympathetic environment and bear fruit that "will abide" (v. 16). He does not order them to retreat from the world and establish a secure community for themselves in the desert as the Essenes did, far away from the corruptions of the world.[12]

When Jesus tells his friends, "If you abide in me, and my words abide in you, ask whatever you will and it will be done for you" (v. 7), he is promising them that the Father will hear them just as he heard his Son during his mission in the world. The disciples will do the works that their Master has done in the world, and even "greater works" because he is going to the Father (14:12–14). The Spirit-Paraclete is coming, and will guide them when they go face-to-face against the dark powers of the world (v. 26). Jesus's disciples identify with him, and he identifies with them. Indeed, he abides in them. His redeeming work is to be carried forward as they confront the world on its own ground, in spite of its evil power and its threats. The world hates them, but they are not to hate the world. Indeed, the opposite is true. God loves the world so much that he sent his Son to save it, and now God's Son sends them. The risen Lord will proclaim this explicitly on the evening of the day of resurrection, when he comes to the disciples, hiding behind locked doors, and tells them, "Peace be with you. As the Father has sent me, even so I send you" (20:21), and then breathes upon them his Spirit.

The challenge of Christ to his disciples in our time is for us to become courageously counter-cultural. We must change some of our old habits. This requires us to turn away from the money-and-power oriented techniques and authoritarian methods that have dominated the church's life since the time of Constantine. Jesus invites contemporary disciples to shape our common life and direct our common mission by renewed dedication to the example of the incarnation we see portrayed in the Fourth Gospel. This is a picture of God's love enfleshed in Jesus, his Son, who comes among us to share our human condition, and dies to save the world that rejects

---

12. The Essenes were a contemporary Jewish sect who lived a monastic existence. They established houses in many Judean villages and had a larger community in Jerusalem. Some Essenes retreated into the wilderness and established a large monastic community at Qumran in a barren valley on the western side of the Dead Sea. (See Capper, "Holy Community," 115–18; and Capper, "Essene Community Houses," 478–79.)

him—never losing confidence that he is implementing his Father's plan for this, his Father's world.[13]

Doing Your Own Theology

Questions for reflection after reading John 15.

- Jesus applies to himself an image which was traditionally used to describe the whole community of Israel. He says, "I Am the true vine." This usage is a significant expression of John's theology: the union between the divine Son and those who believe in him is deep and personal. Just as the Father and the Son are one, so the Son and his disciples are one, he in them and they in him (v. 5). Jesus says, "I am the vine, you are the branches. He who abides in me, and I in him, he it is that bears much fruit, for apart from me you can do nothing" (v. 5).—*Do you feel as if sometimes you're abiding in Jesus and at other times disconnected from him? What helps you stay connected to Christ? What disconnects you from him? But perhaps abiding in Jesus has nothing to do with how we feel from day to day, but is rather a gift of God, a status bestowed upon us by the Lord. What do you think?*

- Jesus tells the disciples that his Father is the vinedresser, the master gardener, the owner and guardian of the vineyard. The master gardener comes to his precious vine looking for fruit, and cuts off any branches that aren't producing. Those bearing at least some fruit don't get removed, but they do get docked. Pruning stimulates a grape vine to produce better quality grapes. (It is important for us to remember that the Greek word for "pruning" is the same as the word for "cleansing.")—*How have you experienced visits from the vinedresser, the master gardener? To extend this metaphor, who has most often represented the master gardener in your life? Pruning does not happen only once in the life of a grape vine; it happens at least annually. Sometimes pruning may be severe, sometimes not. What was your most recent pruning like? How would you describe your fruitfulness prior to the pruning and afterwards?*

- Jesus wants his disciples to realize the depth of his love for them and how vital it is for them to love one another as much as he loves them. He tells them that they are no longer merely his apprentices, his servants. They are his *friends*. Their bond with him is deep and will become even deeper. He will always be loyal to them, and they must be equally dedicated to one another, for that is how friends behave. Jesus has given them one example to imitate: he has washed their feet. On Friday he will give them another: "Greater love has no man than this, that a man lay down his life for his friends" (v. 13).—*Who are your closest friends? What*

13. See O'Day, *Gospel of John*, 768.

qualities do you expect from these friends? What would you do for them? In what way do you think of Jesus as your friend, perhaps your best friend? If you are Jesus's best friend, what does he have a right to expect from you?

Chapter Sixteen

John 16:1–33. The Farewell Discourse concludes: Jesus promises his friends that they will see him again soon.

Vv. 1–15. "When the Spirit of truth comes, he will guide you into all the truth."

INTRODUCTION. The material in vv. 1–4*a* continues the theme of 15:18–31. Jesus explains that he is speaking thus with his disciples to encourage them in view of tribulations that are sure to come. Jesus warns of coming persecution in the Synoptic gospels also (see Mark 13:9–13; Matt 10:17–22; Luke 12:4, 11–12). Scholars debate whether Jews could have threatened Jesus's disciples with death for believing in him, since the Romans did not allow Jewish authorities to inflict the death penalty. However, Acts tells us that not only threats, but actual executions took place—citing the stoning of Stephen by a Jerusalem mob and the execution of James the brother of John by Herod Agrippa I.[1] As Jesus is aware of the arrival of his hour, so his followers are to anticipate their own hour—and for disciples as for their Master, the hour is one of confrontation with the power of Satan.

In this section, Jesus reiterates some points made earlier in the Farewell Discourse (e.g., 14:16, 26–28; 15:26–27), but with slightly different emphases. Some readers might assume v. 5 contradicts 13:36 or 14:5, but the implication in this context, with its reference to the sorrow that fills their hearts (v. 6), is that Jesus's friends are so weighed down by sadness that they do not ask him to be specific about where he is going. He tells them he is going to his Father, but he does not specify that death will be his path. Jesus describes the future ministry of the Spirit-Paraclete as two-fold—to the world (vv. 8–11) and to the community of believers (vv. 12–15). Jesus has already

---

1. Smith, *John*, 291–93; Martyn, *History*, 67–68; Keener, *Gospel of John*, 2:1026–27. See Acts 7:54—8:3; 12:1–3. Roman authorities tended to show indifference to mob actions, such as the stoning of Stephen; and Rome allowed Herod Agrippa (r. 41–44 CE) the right of capital punishment within his kingdom, which included both Judea and Galilee. Both events probably occurred at least a decade after the resurrection.

said the world is unable to receive the Paraclete (14:17), which means the ministry of the Spirit to the world will be through the work of the community—the preaching and testimony of his disciples and the power of their love for one another.[2]

In this portion of the Farewell Address, Jesus implies that when the Paraclete comes, he will provide the disciples with what one writer calls "supplementary revelations."[3] These are things his friends "cannot bear now" (v. 12). Experts differ on whether this refers to a prophetic gift of the sort alluded to by Paul (1 Cor 12:10 and 14:1–3) or to a revelation of the deeper meaning of things Jesus has already told them. In the theology of the Fourth Gospel, Jesus *is* the truth; therefore, what the Spirit of truth will reveal must be connected in some way with Jesus's own message. What the Spirit tells the disciples will be a "fuller disclosure of that which was true of Jesus all along, and what his earthly activities actually portended."[4] Yet it also seems that he will declare new things: "When the Spirit of truth comes, he will guide you into all the truth; for he will not speak on his own authority, but whatever he hears he will speak, and he will declare to you the things that are to come" (v. 13).[5]

[16:1–15] [1] *"I have said all this to you to keep you from falling away.* [2] *They will put you out of the synagogues; indeed, the hour is coming when whoever kills you will think he is offering service to God.* [3] *And they will do this because they have not known the Father, nor me.* [4] *But I have said these things to you, that when their hour comes you may remember that I told you of them.*

"I did not say these things to you from the beginning, because I was with you. [5] *But now I am going to him who sent me; yet none of you asks me, 'Where are you going?'* [6] *But because I have said these things to you, sorrow has filled your hearts.* [7] *Nevertheless I tell you the truth: it is to your advantage that I go away, for if I do not go away, the Counselor will not come to you; but if I go, I will send him to you.* [8] *And when he comes, he will convince the world concerning sin and righteousness and judgment:* [9] *concerning sin, because they do not believe in me;* [10] *concerning righteousness, because I go to the Father, and you will see me no more;* [11] *concerning judgment, because the ruler of this world is judged.* [12] *"I have yet many things to say to you, but you cannot bear them now.* [13] *When the Spirit of truth comes, he will guide you into all the truth; for he will not speak on his own authority, but whatever he hears he will speak, and he will declare to you the things that are to come.* [14] *He will glorify me, for he will take what*

2. An excellent brief theological excursus on John's portrayal of the Paraclete is found in O'Day, *Gospel of John*, 774–78.

3. Burge, *Anointed Community*, 214.

4. Hurtado, "Remembering and Revelation," 20.

5. Burge, *Anointed Community*, 215–16. See Brown, *John XIII–XXI*, 707; Keener, *Gospel of John*, 2:1036–38.

is mine and declare it to you. ¹⁵ All that the Father has is mine; therefore I said that he will take what is mine and declare it to you.

RESPONSE. Jesus says something emotionally profound to his disciples on this night before he goes to the cross, "I don't call you my servants anymore. I call you my friends" (paraphrase of 15:15). For us, as for people who lived in the New Testament era, true friendship is a gift. Not everyone has someone they can trust as a true friend. I refer to a connection that goes far beyond "hail fellow" camaraderie—the congenial foursome at golf, the bridge group, or the book club—even beyond our relationship with the college friend who hiked up to Machu Picchu with us.

We're truly blessed if we have someone in this life we can count as a true friend, a *soul* friend—someone "who knows all about us, but loves us anyway." If our true friend happens to be our spouse, then we're in an enviable situation indeed. Our true friend shares the secrets of our heart and discloses the depths of his or her own self. Our true friend brings out the best in us. In the presence of such a true friend, we feel safe and peaceful. If our true friend is absent, there is a noticeable void in our life.

This is the kind of friendship—and obviously more—that Jesus has for his disciples. He is the true friend to each of them, although they cannot return the same kind of love that he gives them. When Jesus is with them, life is good and they feel able to tackle any task. When he's absent, they're anxious and start bickering with one another about who among them is the greatest. Jesus's friends are imperfect; but he is aware of their faults, and he loves them anyway. His compassion for them is deep. He will lay down his life for them.

On this night before he goes to the cross, sensing how panicked and afraid his friends will feel when he is taken from them, Jesus promises—as we read earlier—"I will pray the Father, and he will give you another Counselor [*Paraclete*] to be with you forever, even the Spirit of truth, whom the world cannot receive, because it neither sees him nor knows him. You know him, for he dwells with you, and he will be in you" (14:16–17).

John is the only gospel that portrays Jesus as speaking at length about the Holy Spirit, and he does so primarily in this Farewell Discourse. The title he chooses to use for the Spirit is *paraclete*, a Greek word the RSV translates as "Counselor."[6] Paraclete refers to a person to whom one calls for help in the hour of need. Jesus has been his friends' Paraclete for the past three years. On his last night with them he promises he will ask his Father to send them "another Paraclete." And this new Paraclete, this new true friend of their souls, will never leave them. He will, in fact, be "in" them (14:17). I doubt whether the disciples are able to make sense of what Jesus is telling them. Not yet. They clearly don't get it until the Spirit-Paraclete finally comes to them and they experience his presence.

---

6. See General Introduction to the Farewell Discourse, pp. 206–7, above.

What Jesus promises to his friends on this last night with them, and what he also promises to today's disciples, is guidance from the Spirit of truth. He says, "I have yet many things to say to you, but you cannot bear them now. When the Spirit of truth comes, he will guide you into all the truth" (vv. 12–13a). Perhaps the greatest work of the Spirit is to lead followers of Christ further on the path of truth. History shows that in every age humanity is compelled to grapple with newly recognized truth. Pride leads people to suppose we know more than we do, and when our pride is in full bloom we presume ourselves qualified to issue dogmatic definitions with utter certainty. Then God surprises us with a humbling new insight into truth. Because our mortal capacity for understanding is limited, God chooses not to give us more than we can handle at any one time. Thus, Jesus says to his friends, "I have yet many things to say to you, but you cannot bear them now" (v. 12).

The challenge to us and to the church in every age is to allow the Spirit-Paraclete to lead us steadily ever closer to God and not decide we've already gone as far as possible. Here's a depiction of what that looks like to me. I've lived the majority of my adult life in the Rocky Mountains, and I picture us, the community of Jesus's followers, as a gaggle of tourist hikers from the flatlands traversing a mountain trail, following a trustworthy Guide who promises to take us to the top of a mountain from which we will enjoy a view of unsurpassable splendor. Sometimes we fail to follow the Guide as closely as we should. On the lower slopes, we get distracted by wildflowers in a mountain meadow and stop to take pictures, while the rest of the group disappears up the trail. The Guide has to run back and find us. Later we're distracted by looking off at an amazing vista and accidentally slide down into a gully. Our Guide must rescue us. When the trail gets really steep, some of us declare we're too old and tired for such a long hike and we've gone as far as we intend to go. We've seen enough mountain grandeur. But our new best friend the Guide won't let us quit. He encourages us, shares his water and an energy bar, and gets us moving upward again. Even when the trail becomes precipitous, if we listen to the Guide and put our feet exactly where he shows us, we will be safe. He will take us all the way to the peak, where we can behold incomparable beauty, if only we will keep listening and trusting what he tells us.

Reflecting on Jesus's promise of the Paraclete, we logically ask: "How do we develop a relationship with this True Friend of our soul?" Why, we *cry out to him*, of course! The original Greek-speaking audience of the Fourth Gospel could see that clearly in the title Jesus gives the Holy Spirit: the *Paraclete*. Etymologically, a *paraclete* is "called to be with" us. We cry out for his help. We beseech his presence, wisdom, encouragement, and direction. Therefore, the church in its worship for two thousand years has continued to pray, "Come, Holy Spirit, come!" We also sit quietly and listen for his voice. Silence, too, can be a form of prayer. Without prayer, we will not encounter the Spirit. Without prayer, we will not hear the Spirit. Without prayer, we will not know the Spirit, even though he is always near us.

Jesus's promise of the Paraclete offers hope for the church in an era when many old structures, customary rules, and settled understandings seem to be failing. The wisdom of God is greater than our minds can encompass. The Almighty makes all things new. With the guidance of the Paraclete, we can fabricate new wineskins for new wine.[7] Jesus says, "When the Spirit of truth comes, he will guide you into all the truth" (v. 13). Our True Friend will keep us on the trail that leads to the Father's presence. The Paraclete will lead us home to God and will equip us to do the Lord's redeeming work during the journey that takes us there.

Vv. 16–33. "Be of good cheer. I have overcome the world."

INTRODUCTION. In this final portion of the Farewell Discourse, we hear the voices of the disciples again for the first time since 14:8. Their remarks are formulated as questions to one another, whispered asides which readers of the gospel can overhear, "What is this that he says to us, 'A little while, and you will not see me, and again a little while, and you will see me'; and, 'because I go to the Father'?" (v. 17). They don't know what he means (v. 18), and they are afraid to ask him. However, since Jesus knows their hearts and perceives what his friends are thinking, he answers their questions. What he says addresses again the matter of his going to the Father and his return to them—their certain grief at being parted from him, and their assured joy at his coming back to them (vv. 19–22). To describe what their emotional state will be like, Jesus borrows the familiar Old Testament metaphor of a mother in labor: the pain of her labor is indeed grievous, but it is relatively brief and all but forgotten in the gladness that her baby has been born.[8]

Jesus tells them, "You have sorrow now, but I will see you again and your hearts will rejoice, and no one will take your joy from you" (v. 22). He does not say, "You will see *me* again," but rather, "I will see *you* again." Meeting their risen Lord will not be an encounter with an apparition, not a spectral visitation, but rather a face-to-face reunion of friends. John wants his readers to recognize this. The disciples will see Jesus, and he will see them.[9] They will truly be together again, conversing together face-to-face, and the delight of that meeting will remain with them forever. This promise will be fulfilled in the Easter narratives (20:20–29).

The Farewell Discourse is positioned as it is in John's Gospel, as conversation with his disciples after the Last Supper, because Jesus is about to die. He wants to prepare his disciples for this stunning blow and the drastic change it will mean for them, for their life together, and for their future mission. Jesus employs a variety of allusions and different figures of speech to depict his friends' relationship with him and

---

7. Mark 2:22.

8. Isa 13:8; Hos 13:13; Mic 4:9.

9. Kysar comments regarding v. 22 that "even if believers do not see (20:29), they can trust that God *sees them*." Kysar, *John*, 251.

what the future will bring. Much earlier, he describes himself as a shepherd with his flock (10:1–18); now, at the Supper, first he pictures himself as a vine with its branches (15:1–8) and afterwards portrays the disciples' feelings as akin to those of a woman in the pains of labor. Although Jesus said to the Passover throng four days earlier, "unless a grain of wheat falls into the earth and dies, it remains alone, but if it dies, it bears much fruit" (12:24), and he tells his followers several times this evening that he is "going away," he never says unambiguously, "tomorrow I will die." Jesus promises, however, that the time is coming when he will speak plainly to them about the Father. That will happen after he is crucified and raised from the dead. Then, "in the person of the Spirit, he will be able to speak directly of what 'going to the Father' has meant."[10]

Jesus's hour has now struck (v. 32). Although his chosen disciples will soon abandon him in fear for their own safety, the Johannine Christ faces the next day with serenity. His dearest friends may forsake him, but he will never be alone because his Father is always with him (v. 32). When John tells the story of the crucifixion (19:17–30), no cry of dereliction is heard from Jesus's lips. Indeed, on this night before he suffers, Jesus speaks peace to his friends and confidently assures them that his triumph is already complete, "In the world you have tribulation; but be of good cheer, I have overcome the world" (v. 33). The overcoming that Jesus anticipates is not to be a crushing defeat of the world, but rather its final liberation from bondage to the Evil One. The mission of God's Son described in 3:17 will be fulfilled: "God sent the Son into the world, not to condemn the world, but that the world might be saved through him."

[16:16–33] [16] *"A little while, and you will see me no more; again a little while, and you will see me."* [17] *Some of his disciples said to one another, "What is this that he says to us, 'A little while, and you will not see me, and again a little while, and you will see me'; and, 'because I go to the Father'?"* [18] *They said, "What does he mean by 'a little while'? We do not know what he means."* [19] *Jesus knew that they wanted to ask him; so he said to them, "Is this what you are asking yourselves, what I meant by saying, 'A little while, and you will not see me, and again a little while, and you will see me'?* [20] *Truly, truly, I say to you, you will weep and lament, but the world will rejoice; you will be sorrowful, but your sorrow will turn into joy.* [21] *When a woman is in travail she has sorrow, because her hour has come; but when she is delivered of the child, she no longer remembers the anguish, for joy that a child is born into the world.* [22] *So you have sorrow now, but I will see you again and your hearts will rejoice, and no one will take your joy from you.* [23] *In that day you will ask nothing of me. Truly, truly, I say to you, if you ask anything of the Father, he will give it to you in my name.* [24] *Hitherto you have asked nothing in my name; ask, and you*

10. Marsh, *Saint John*, 544.

will receive, that your joy may be full. ²⁵ "I have said this to you in figures; the hour is coming when I shall no longer speak to you in figures but tell you plainly of the Father. ²⁶ In that day you will ask in my name; and I do not say to you that I shall pray the Father for you; ²⁷ for the Father himself loves you, because you have loved me and have believed that I came from the Father. ²⁸ I came from the Father and have come into the world; again, I am leaving the world and going to the Father." ²⁹ His disciples said, "Ah, now you are speaking plainly, not in any figure! ³⁰ Now we know that you know all things, and need none to question you; by this we believe that you came from God." ³¹ Jesus answered them, "Do you now believe? ³² The hour is coming, indeed it has come, when you will be scattered, every man to his home, and will leave me alone; yet I am not alone, for the Father is with me. ³³ I have said this to you, that in me you may have peace. In the world you have tribulation; but be of good cheer, I have overcome the world."

RESPONSE. I don't know anybody who happily anticipates the arrival of life's most painful episodes—the inevitable heartbreaks, frustrations, disappointments, and failures that every living soul experiences. We'd like to sidestep all of them. We know the trite maxim is true, "Into every life a little rain must fall." But if we were allowed to have our way there'd be blue skies and sunshine 365 days a year, and we'd die peacefully in our sleep after living a hundred healthy, vigorous years. Who among us would not gladly bypass the ordinary miseries of life? Sometimes we feel particularly singled-out by God—or fate, or the Devil—to undergo even worse situations than other people face. At such times we compare ourselves with peers who seem to be coasting through life with nary a care. Then we complain to God, "Why me, Lord? Why does Mary Lou never have my problems? Why does Joe always seem to come out on top?" A reality check shows us that everyone has pains and problems, and no one wins every battle.

The last sentence of Jesus's Farewell Discourse offers subject matter for our prayer and pondering: "In the world you have tribulation; but be of good cheer, I have overcome the world" (v. 33). Jesus does not soft-peddle this prediction of the future for his friends. He doesn't give them a mild and understated warning, like "There may be some rough spots for you down the road." Or, "It's reasonable to assume the chief priests and Pharisees will create problems." No, he tells them flatly, "In the world you have tribulation." In other words, "Do not doubt the nature of life in the world. In this world, there *is* and always *will be* pain, anguish, and grief. These are certainties of mortal life." Following Jesus does not earn anyone exemption from the ordeals of everyday human existence or guarantee them a lifetime of unbroken spiritual bliss.

John's Gospel speaks of "the world" much the same way as it speaks of "the Jews;" both expressions are often employed in either ambivalent or ambiguous ways. The Jews are frequently portrayed as Jesus's enemies—constantly seeking to do him harm. Yet, Jesus is a Jew, as are all of his disciples, and he tells the woman at the well in

Samaria that "salvation is from the Jews" (4:22). The community of believers gathered around Jesus is not being shaped to annihilate Judaism, but rather to renew it and perfect it. The verse of John's Gospel that we know best begins with the words, "For God so loved the world that he gave his only Son" (3:16). Yet here, at the end of the Farewell Discourse, he tells his friends that he has "overcome the world."

As we read this conclusion to the Farewell Discourse and Jesus's great prayer that follows in chapter 17, we must not forget to keep the author's rhetorical ambiguities and ambivalences in mind. The Word (the *Logos*) is God's agent in the creation of the world (1:1–3). God loves the world and sends his Son, the incarnate Word, to save it. At the same time, John perceives the world as the stage on which the cosmic struggle between the life-giving, self-offering love of God and the death-dealing selfishness of the Evil One is being played out. Disciples of Jesus are in the world, on that stage, and engaged in that struggle as agents of God's grace. To *overcome the world*, as Jesus does, and as his faithful followers are summoned to do in his name, does not mean to destroy or demean the world, but to defeat the world's rebellion and completely redeem and restore it. To fulfill our calling, we who are disciples of Jesus must be willing to play the role our Master plays. Jesus's victory will be total, yet it cannot be complete until he dies on the cross.

The poet Gerard Manley Hopkins comes to my mind as a disciple who perseveres to his life's end in faithfulness to the example of his Savior, in spite of numerous personal failures, disappointments, bouts of depression, and spiritual aridity. An upper middle-class Victorian Englishman, Hopkins converts to Roman Catholicism while he is a student at Oxford, which estranges him from his Anglican family and many of his friends. Later, under the influence of John Henry Newman, he becomes a Jesuit priest and serves in a variety of different school and parish assignments around England before spending the last five years of his life as professor of Greek and Latin literature at Cardinal Newman's newly founded Catholic University College in Dublin. It's sufficient for my purposes simply to point out that, once he finishes his studies, Gerard Manley Hopkins fails to find much success in anything.

He earns no recognition as a pastor in the slums, or as a preacher, retreat leader, theologian, or teacher, even though he throws all his energy into every task assigned him and habitually works to exhaustion. Neither is he much appreciated for his poetry until long after he is dead. Hopkins suffers greatly from depression and melancholy during the latter years of his life, at one point finding himself unable to feel close to God even in prayer. He sometimes worries he is losing his mind. In those trying and difficult times the poet "screams out his pain in anguished—and brilliant—sonnets like 'I wake and feel the fell of dark' and 'No worst, there is none.'"[11]

Yet, in spite of his many frustrations, oppressive mental darkness, and personal disappointments, Hopkins' final words before dying of typhus at age forty-five seem full of what can only be called supernatural peace. He says to those at his bedside, "I

11. Feeny, "Praise Him," 1.

am so happy. I am so happy. I loved my life."[12] The personal history of Gerard Manley Hopkins is testimony to a life of paradox: a depressed, ascetic priest and poet who on his deathbed declares himself a very happy man.—How could such an outcome be possible?

When we read his dark sonnets, the man's melancholy is apparent. Still, when we read his spiritual poems, the depth of his passion for Christ cannot be missed. I have no doubt that Hopkins felt in his soul the reality of what Jesus told his friends at the end of his final talk with them: "In the world you have tribulation; but be of good cheer, I have overcome the world." The poet priest drank deeply from the cup of this world's tribulation, yet his final cry was a shout of joy. He tasted Christ's victory. Hopkins proved himself to be a disciple like his Teacher, a servant like his Master. (See Matt 10:25*a*.)

Doing Your Own Theology

Questions for reflection after reading John 16.

- Earlier, Jesus told those who believed in him, "You will know the truth, and the truth will make you free" (8:31–32). Now Jesus, who just said, "I am the way, and the truth, and the life" (14:6), promises to send his followers the "Spirit of truth," who will guide them "into all the truth" (v. 13). History shows that in every age humanity is compelled to grapple with newly recognized truth. Pride causes us to imagine we know more than we do, and when our arrogance is in full bloom we presume ourselves qualified to issue dogmatic definitions with bold certainty. Then God surprises us with humbling new insights into the truth. Because our mortal capacity for understanding is limited, God chooses not to give us more than we can handle at any one time.—*To be guided "into all the truth" implies a process, a progressive deepening of engagement with truth. Has your own experience of the Spirit's guidance been characterized by gradual, progressive growth? What have been the stages of your growth? From what previous limitations (e.g., deceptions, fears, obsessions, and sins) are you slowly or suddenly experiencing freedom through the Spirit's work?*

- In the final verse of chapter 16, we should not pass quickly over a compassionate statement of Jesus that immediately precedes the triumphant assurance, "be of good cheer, I have overcome the world." The preceding statement is, "I have said these things to you that in me you may have peace" (v. 33*a*). As we contemplate that conclusion to the Farewell Discourse from a post-Easter perspective, we may miss what the promise of *peace* actually meant for the disciples as they lived

---

12. Wiman, *Bright Abyss*, 35. Wiman reflects on Hopkins' life on pp. 35–37.

in the moment. Shortly after Jesus spoke these words, they witnessed (rather, fled from) Christ's horrifying crucifixion and death—an event none of them anticipated and which they would come to understand until much later.—*If you felt troubled or afraid at any time during your reading of John, did you find in this gospel any words of Jesus that gave you peace or encouragement, particularly verses to which you are likely to turn again in a time of need? Which words of Jesus touched you in that way? How do you describe the peace that Christ gives you?*

- To "overcome the world" (v. 33), as Jesus does, and as his faithful followers are summoned to do in his name, does not mean to destroy or demean the world, but to defeat the world's rebellion and completely redeem and restore it. To fulfill our calling, we who are disciples of Jesus, must be willing to play the role our Master plays. His victory is total, yet it is announced as he dies on the cross. "God so loved the world that he gave his only Son" (3:16). The personal history of Gerard Manley Hopkins (described above in the response to vv. 16–33) is testimony to a life of paradox. Hopkins was a depressed, ascetic priest and poet who experiences rejection, hardship, frustration, disease, and repeated failure in life, yet—as he is dying from typhus in only his mid-forties—he declares himself a very happy man, reportedly saying "I loved my life." Indeed, many of his poems glow with the joy of his faithful devotion to Christ.—*What might a life of perseverant faith like that of Gerard Manley Hopkins signify to a person who is experiencing similar misfortunes? What spiritual resources enable a believer to "overcome the world"? Have you known anyone who exhibited a similar strength of soul?*

Chapter Seventeen

John 17:1–26. Jesus's "High Priestly" Prayer.

Vv. 1–8. "Father, the hour has come;
glorify thy Son that the Son may glorify thee."

INTRODUCTION. At the end of his Farewell Discourse (chapters 14–17), still in the presence of his friends, Jesus lifts his eyes to heaven and prays aloud to his Father. This is the longest prayer attributed to Jesus in any of the Gospels. Since the Protestant Reformation it has borne the label, Jesus's "High Priestly Prayer." Such a label imagines Jesus in the role of the "great High Priest who has passed through the heavens," described in Hebrews 4:14, communing with his Father both from within time and outside time, both "in the world" (v. 18) and yet "no longer in the world" (v. 11).[1] Jesus ceases to address his friends directly at 16:33 and from 17:1 to 26 speaks only to his Father with deep intimacy and trust. This lengthy prayer provides John's readers with a theological exposition of the Fourth Gospel. It is somewhat circular and repetitive, and commentators analyze it in various ways. The simplest way is to see it as a prayer with three related subjects: Jesus prays for himself and his work (vv. 1–8), for the future life of his followers (vv. 9–23), and expresses the intimate connection of will which he shares with his Father (vv. 24–26).[2]

Jesus's *hour* is first mentioned in 2:4, at the time of his first miracle at Cana in Galilee. Readers await the arrival of the hour, until 12:23, when—after his triumphal entry into Jerusalem and after learning that some Greeks want to see him—Jesus tells the disciples, "The hour has come for the Son of Man to be glorified." Everything we read from that point until the morning of the resurrection must be understood as encompassed within Jesus's metaphoric hour, the divinely appointed time when the glory of the Son of God is fully disclosed in his acceptance of a shameful death at the

---

1. This title was apparently first applied to ch. 17 by Lutheran theologian David Chytraeus (1531–1600). See Keener, *Gospel of John*, 2:1051.

2. See O'Day, *Gospel of John*, 788–96. Other commentators propose slightly different divisions.

hands of the Evil One's human agents and his being raised from death to life by the power of the Father.

The glorification of God's Son is not an end in itself, but rather the means by which the Father will be glorified. In John, *glory* is God's majesty deliberately made visible to mortals through an act of God's power.[3] Concerning the Son of God, John tells us in the prologue that by virtue of the incarnation "we have beheld his glory" (1:14). In 2:11 John states that by his first sign, performed at Cana, Jesus "manifested his glory." Therefore, we understand the glorification for which Jesus prays is a glory exceeding any that has already been revealed. Jesus's resurrection from the dead and the gift of eternal life will be the supreme revelation by which God makes his glory known through his Son.

Commentators have a great deal to say about v. 3, "And this is eternal life, that they know thee the only true God, and Jesus Christ whom thou hast sent." The majority agree that this verse is probably a theological explanation inserted by the narrator—something modern writers would put in a footnote. (Jesus never speaks of himself in the third person as "Jesus Christ," an expression found only here and in 1:17 in John.) When John tells us that eternal life is "to *know* thee, the only true God," he employs the verb *know* in a distinctly biblical and Hebrew way, as a reference to *intimate relationship*. He does not use "know" the way Greek philosophers do, referring to comprehension of concepts. For John's Gospel, to know the Father and the Son is to be united with them. The Johannine understanding of eternal life permits readers to perceive it not only as a future hope but a present possession for those whom the Father has given to his Son (v. 2), for those who believe in him, his little flock.[4]

We can only speculate about the deeper meaning of v. 5, "Father, glorify thou me in thy own presence with the glory which I had with thee before the world was made." Does this petition of Jesus's prayer simply anticipate the return of God's eternal *Logos*, his Son, to the glorious status which he laid aside to become incarnate as a mortal man? Or is this petition meant to draw readers' attention to the profound mystery of the resurrection of the Son of God/Son of Man and the full incorporation of his transformed humanity into the primordial glory of the *Logos*?

The true meaning of all Jesus asks in v. 5 depends on something only the Spirit-inspired author of the Fourth gospel might be able to tell us, if we were able to question him. When John writes that Jesus prays for himself, saying, "Father, glorify thou *me*," is the "me" in question understood to be Jesus of Nazareth, fully divine *and* fully human? If not, then why is Jesus's tomb left empty on the morning of the third day? Christian faith does not regard the incarnation as merely a temporary expedient adopted by God as means to a greater end. The incarnation of God's Son is an end in itself, the Father's eternal choice, his plan for the redemption of humanity. The New Testament portrays the *body* of Jesus as raised from death on the third day and

---

3. Brown, *John XIII–XXI*, 751.

4. Köstenberger, *Encountering John*, 488.

ultimately taken into heaven (see 20:17; cf. Luke 24:50–52; Acts 1:9–11), where—in his resurrected flesh—Jesus is "exalted at the right hand of God" (see, e.g., Acts 2:33; cf. Mark 16:19; Acts 5:30–31; Heb 10:12).[5]

When Jesus says, "I have manifested thy name to the men whom thou gavest me out of the world" (v. 6), one obvious assumption is that the name he manifested (that is, the "person" that he revealed) is God, whose sacred name, *I AM*, Jesus intentionally claims for himself (e.g., 4:26; 6:20; 8:24, 58; 13:19).[6] Or we might understand God's "name" here in the purely Hebraic sense, referring to God's "character and identity."[7] It also appears obvious that in the Fourth Gospel Jesus reveals to his followers God's name as "Father," doing so in a way that invites them also to call God their Father (14:6; and see, e.g., 20:17).

> **[17:1–8]** *¹ When Jesus had spoken these words, he lifted up his eyes to heaven and said, "Father, the hour has come; glorify thy Son that the Son may glorify thee, ² since thou hast given him power over all flesh, to give eternal life to all whom thou hast given him. ³ And this is eternal life, that they know thee the only true God, and Jesus Christ whom thou hast sent. ⁴ I glorified thee on earth, having accomplished the work which thou gavest me to do; ⁵ and now, Father, glorify thou me in thy own presence with the glory which I had with thee before the world was made.*
>
> *⁶ "I have manifested thy name to the men whom thou gavest me out of the world; thine they were, and thou gavest them to me, and they have kept thy word. ⁷ Now they know that everything that thou hast given me is from thee; ⁸ for I have given them the words which thou gavest me, and they have received them and know in truth that I came from thee; and they have believed that thou didst send me.*

RESPONSE. When we get old enough to know we have relatively few years left to live, if we have children we begin to think about what sort of personal legacy we want to leave to our descendants. I'm not referring to bequests of material wealth—money, land, old jewelry, or antique furniture. I'm thinking about wealth of a different sort, the legacy of wisdom and faith—or both—we might pass along both to the next generation and those who come after them.

I've written a number of things, including this book, and what I have written is part of my legacy of faith. I've thought about also composing a personal prayer for my children and grandchildren. This would not be something for publication, but a prayer I would print and seal in an envelope to be opened after I'm gone. It might possibly be inspiring for my children and grandchildren to read what I asked the Lord on their behalf back in the days when I was still with them. My prayer would be part

5. The New Testament's best explanation of these matters is offered by Paul in 1 Cor 15:12–50.

6. Keener, *Gospel of John*, 2:1056.

7. O'Day, *Gospel of John*, 791.

of my personal legacy of faith, and perhaps it might give them some inspiration for their own lives.

As I consider this, I wonder, "Will I pray differently for them, knowing they're in a sense going to be 'listening' to my prayer, than I would if I kept that prayer totally secret, just between the Lord and me?" Jesus's High Priestly Prayer is a bit like what I'm considering—a prayer written for his disciples to read and ponder after he was crucified, resurrected, and raised to the Father's right hand. I'm not saying that's exactly what we find here in John, but I suspect it might be close to what the author of the gospel had in mind.

Jesus prays, "Father, the hour has come; glorify thy Son that the Son may glorify thee, since thou hast given him power over all flesh, to give eternal life to all whom thou hast given him. And this is eternal life, that they know thee the only true God, and Jesus Christ whom thou hast sent" (vv.1*b*–3). Jesus prays to God as his own Father, which is not the way Jewish people in his time usually prayed. Most of the time they did not call God "Father." We learn elsewhere that Jesus often addressed God as "*Abba*," the special name only a Jewish man's own children would use for their father. It's a name that expresses great intimacy, a name that assumes a special, close, and loving parent-child bond.

We typically permit our children liberties we wouldn't allow other people. We listen to them and care about them and sacrifice for them in ways we're not likely to do for other people. For Jesus to know God as his *Abba* was unprecedented. That makes all the more significant the great legacy which Jesus left his disciples and us—to know the Creator of the Universe as our own dear Father, our own *Abba*. Outside the empty tomb on Easter morning, when he appears to Mary Magdalene, Jesus tells her, "Go, and tell my brothers that I'm ascending to my Father and your Father, to my God and your God" (20:17).

Jesus went to great lengths to explain to his disciples that if they really know *him*, they can be certain they know his Father also, because the two are united. Jesus is the human face of God, the one whom Paul calls "the image of the invisible God" (Col 1:15). If his friends understand how much Jesus loves them, then they can be positive that's how much *God* loves them. If Jesus is patient and understands them in spite of their mistakes and their foolishness, if Jesus is willing to forgive their pettiness and squabbling with one another, then they can know their heavenly Father is likewise merciful and forgiving. They need not be afraid of being caught short on some awful future day of judgment and condemned to everlasting punishment. As John will say in his First Letter, "There is no fear in love, but perfect love casts out fear" (1 John 4:18).

John tells us what eternal life is: a life in relationship with the Father and the Son, a life in which Jesus's disciples *know* God, who has disclosed himself in Jesus. This way of knowing God does not mean having information about God, but rather having a deep personal relationship with God. Here's an analogy that might help us understand this better. From conception each one of us is deeply connected with our mother.[8] We *know* our mothers. Hers is the first voice we learn to recognize. Even though when we're very young we don't have much factual knowledge *about* mom (like her shoe size or the name of her best friend in middle school), we *do* know her. Our relationship with her is intimate. We know mom's touch. We know the light in her eyes when she looks at us. And we know she knows *us*—and that she loves us totally. Eternal life means knowing our heavenly Father the same way we know our mothers when we're little children—with exactly the same assurance of being loved, protected, and safe. Jesus is thankful that the Father has given him power to give his disciples this gift of "eternal life," an everlasting relationship with God as their loving Father. *And they have it already.* They don't have to die and go to heaven in order to receive it.

In the Old Testament story about Moses's encounter with the burning bush, Moses asks God to tell him his name. God tells Moses his name is "I-AM-THAT-I-AM," which can also be translated as "I-will-be-what-I-will-be" (Exod 3:14). Jews, however, were not permitted to pronounce the sacred name of God. Only the high priest was allowed to do that, and then only once a year. But Jesus revealed to his friends what we might describe as God's "human" name, *Father.* God had said to Moses, "My name is 'I-will-be-what-I-will-be,'" and now God tells his Son Jesus that he is going to be, for all time, "Father" to those who put their trust in him. And they may call him *Abba,* too, anytime they wish.

As we read Jesus's High Priestly Prayer, we can recognize that our Lord wishes for us most of all to have the same intimate relationship with the Father that he had during his earthly ministry—the same intimacy, the same mutual love, and the same ability to demonstrate the mercy of God in our dealings with other people. If we will but claim it, the legacy Christ has given his sisters and brothers is to be like him in this world.

Vv. 9–26. "Holy Father, keep them in thy name . . . that they may be one, even as we are one."

INTRODUCTION. As Jesus prays for his disciples in vv. 9–25, we notice some of John's most negative language about the world. Jesus refuses to pray for the world (v. 9); the world hates his disciples, "who are not of the world, even as I am not of world" (vv. 14, 16); and the world "has not known" the Father (v. 25). Still, his prayer makes obvious that Jesus perceives his disciples' mission as being *to* the world, precisely as Jesus's own mission has been *to* the world (vv. 11, 18, 21, 23; cf. 20:21). John understands Jesus as the great high priest who offers himself (the Lamb of God) as the sacrifice that takes away the sin of the world and who sets for his disciples an example of

---

8. The intimate bond between a child and the child's *mother*, rather than its father, provides a better analogy for the Johannine picture of the relationship between a believer and God. Because God has no gender, the scriptural characterization of God as "Father" does not exclude God's obvious *maternal* qualities.

self-sacrifice which they will reproduce. He says, "For their sake I consecrate myself, that they also may be consecrated in truth" (v. 17). To "be consecrated" means to be set apart for God as an offering, a sacrifice.

In the mind of John, at least, if not also in the mind of Christ himself, the world is a hostile and largely godless milieu, where the community of Jesus's disciples must engage in a constant struggle with the agents of the Evil One (see 1 John 2:15–16). In spite of this, the Fourth Gospel's confidence in ultimate victory over the world is never abandoned. John proclaims it at the beginning of the prologue (1:5), when readers are assured that the light will always triumph over darkness, and repeats it at the end of the Farewell Discourse (16:33), when the disciples on the eve of Jesus's crucifixion are assured that he has overcome the world. In Christian history, recognition of the world's hostility to the gospel has produced at various times either a siege mentality, vigilant in guarding against the world's wickedness, or an aggressive attitude, commit- ted to winning the world for Christ.[9] Both have been evident in the past, and both can still be seen today.

The last part of Jesus's prayer has become the favorite gospel of the modern ecu- menical movement: "I do not pray for these only, but also for those who believe in me through their word, that they may all be one; even as thou, Father, art in me, and I in thee, that they also may be in us, so that the world may believe that thou hast sent me" (vv. 20–21). This reminds us of what Jesus says earlier in the allegory of the shepherd and his sheep, keeping in mind the unique Hebraic meaning of intimate relationship implied by the use of the verb *know,* "I am the good shepherd; I know my own and my own know me, as the Father knows me and I know the Father; and I lay down my life for the sheep. And I have other sheep, that are not of this fold; I must bring them also, and they will heed my voice. So there shall be one flock, one shepherd" (10:14–16).

Jesus's prayer for his disciples—including both those who are with him at the moment and those who will ultimately come to believe in him through their testimo- ny—is rooted in the analogy between his relationship to the Father and his disciples' relationship to Jesus. It is essential that his own loving unity with the Father be reflect- ed in his followers' unity with one another in him (see 14:18–24). The salvation of the world ("that the world may believe," v. 21) hinges on this unity, because a fragmented Christian community "denies by its behavior the message which it proclaims."[10] A perfectly united body of believers will provide a living witness to the truth that Jesus was sent from the Father and that the Father loves those who believe in the Son exactly the same way that he loves the Son himself (v. 23). All unity proceeds from love. The world has not known the Father (v. 25), but Jesus knows the Father, and his disciples know Jesus. The Savior's hopes for the world depend on the disciples.

---

9. Brown, *Community,* 63–66, offers a helpful analysis of the Johannine community's sensitivity to the hostility of the world.

10. Lindars, *Gospel of John,* 530.

[17:9–26] *⁹ I am praying for them; I am not praying for the world but for those whom thou hast given me, for they are thine; ¹⁰ all mine are thine, and thine are mine, and I am glorified in them. ¹¹ And now I am no more in the world, but they are in the world, and I am coming to thee. Holy Father, keep them in thy name, which thou hast given me, that they may be one, even as we are one. ¹² While I was with them, I kept them in thy name, which thou hast given me; I have guarded them, and none of them is lost but the son of perdition, that the Scripture might be fulfilled. ¹³ But now I am coming to thee; and these things I speak in the world, that they may have my joy fulfilled in themselves. ¹⁴ I have given them thy word; and the world has hated them because they are not of the world, even as I am not of the world.*

¹⁵ I do not pray that thou shouldst take them out of the world, but that thou shouldst keep them from the evil one. ¹⁶ They are not of the world, even as I am not of the world. ¹⁷ Sanctify them in the truth; thy word is truth. ¹⁸ As thou didst send me into the world, so I have sent them into the world. ¹⁹ And for their sake I consecrate myself, that they also may be consecrated in truth.

²⁰ "I do not pray for these only, but also for those who believe in me through their word, ²¹ that they may all be one; even as thou, Father, art in me, and I in thee, that they also may be in us, so that the world may believe that thou hast sent me. ²² The glory which thou hast given me I have given to them, that they may be one even as we are one, ²³ I in them and thou in me, that they may become perfectly one, so that the world may know that thou hast sent me and hast loved them even as thou hast loved me. ²⁴ Father, I desire that they also, whom thou hast given me, may be with me where I am, to behold my glory which thou hast given me in thy love for me before the foundation of the world. ²⁵ O righteous Father, the world has not known thee, but I have known thee; and these know that thou hast sent me. ²⁶ I made known to them thy name, and I will make it known, that the love with which thou hast loved me may be in them, and I in them."

RESPONSE. We live in a fragmented world, there's no arguing with that. On our planet we have different countries, different cultures, different races, and different religions. We also have different economic systems, different political systems, and different ideas about the right way to do things. Here in our own country we divide ourselves into liberals and conservatives, progressives and traditionalists, "those who have it right," and "those who have it wrong" (depending on one's partisan allegiance). It seems we're obsessed with our *differences*, labeling winners and losers, and deciding who are the "good guys" and who are the "bad guys." A couple of years ago I read a survey that said the only areas of broad agreement in the world are about movies and pop music. (That can't be a good sign.) We're exhausted by this discord and fragmentation, and it's especially painful when our divisions are celebrated in the name of God or truth. In the name of God, people demean, ignore, or even use violence against those who aren't part of their faction.

As we read Jesus's High Priestly Prayer, we see him interceding not only for the disciples with him that night after the Last Supper, but for us—for all those down through the centuries who will ultimately come to believe in him because of the testimony that will be given by his disciples there at the table with him (v. 20). The heart of his prayer is that his disciples might "all be one." As John tells it, the last thing on Jesus's heart, the deepest prayer of his soul, is "that they may all be one; even as thou, Father, art in me, and I in thee, that they also may be in us, so that the world may believe that thou hast sent me" (v. 21).

We have a tendency to idealize Jesus's first disciples: Peter and Andrew, James and John, Thomas, Nathaniel and the others. But there's evidence that these men disagreed with one another regularly. When Jesus was with them in the flesh and they were paying attention to him, they got along. But when Jesus went away even for a little while they began to argue about foolish things—such as which one of them was "the greatest."

The disciples could behave badly towards one another. So, there's a good reason that Jesus's last *instructions to* them are to love one another as he loves them (13:34–35), and that his final *prayer for* them is that they might be united. If they were already living in unity and loving one another, these final instructions and last prayer would have been superfluous.

Notice this: when Jesus is about to depart from his disciples to return to the Father, he *commands* them to love one another, but he *prays* that they might be one. There's a subtle but significant distinction in this. Jesus does not *command* his disciples to be one, because the unity he wants for them is not something they will be able to manufacture on their own as an act of simple obedience. Unity can only come from the Father as a work of the Spirit. For Christians in our time, just as for Jesus's first disciples, unity will not happen unless we submit ourselves to the Spirit of God. It will never be our own achievement. Thus, the final petition of Jesus's prayer remains unfulfilled, not because the Father closes his heart to the entreaty of his Son, but because Christians persistently refuse to yield themselves to the Spirit—who entreats, inspires, encourages, counsels, and consoles, but never *compels* us to do anything.

History shows that Christians have long sought what we imagined to be unity. For centuries we dreamed that we could somehow *impose* unity on one another—that our unity could somehow be engineered. The Nicene Creed was intended to bring unity. Obedience to the Pope was supposed to create unity. Enforced forms of worship were designed to produce unity. Agreement that the Bible is the Word of God and contains all things needed for salvation was supposed to build unity too. But none of these efforts accomplished the task. The best we've been able to do with our popes, primates, creeds, catechisms, liturgies, vows, and laws has been to compel a certain degree of *uniformity* here and there. But that is not *unity*. We do not see Jesus praying for uniformity among his disciples just before he leads them out to the Mount of Olives on his last evening with them. No, Jesus prays that the oneness of the Father and the Son, bound together in mutual love, will be matched by unity and love among those who believe in him.

Nothing the church has produced until now is able to generate the unity Christ sought on his last night with the disciples.—And why is that? Why have we failed? We have failed because for more than a millennium and a half—since Christianity became a legal religion in the Roman Empire—the church has clung to a worldly, "managed" picture of what we imagine Christian unity ought to look like, i.e. *uniformity*. We have attempted to turn our fantasy of uniformity into reality by using every coercive or manipulative device available, and we have failed. Instead of achieving unity, Europe has had heresies, wars of religion, mutual hatred, and conflict followed by exhaustion, then finally—in our age—apathy. Today, once-Christian Europe is the most thoroughly secular culture on earth. While America is somewhat less secularized than Europe in these early decades of the third Christian millennium, American Christians are even more fragmented than our European sisters and brothers.

Jesus prays that his disciples will be "one." He does not pray that they concur on all interpretations of Scripture or be submitted to any particular church order. Jesus's frame of reference in the prayer we read in chapter 17 of John is not dogmatic or jurisdictional. Jesus's frame of reference is *his own identity and relationship with God*. It is the deep intimacy and communion he has with the Father. He wants his disciples in ages to come to share that with him and with one another and, ultimately, with as many people in the world as they possibly can. The unity Jesus prays for is for the sake of his followers' mission in the world, so the world may believe that God sent his Son into it to save it—the very realm that turned its back on its Creator.

God's answer to Jesus's prayer is to send the Spirit. The Spirit of God, working in the lives of Jesus's disciples, is the only thing that has ever brought Christians together in anything approaching the kind of loving unity our Lord seeks. That's a unity not based on who we are, but on who God is.

Jesus does not pray for unity without also acknowledging what we might call God's "disposition," or character—namely, that the Father is one with his Son, Jesus, and that God loves Jesus's friends in exactly the same way he loves Jesus (v. 23). The unity the Lord wants for us is not uniformity in our expressions of Christian faith. Unity is not defined by the absence of diversity or even the absence of disagreement. Unity arises out of authentic submission to the Spirit of Christ, *who moves us to love one another in spite of our differences*. The church of Jesus Christ is meant to be the community where all are invited to come and discover a new life—a life characterized by healing, reconciliation, and the love of God.

Doing Your Own Theology

Questions for reflection after reading John 17.

- At the beginning of Jesus's High Priestly Prayer, the narrator of the Fourth Gospel inserts his own theological definition of eternal life, (composed of material that would probably be found in a footnote if John's Gospel were a book written in our time): "And this is eternal life, that they know thee the only true God, and Jesus Christ whom thou hast sent" (v. 3). From the first mention of eternal life in John (found in 3:15–16), it is clear that Jesus employs the expression eternal life to mean a state of personal communion with God that begins now for the believer and continues into eternity. Eternal life is to *know* the Father and the Son, not in the sense of having information, but of having *connectedness*, relational intimacy with God.—*Reflecting on what you have read in the Fourth Gospel to this point, by what ways does John say believers come to know the Father and the Son? What role is played by the Spirit-Paraclete in this process? What role is played by other believers? Would you feel comfortable saying, "I know the Lord," or would you regard such a declaration as presumptuous or prideful?*

- Jesus prays, "Father, glorify thou me in thy own presence with the glory which I had with thee before the world was made" (v. 5). The true meaning of this petition depends on something only John himself might tell us if we were able to question him. When the author tells us Jesus prays for himself, saying, "Father, glorify thou *me*," who precisely does he mean? We must assume that *me* means Jesus of Nazareth, fully divine *and* fully human, since Jesus's tomb is empty on the day of resurrection. Christian faith does not regard the incarnation of God's Son as merely a temporary expedient. The risen Lord does not leave his human body behind, instead the New Testament portrays the *body* of Jesus as raised from death and ultimately taken into heaven (see 20:17; cf. Luke 24:50–52; Acts 1:9–11), where—in his resurrected flesh—Jesus is eternally "exalted at the right hand of God."—*Realizing that this question calls for a bit of mystical speculation, what do you imagine as the glory Jesus asks for in this prayer? What does the ultimate glorification of the resurrected Son of God/Son of Man imply for his followers, his totally human sisters and brothers? What hint does this give us about John's understanding of the full potential and destiny of humankind?*[11]

- The last part of Jesus's High Priestly Prayer has become the gospel of the modern ecumenical movement, "I do not pray for these only, but also for those who believe in me through their word, that they may all be one; even as thou, Father, art in me, and I in thee, that they also may be in us, so that the world may believe that thou hast sent me" (vv. 20–21). Divisions within the body of believers have been evident in various ways since the second century. Jesus prays that all

11. This relates to the Eastern Orthodox doctrine of *theosis* (or "divinization").

who believe in him "might be one," yet history is witness to more than seventeen centuries of increasing fragmentation, until the birth of the modern ecumenical movement in 1910. The unity that Jesus prayed for is slow in coming.—*All real unity proceeds from love. Is our failure truly to love one another the reason that the world-wide body of believers is not united? Are there other reasons for divisions between Christians? How is it possible for Christians to have unity without uniformity? Do you see signs of hope for Christian unity today?*

Figure 10. Israel Museum scale model of Herod's Palace in Jerusalem. Herod's fortress-palace was the second most impressive building in Jerusalem, after the temple. It was built on the highest point in the city, atop Mount Zion, with thick walls over forty feet high, including three high, independently fortified towers. The complex included two elaborate, ostentatiously furnished multi-storied matching residences (each capable of housing a hundred guests) facing one another north and south across a broad expanse of gardens, colonnades, porticoes, and cisterns, ornamented with numerous bronze statues and fountains.[1] The Israel Museum scale model only suggests the complexity of the palace; it does not portray the details, although it does indicate the massive fortifications. The palace was undoubtedly used by Pilate as his *praetorium*. It is only about a thousand yards from the traditional site of Jesus's crucifixion.

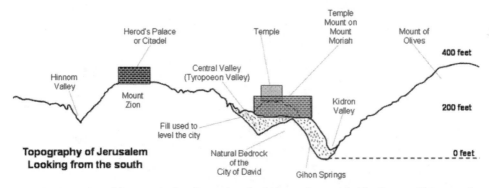

Figure 11. Diagram of the topography of Jerusalem, looking south to north. The diagram illustrates the difference in height between Mount Zion, upon the summit of which Herod built his fortress-palace, and Mount Moriah, the site of the temple. This diagram portrays the "box" composed of enormous limestone ashlars with which Herod's engineers surrounded the summit of Mount Moriah in order to expand the temple platform. The largest of these ashlars, in the foundation course of the temple platform sustaining wall, were each almost forty feet long, weighing eighty tons.

1. See Josephus, *Wars*, V.iv.4, 553–54.

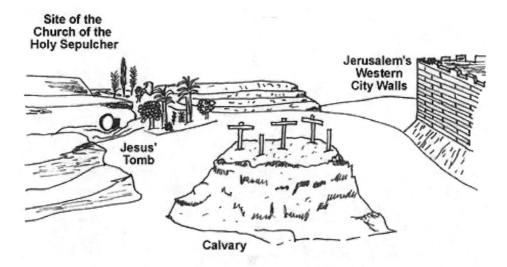

Figure 12. Diagram showing Jesus's tomb and Calvary (Golgotha), both of which were in an abandoned quarry. Calvary/Golgotha was a cranium-like knob of stone the quarrymen had rejected. Both sites lie within the ancient shrine church originally built by Constantine between 325 and 335 CE, originally called the Church of the Resurrection (*Anastasis*), later called the Church of the Holy Sepulcher by the Crusaders. This complex, damaged by earthquakes and wars and reconstructed a number of times still stands on its original site.

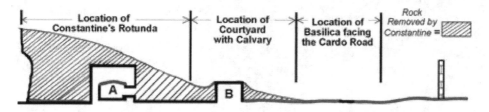

Figure 13. Profile diagram showing Jesus's tomb (A) and Calvary (B). The shaded portion is the rock cut away by Constantine's engineers to leave the tomb of Christ and the rock of Calvary (unshaded) as freestanding elements to be enclosed in Constantine's shrine church, as shown in Fig. 14, below.

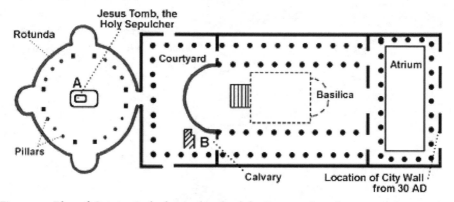

Figure 14. Plan of Constantine's shrine church of the Resurrection, the courtyard *martyrium* of Calvary, and the attached basilica, ca. 335 CE.

Figure 15. The Church of the Holy Sepulcher today. The dome on the left covers Constantine's ancient rotunda of the *Anastasis*; the dome on the right is above the rock of Calvary.

Figure 16. The Aedicule enclosing what remains of the tomb of Christ today in the Church of the Holy Sepulcher. This is the sepulcher which gives its name to the church. The freestanding tomb as left by Constantine's engineers was pounded to rubble in 1009 by soldiers of the Fatimid Caliph Al-Hakim, but the lowest portions and the actual shelf on which the body of Christ was laid remained under the debris. These were ultimately sheathed in marble to deter relic hunters from chipping away fragments, and they remain within this ornate nineteenth-century aedicule. Some of the visible columns of the rotunda still remain from Constantine's original shrine, although each column is only half the height of the original.

A General Introduction to Chapters 18–19.
John's Passion Narrative

The oldest parts of the gospel tradition are two bodies of narrative material we know as stories of the passion of Christ and stories of his resurrection.[1] The first describe the events of Jesus's life on Thursday night and Friday of his last week (beginning with the Last Supper and ending with his death and burial), and the second depict what took place on Sunday morning (beginning with the women's discovery of the empty tomb and including various appearances of the risen Christ). Accounts of Jesus's suffering, death and resurrection begin to circulate soon after the events, offered first by eyewitnesses and then retold by others. The various narratives take shape so early and are repeated so often that they become the heart of the Christian proclamation, the core of the gospel. This is evident in Paul's First Letter to the Corinthians (written only about twenty years after the resurrection). The apostle writes of what he has "received" and has "delivered" to the Corinthians—meaning the traditions about Jesus he has been taught and which he has passed along to his converts. The historical events he mentions all are drawn from narratives of the passion and the resurrection—the Lord's Supper, betrayal, crucifixion, and rising from the dead (see 1 Cor 11:23–25 and 15:1–11). Paul's theological teaching in the letter focuses on Christ crucified and Christ risen. The earliest known Christian creed comes from mid-second century Rome, and it supports our sense that the stories of Christ's incarnation, passion, and resurrection/ascension are the essential elements of the gospel. That first creed says about the life of Jesus only that he was: "born of the Holy Spirit from the Virgin Mary, crucified and buried under Pontius Pilate, on the third day rose from the dead, [and] ascended into heaven."[2]

Scholars debate how quickly any of the stories of the passion and resurrection are put into writing. Theories abound concerning sources used by the gospel writers as well as about other early and presumably lost gospels. Nevertheless, by the time the canonical gospels begin to circulate, the known sequence of events of Thursday, Friday and Sunday have acquired a more or less fixed form.[3] Because John's work is most likely the last of the four canonical gospels to be published, we can be confident that both its author and his intended audience are by now familiar with the stories of Jesus's passion and resurrection. Our author writes his gospel in order to communi-

---

1. "Passion" derives from the Latin word *passio*, meaning "suffering," which is cognate with the Greek verb *paschō*, "to suffer."

2. Kelly, *Early Creeds*, 102.

3. See Lindars, *Gospel of John*, 533–34; Keener, *Gospel of John*, 2:1067–73.

cate and preserve the unique theological perspective of the Beloved Disciple regarding the person and work of Christ. He tells stories which have already become familiar in a way he believes will most effectively communicate his inspired personal understanding of these events and their significance.

We previously noted that John's Gospel differs in many ways from the three Synoptics. For example, John follows an alternate chronology, focuses Jesus's ministry in Jerusalem rather than Galilee, includes accounts of relatively few miracles and no exorcisms, makes use of few extended parables, and portrays Jesus as speaking early and often about his divine Sonship but rarely giving ethical instruction. John's Passion Narrative, however, is virtually forced to follow the same basic outline as the other gospels because the actual course of events leading to Jesus's death and resurrection are widely known among Christians. John begins with the disciples' exit from the city after supper to a place on the eastern side of the Kidron (though only John calls it a garden, using a Greek word that usually applies to a walled agricultural area). It continues with Jesus's arrest by a detachment of armed men guided to the garden by Judas Iscariot, a hearing before the high priest into which is woven the story of Peter's three-fold denial, a trial before the Roman governor (the dramatic centerpiece of John's story), Jesus's crucifixion and death with two others on Golgotha, and ends with his immediate burial in the rock-hewn tomb of a rich sympathizer named Joseph of Arimathea.

Though the outline of John's Passion Narrative is similar to the Synoptics, there are differences in a great many details. The most obvious difference is that the Johannine Jesus demonstrates no evidence of suffering. In spite of what he experiences, Jesus displays such serenity that for us even to label John's account a "*Passion* Narrative" seems wrong. John's only acknowledgment of what the other gospels portray as Jesus's psychological or physical agony is contained in the proclamation Jesus makes in the temple on the previous Sunday after his triumphal entry, "Now is my soul troubled. And what shall I say, 'Father, save me from this hour'? No, for this purpose I have come to this hour. Father, glorify thy name" (12:27–28).

Chapter Eighteen

John 18:1–40. John's Passion Narrative begins: Jesus is arrested, interrogated by the high priest, then taken to Pilate.

Vv. 1–11. "Shall I not drink the cup which the Father has given me?"

INTRODUCTION. In John's telling of what transpires in the garden on Thursday night, Jesus displays no behavior one might construe as symptomatic of the anxious emotional turmoil portrayed in the Synoptics. John undoubtedly has heard the story recorded in Mark 14:32–42, but he includes no similar tale of Jesus exhorting sleepy disciples to stay awake and watch with him while he goes off alone to wrestle in prayer with his submission to the Father's will. John presents his readers with no "agony in the garden." Throughout John's Gospel, Jesus's will and his Father's will are *always* united (4:34). If the Johannine Jesus is indeed "troubled," it is only on the preceding Sunday (12:27). By the time Thursday night arrives he is calm, composed, and fully in charge of everything. At the end of the arrest story, after Peter lashes out with a blade in defense of his Master and wounds a servant of the high priest, Jesus orders him not to resist those who have come to seize him, saying, "Put your sword into its sheath. Shall I not drink the cup which the Father has given me?" (v. 11).[1]

John shows Jesus possessing the initiative in every circumstance, according to his Father's will, including managing the timing of events. Earlier, at the supper, Jesus dips a morsel of bread and gives it to Judas who is seated beside him in the place of honor, saying, "What you are going to do, do quickly" (13:27). The traitor, having already yielded himself to the Devil (13:2), then goes away from the light of Christ into the night. In v. 2, Judas and those with him find their way to the garden by the light of lanterns and torches—a bit of Johannine irony, since these men who are moving stealthily through the darkness are trying to capture one who is, in truth, "the light of the world."

---

1. The Greek word for Peter's weapon would better be translated as "dagger," not "sword."

The armed men accompanying Judas are most likely a group drawn from the temple's Levite guards, a security force we might call the temple police or sergeants-at-arms. They are very unlikely to be Roman soldiers as a number of writers propose.[2] Pilate, a military prefect, would never have put his own troops under even the indirect command of the Jewish chief priests. John tells us that the company with Judas is sent "from the chief priests and the Pharisees" (v. 3). This is the final mention of Pharisees in John's Gospel. None of the other gospels records that the Pharisees are involved with Jesus's death, and in that context John mentions them only here. John invariably describes Pharisees as among Jesus's bitterest theological adversaries, but does not implicate them in the crucifixion. John portrays Jesus's judicial execution as contrived by the chief priests—who at that time belong to four aristocratic families, the most powerful of which is the bet Hanan family, whose patriarch is Annas ben Seth, (high priest from 6 to 15 CE).[3]

When Judas arrives with the posse sent to arrest him, "Jesus, knowing all that was to befall him," comes forward and asks them, "Whom do you seek?" (v. 4). This question takes us back to a story told in the gospel's opening chapter. It is the same question Jesus asks the two men who left the company of disciples around John the Baptist and started following Jesus (1:38). It is also the question that—by implication—the Beloved Disciple is addressing to all who read his testimony.

This is a decisive moment, unique to John's narrative and consistent with his understanding of Jesus as the divine Son of God. To the question, "Whom do you seek," the arresting officers reply, "Jesus of Nazareth." Jesus then responds, "I Am [he]" (v. 5), using a self-designation we know is theologically significant to this gospel writer. Although the RSV inserts the pronoun "he," there is no pronoun in the Greek. It is intended as another absolute claim to God's name, *I Am*.[4] This fulfills the prediction Jesus makes at the supper concerning his betrayal, "I tell you this now, before it takes place, so that when it does take place you will know that I Am [he]" (13:19). The traitor and those with him step back and fall to the ground at the announcement of the sacred name (v. 6)—which is an indication that all members of the company are Jews, since the name would be unintelligible to Gentiles.

Those who come to the garden to apprehend a man supposed to be a dangerous enemy of true religion are confronted—stunningly—by God incarnate. Rather than striking them down for their impudence, he willingly yields himself into their hands, but only after first making sure his disciples are set free. He tells them, "If you seek me, let these men go" (v. 8). Jesus will lay down his life of his own accord; no one can take it from him (10:18). Jesus will die, but now his followers will live because he peacefully

2. Keener, *Gospel of John*, 2:1078–80; Malina and Rohrbaugh, *Social Science Commentary*, 252.

3. Smith, *John*, 329, 332–34; O'Day, *Gospel of John*, 805–8. Keener, *Gospel of John*, 2:1073, says some priests were sympathetic to the Pharisees (notably the *Sagan*, sometimes called "the captain of the temple," who was in charge of the temple's corps of Levite police).

4. Brown, *John XIII–XXI*, 818.

gives himself up to death. In this way, John's Passion Narrative makes clear the saving effect of Jesus's sacrifice.[5]

> **[18:1–11]** *¹ When Jesus had spoken these words, he went forth with his disciples across the Kidron valley, where there was a garden, which he and his disciples entered. ² Now Judas, who betrayed him, also knew the place; for Jesus often met there with his disciples. ³ So Judas, procuring a band of soldiers and some officers from the chief priests and the Pharisees, went there with lanterns and torches and weapons. ⁴ Then Jesus, knowing all that was to befall him, came forward and said to them, "Whom do you seek?" ⁵ They answered him, "Jesus of Nazareth." Jesus said to them, "I am he." Judas, who betrayed him, was standing with them. ⁶ When he said to them, "I am he," they drew back and fell to the ground. ⁷ Again he asked them, "Whom do you seek?" And they said, "Jesus of Nazareth." ⁸ Jesus answered, "I told you that I am he; so, if you seek me, let these men go." ⁹ This was to fulfil the word which he had spoken, "Of those whom thou gavest me I lost not one." ¹⁰ Then Simon Peter, having a sword, drew it and struck the High Priest's slave and cut off his right ear. The slave's name was Malchus. ¹¹ Jesus said to Peter, "Put your sword into its sheath; shall I not drink the cup which the Father has given me?"*

RESPONSE. If there is an authentic villain in John's dramatic Passion Narrative, it's not the high priest or the Roman governor. It's Judas Iscariot, the betrayer. The Fourth Gospel depicts Judas as one of Jesus's intimate friends, part of his inner circle, possibly even Jesus's most trusted companion. John says that at the Last Supper Judas reclines in the place of honor at Jesus's left just as the Beloved Disciple does at Jesus's right (see pp. 198–99, above). Jesus and the others obviously have total confidence in Judas because they put him in charge of the money they possess in common (12:6). Only someone whose honesty and fidelity are proven would be awarded that responsibility. Jesus and his disciples trust and respect Judas. Jesus loves Judas and honors him. Judas, in turn, must be aware that if he betrays that trust and love, he dooms himself to a life of shame. If he hands Jesus over to people who want to kill him, his name will become an epithet.—Who would choose that for himself? What makes Judas willing to betray Jesus and deliver him to those who wish him dead? How can we learn from reflection on Judas's villainy?

Through the centuries, various explanations for Judas's betrayal have been proposed. The earliest, easiest, and most common is "the Devil made him do it." Rather than immediately discard that hypothesis as purely mythical and unhistorical, let's

---

5. Unlike the Synoptics, John gives no description of the disciples abandoning Jesus in the garden, but earlier that evening Jesus tells them, "The hour is coming, indeed it has come, when you will be scattered every man to his home, and will leave me alone; yet, I am not alone, for the Father is with me" (16:32). Verses 8–9 could logically be interpreted as implying that the temple police told Jesus's disciples to leave the garden and go home.

stay with it for a while. Maybe it's correct. After all, it *is* what our gospel writer tells us. Whether or not we privately believe in the existence of an incorporeal entity called the Devil or Satan, none of us denies the reality of evil or the pervasiveness of temptation. The story of our Lord's betrayal by one of his most intimate friends invites us to contemplate the power of temptation and the evil that can arise from the human heart in response to temptation.

The first time Judas is mentioned in the Fourth Gospel, Jesus says, "Did I not choose you, the twelve, and one of you is a devil?" The gospel adds, "He spoke of Judas the son of Simon Iscariot, for he, one of the twelve, was to betray him" (6:70–71). Later, at the supper, Jesus identifies the betrayer to the Beloved Disciple as the one to whom he gives a morsel of bread after he dips it in the bowl. Jesus hands the morsel to Judas. John then says, "After the morsel, Satan entered into him" (13:27).

An episode in the life of Christ mentioned in all three Synoptic gospels and described in detail by Matthew and Luke is the familiar one usually called Jesus's "temptations in the wilderness" (Matt 4:1–11; Mark 1:9–11; Luke 4:1–13). Hebrews doesn't mention that confrontation of Jesus with Satan, but it does say that Christ suffered and was tempted just as we are (Heb 2:18; 4:15). John's Gospel, however, not only omits the temptations in the wilderness, it evades specifying any circumstances in which Jesus faces temptation, just as it circumvents direct reference to Jesus's suffering. This is not because the writer of the Fourth Gospel imagines Jesus was never tempted or never suffered. Far from it. He knows very well that Jesus was tempted and that Jesus suffered, but he chooses to tell the story of Jesus's passion in his own unique way. In a sense, John honors his Lord by veiling Jesus's temptation and suffering. Readers of his gospel must lift that veil in order to see what John disguises, and that's what I will attempt. My theory about this is obviously mere speculation, but speculation can often lead us to deeper understanding.

The one time John uses the name "Satan" is in connection with Judas, as noted above (13:27). He mentions "the Devil" only three times; two of these refer to Judas (6:70; 13:2) and one refers to the Devil as father of the Jews who refuse to believe in Jesus and want to stone him (8:44). Here is part of the "veil" we want to lift. John chooses to show us Jesus's very real confrontation with the tempter, not head-on, as the Synoptics do with their story of the temptations in the wilderness, but obliquely. John's account implies that through three years of day-to-day ministry, Jesus deals continually with a trusted disciple, a dear friend, who is at the same time "a devil" (6:70), an agent of the tempter. Perhaps there are times when this friend encourages Jesus to make choices that might appear prudent or even beneficial, but which conflict with what Jesus knows is the Father's will. At other times he vocally objects to Jesus's priorities, such as when his Master allows Mary of Bethany to bathe his feet with costly ointment rather than insist it be sold and the proceeds given to the poor (12:3–8). Observing that Judas might play a devilish role does not foreclose the possibility that another disciple might also serve the tempter's cause. Matthew tells us Peter once fell into Satan's snare.[6] The Devil finds many unwitting allies. In a veiled way, John wants to show that Jesus deals with temptation all through his life. It's logical to conclude that the occasion of his betrayal, arrest, trial, and crucifixion—his passion—is a time when temptation is certain.

We miss the ubiquity of temptation if we associate it exclusively with seductions of the flesh or crude enticements of wealth or power. Those are real of course, but people who are able to resist such temptations may succumb to others. There is, for example, the common enticement to choose a lesser good over a greater one, or to see God's will operating in outcomes that yield us personal advantage more quickly than we see it in outcomes that yield us no reward, but only rejection or humiliation. There also comes to all of us, depending on the situations we face, the temptation to anger or an equally potent temptation to despair.—Can we honestly imagine that the man Jesus of Nazareth was exempt from any of these?

We can only be tempted by something we desire, something we want to have or something we want to do. James spells this out (1:14*a*), "each person is tempted when he is lured and enticed by his own desire." A successful "devil" only has to put us in a situation where we must do battle with our darker cravings; we do the rest. As James writes (1:14*b*), "Desire, when it has conceived, gives birth to sin; and sin, when it is full-grown, brings forth death." Our dark desires are not inevitably for wealth, power, sex, gourmet delights, drugs, or fame, but sometimes for adulation, vindication, pity, or revenge. Most days I say an old prayer that, in part, asks God to "drive far from us all wrong desires."[7] Our "wrong desires" open the door to the tempter.

Every temptation that comes to us, either small or great, tests our faith in God. Only faith can bring a believer to victory over the tempter; and for the Fourth Gospel, Jesus is the archetypal believer. The events of his passion are the supreme test, the painful trial of Jesus's trust in the goodness and rightness of his Father's will. In the episodes of his passion, brutal experiences will be visited upon Jesus, experiences with power to drive anyone to despair, anger, or terror. Judas is the Devil's agent who—not for thirty pieces of silver, but for the satisfaction of his own unknowable needs—chooses to hand over his friend and Teacher to these experiences.

Vv. 12–27. Peter denies that he is Jesus's disciple.

INTRODUCTION. This portion of the Passion Narrative shows the fulfillment of what Jesus foretold concerning Simon Peter earlier that same evening, when at the supper he proclaims himself willing to die for Jesus. His Master says to him, "Will you lay down your life for me? Truly, truly I say to you, the cock will not crow till you have denied me three times" (13:36–38).

6. See Matt 16:21–23. Jesus calls Peter "Satan" because the disciple denies the need for his Master to suffer and die.

7. "A Collect for the Renewal of Life," in *The Book of Common Prayer*, 99.

Following the same Passion Narrative outline as the Synoptics, John reports that the temple guards and their officers and leaders tie Jesus up and take him from the garden on the Mount of Olives into the city.[8] In a departure from the Synoptic narrative, however, John tells us they take Jesus first of all to the palace of the high priest, to be interviewed by him. Unlike the Synoptics, John does not describe the occasion as an official hearing, much less an actual trial before the Sanhedrin. The "court of the High Priest" (v. 15) refers only to a courtyard area of the high priest's elegant private residence, not to the gathering place of a judicial body. John lays out the familiar story of Peter disowning Jesus almost as if it were part of what we would recognize as the script for a movie, with the camera shifting back and forth between the courtyard and the high priest's inner chamber.

The chief priests and other Jerusalem aristocrats have magnificent houses in a quarter of the city immediately southwest of the temple, near the residence of Annas and not far from the fortress-palace built by Herod the Great.[9] Annas, who was high priest from 6 to 15 CE and is patriarch of the bet Hanan high priestly family, may share his palatial home with the ruling high priest, Caiaphas, his son-in-law.[10] Peter and a second disciple trail along behind the officers who have taken Jesus captive and arrive shortly after at the high priest's compound. The identity of the "other disciple, known to the High Priest" (v. 15) is debated by commentators. Some assume that he is the Beloved Disciple, though this seems unlikely to others. Perhaps this other disciple is someone prominent enough to be a member of the high priest's aristocratic circle of personal acquaintances.

John deftly incorporates the story of Peter's denial into his account of Jesus's appearance before Annas and Caiaphas, and he tells that part of the story in much the same way as Mark (Mark 14:66–72). Since the disciple known to the high priest is not mentioned again, we may imagine that he is not only allowed through the gate into the courtyard but has high enough social standing to be permitted to enter the palace itself. Peter must remain in the courtyard, standing with the guards and servants,

8. In v. 12 John refers to "the band of soldiers and their captain and the officers of the Jews," using "the Jews" (as he frequently does) to mean only the high priest and his allies—not the entire Jewish people. Elsewhere in the trial scene when the gospel writer mentions "the Jews," the reference is still only to the priestly leaders of the elite.

9. See Fig. 10, p. 249. Archaeologists have recently identified what appears to be the remains of an elaborate priestly residence from the Second Temple era. See UNC–Charlotte publicity release, "Mt. Zion Dig." See also Smith, "House of Sedition."

10. See Reicke, *New Testament Era*, 141–43. Because the high priest is a powerful, princely figure, Judea's imperial overlords, the Romans, take control of the office when they remove Herod's son, Archelaus, as king in 6 CE and assume direct oversight of the province. The Roman prefects of Judea (or their superiors, the Roman legates of Syria) thereafter appoint and remove high priests for their own reasons, regardless of the Jewish law that a high priest should serve for life. Annas has five sons and a son-in-law (Caiaphas), all of whom serve as high priest in this era. Caiaphas, who has a good working relationship with Pilate, holds the high priesthood during Pilate's entire administration from 18 to 36 CE, but Reicke says that Annas remains the dominant power in the Sanhedrin until his death in the year 35.

conversing with them and warming himself by their charcoal fire. It is to one of them, "the maid who kept the door" (v. 17), that he makes his first denial. She says to him, "You're not also one of that man's disciples, are you?" Peter answers, "No, I'm not" (paraphrase of vv. 17–18). The grammar of the Greek sentence suggests the door-keeper's question is one that assumes a negative answer.[11] The maid's query implies that she recognizes that Peter's companion is a disciple of Jesus. (Keep in mind that John's Gospel uses the word "disciple" to identify members of a much larger group than the twelve.)

Because Annas is a former high priest—and continues to exercise decisive influence in Jerusalem affairs—he apparently continues to be known by his former title.[12] John reports that "the High Priest questioned Jesus about his disciples and his teaching" (v. 19). Annas interrogates Jesus in a private setting, not a courtroom. Guards and slaves and maybe a few of Annas's important cronies are with them, of course. Great men in that era are almost never alone. The questions Annas asks seem intended to uncover whether Jesus of Nazareth has a clandestine political agenda underlying his public claim to be the Son of God. Does he have other disciples than the ones the chief priests already know about, perhaps some firebrands from among the nationalistic group known as Zealots (who will ultimately incite war with Rome in 63)?

Jesus, still bound and under guard, gives old Annas a crisp rejoinder. He is hiding nothing; his teaching has always been in public; and he has "spoken openly to the world" (v. 20). Remembering John's portrayal of "the world" as the realm of those who live in spiritual darkness, Jesus says, in effect, that he has been bringing light into dark places, not hiding in the shadows, concocting a plot. Powerful men like Annas are accustomed to common people cowering obsequiously in their presence. Jesus addresses the elderly ex-high priest as if he were a social equal and so earns himself a blow from one of the guards. He responds to the physical assault candidly, not cringingly, wherewith the old man dispatches the Galilean troublemaker off to his son-in-law, the sitting high priest.

The scene changes to where Peter is still shivering in the courtyard with the guards and servants, trying to get warm beside their fire. In quick succession, two of the people standing around ask him again if he is not one of Jesus's followers. The first asks a question identical to that of the doorkeeper. The second, however, was in the garden and witnessed Peter's role in the scuffle there; the form of his question indicates that he expects an affirmative answer. He definitely recognizes Peter.[13] Nevertheless, Peter firmly rebuffs all attempts to associate him with the high priest's prisoner. Then the cock crows, fulfilling Jesus's prophecy at the supper. John does not join Matthew in

---

11. O'Day, *Gospel of John*, 808.

12. At least Annas is identified in the New Testament by the Greek term customarily used in that language for the high priest.

13. Ibid., 810.

describing Peter as weeping bitterly when he hears it (Matt 26:75). Evidence of Peter's remorse will not be demonstrated until the epilogue (21:15–19).

Peter's disowning of Jesus is almost as shameful as Judas's betrayal. It would be shameful even if Peter had not earlier in the evening promised Jesus in front of the other disciples that he would defend him to the death. To repudiate one's close friend in his hour of need—and especially one's teacher—is both dishonorable and cowardly. Peter's behavior aligns him with the enemies of Jesus. Rather than proclaim his loyalty to Jesus, he seeks the favor of the high priest's circle. Peter compares unfavorably with the man born blind, who clings faithfully to his relationship with Jesus even when that allegiance results in his being cast out of the synagogue (9:24–34).[14]

[18:12–27] *[12] So the band of soldiers and their captain and the officers of the Jews seized Jesus and bound him. [13] First they led him to Annas; for he was the father-in-law of Ca'iaphas, who was High Priest that year. [14] It was Ca'iaphas who had given counsel to the Jews that it was expedient that one man should die for the people.*

[15] Simon Peter followed Jesus, and so did another disciple. As this disciple was known to the High Priest, he entered the court of the High Priest along with Jesus, [16] while Peter stood outside at the door. So the other disciple, who was known to the High Priest, went out and spoke to the maid who kept the door, and brought Peter in. [17] The maid who kept the door said to Peter, "Are not you also one of this man's disciples?" He said, "I am not." [18] Now the servants and officers had made a charcoal fire, because it was cold, and they were standing and warming themselves; Peter also was with them, standing and warming himself.

[19] The High Priest then questioned Jesus about his disciples and his teaching. [20] Jesus answered him, "I have spoken openly to the world; I have always taught in synagogues and in the temple, where all Jews come together; I have said nothing secretly. [21] Why do you ask me? Ask those who have heard me, what I said to them; they know what I said." [22] When he had said this, one of the officers standing by struck Jesus with his hand, saying, "Is that how you answer the High Priest?" [23] Jesus answered him, "If I have spoken wrongly, bear witness to the wrong; but if I have spoken rightly, why do you strike me?" [24] Annas then sent him bound to Ca'iaphas the High Priest.

[25] Now Simon Peter was standing and warming himself. They said to him, "Are not you also one of his disciples?" He denied it and said, "I am not." [26] One of the servants of the High Priest, a kinsman of the man whose

---

14. Keener, *Gospel of John*, 2:1091–92; Malina and Rohrbaugh, *Social Science Commentary*, 253–54.

ear Peter had cut off, asked, "Did I not see you in the garden with him?"
²⁷ *Peter again denied it; and at once the cock crowed.*

RESPONSE. There is no doubt about the authenticity of the story of Peter disowning his Lord. It's found in the earliest layer of the gospel tradition. Because such a denial was a dishonorable act of cowardice, it's not something the early church would publicize unless there was no choice in the matter. And it's certainly not a fiction someone dreamed up in order to add still more drama to the Passion Narrative. All four gospels include the story because it really happened. All the earliest Christians know about it, and although the episode shows the spokesman of the apostles in a bad light, the gospel writers have no choice but to admit its truth.

There is an alternate theory put forward by some who are unwilling to accept that Peter denies knowing Jesus because he is afraid of sharing Jesus's fate. Authors of this theory fantasize that Peter lies about being a disciple because he is in the courtyard to find a way to rescue Jesus or at least strike another blow on his behalf. This scheme requires him to remain incognito.—That theory might make an interesting plot for a movie, but it's not a theologically satisfactory explanation of what John wants readers to learn from his account of Peter denying his Master. John records a true story about what it means to be human. The account of Peter's behavior in the high priest's courtyard, is about a good man with high ideals and noble intentions who feels so scared and intimidated that he betrays his deepest convictions.

There are few people reading John's Gospel today who have not at some time in our lives displayed weakness of character. When we read the passion story, we have little trouble identifying with Simon Peter. We say to ourselves, "That could be me." Peter's bravado at the supper table sustains his willingness to start a brawl in the garden when Judas comes with the temple guards to seize Jesus. Boldness in the garden is easier than it will be in the high priest's courtyard, since Peter's comrades are beside him there and—most of all—his Master, the Son of God, is with him.

After Jesus arranges the release of his followers, Peter and the other disciple follow along to the high priest's residence out of natural curiosity, to see what will happen to their friend. The other man departs, leaving the once-bold Galilean fisherman standing alone on his enemies' turf. Since his influential companion is gone, Peter is by himself in the midst of the high priest's servants and armed retainers—including some who just arrested Jesus. Peter is fortunate that it's dark and faces are obscured by flickering shadows. When people start to ask whether he's not also one of the Nazarene's disciples, Peter grows uneasy. Threatened by the hostile setting, he twice denies knowing Jesus. When a kinsman of the fellow he wounded comes over, peers closely at him and says, "I saw you there. You *are* one of this man's followers," Peter knows he's in danger. He quickly disowns Jesus again and then gets out of the courtyard as quickly as he can.

The Fourth Gospel is tightly constructed. Those who read about Peter's shameful behavior in 18:12–27 will soon read the account of his forgiveness and rehabilitation in 21:15–19. Readers must see these two episodes as two sides of a coin: one side is Peter's sin, the other is Jesus's mercy. An influential school of Johannine scholars believes that the Beloved Disciple writes his gospel for a small sect of Greek-speaking Jews who worship Jesus as Messiah and Son of God. Many of them have already faced rejection by their families and expulsion from their local synagogues because of their faith in Jesus. Some of them, however, and probably a number of others outside their circle, conceal their convictions about Jesus in order to remain in the good graces of their parents, siblings, and neighbors. These people worship in the synagogue on the Sabbath with their families and fellow Jews just as they have done all their lives. But they gather on the Lord's Day, the first day of the week, to break bread and pray with the despised followers of Jesus of Nazareth, a group that includes not only Jews by birth but also Gentiles. These people are secret Christians.[15]

No doubt some of strictest of their openly Christian friends regard these secret Christians as hypocrites, and some of the secret Christians have troubled consciences because of their duplicitous behavior. It's easy for us to sit in judgment on the secret Christians of the New Testament era, just as it's easy to see Peter's denial of Jesus as a shameful act of cowardice. However, we live in a world where—in certain contexts—explicit profession of Christian faith is not only a hindrance to progress towards higher education, or an obstacle to promotion at work, or a barrier to election to public office, but also puts believers' physical safety and the well-being of their families at risk. Our churches honor the memory of the martyrs, including those from this week's cable news stories as well as those from the early days of the Christian era. We do not usually show much compassion for compromisers, though. We do well to learnempathy for people who, just like Peter, get scared and pretend not to be believers. They are our brothers and sisters.

From the comfort of our suburban American church pews or while nibbling doughnuts with our neighborhood Bible study groups, it's easy to imagine that we would never disown the Lord Jesus as Peter does and some secret Christians of the first century did (and as others in our own century might do). But would we, in fact, prove braver than Peter? What would we do, faced with circumstances identical to his?

Vv. 28–40. Jesus goes on trial before Pilate.

INTRODUCTION. John's story of Jesus's trial before Pilate is the dramatic centerpiece of his Passion Narrative. Half of the trial is described in this chapter and half in chapter 19. Although it is only the prelude to the crucifixion, the trial is the

15. See Brown, *Community*, 71–81.

acknowledged masterpiece of John's literary artistry. The dialogue between Jesus and the Roman governor demonstrates Jesus's command of the situation. Even though he is a prisoner on trial for his life, John shows that Jesus is in fact the true Judge, both of his accusers and of the Roman prefect who has power to decide his fate. Although the Synoptics describe the kingdom of God as the focus of Jesus's preaching, in the Fourth Gospel Jesus refrains from making any mention of the kingdom of God except in his conversation with Nicodemus (3:3–5). Jesus's explanation of his kingship to Pilate during the trial helps us better understand what Jesus says earlier to the sympathetic Sanhedrin elder, Nicodemus, "Truly, truly, I say to you, unless one is born anew he cannot see the kingdom of God" (3:3). The trial before Pilate lays bare Jesus's identity as the true King of Israel (the Messiah) and "King of Truth," even though the Roman governor himself never perceives what is truly at issue in the conflict between the humble defendant and his high-ranking accusers. D. Moody Smith writes,

> The kingship of Christ in John replaces the kingdom of God in the teaching of Jesus, because in John, Christ is, in his historic revelation, his ministry, death and resurrection, the manifestation of God (1:18). No one comes to the Father except through him (14:6). Thus, "the Jews," who by definition reject Jesus, in a certain sense understand the meaning of the claims they do not accept. Pilate, on the other hand, remains uncomprehending.[16]

The Synoptic gospels describe a trial of Jesus before the Sanhedrin; John does not. The Fourth Gospel has already described Jesus's religious "trial" in great detail. As far as John is concerned, that trial begins in 5:15, after he heals a paralyzed man on the Sabbath at the Bethesda Pool, and is thereafter confronted in the temple by representatives of the religious authorities. It continues, on and off, until 11:53, when Jesus is condemned by the religious leaders of his nation.[17] All that remains is for Caiaphas and his colleagues to devise a way to bring about the punishment to which they have already agreed.

John tells us that "they"—presumably meaning the high priest and other chief priests, along with their servants and a squad of temple police—"take Jesus from the house of Caiaphas to the praetorium" (v. 28). *Praetorium* is the word for a Roman commanding officer's headquarters, wherever his duty takes him. It could be a tent, or a fort, or a palace. Pilate's praetorium in Jerusalem is wherever he chooses to reside in the city. Prefects habitually commandeer the vast, magnificent well-fortified palace Herod the Great built for himself along the western wall of the city. Herod's Palace is very near the high priest's residence and is surely the place to which Jesus's accusers bring him very early in the morning on the day of preparation, the day when at noon priests in the temple will begin killing the Passover lambs.[18]

16. Smith, *John*, 353.

17. Kysar, *John*, 271; Lindars, *Gospel of John*, 545–47. See also Smith, *John*, 338–39.

18. Josephus, *Wars*, V.iv.4, 553–54. A large imaginative reconstruction of Jerusalem in the time of

The Roman governor's business day routinely begins at first light, and some of his officials are busy before that.[19] Roman judicial proceedings are routinely held in the open air or in a portico. This venue suits Jesus's accusers well, since if they must enter the Gentile's domicile they will be ritually defiled and unable to eat the Passover meal (v. 28). John's irony is very evident here. The chief priests are hypocrites, concerned about preserving their ritual purity but oblivious to the moral defilement they incur by conspiring to make the Roman governor execute an innocent man.

Some commentators describe John's portrayal of the trial before Pilate (which continues into chapter 19) as consisting of a series of scenes, distinguished from one another by Pilate's movements into and out of the praetorium.[20] His exchanges with the Jewish leaders occur outside, and his private conversations with Jesus are inside the palace. John's description of the trial, with its dramatic and theologically fraught language, is the supreme example of this gospel writer's literary craftsmanship. It has the characteristics of a contemporary, Oscar-winning historical film. We assume the dialogue between Jesus and Pilate—which is the heart of the story—is a product of John's inspired imagination. However, it is conceivable that our gospel writer has access to an eyewitness report—since a Roman governor conducting official business inevitably has a secretary beside him to take notes and prepare legal documents as well as an assortment of adjutants, guards, and slaves to carry out his orders.[21]

John's story infers that Pilate has heard nothing about who Jesus is or what he might have done to offend the leaders of the Jews. The appearance of the high priest and his entourage with a prisoner in tow appears to take the prefect by surprise. He opens the proceedings by treating their application for Roman justice as out of order, assuming the issue is purely a matter of Jewish religious laws (vv. 30–31). When the accusers inform Pilate that they have brought their prisoner to him because they are

the Second Temple, a permanent exhibition at the Israel Museum in Jerusalem, portrays how extensive Herod's palace was. (See Figs 3–5 and 9, pp. 27–29, and Fig 10, p. 257, above.) Older commentaries assume that Jesus's trial before Pilate occurs at the Antonia fortress, adjacent to the temple, but recent research demonstrates that to be unlikely. Nevertheless, the effectiveness of John's dramatic trial scene does not hinge on a particular, historically verifiable setting. See Charlesworth, "Jesus Research and Archaeology," 34.

19. Brown, *John XIII–XXI*, 808; Keener, *Gospel of John*, 2:1098. For this introduction I rely on Keener's commentary, which includes an extensive and carefully documented account of interactions between Roman governors and provincial élites in general as well as between the prefects of Judea and local Jewish authorities in particular. Keener also provides a summary of Pilate's checkered career as governor of the province. See Keener, *Gospel of John*, 2:1103–9.

20. Archaeologist Shimon Gibson appears in a brief video recorded by Kenneth Hanson on the site of Herod's Palace in which he points to the placement of the prefect's seat, the Jewish leaders, and Jesus. See Hanson, "Shimon Gibson Jerusalem." Reicke, *New Testament Era*, 184, theorizes that the actual trial is held in the Antonia fortress and then Jesus is taken to the praetorium, the Palace of Herod, where he is mocked by the prefect's praetorian guard company before being led to Golgotha. This is very unlikely; the entire proceeding was probably held in the vast Palace of Herod.

21. A system of shorthand was in common use in Rome from the middle of the first century BCE. It was invented in order to provide transcriptions of speeches. Stenographers were typically highly skilled slaves.

not permitted to put him to death (v. 31), they get Pilate's attention. They warn the governor that Jesus's offense, whatever it might be, somehow threatens Rome's authority.[22] Although John focuses on the role of the Jewish elite in bringing Jesus to the cross, he affirms that it is the Romans who play the decisive part. There is no public crucifixion in a Roman province unless a sentence is pronounced by a Roman judge. When the Romans allow their Jewish vassals to inflict a death sentence, the victim is stoned, not crucified. Jesus has already foretold how he will die—he will be "lifted up," that is, crucified (12:32–33, to which John refers in v. 32). The high priest and his associates engineer the process, but the Romans will do the deed.

Pilate asks Jesus if he is "*the King of the Jews*." The Roman governor undoubtedly knows the Jews expect that someday a Messiah will arise. Pilate's question is likely an effort to discern whether Jesus thinks of himself as that Messiah. A man named Judas had been called "the Messiah" and led an armed rebellion twenty five years earlier (see Acts 5:37). A previous governor disposed of Judas and many of his followers. King of the Jews might be Pilate's own idea of what a would-be Messiah might call himself. To claim that designation would be an overtly rebellious act, since King of the Jews is the title the Roman Senate bestowed on Herod the Great.[23] In Pilate's question, "Are you the King of the Jews" (v. 33) the pronoun "you" could be read as emphatic in the Greek sentence. It is unclear whether that emphasis means to indicate Pilate's surprise that a man such as Jesus might claim to be the Messiah.[24]

Pilate seems unaware that when the Davidic Messiah appears, he will be King *of Israel*—the title of David and Solomon—not King *of the Jews*. Readers of John recall that in 1:49–50, Nathanael, an early disciple, tells Jesus, "Rabbi, you are the Son of God! You are the King of Israel!" Jesus then answers him, "Because I said to you, I saw you under the fig tree, do you believe? You shall see greater things than these." John intends his readers to see that Jesus is, indeed, both Son of God and King of Israel—but he is *not* the kind of Messiah the Jewish public wants (see 6:15).

Jesus responds to Pilate's question in the same fearless, self-confident manner he exhibited earlier in his interview with Annas. Pilate encourages him to keep talking, so the Roman guards do not strike him for his impertinence. The prefect is probing for an explanation of what Jesus has done to bring upon himself the wrath of the Jewish hierarchy (vv. 34–35). This allows Jesus to explain the nature of his kingship, which is "not of this world" (v. 36). The title people use for him does not matter a great deal to Jesus. His mission is what matters: "I was born and came into the world to bear

22. Welch, "Miracles," 350–52, proposes that the chief priests were very concerned by Jesus's miracles (particularly the raising of Lazarus) and deemed him guilty of engaging in magic, an offense deserving death under their Law. They hoped Pilate would find him guilty of "sedition (*crimen maiestatis*) through illicit magical wonder-working (*maleficium*)," which was a capital offense according to Roman law.

23. Josephus, *Wars*, I.xiv.4, 444–45. Raymond Brown thinks the title seems to have been one used by foreigners, not by Jews themselves. See Brown, *John XIII–XXI*, 850–51.

24. Marsh, *Saint John*, 600.

witness to the truth" (v. 37). To these words Pilate gives his infamous reply, "What is truth?" (v. 38a). We may treat Pilate's response as merely a crass Roman politician's cynicism, or—more importantly—we might recognize it as a question John wants his readers to think about. Our author is an expert at crafting scenes in which a single phrase conveys multiple layers of possible meaning.

Pilate goes back outside and tells the Jews he does not find Jesus guilty. He recognizes that even if this man thinks of himself as some kind of "Messiah," he represents no military challenge. He then mentions to Jesus's accusers his custom of releasing a prisoner during the Passover festival and asks—deliberately taunting the Jews with his sarcasm—whether they would like him to release for them "the King of the Jews." They shout back, "Not this man, but Barabbas!'" (v. 40a).[25] John's Gospel adds, "Barabbas was a robber" (v. 40). To understand John clearly here we must observe that although the Greek word *lēstēs* does indeed sometimes mean "highwayman," "robber," or "bandit," it is also the word first century writers use for "insurrectionist," "revolutionary," or "social bandit."[26] The Roman governor only concerns himself with malefactors of the latter sort. Ordinary civil courts deal with ordinary robbers; Barabbas is a revolutionary already tried and condemned by the prefect.

In this trial, Pilate does not care deeply about whether he protects Jesus from death, even though he states several times during the trial that he does not find Jesus guilty (v. 38; and 19:4, 6, 12). The prospect of crucifying one more Jew gives the Roman governor no qualms of conscience. Whether Jesus actually thinks himself as "King of the Jews" makes no difference to him. For Pilate, Jesus is but a pawn to be played in a continuing political chess match with the high priest and his colleagues.[27]

> [18:28–40] [28] *Then they led Jesus from the house of Ca'iaphas to the praetorium. It was early. They themselves did not enter the praetorium, so that they might not be defiled, but might eat the passover.* [29] *So Pilate went out to them and said, "What accusation do you bring against this man?"* [30] *They answered him, "If this man were not an evildoer, we would not have handed him over."* [31] *Pilate said to them, "Take him yourselves and judge him by your own law." The Jews said to him, "It is not lawful for us to put any man to death."* [32] *This was to fulfil the word which Jesus had spoken to show by what death he was to die.* [33] *Pilate entered the praetorium again and called Jesus, and said to him, "Are you the King of the Jews?"* [34] *Jesus answered, "Do you say this of your own accord, or did others say it to you about me?"* [35] *Pilate answered, "Am I a Jew? Your own nation and the chief*

25. The earliest readers of John's Gospel, if they know some Hebrew or Aramaic, will understand that the patronymic "Barabbas" means "son of the father," another bit of irony. A man who is called "son of the father" is released in preference to the one who is the true Son of the Father.

26. Malina and Rohrbaugh, *Social Science Commentary*, 262–63; Danker, *Greek-English Lexicon*, 594.

27. O'Day, *Gospel of John*, 815.

priests have handed you over to me; what have you done?" [36] *Jesus answered, "My kingship is not of this world; if my kingship were of this world, my servants would fight, that I might not be handed over to the Jews; but my kingship is not from the world."* [37] *Pilate said to him, "So you are a king?" Jesus answered, "You say that I am a king. For this I was born, and for this I have come into the world, to bear witness to the truth. Every one who is of the truth hears my voice."* [38] *Pilate said to him, "What is truth?"*

After he had said this, he went out to the Jews again, and told them, "I find no crime in him. [39] *But you have a custom that I should release one man for you at the Passover; will you have me release for you the King of the Jews?"* [40] *They cried out again, "Not this man, but Barab'bas!" Now Barab'bas was a robber.*

RESPONSE. Can any thoughtful person read John's Passion Narrative and not be affected by it? Even a reflective non-Christian who reads this story merely as a famous work of literature like *The Iliad* or *Hamlet* is challenged to contemplate some serious existential questions: How do I recognize truth? What kind of power is most important? And, to whom (or what) do I owe my deepest allegiance?

Vv. 33–37 of this text is read every three years in the Revised Common Lectionary on the last Sunday before the beginning of Advent, a Sunday many churches call "the Feast of Christ the King." It's an occasion to ponder what we're asking for when we pray, "Our Father who art it heaven, hallowed be thy name; thy kingdom come, thy will be done on earth as it is in heaven." What *is* this "kingdom" we seek? We're Americans. We live in a republic. Virtually none of us has any experience of living in an absolute monarchy, which was the only sort of kingdom that existed from antiquity until early modern times.

Pundits often describe the President of the United States as "the most powerful person in the world." That may or may not be true. The Fourth Gospel's Passion Narrative introduces Pilate to us. He is the Roman military prefect of Judea, local personal representative of Tiberius Caesar, who arguably *is* the most powerful man in the world. Judea is a third class imperial province—small, poor, and producing little revenue for Rome. It also has a restless, difficult, multi-ethnic population. Pilate has some auxiliary troops under his command—numbering at most half a legion in size.[28] If things get out of hand in Judea, he normally would appeal to his superior in Antioch, the legate of Syria, who has four whole legions at his disposal. Unfortunately for Pilate, the legate has been detained in Rome for several years. If a rebellion were to take place in Judea right now, the prefect can't count on help coming very soon from

---

28. Under Tiberius (r. 14–37 CE) a legion was typically 5,000. Each legion would be paired with a similar-sized body of auxiliary troops (provincials, not Roman citizens). For a description of Roman armies in Judea, see Josephus, "War," III.v–vi, 505–7.

Antioch. He'll be forced to manage with his small body of troops.[29] Pilate must be cautious.

It's good for us to know these bits of historical trivia, because they reveal that Pilate is a man who always needs to be aware of where power lies. His little province seethes with unrest. Even though Jews despise Romans and Romans despise Jews, the Roman occupiers depend on the power of the Jewish high priest and his fellow aristocrats to manage day-to-day affairs and support the empire's interests, while the Jewish elite depend on the Romans' military power to keep them in their place atop the provincial social pyramid. A *Messiah*—whether actually sent from God (which Caiaphas and his colleagues do not expect) or self-designated—will prove extremely inconvenient for both sides. A Messiah will compete for power with both governor and high priest.

It's important for Pilate to determine whether Jesus presents himself as a "real" *king*—like Herod once was. That's why he asks if he is "King of the Jews," Herod's old title. Is Jesus a pretender to that throne? Pilate doesn't care what title this man wants to use, as long as he doesn't aspire to the kind of authority Pilate worries about, authority to give orders that many other Jews will obey. If Jesus lacks ability to change the status quo in Judea, if he has no political power, then he presents no problem for Pilate.

Jesus doesn't deny being a king, but he shows no interest in Herod's defunct title. He seems to imagine himself as a king unlike any of which Pilate has ever heard. If Jesus wanted to be the sort of king Pilate understands, he'd already be imitating Judas the Galilean "Messiah" who appeared twenty-five years before. He'd have a small army at his back, and the Romans would have to fight them. But Jesus tells the governor, "My kingship is not of this world; if my kingship were of this world, my servants would fight, that I might not be handed over to the Jews; but my kingship is not from the world" (v. 36). "So," Pilate thinks, "This man *is* a 'king,' but his sort of king is 'not *of* this world' and 'not *from* the world.' Fine. His sort of king has no power." The governor is surprised and relieved to learn that Jesus does not aspire to be a *real* king.

We know what John means when he refers to the world. He means the sphere of affairs in which the Devil currently has the upper hand, the human realm which turns its back on God and will not heed God's incarnate Word. Pilate is "of this world" and so are the priestly aristocrats who bring Jesus to Pilate for judgment. For the Fourth Gospel, Pilate represents a very particular dimension of the world. He stands for the Gentile world, the Roman world, a world very much like our own, one that imagines itself able to make and unmake gods. (What does the television program, *American Idol*, really represent in our society? Do we ever think seriously about the "idols" we sometimes worship?) Pilate's response to Jesus is nothing like that of the Samaritan villagers who earlier in John's narrative listen to Jesus and recognize that he is the Savior of the world (4:42).

29. Bond, "Pontius Pilate."

Once he learns that Jesus has no aspiration to political power—that is to say, he has no army—Pilate stops listening. He says to the prisoner, "So, you *are* some kind of king." Jesus answers, "You say I am a 'king.' I was born and came into the world for one reason: so that I might bear witness to the truth. Everyone who cares about truth listens to what I say" (paraphrase of v. 37). Then Pilate replies, "What is truth?" (v. 38).

What does "truth" look like to Christians today? What does it mean for us to think about Jesus, not as King of the Jews, but as King of Truth? Does Jesus's truth have the power to change our status quo? We, his disciples, are the community that believes in him, the community that knows him. We're convinced that the birth of Jesus, the acts of Jesus, the words of Jesus, and the death and resurrection of Jesus reveal God. His person shows us truth, and to encounter him, in the power of his Spirit, is to come face-to-face with a reality that transforms us and makes living a fulfilled and morally meaningful life possible, makes hope possible, and makes courage in the face of death possible. Those who serve the King of Truth have these convictions. One may test the truthfulness of any set of convictions by examining the sort of life they produce. King Jesus summons us to listen to him, believe in him, know and love him, and—thus—to know the truth that sets us free (see 8:31–32).

Jesus's kingship is not of the world or from the world, but it is *in* the world. It has power to change the world—though it's not a kind of power that Pilate understands. Those who are "of the truth" listen to Jesus. Pilate is not "of the truth," and neither are Caiaphas and his colleagues, the Jerusalem old guard. But the truth is now loose in the world, and it cannot be silenced. The truth has a power that cannot be quantified. It cannot be measured by the number of soldiers in an army, or by the size of a nation's GDP, or by the count of a politician's followers on Twitter. The power of truth lies in its ability to shape the heart and focus the will. When truth is embraced, life is changed forever.

For the Beloved Disciple, Jesus is both "True King" and "King of Truth." When Jesus tells Pilate that his kingdom is "not of this world" he doesn't mean it isn't real, or has no power. Jesus's kingdom does not originate *from* the world, but does exist *in* the world. His kingdom is not merely a utopian ideal, or a state of being which will be realized only in a future age beyond history. The kingdom of God that Jesus announces—and which he personally embodies in the days of his flesh—is what life could be here and now, if God were the King whose voice people heeded and whose laws they obeyed. This is why Jesus teaches his disciples to pray, "Thy kingdom come, thy will be done on earth as it is in heaven" (Matt 6:10). What would our life be like if God's will were done on earth as it is in heaven?[30] We prove that Jesus is our king when we demonstrate our willingness to do what he commands.

The trial is not yet ended. Before it ends, Pilate will mock Jesus's kingship. He will make a brutal joke of it, a sadistic parody. And the King of Truth will grow silent in his dignified endurance. He has spoken and no one has listened. No one has understood.

30. Clendinin, "Yes, I Am a King."

There is little more to say. The victory of the King of Truth does not depend on his escaping the cross, but—paradoxically—it depends on his accepting the cross. It is his throne. The words of the Good Friday hymn, "To Mock Your Reign," come to my mind:

> *They did not know, as we do now,*
> *though empires rise and fall,*
> *Your Kingdom shall not cease to grow,*
> *till love embraces all.*[31]

Doing Your Own Theology

Questions for reflection after reading John 18.

- The oldest known Christian creed, from which our Apostles' Creed derives, comes from mid-second century Rome, and it supports a sense that the stories of Christ's incarnation, passion, and resurrection/ascension are the essential elements of the gospel. That creed says about the life of Jesus only that he was "born of the Holy Spirit from the Virgin Mary, crucified and buried under Pontius Pilate, on the third day rose from the dead, [and] ascended into heaven." The heart of what we understand as Christian faith lies in the accounts of Jesus's suffering, death, and resurrection—*not* in the specific content of his moral teaching, such as we find, for example, in the Sermon on the Mount (Matt 5–7) or the parable of the Good Samaritan (Luke 10:25–37). Nevertheless, the reality of Jesus's incarnation, passion and resurrection give authority to his moral teaching.—*Would you agree that Jesus's moral teaching derives its authority from his incarnation, passion, and resurrection? Why or why not? Why do you suppose that, as scholars suggest, the stories of Jesus's suffering, death, and resurrection were the first gospel traditions to be put into writing? How do the stories of Jesus' suffering and death speak to his nature as both fully human and fully divine?*

- This portion of the Passion Narrative shows the fulfillment of what Jesus foretold concerning Simon Peter earlier that same evening, when at the Supper he proclaims himself willing to die for Jesus. His Master says to him, "Will you lay down your life for me? Truly, truly I say to you, the cock will not crow till you have denied me three times" (13:36–38). There is no doubt about the authenticity of the story of Peter disowning his Lord. It's found in the earliest layer of the gospel tradition. Because such a denial was a dishonorable act of cowardice, it's not something the early church would be proud to publicize unless there was no choice in the matter. And it's certainly not a fiction someone dreamed up in

31. Green, "To Mock Your Reign."

order to add still more drama to the Passion Narrative. All four gospels include the story because it really happened.—*How can meditating on the story of Peter's denial be of benefit to a contemporary reader of John? Does it inspire you in any way? Are you able to identify with Peter? Why or why not? Have you ever denied Christ as an act of self-protection, in response to outside threats?*

- John's story of Jesus' trial before Pilate is the dramatic centerpiece of his Passion Narrative. Although it is only the prelude to the crucifixion, the trial is the acknowledged masterpiece of John's literary artistry. Jesus's explanation of his kingship to Pilate during the trial helps us better understand what he said earlier to the sympathetic Sanhedrin elder, Nicodemus, "Truly, truly, I say to you, unless one is born anew he cannot see the kingdom of God" (3:3). The trial before Pilate lays bare Jesus's identity as the true King of Israel (the Messiah) and "King of Truth."—*Even a reflective non-Christian who reads this story of Jesus's trial before Pilate merely as a famous work of literature like "The Iliad" or "Hamlet" is challenged to contemplate serious existential questions, such as, how do I recognize truth? What kind of power is most important? And, to whom (or what) do I owe my deepest allegiance? How do you imagine an atheist would answer those questions? How would you, a believer, answer them?*

Chapter Nineteen

John 19:1–42. John's Passion Narrative concludes: Pilate sends Jesus to die. The crucifixion and burial of the Lord.

Vv. 1–16. Pilate condemns Jesus.

INTRODUCTION. After the chief priests and their officers demand that Pilate release the insurrectionist, Barabbas, for them instead of "the King of the Jews," John tells us "Pilate took Jesus and scourged him" (v. 1). The governor does not personally whip the prisoner; his soldiers do so—somewhere within the precincts of the palace, not outside in full view of the Jewish officials. Scourging of the kind Jesus endures is a sadistic, sometimes fatal punishment. It is important to note that none of the Gospels dwells on the details of the physical abuse directed at Jesus. The gospels' first readers need no descriptions, since they live in the same brutal age into which God sent his Son. If they wish, they have multiple opportunities to witness first-hand the beatings, beheadings, crucifixions and other grisly torments inflicted by the Romans. During the Jewish War of 67–73, the Romans crucified ten thousand victims in a great ring around the besieged city of Jerusalem. Reading of Jesus's passion reminds John's audience that he is with them in their suffering. Victims of Roman cruelty are sustained in the knowledge that their Master walked that way before them.

After the scourging, Pilate's soldiers, who have been told Jesus claims to be the rightful "King of the Jews," make fun of him by conducting what we would call a mock coronation. John says they plait a wreath of thorns—imitating the laurel garland that would adorn the head of a victorious Roman general in his triumph. They place a soldier's voluminous red cape around him (certainly not "purple," as John says, since purple-dyed apparel was costly and not found among common soldiers), and they come up to him, striking him, and saying, "Hail, King of the Jews!" (v. 3). The soldiers' cruel joke is a parody of what actually happened when a Roman legion decided to proclaim its victorious commander as emperor.

John implies that the whipping and mock coronation by the soldiers are part of a plan by Pilate to secure Jesus's release. Such a flogging is a formal punishment in itself. Since Pilate, both before (18:38) and after the scourging (v. 4), tells the chief priests that he regards Jesus as innocent of anything deserving death, John might wish us to see that the governor regards the whipping and mockery as a sufficiently shameful punishment for this prisoner.[1] More importantly, he wants to ensure that his will prevails over whatever the chief priests demand. Their alliance is a wary one, and the two are frequent antagonists. Pilate brings Jesus out of the praetorium—beaten bloody and dressed in the soldiers' parody of regal attire—and shows him to the Jewish leaders, saying, "Here is the man!" (v. 5). We recall that Jesus's usual self-designation in the Fourth Gospel is "Son of Man" and that John teaches us to see Jesus as the Son of Man to whom God will ultimately give universal dominion (9:35–36; cf. Dan 7:13–14). That Pilate could possibly be aware of this is unlikely; nevertheless, it constitutes one more piece of Johannine irony. Pilate, who explicitly rejects the truth of Jesus, admits that same truth without knowing what he is saying.

The chief priests and officers of the temple refuse to accept any punishment except death by crucifixion for their prisoner. It is logical for us to ask why they insist that Jesus die on a cross. If the Jewish leaders want Jesus dead, why does the high priest not petition the governor for permission to have Jesus executed by stoning? The Romans permit the temple authorities to execute Jews who violate their most serious religious laws. Such a request would be in order, and the prefect would certainly consent. It is clear the chief priests want Jesus executed, not by them, but by the Romans. And they specifically want the Romans to crucify him—to inflict on him the Roman punishment for a rebellious slave, a punishment that permanently taints the memory of the dead man in the eyes of Jew and Gentile alike, rendering him an object of shame and embarrassment to his family and friends forever. In addition, crucifixion brings upon the victim the curse of heaven, since it is written in the Law: "a hanged man is accursed by God" (Deut 21:23; cf. Gal 3:13).

When Pilate brings Jesus out, obviously the victim of a vicious scourging and dressed as a buffoon king, they shout, "Crucify him! Crucify him!" Unlike the Synoptics, John makes clear that "the Jews" who are calling for Jesus's crucifixion are exclusively the leading priests and their retainers, not the ordinary people. Pilate tells them to take their prisoner and crucify him themselves, because he, the Roman governor and proper judge of these matters, finds no case against him (v. 6). "The Jews" do not take Pilate literally; instead, they try a new tactic, presenting another complaint against Jesus—one we already have heard—blasphemy (10:31–33), "He has made himself the Son of God" (v. 7). This is their true grievance, and it sums up their whole case.[2]

The priestly rulers of the Jews assert that the prisoner Pilate has just flogged claims not only to be a king, but a divinity. This initiates what some have called a new

---

1. Brown, *John XIII–XXI*, 886.
2. Smith, *John*, 347.

trial on a new charge, with a new examination of Jesus by the prefect.[3] Pilate is familiar with the title "son of [the] god" (Latin, *divi filius*) since it is borne by his master Tiberius, as it was by Tiberius' foster father, Augustus. Caesar's divine title is an honor granted by vote of the Roman Senate. But, could his strange prisoner be a *real* god or demi-god appearing in human form? Greco-Roman mythology includes many stories of such entities, and Pilate's aides inform him that the priests believe the Galilean has magical powers. The superstitious Roman is nervous.

When the governor asks Jesus, "Where are you from," the gospel writer reminds us of earlier dialogues between Jesus and his opponents (see 7:25–30; 8:14–23). Jesus does not reply. This provokes Pilate, who says, "How dare you not answer me? Don't you realize I have power to set you free and power to crucify you?" (paraphrase of v. 10). Now Jesus speaks for the first time since prior to the scourging, pointing out to Pilate that any power Caesar's representative might have over him comes "from above." The governor knows that by "from above" Jesus is not referring to Caesar. Pilate is "of the world" and speaks on a worldly level concerning political power and brute force. Jesus, whose kingdom is not of this world, speaks on the level of truth, concerning the highest of all powers, the will of God.[4] We are back to Pilate's essential concern, which we saw at the beginning of the trial: maintaining the delicate balance of power in Judea.

After this exchange with Jesus, Pilate tries once again to release him, but to no avail. His own worldliness makes the prefect susceptible to manipulation by the chief priests, who quickly strike a blow at the point where he is most vulnerable. If he releases a man who claims to be a king he will show he truly is "not Caesar's friend." *Amicus Caesaris* ("Friend of Caesar") is a title bestowed by the emperor on trusted servants, and withdrawal of the title is tantamount to being condemned as a traitor. Tiberius does not tolerate rivals. That threat forces Pilate's hand.[5]

The governor sits down on his curule chair, the official portable "judgment seat" carried about by every Roman magistrate holding absolute authority. He orders Jesus brought out, still dressed as a clown king, to face "the Jews."[6] John, writing as if he were a clerk of the court, enters the date, hour, and place of the judge's decision into

3. Malina and Rohrbaugh, *Social Science Commentary*, 260.

4. Brown, *John XIII–XXI*, 892–93.

5. Burge, *Roman Centurion*, 161–62.

6. There is debate among commentators concerning precisely who sits on the curule chair. In the sentence, "He brought Jesus out and sat down on the judgment seat" (v. 13), the Greek verb for "sat down" may be translated as either transitive or intransitive. The two forms are identical. If it were translated as transitive, which is syntactically possible, the sentence would read, "He brought Jesus out and *sat him down* on the judgment seat." This would put Jesus, the King of the Jews, literally in the official seat of the judge, confirming John's portrayal of Jesus's role as true judge of the world (see 5:22; 9:39; 12:47). Although some commentators are fond of this interpretation, it is unthinkable that a Roman governor would make such a clownish gesture using his curule chair, a potent, quasi-sacred symbol of Roman authority. And there would be no other seating on the elevated tribunal other than the governor's curule chair. (See, e.g., Brown, *John XIII–XXI*, 880–81; O'Day, *Gospel of John*, 823, 825.)

the record of proceedings.[7] It is high noon on the day of preparation of the Passover, the time when the priests in the temple, just a short distance away, will begin to sacrifice the Passover lambs.

Pilate, in a final gesture of sarcastic defiance to the high priest and his cronies, declares to them, "Behold your King!" (paraphrase of v. 14). The religious leaders of the nation shout, "Away with him, away with him. Crucify him!" Pilate ridicules them with his response (v. 15*b*), which in Greek emphasizes the word king: "Your king— shall I crucify him?"[8] The chief priests seal their apostasy with the answer, "We have no king but Caesar!" (vv. 14–15). Pilate "then handed him over to them to be crucified" (v. 16), not meaning the Jews physically took charge of Jesus's execution, but John wishes his readers to understand that Jesus is crucified because it is insisted upon by the chief priests. By their declaration of commitment to Caesar as their only king, "the Jews" renounce their covenant with God at the very moment the priests and Levites are beginning preparation for Passover, the annual festival celebrating that covenant. Raymond Brown comments concerning the leaders of Israel,

> By the blood of the lamb he marked them off to be spared as his own, and now they know no king but the Roman emperor . . . They think of Passover as a traditional time for God's judgment of the world, and on Passover Eve they have judged themselves by condemning the one whom God sent into the world, not to judge it but to save it.[9]

[19:1–16] *¹ Then Pilate took Jesus and scourged him. ² And the soldiers plaited a crown of thorns, and put it on his head, and arrayed him in a purple robe; ³ they came up to him, saying, "Hail, King of the Jews!" and struck him with their hands. ⁴ Pilate went out again, and said to them, "See, I am bringing him out to you, that you may know that I find no crime in him." ⁵ So Jesus came out, wearing the crown of thorns and the purple robe. Pilate said to them, "Behold the man!" ⁶ When the chief priests and the officers saw him, they cried out, "Crucify him, crucify him!" Pilate said to them, "Take him yourselves and crucify him, for I find no crime in him." ⁷ The Jews answered him, "We have a law, and by that law he ought to die, because he has made himself the Son of God." ⁸ When Pilate heard these words, he was the more afraid; ⁹ he entered the praetorium again and said to Jesus, "Where are you from?" But Jesus gave no answer. ¹⁰ Pilate*

---

7. Despite older commentators' oft-repeated assertion that the place called in v. 13 "The Pavement" (Greek, *lithostrotos*) or "*Gabbatha*" (Hebrew for "height" or "raised place") must be located in the vicinity of the Roman fortress called the Antonia, recent research points to the vicinity of Herod's palace, the highest point in the city where bedrock is exposed (having an elevation slightly higher than the temple itself), rather than the Antonia fortress as the place where Jesus was put on trial before the Roman prefect. See von Walde, "Archaeology and John's Gospel," 573–75.

8. Kysar, *John*, 284.

9. Brown, *John XIII–XXI*, 895.

therefore said to him, "You will not speak to me? Do you not know that I have power to release you, and power to crucify you?" [11] Jesus answered him, "You would have no power over me unless it had been given you from above; therefore he who delivered me to you has the greater sin."

[12] Upon this Pilate sought to release him, but the Jews cried out, "If you release this man, you are not Caesar's friend; every one who makes himself a king sets himself against Caesar." [13] When Pilate heard these words, he brought Jesus out and sat down on the judgment seat at a place called The Pavement, and in Hebrew, Gab'batha. [14] Now it was the day of Preparation of the Passover; it was about the sixth hour. He said to the Jews, "Behold your King!" [15] They cried out, "Away with him, away with him, crucify him!" Pilate said to them, "Shall I crucify your King?" The chief priests answered, "We have no king but Caesar." [16] Then he handed him over to them to be crucified.

RESPONSE. This portion of his gospel is called "the Passion Narrative," but John makes no effort to draw our attention to the physical and psychological anguish the Lord experiences. He isn't creating a scene of pathos contrived to extract sympathetic tears from his readers. His text is in no way manipulative. John's Gospel has nothing in common with Mel Gibson's mawkish cinematic portrayal, *The Passion of the Christ*.[10] In fact, those who have little knowledge about daily life in a first century Roman province can easily miss the banality of the suffering Jesus endures, its very ordinariness in the context of the time.

In that cruel and callous age, the abuse and pain which Jesus undergoes is typical, not unusual or worse than what other victims of the Romans suffer. It is typical, too, of what still happens. In the modern era, analogous atrocities have been and are still inflicted on prisoners. Such things did not only occur in the last century under communist or fascist dictators, but they take place even now—sometimes authorized by our own democratically-chosen government, as well as by the terrorists whom we battle.[11] Pilate's sadistic troops have contemporary counterparts. As the French epigram famously puts it, "the more things change, the more they stay the same."[12] Caesar is long-gone, but his successors' tactics are not categorically different.

At the end of the gospel, in his narrative of the passion of Christ, John once more calls our attention to the gritty reality of the incarnation he proclaims in the prologue: "the Word became flesh and dwelt among us" (1:14). The Word made flesh shares every painful circumstance, every bitter experience of the ordinary humble, human child of God. In the Fourth Gospel Jesus habitually calls himself "the Son of Man" because for our sake he has become "Everyman."—Have we ever been the victims of

10. See Internet Movie Database, *The Passion of the Christ* (2004), directed by Mel Gibson.

11. *Wikipedia.com*, s.v. "Abu Ghraib Torture and Prisoner Abuse."

12. *Plus ça change, plus c'est la même chose.*

injustice? So has Jesus. . . . Have we ever been abandoned by our friends and left to face our enemies without comrades at our side? So has Jesus. . . . Have we ever been mocked and made the butt of cruel ridicule? So has Jesus. . . . Have we ever been subjected to physical torture by people who derive pleasure from our pain? So has Jesus.

John's passion story is a demonstration of the total immersion of God in our human condition, an immersion undertaken deliberately, willingly, and redemptively. There is a profound, logical reason some of us fall to our knees or bow deeply when in our liturgies we recite the words of the Nicene Creed, "for us and for our salvation he came down from heaven; by the power of the Holy Spirit he became incarnate from the Virgin Mary, and was made man." Kneeling or bowing at those words is an act of gratitude and reverence offered because, in his great love for us, God himself assumed our flesh. In the person of his Son, God became subject to every evil we routinely visit upon one another. He is our fellow-sufferer.

To fulfill his Father's plan for the healing and renewal of humankind, Jesus is willing to undergo the tribulations of the passion John describes for us in his uniquely serene and *dis*passionate way. Not only Jesus's death, but every other aspect of the incarnation must be understood as God's redeeming, healing work. Gregory Nazianzus, a famous fourth century theologian, explains this very succinctly: "That which he has not assumed he has not healed."[13] Jesus assumed the fragility of our human condition in every respect.

At the very end of the trial, the chief priests and their officers finally maneuver the worldly Roman governor into giving them what they want—the crucifixion of the Son of Man/Son of God, the King of Truth. Before he passes sentence, Pilate points to the bruised and bloodied yet still dignified victim, standing before them in his mock-regal vesture, and says, "Behold, your King!" They reply, "Away with him! Get rid of him! Crucify him." The governor sarcastically asks the priests, "Your King—shall I crucify him?" And they answer, "We have no king but Caesar" (paraphrase of vv. 14–15). Now the chief priests choose Caesar as their friend, instead of Jesus.[14]

Certain Roman emperors were treated as divine, which meant something different in the first century from what modern people generally mean when we use the word "god."[15] When the chief priests tell Pilate they have no king other than the Roman emperor, it is tantamount to admitting they also have no other God but Caesar, since they recognize that only Caesar (or his agent) has the power to make a difference in their world. If we were to transform the words of the Jewish leaders into a theological statement, it would be a declaration that Tiberius Caesar is the son of

13. Gregory Nazianzus, "To Cledonius," Epistle 101.

14. Kysar, *John*, 285.

15. Being made a state divinity (*divus*) by senatorial decree was something like being legally declared "larger than life" and, therefore, worthy of worship. Temples were built everywhere in the empire to honor the divinities of the imperial cult, including the current ruler, Tiberius, his foster-father Augustus, and Julius Caesar. Herod the Great, who built the temple in Jerusalem, also built a temple in Caesarea to the deified Augustus.

God. Jesus cannot be their king, for they have only *one* king, Caesar! When I hear the chief priests tell Pilate, "We have no king but Caesar," I wonder what in our modern churchly sphere might be considered a counterpart to the Jewish leaders' repudiation of Yahweh as their King. I find the analogue in an assertion I have sometimes heard even in church gatherings from church leaders—a declaration that the faith we need most these days is *faith in ourselves*. When church leaders adopt such thinking, their faith is reduced, in practice, to functional atheism. They speak about God, but behave as if God were powerless. Parker Palmer describes functional atheism as "the belief that ultimate responsibility for everything rests with us. This is the unconscious, un-examined conviction that if anything decent is going to happen here, we are the ones who must make it happen—a conviction held even by people who talk a good game about God."[16]

In contemporary American society, ruling power is not vested in a monarch, but in the cultural, economic, social, and political entities that provide the public what it wants. We are a market-driven society, and public taste is fickle; therefore, our "ruling powers" are made and unmade swiftly, much as Roman emperors were. What the public appears to crave most right now is entertainment. Amusement. Ruling power, in a sense, belongs to the entities that provide us with entertainment in any of its popular, varied forms.

These reflections bring to mind the challenges articulated more than sixty years ago by H. Richard Niebuhr his classic study, *Christ and Culture*.[17] How do the "rul-ing powers" of our culture affect our practice of Christian faith? Should the world's prevailing value system define our Christian practice? Do we intentionally seek Christ to be formed in us (to borrow Paul's words from Gal 4:19), taking the servant Lord we see in John's Gospel as our model? Or do we allow our personal aspirations to be guided by the ever-shifting "ruling powers" of the world around us?

We live *in* the world, even if we do not want to be *of* it. Christians will be forced to retreat to hermitages or wall ourselves off from the rest of society if we insist on not being affected by the world. Christ does not call us to withdraw from engagement with the world and its culture, but to resist being controlled by its power. Therefore, why should we worship at its shrines? We will be influenced by our culture; this is inevitable. But we have seen, heard, received, and believed in the incarnate Word of God, and we cannot "unsee" him. We cannot "unhear" him. The follower of the Beloved Disciple who became the final editor of his gospel is probably the author of these words:

> From the very first day, we were there, taking it all in—we heard it with our own ears, saw it with our own eyes, verified it with our own hands. The Word of Life appeared right before our eyes; we saw it happen! And now we're telling you in most sober prose that what we witnessed was, incredibly, this: The infinite Life

16. Palmer, *Let Your Life Speak*, 88–89.

17. Wax, "Overview." See also Niebuhr, *Christ and Culture*, foreword by Martin Marty, xiii–xix.

of God himself took shape before us. We saw it, we heard it, and now we're telling you so you can experience it along with us, this experience of communion
with the Father and his Son, Jesus Christ. Our motive for writing is simply this:
We want you to enjoy this, too. Your joy will double our joy! This, in essence, is
the message we heard from Christ and are passing on to you: God is light, pure
light; there's not a trace of darkness in him (1 John 1:1–5).[18]

As disciples of Christ the King of Truth, our vocation is not to abandon the
world, but to seize every occasion to *shape* the world's culture more than it shapes us.

Vv. 17–37. "It is finished." Jesus dies on the cross.

INTRODUCTION. It is difficult for modern people formed by a Christian culture
to grasp the depth of shame and dishonor applied in the first century to a death by
crucifixion. This was not only deemed the most painful of deaths, it was also the
punishment reserved by Rome for rebellious slaves and others whose crimes were
the vilest.[19] For their Lord to be crucified was a stigma the earliest Christians had
to overcome. It was an immediate psychological obstacle for potential new disciples.
Martin Hengel writes,

> People were all too aware of what it meant to bear the cross through the
> city and then be nailed to it and [they] feared it; they wanted to get away
> from it . . . Death on the cross implied extreme humiliation, shame, and tor-
> ture . . . That this crucified Jew, Jesus Christ, could truly be a divine being sent
> on earth, God's Son, the Lord of all, and the coming judge of the world, must
> inevitably have been thought by any educated man to be utter 'madness' and
> presumption.[20]

Willingly to identify oneself as the disciple of a crucified criminal who died a slave's
death—treating him as a model worthy of imitation—called not only for genuine faith
but also a remarkable measure of social courage.

We can best understand the differences between John's story of the crucifixion
and the Synoptic accounts if we recognize the intention of the Fourth Gospel to carry
forward the themes already introduced. John does not include details that could de-
tract from his theological motifs of Jesus as high priest (chapter 17) and King (chapter
18). The crucifixion is the symbolic enthronement of Jesus as King. Although he is
undoubtedly aware of the story about Simon of Cyrene carrying Jesus's cross for him
(Matt 27:3; Mark 15:21; Luke 23:26), John pointedly tells his readers that "Jesus went
out, bearing his own cross" (v. 17). The initiative belongs entirely to Jesus. He is sov-
ereign. He lays down his life; no one takes it from him (10:18). Like Isaac, who carries

---

18. *The Message*, 1687.

19. Hengel, *Crucifixion*, 51–63.

20. Ibid., 62, 83.

the wood for the sacrifice planned by his father Abraham (Gen 22:6), Jesus carries the wood of his own cross, while he is also the lamb which God provides for the sacrifice (Gen 6:8).[21] John's mention of Jesus's tunic "without seam, woven from top to bottom" (v. 23), advances the image of Jesus as great high priest, since the high priest's linen vestments include a seamless tunic woven top to bottom.[22]

Although John does not mention their participation in the parade of victims, we can assume that the two others crucified with Jesus walk with him, carrying their crosses out to "the place of a skull, which is called in Hebrew, Golgotha" (v. 17). Barabbas also would have been in that sad parade, had he not been released at the behest of the chief priests. Those led out for crucifixion carry only the transverse beam of the cross (Latin, *patibulum*), laid across their shoulders. Victims' hands would be tied to the opposite ends of this crosspiece, making it difficult for them to maintain their balance on the death march.[23]

Rome would adopt a spot in every city for judicial crucifixions and use it repeatedly, leaving in place several large, notched vertical posts for crosses. Because it usually takes several days for victims to die, an execution site adjacent to a busy road is invariably selected. Crucified men suffering for days in public view provide passersby a vivid reminder of the fate in store for all who provoke the empire's wrath. The location of Jerusalem's "place of a skull," is well-known, since it now lies within the ancient Church of the Holy Sepulcher, a site just outside the Gennath Gate of the city wall at the time of Jesus's death, roughly a thousand yard walk from Pilate's judgment seat.[24] (See Figs. 12–13, p. 255, above.) The hill named Golgotha is skull-like in the sense of being a rocky knob like a human cranium, located in what once was a quarry. The bare hillock was probably left unquarried because of the poor quality of its stone.[25]

A person being crucified is stripped naked, then nailed (or occasionally tied) to the crosspiece.[26] The soldiers would hoist up the crosspiece with their victim attached and slot it into the upright. It is to this "lifting up" that Jesus refers when he says on the preceding Sunday, "I, when I am lifted up from the earth, will draw all men to myself"

21. Brown, *John XIII–XXI*, 917–18. Brown points out that there was a rabbinical tradition associating the Passover lamb with the sacrifice of Isaac.

22. Lindars, *Gospel of John*, 578. The tunic had a vertical slit for the head and slits at the sides for the arms.

23. The Romans used many different shapes of crosses, and when crucifying large numbers of people at once—which sometimes happened—soldiers nailed victims to trees, walls, or trellises in various positions, including head-down. See Keener, *Gospel of John*, 2:1136; Hengel, *Crucifixion*, 24–31.

24. A few archeologists in the past decade have suggested that the actual site of Golgotha was much larger and that the site of Jesus's crucifixion was probably several hundred meters further south, near a crossroad and, thus, exposed to a greater number of passersby. See Taylor, "Golgotha."

25. This is a fact which happens to align with Ps 118:22–23, "The stone which the builders rejected has become the head of the corner. This is the Lord's doing; it is marvelous in our eyes." (See Acts 4:11.)

26. Hengel, *Crucifixion*, 32, says the use of nails was routine; tying the victim to the cross with only bonds was exceptional. Some were both tied and nailed.

(12:32). The victim's feet are then nailed to the lower part of the upright. Crosses are only high enough to get a victim's feet off the ground with his knees bent. Jesus's cross is probably about seven feet high—almost eye-level with anyone standing close by.[27]

Except on the occasion of mass crucifixions, the Romans usually display a tablet on which is written the victim's crime. This *titulus* is affixed to his cross. Pilate orders that the tablet for Jesus should state, "Jesus of Nazareth, King of the Jews" (v. 20). In this way the prefect reaffirms Jesus's kingship, announced earlier to the chief priests and mocked by Pilate's soldiers with their cruel parody of a coronation. To Pilate, Jesus is the Jews' Messiah. Rejecting the chief priests' objections, Pilate intends that every literate person watching Jesus die should know exactly who he is. John wants his readers to know that the cross is Jesus's chosen throne. The titulus is written in Aramaic, the local language; Greek, the lingua franca of the eastern Mediterranean; and Latin, the administrative language of the empire. By this act, Pilate proclaims to the world that Jesus's title is true and unalterable. Like v. 14, this is another display of Johannine irony: an unwittingly true proclamation by the Roman prefect who had earlier claimed not to know the meaning of truth.[28]

John's depiction of the company around the cross differs from those of the Synoptics. Other than the soldiers, the Fourth Gospel mentions no one except the Beloved Disciple and four women—Jesus's mother, her sister, and two other women named Mary, Mary the wife of Clopas and Mary Magdalene. John conveys his esteem for the significant role of Jesus's female followers. Their courage casts shame on the male disciples who—except for the Beloved Disciple—have abandoned their Master. If Jesus's cross is the ordinary sort, these five are almost face-to-face with him. They can hear clearly as Jesus designates his own mother to become adoptive mother to the Beloved Disciple and that disciple now to become her son and protector—thus making the disciple his brother (vv. 25–27). Here the Fourth Gospel shows that true disciples adopt the concerns of Jesus as their own and follow in his footsteps (see 1 John 2:6).[29] The oldest son is responsible for the welfare of his mother. Although Jesus's mother is losing this Son, he gives her a new son, one who shares the mind of Jesus, his brother and Lord. This is a touching act of compassion on the part of the man suffering the ordeal of crucifixion. It underscores Jesus's depiction of his death—his "going away"—as a benefit to those who love him (16:7–11).[30] Like his other words and deeds in John's Passion Narrative, Jesus offers these with quiet dignity, compassion, and simplicity—but without emotionalism.

27. Keener, *Gospel of John*, 2:1136. Romans used tall crosses to display more visibly the death of notorious or politically prominent subjects of their retribution, but we cannot assume Pilate regards Jesus as that important. Furthermore, since this day's victims must be removed from their crosses before sunset because of the Passover, using a high cross will slow the soldiers' work and the prominent subject's short time on the cross will nullify the political effect of such a display.

28. Lindars, *Gospel of John*, 576; Brown, *Crucified Christ*, 64.

29. Keener, *Gospel of John*, 2:1144.

30. Lindars, *Gospel of John*, 579.

Like the Synoptics, John sees events on Golgotha as fulfilling predictions in Scripture—naming specifically the casting of lots for shares of Jesus's clothing (vv. 23–24), fulfilling Ps 22:18; and the offering of sour wine to Jesus (vv. 28–30), fulfilling Ps 69:21. The Gentile soldiers also unknowingly carry out another scriptural mandate, the one which forbids the tearing of a high priest's clothing (Lev 21:10). In addition, John tells us they use hyssop to give Jesus a sponge soaked in their vinegary wine (v. 29), choosing the same kind of branch used to sprinkle the blood of the Passover lamb on the door posts of Hebrew homes at the exodus (Exod 12:22).

John emphasizes the fulfillment of scriptural predictions more often in his Passion Narrative than in any other part of the gospel. But we must not have the idea that the man dying on the cross is at the same time thinking about what prophecies he must fulfill. These references are all observations of the narrator, conclusions drawn following years of meditation on the death of his Lord. After Jesus receives the sour wine, thus fulfilling another ancient prophecy, he says, "It is finished," bows his head, and hands over his spirit to the Father (v. 30). The word translated "finished" is of signal importance. It is a cry of triumph, indicating that everything the Father sent his Son to do in his great redeeming work has now been accomplished. The word means "achieved," "fulfilled," and "completed." In keeping with the way the Fourth Gospel tells the story of the passion, Jesus remains in control. He decides when his work is done.

John's Gospel, more than the others, emphasizes the intimate connection between Jesus's death and resurrection and the bestowing of the Holy Spirit, which the Fourth Gospel explicitly describes as Jesus's own Spirit. John tells us in 7:39 that the Spirit does not become real for Jesus's followers until he "is glorified." When Jesus dies on the cross, he marks the fulfillment of his earthly work. This is the high moment of his glory until he is raised from the dead. The RSV says Jesus "gave up his spirit," but the word literally means "handed over." Many commentators draw attention to the Greek word John uses here, a word employed repeatedly in the passion story.[31] Judas hands Jesus over to the chief priests; the chief priests hand him over to Pilate; Pilate hands him over to the executioners. Now the Son of God hands over his spirit to the Father who—in a sense—has "handed over" his Son to give his life for the salvation of the world. We may also see Jesus's dying breath as a symbolic exhalation of the Spirit, anticipating the dramatic gesture by which the risen One will breathe the Spirit upon his disciples on Sunday evening when he sends them into the world in the same way the Father sent him (20:22).[32]

The final verses of this section deal with the treatment of Jesus's dead body, and the gospel writer—or his editor—emphasizes that these details concerning Jesus's death are the testimony of a trustworthy eyewitness (v. 35). Because it is afternoon on the day of preparation, the bodies must be taken down from the crosses before

31. Kysar, *John*, 290; Lindars, *Gospel of John*, 582–83; Brown, *John XIII–XXI*, 931.

32. Brown, *Crucified Christ*, 66.

sundown. Romans often break the legs of crucifixion victims when it seems essential to hasten their deaths. This they do to the two men crucified with Jesus, and the soldiers are prepared to do the same for the King of the Jews. However, since he is already dead, they do not break his legs. John notes this as another fulfillment of Scripture, an allusion to Christ as the Passover Lamb (v. 36), since the Law instructed that none of its bones should be broken (Exod 12:46; Num 9:12). Nevertheless, even though Jesus seems to be dead, they thrust a spear into his side to make sure. From that spear wound comes a flow of what appears to be blood and water (vv. 33–34). Medical experts say that such a flow would be fluid that has collected in Jesus's lungs. John may intend for his readers to see this as a symbolic pouring out of the benefits of Jesus's death for believers.

[19:17–37] *17 So they took Jesus, and he went out, bearing his own cross, to the place called the place of a skull, which is called in Hebrew Gol'gotha. 18 There they crucified him, and with him two others, one on either side, and Jesus between them.*

19 Pilate also wrote a title and put it on the cross; it read, "Jesus of Nazareth, the King of the Jews." 20 Many of the Jews read this title, for the place where Jesus was crucified was near the city; and it was written in Hebrew, in Latin, and in Greek. 21 The chief priests of the Jews then said to Pilate, "Do not write, 'The King of the Jews,' but, 'This man said, I am King of the Jews.'" 22 Pilate answered, "What I have written I have written." 23 When the soldiers had crucified Jesus they took his garments and made four parts, one for each soldier; also his tunic. But the tunic was without seam, woven from top to bottom; 24 so they said to one another, "Let us not tear it, but cast lots for it to see whose it shall be." This was to fulfil the Scripture, "They parted my garments among them, and for my clothing they cast lots."

25 So the soldiers did this. But standing by the cross of Jesus were his mother, and his mother's sister, Mary the wife of Clopas, and Mary Mag'dalene. 26 When Jesus saw his mother, and the disciple whom he loved standing near, he said to his mother, "Woman, behold, your son!" 27 Then he said to the disciple, "Behold, your mother!" And from that hour the disciple took her to his own home.

28 After this Jesus, knowing that all was now finished, said (to fulfil the Scripture), "I thirst." 29 A bowl full of vinegar stood there; so they put a sponge full of the vinegar on hyssop and held it to his mouth. 30 When Jesus had received the vinegar, he said, "It is finished"; and he bowed his head and gave up his spirit.

31 Since it was the day of Preparation, in order to prevent the bodies from remaining on the cross on the Sabbath (for that Sabbath was a high day), the Jews asked Pilate that their legs might be broken, and that they might be taken away.

32 So the soldiers came and broke the legs of the first, and of the other who had been crucified with him; 33 but when they came to Jesus and saw that he was already dead, they did not break his legs. 34 But one of the soldiers pierced his side with a spear, and at once there came out blood and water. 35 He who saw it has borne witness--his testimony is true, and he knows that he tells the truth--that you also may believe. 36 For these things took place that the Scripture might be fulfilled, "Not a bone of him shall be broken." 37 And again another Scripture says, "They shall look on him whom they have pierced."

RESPONSE. I am an Episcopal priest. In our church, the centerpiece of the yearly Good Friday Liturgy is a solemn reading of the entire Passion according to John. The congregation sits until the verse that says, "So they took Jesus, and he went out, carrying his own cross, to the place called the place of a skull, which is called in Hebrew Golgotha" (v. 17). Then everyone stands and remains standing until the end, when Christ's body is laid in the tomb. The verses I am responding to at the moment, vv. 17–37, constitute the core of John's Passion Narrative. He tells this crucial part of Jesus's story in a concise way, but the Apostles' Creed is even briefer: "he suffered under Pontius Pilate, was crucified, died, and was buried." That's the simplest possible account of the cosmic event which Christians believe was the pivotal moment of human history.

Good Friday no longer seems to be a day when most Episcopalians go to church. I suspect that holds true for many other Christians in our country, regardless of their denominational connections. All churches are still packed on Easter, though. Has this change occurred because Americans now have more difficulty dealing with death than we once did? Anybody's death—not just the death of Jesus? Maybe so. We certainly seem to have expunged the word "funeral" from our ecclesiastical vocabulary. We want to celebrate life and avoid references to dying. We're motivated to make Easter worship as beautiful, uplifting, and colorful as possible. Brass ensembles support choirs singing the "Hallelujah Chorus," bright spring flowers adorn every altar, and churches are filled with happy, smiling people wearing their prettiest clothes. After services are over, there are Easter egg hunts on the lawn for the little ones and delectable goodies in the parish hall for everybody. Easter is a lovely, happy, very special day—the day of resurrection. Even church drop-outs tend to show up on Easter.

However, for many contemporary Christians Good Friday services feel dark, heavy, and sad, "like a funeral." (Nobody likes to go to funerals; that's why we avoid the word.) To be fair, there's a faithful remnant of churchgoers deeply committed to worship on Good Friday, but they compose a distinct minority. A few of those who choose to celebrate Easter but skip Good Friday tell me there is too much going on in the world that already makes them sad. They don't want to come to church, sing gloomy songs, and weep because it's the day Christ died. Last year on Good Friday my wife and I were invited to a cocktail party and fish fry at a nearby country club. I guess that's a sign of the times. (We didn't attend.) Alas, by missing the opportunity to enter deeply into the heart of the gospel—the passion of Christ—"Easter only" Christians forego the opportunity to learn first-hand why we call the day Jesus died *Good* Friday.

I concede that Good Friday is sad. And dark. It's definitely not "upbeat," and we Americans are a people who want everything to have a "positive vibe," if possible. Of course, when challenged to think about it, most people agree that real life is *not* always happy and cheerful. Our lives invariably include incidents of pain, loss, and grief. But it's a profound truth that facing painful experiences—including tragedies—shapes the soul. Furthermore, we often feel much closer to people with whom we share an occasion of loss or heartbreak than to people with whom we only share a pleasant holiday.

By the same token, symbolically walking the Way of the Cross with Jesus in his passion creates a unique bond between the Christians who experience it. It links us with one another as followers of the Son of Man who laid down his life for us. It certainly gives us a personal connection with the classic spiritual, "Were you there when they crucified my Lord?" If we listen closely to the passion according to John and use our imagination, we *will* be affected. Picture yourself in Pilate's praetorium as he asks the chief priests, "Shall I crucify your King?" Visualize yourself standing at the roadside as Jesus stumbles by carrying his cross to Golgotha. Imagine how you might feel coming quietly alongside the Beloved Disciple, Jesus's mother, and the faithful women as they keep their death watch at the cross. John's Gospel *connects us* to the Savior in his supreme act of love for the world.

I want to summarize this portion of John's story for you, using language appropriate to the Fourth Gospel's symbolic, mythic world: The city of Jerusalem, and in particular Skull Hill just outside its walls, is the stage for the definitive struggle between Truth and Falsehood, Light and Dark, the kingdom of God and the kingdom of the Evil One. It has been God's plan from the beginning that this bare rock knob should be the spot where, at Passover (and it *must* be at Passover), God's incarnate Son, the King of Truth, engages in single combat with his spiritual foe, the invisible but insidiously powerful King of Lies. There is an epic clash, and at its conclusion the King of Truth dies—though calm and courageous to the end. Once Jesus breathes his last, the King of Lies seems victorious. He declares himself the winner and pronounces the dead King of Truth, the loser. The body of the dead King of Truth is carried from the battlefield to his tomb and laid to rest by a handful of brave, loyal friends, with all the honors due such a King.

The King of Lies congratulates himself on his triumph. But he is wrong, oh so wrong. He may indeed seem the winner of this epic contest—but the illusion only lingers until Sunday morning. The King of Truth has indeed laid down his life, but he has not surrendered. He is not defeated. The willing self-sacrifice of the righteous and innocent Son of God—True King of Israel and King of Truth—is the act of peaceful power that demolishes the authority of the King of Lies for all time. (The King of Lies works through many surprising agents, but in our story his primary earthly representative is Caesar—the proud, earthly monarch who wants to be considered divine.)

Thirty-odd years before John's Gospel was put in final form, the apostle Paul wrote these words,

> We preach Christ crucified, a stumbling block to Jews and folly to Gentiles, but to those who are called, both Jews and Greeks, Christ the power of God and the wisdom of God. For the foolishness of God is wiser than men, and the weakness of God is stronger than men . . . None of the rulers of this age understood this; for if they had, they would not have crucified the Lord of glory (1 Cor 1:23–25; 2:8).

Had the powers-that-be, the agents of the King of Lies whom Paul labels elsewhere as "the world rulers of this present darkness" (Eph 6:12), perceived that they could possibly suffer a decisive defeat through Jesus's dying on a Roman cross, they would not have crucified him. They'd have manipulated things to ensure that he was set free and written off as a harmless Galilean preacher. After all, what was Jesus, *really*? A rural prophet whose disciples were a gang of powerless peasants and tradesmen. Even if he fancied himself the long-awaited Messiah, this Jesus was clearly a peaceful fellow, not a soldier—and certainly no threat to the powers-that-be. If the powers-that-be were as wise as they imagined themselves to be, Barabbas would have been crucified between the two others on Skull Hill, not Jesus. But *this* was God's plan, God's wisdom. As Paul said, "The weakness of God is stronger than men" (1 Cor 1:25).

The chief priests want Jesus crucified because nothing in their cultural context more explicitly shames and degrades a person than crucifixion. They're convinced that having the Romans nail Jesus to a cross will make his memory odious. No Jew will want to be identified as a disciple of someone who dies an accursed death, hanging on a cross. And no Gentile will be attracted to one who suffers the death of a rebellious slave, the death of someone guilty of the foulest of crimes. In addition, their scheme to force Jesus's crucifixion will have the secondary and positive effect of putting blame for Jesus's death squarely on the Romans.

As it turns out, the chief priests are sorely mistaken. Jesus predicted his victory in the courts of the temple a few days earlier, on the home turf of the leaders of the nation who rejected him: "I, when I am lifted up from the earth, will draw all men to myself" (12:32). What on Friday seems to be a cruel mockery of his kingship is actually his coronation, and that which appears to be the vicious instrument of his death is truly his throne. What looks like a defeat for the King of Truth is in fact his triumph. Ironically, Pilate, the local arch-agent of "the world ruler of this present darkness" personally decrees that the King's throne be clearly marked as such with a sign written in Hebrew, Greek and Latin, so no literate passersby might fail to know precisely who occupies it. What the powers-that-be determine will be the end of the road for Jesus in fact becomes the pinnacle of his glory. The death cunningly designed to make him repellant to all potential followers has an opposite effect. The cross shows Jesus a hero worthy of imitation.

Some gospel texts are most effective for me, spiritually, when I am able to find a character in the text with whom I identify. John's passion offers readers a number of dramatically delineated characters. In order of their appearance, we see Judas the betrayer; weak, fickle Peter; the wily, worldly chief priests; Pilate, the vacillating judge who proclaims Jesus innocent three different times but sends him to die anyway; the callous soldiers of the crucifixion squad who drink and throw dice at the foot of the cross, oblivious to everything that's going on; the Beloved Disciple and the Lord's mother, who watch and weep and are bonded to Jesus and one another in a new way; Mary Magdalene, who does not yet know that she will be the primary witness to Jesus's resurrection; and, finally, the two other compassionate women who show themselves to be Jesus's only faithful friends.

Maybe we who read John's story can see something of ourselves in all of them. (Do you?) I must confess, I *did* leave one character out. He has only a tiny part in this drama. He never even appears "on stage." But I must bring him in, because *he's* the one with whom I have come personally to identify. I'm talking about Barabbas. Barabbas is truly guilty of everything Jesus is falsely accused of. Our English translation of John labels Barabbas a "robber" (18:40), but "robber" is a poor translation of the word's meaning in this context. The Roman governor of Judea does not deal personally with thieves; he has too much else to do. Ordinary criminals are left to the high priest and the regular Jewish courts; they, not Pilate, administer day-to-day justice.[33] The only Jewish prisoners brought before the Roman governor for trial are capital offenders: rebels, revolutionaries, and assassins of Roman tax collectors—obvious enemies of Caesar. You and I would call Barabbas a convicted terrorist, and so are his two companions. They have already been tried by the governor, found guilty, and sentenced to die on the cross. John merely omits a description of their trial. Barabbas is most likely a zealot, perhaps an assassin, and he is slated to occupy one of the crosses on Skull Hill that day. However, by the will of God, Barabbas is set free, and Jesus dies in his place.

The humble preacher from Nazareth—whose touch healed the paralyzed man at the Bethesda pool, who gave sight to the man born blind, and who raised Lazarus to life—stretches out his innocent hands and dies on the cross where Barabbas belongs. By popular demand the guilty man is released and the only sinless mortal who ever lived is executed in his place. How ironic, and appropriate too, that the one who has obeyed his heavenly Father faithfully all through his life should be put to death in the place of another man whose surname in Hebrew means *"son of the father."*

---

33. Reicke, *New Testament Era*, 141, describes how the Romans left civil administration in the hands of the Jewish authorities.

"Son of the Father," that's who I am. I bear that name. It gave me a chill when I first realized that "son of the father" is the precise meaning of my Scottish surname. In my ancestors' native tongue, our clan name literally means, "children of the father." So, I *am* Barabbas—in more ways than one. The chief priests shout in sympathy for me. They identify with me because they know they're really just as guilty as I am. Now, because innocent Jesus hangs there in my place and *his* blood trickles down the wood of the cross instead of mine, I'm free to go. I am Barabbas, a "son of the Father." So are you. All of us are "children of the Father," and because we are, there's hope for us.

When Jesus says, "It is finished," then bows his head and hands over his spirit to God, he does not utter an expression of weary resignation, but one of triumph. He's not saying, "I'm exhausted; I'm worn out; I'm done." Instead, Jesus is telling his Father, who is always with him (16:32), "Everything you sent me to do is now accomplished." He has said only what his Father has given him to say, and he has done only what his Father has given him to do. Now Jesus—the incarnation of the Word that "was in the beginning with God," the one "through whom all things were made"—will become the author of a *new* creation.

On Friday afternoon, with the Sabbath drawing nigh, Jesus says to the Father, "It is finished." Refer to the end of the Genesis creation story, where we read, "on the seventh day, God *finished* his work which he had done, and he rested on the seventh day" (Gen 2:2). The same word; the same message: *It is finished.* The work God sent his Son to do is now done. The story of the old world, the old covenant, has reached its climax. The new creation, the new world will dawn on Sunday morning.[34] For John's Gospel only a gauzy partition separates Jesus's death on Friday afternoon from his resurrection on Sunday morning. They are two faces of a single coin. The resurrection life can only be real if there is also a *real* death.

Jesus's labor is over. He has been a good shepherd of his Father's flock. He now has permission to depart in peace. What happens next is entirely in the Father's hands.—This Sabbath, the Man of Faith, the King of Truth, the Son of God, will rest in the tomb.

Vv. 38–42. Jesus receives a kingly burial at the hands of two members of the Sanhedrin.

INTRODUCTION. John's Passion Narrative closes with a short description of Jesus's burial at the hands of two rich men. One of the two appears earlier in the Fourth Gospel, Nicodemus, with whom Jesus engages in a night-time dialogue (3:1–15) and who later challenges the Pharisees of the Sanhedrin to give the prophet from Galilee a hearing (7:50–52). The second, Joseph of Arimathea (described in Mark 15:43 as "a respected member of the council, who was also himself looking for the kingdom

34. Wright, *How God Became King*, 78–79.

of God"), is mentioned in all four gospels only in the context of Jesus's burial. These two wealthy members of the Jerusalem elite, Joseph, a secret disciple, and Nicodemus, another secret disciple—though known to be sympathetic to Jesus—confirm the crucified man's kingship by giving him a regal interment. Our gospel writer may be implying that Jesus's death on the cross brings these two "closet disciples" to make public confession of their faith. Nicodemus brings fine linen burial cloth and a mixture of myrrh and aloes, "about a hundred pounds' weight" (v. 39).[35] Such a quantity of these fragrances cost a fortune. The ointment with which Mary of Bethany bathes Jesus's feet on the preceding Sunday is appraised by Judas Iscariot as worth 300 denarii, a year's wages for a working man (12:5). The value of the precious burial spices Nicodemus provides for Jesus's interment is a hundred times greater than that.[36]

All four gospels ascribe to Joseph of Arimathea the initiative in asking Pilate for permission to remove the body of Jesus from the cross for burial (see Matt 27:57–61; Mark 15:42–47; Luke 23:50–56). The governor has no reason to deny a request from such an important man. All four gospels also indicate that the tomb is new, but only Matthew says the tomb belongs to Joseph. John alone records Nicodemus's involvement in the burial and alone says Jesus was buried in this new tomb because it was late on the day of preparation and the tomb was "close at hand" (v. 42).[37]

The Fourth Gospel says Mary Magdalene comes to the tomb early the next morning (20:1), which means that at least she—and probably the others—watch as Jesus's body is taken down from the cross and placed in the tomb.

> **[19:38–42]** [38] *After this Joseph of Arimathe'a, who was a disciple of Jesus, but secretly, for fear of the Jews, asked Pilate that he might take away the body of Jesus, and Pilate gave him leave. So he came and took away his body.* [39] *Nicode'mus also, who had at first come to him by night, came bringing a mixture of myrrh and aloes, about a hundred pounds' weight.* [40] *They took the body of Jesus, and bound it in linen cloths with the spices, as is the burial custom of the Jews.*
>
> [41] *Now in the place where he was crucified there was a garden, and in the garden a new tomb where no one had ever been laid.* [42] *So because of the Jewish day of Preparation, as the tomb was close at hand, they laid Jesus there.*

RESPONSE. Just as Nicodemus, the wealthy, aristocratic rabbi and Sanhedrin elder, once came to call on Jesus by night, accompanied by his own disciples and an entourage of attendants, so in this case the Jerusalem magnate does not act alone. Imagine the scene on Golgotha. It is late on the day of preparation. The body of Jesus must

35. A hundred Roman pounds would be about seventy-five modern pounds.

36. Kysar, *John*, 293–94; Keener, *Gospel of John*, 2:1163–64.

37. In the Church of the Holy Sepulcher it is roughly 70 paces from the Rock of Calvary to the Aedicule which marks the tomb of Christ.

be taken down from the cross and buried before the Sabbath begins at sunset. Two prominent and elderly noblemen, Joseph of Arimathea and Nicodemus, arrive at the well-known public execution site, accompanied by bodyguards, attendants, and four or five servants carrying bags of costly, precious, aromatic spices and the burial linens. The servants carefully and respectfully remove the body of Jesus from the cross and bear it to the tomb, where they wrap it in alternating layers of linen and spices before sealing the entrance with a stone. All of this is done under the watchful eyes of Joseph and Nicodemus, while the Beloved Disciple, Jesus's mother, and the other women look on. Then, after expressing their condolences and probably weeping with Jesus's mother and her companions, the two elders depart.

Since the Fourth Gospel does not describe a "trial" of Jesus before the Sanhedrin, it is likely—at least in John's story world—that neither of these two distinguished secret disciples knows what is afoot until it's too late to stop it. We assume that if there had been a hearing and the two were present, they would have spoken up on Jesus's behalf. (John tells us Nicodemus did so on an earlier occasion.) On the other hand, it is legitimate to ask whether the crucifixion either could or should have been stopped. Writing years before any of the Gospels took shape, Paul tells the Corinthian believers that the death of God's Son on a Roman cross is a demonstration of God's wisdom, part of his mysterious plan for the redemption of the world (1 Cor 1:20–25). John assures his readers the cross is Jesus's choice. By willingly laying down his life for those he loves, Jesus reveals his glory. Indeed, this act is the consummation of that revelation.

These last verses of the Passion Narrative tell us clearly that the self-offering love of Christ is compellingly attractive. He had said, "I, when I am lifted up from the earth, will draw all men to myself" (12:32). The cross draws these two aristocratic secret disciples into a public display of their devotion to Jesus. They have perhaps tried to straddle the fence politically until now, but the cross has made all the difference. Whatever fear they may have had earlier is gone. Come what may, the governor, the high priest, and all Jerusalem will know they count themselves willing subjects of the king whom they have honored at his burial.

As the great stone is rolled in front of the tomb's entrance, Joseph, who prepared this tomb in preparation for his own death, may console himself with the thought that one day—perhaps soon—he will lie in this same tomb, with Jesus.

Joseph can't imagine the surprise Sunday morning will bring.

Doing Your Own Theology

Questions for reflection after reading John 19.

- The moment when the chief priests tell Pilate they "have no King but Caesar" (v. 15*b*), they repudiate the reign of God. Their statement is tantamount to an admission that they have no other God but Caesar, since they recognize that only Caesar (or his agent) has the power to make a difference in their world. These same men will leave the governor's tribunal and go directly to the temple to preside at rites meant to celebrate and renew Israel's covenant with her God. They are priests, spiritual leaders, but they practice "functional atheism . . . the unconscious, unexamined conviction that if anything decent is going to happen here, we are the ones who must make it happen."[38] Acknowledging God's absolute power is, in principle, an acknowledgement of our own true powerlessness. In practice, however, we often pay lip service to the power of God while behaving as if every good thing depends entirely on our human efforts.—*How can individual believers avoid being trapped by functional atheism? How can our churches demonstrate authentic reliance on God rather than on the purely worldly resources of showmanship, money, political favor, and strategic marketing plans? It has been said that true power comes from submission to God. Do you agree or disagree? Why?*

- On the Sunday before he goes to the cross, Jesus announces to the Passover throng in the temple, "Now is the judgment of this world, now shall the ruler of this world be cast out; and I, when I am lifted up from the earth, will draw all men to myself" (12:31–32). John's Passion Narrative is full of irony and paradox. Jesus, the humble Galilean prophet and teacher is denounced and rejected by the leaders of his nation. They will not have this man as *their* King! But the Romans "lift him up" on a cross that becomes his royal throne. They even mark his throne with an official proclamation issued by Caesar's personal representative, announcing in three languages his true identity, "Jesus of Nazareth, the King of the Jews." By crucifying Jesus, the Romans mock an apparently helpless, failed Messiah. But God—who uses "what is weak in the world to shame the strong" (1 Cor 1:27)—decrees that the instrument of his Son's intended degradation shall instead win his eternal victory.—*The apostle Paul wrote these words to his Corinthian converts: "When I came to you, brethren . . . I decided to know nothing among you except Jesus Christ and him crucified" (1 Cor 2:1–2). How does John's Passion Narrative help you understand Paul's thinking? How does the cross display the wisdom of God for you? Is that a wisdom you can incorporate into your own life choices? What is the message of the cross for you?*

38. Palmer, *Let Your Life Speak*, 88–89.

- On Friday afternoon, with the Sabbath drawing nigh, Jesus says to the Father, "It is finished." Refer to the end of the Genesis creation story, where we read that "on the seventh day, God *finished* his work which he had done, and he rested on the seventh day" (Gen 2:2). The same word; the same message. *It is finished.* The work God sent his Son to do is now done. The story of the old world, the old covenant, has now reached its climax. The new creation, the new world will dawn on Sunday morning. In John's Gospel only a gauzy partition separates Jesus's death on Friday afternoon from his resurrection on Sunday morning. They are two faces of a single coin. The resurrection life can only be real if there is also a *real* death.—*In your own words, tell why Jesus had to die. Can you understand Jesus' final words, "It is finished," as both a cry of triumph and the announcement that the old world has ended and the new world has dawned? If you are able to see it this way, does it modify your understanding of Jesus's life and death?*

A General Introduction to Chapters 20 and 21.

John's Two Resurrection Narratives

The accounts of Jesus's suffering, death, and resurrection constitute a single body of testimony. As pointed out in the introduction to John's Passion Narrative (see p. 257, above), the resurrection stories, like the passion stories, are first told by eyewitnesses to the events, then re-told by those who hear them. Within a relatively short time— possibly only a decade—versions of these oral accounts are put in writing, probably first as *aides-memoire* for the eyewitnesses and later as proto-gospels. The primary function of the written gospels (of which Mark is probably the first) is to preserve the authoritative testimony of Jesus's disciples, those who heard him speak and were witnesses to the events of his life, death, and resurrection. The Passion/Resurrection Narratives, although compiled from oral accounts, never take the form of folklore. Folklore is made up of anonymous tales passed on by word of mouth from generation to generation within a culture, embroidered and reimagined by successive cohorts of storytellers. Such tales evolve over an extended period of time. This is not what happens in the case of the Gospels' Passion/Resurrection Narratives because these narratives assume a written form while numerous eyewitnesses are still available to correct obvious mistakes in the traditions being transmitted within the growing, but still relatively small community of "Jesus people."[1]

The life of the early church cannot be explained apart from the assumption that virtually all members of the first Christian communities believe that Jesus of Nazareth was bodily raised from the dead—not simply resuscitated, like a figure from Greco-Roman literature, but raised to life in a transformed "spiritual body." (See 1 Cor 15:36–56.) Surprisingly, in view of what modern readers anticipate, the gospel narratives of Jesus's rising from the dead do not describe the risen One as appearing dazzling and glorious, although his resurrected body does have unusual properties, such as the ability to pass through locked doors. Instead of appearing superhuman or transfigured, Jesus seems to be among his friends once more simply as "a human being among human beings."[2] Because they did not expect to see him at all, these friends do

---

1. Bauckham, *Jesus and the Eyewitnesses*, 264–318, describes how the authoritative tradition of the Christian community began to develop. That there was a specific body of authoritative testimony being conveyed from person to person within the young church is evident from 1 Cor 11:23–24 and 15:3–8. Likewise, Gal 2:1–10 demonstrates that even an independent-minded evangelist such as Paul felt the need to present the substance of his "gospel" for appraisal by those "who were of repute," James the brother of Jesus, Peter, and John.

2. Wright, *Resurrection*, 605.

not identify him right away. However, they recognize him when they hear him speak and see the identifying marks on his resurrected body.

When we compare the resurrection stories in the four gospels we observe similarities as well as striking differences, just as when we compare the passion stories. The most notable difference among the four sets of resurrection stories is that Mark's gospel describes the women's discovery of the empty tomb, but no resurrection appearances except in its "longer ending" (Mark 16:9–20), which modern experts assume to be a later addition to the text. However, in Mark the angel in Jesus's empty tomb tells the women to "go and tell his disciples and Peter that he is going before you to Galilee; there you will see him, as he told you" (16:7). Therefore, the author of Mark knows of some resurrection appearances, especially in Galilee, but does not describe them.

Despite differences in details (which should always be taken for granted when comparing four different perspectives on a single set of events), the actual core of the Resurrection Narratives is strikingly similar in the four canonical gospels. In all of them, a woman or a group of women discover the empty tomb on Sunday morning and encounter there an angelic figure or figures (Matt 28:1–8; Mark 8:1–8; Luke 24:1–11; John 20:1, 11–18). The fact that women are the first to discover the empty tomb and the first to see the risen One can be assumed as a fact of history, since the society that produces the Gospels is one which discounts the validity of testimony by women. No one feeling inspired to create a fanciful story about these events will choose to make *women* the primary witnesses to the resurrection. After the accounts of the empty tomb, the core of the Resurrection Narratives in Matthew, Luke, and John continue with the risen Lord himself appearing, first to one or more of the women and afterwards to the male disciples (Matt 28:9–10, 16–20; Luke 24:13–49; John 20:14–29; and 21:4–23).

The conviction that God raised Jesus from the dead is central to Christian faith. As James Dunn wrote more than thirty years ago in *The Evidence for Jesus,*

> The belief that God raised Jesus from the dead is, if anything, of even more fundamental importance to Christian faith than the belief in Jesus as the Son of God. If it is untrue, or true only in a very vague sense, a whole range of basic Christian doctrines would have to be rewritten—particularly Christian understanding of who Jesus was and is, of the significance and effectiveness of his death, and of the hope which Christians entertain for themselves and for humanity.[3]

It is safe to say that if Jesus's disciples had never encountered the risen Lord, there would be no "good news" to share, no mission to the world, and no church. Disciples of Jesus might have continued to be identified as such, perhaps ultimately coming to be known as a school within rabbinic Judaism. In time, Israel might have regarded Jesus of Nazareth as a sage greater than Hillel, maybe even as the long-awaited

3. Dunn, *Evidence*, 53.

prophet-greater-than-Moses (Deut 18:15–19). However, minus his resurrection, there is little about Jesus that either Jews or the world at large would perceive as entirely new or unique. In claiming authority to speak to Israel out of an intimate, personal communion with the God of Abraham, Isaac, and Jacob, Jesus resembles Moses, and his ethical precepts fall within the broad parameters of Jewish moral teaching—rooted solidly in Deuteronomy, Jeremiah, Isaiah, and Hosea.

If no one had ever met the risen Christ, any claim that Jesus should be regarded either as the Messiah or the future heavenly Son of Man would have been dismissed. Jesus would, at best, under those circumstances, come to be remembered as a heroic, martyred, wonder-working prophet. If the Beloved Disciple (whoever he was) had not personally encountered his Master raised from the tomb, the Fourth Gospel would never have been created. Neither would the Synoptics. If a book had been written to preserve this Jesus's teaching for later generations in Israel, such a volume would resemble the Old Testament books of the prophets. In no sense would it be a "gospel."

Ancient literature is replete with stories of visions and dreams, voices and visitations of the gods, even resuscitations of people who were buried but not really dead. The Jewish Scriptures themselves contain a story about the shade of the Prophet Samuel summoned up from Sheol by a medium to advise King Saul on the eve of his last battle with the Philistines (1 Sam 28:3–19). If the experiences Jesus's disciples described to others in the months after his crucifixion had fit any of the existing literary or cultural paradigms, no one would have been surprised. Indeed, in that era some tales were expected to arise. There existed, however, no precedent for such stories as Jesus's disciples told about his resurrection.

Jesus's friends, like most Jews, believed the dead would be resurrected at the end of the age. All except the Sadducees expected the dead to be raised to life on the last day in order to receive God's final judgment in their flesh. But no Jew expected *anyone*, no matter how righteous, to be resurrected before the last day.[4] (This conviction is evident in Martha's dialogue with Jesus in 11:21–24.) The gospels' Resurrection Narratives are unique. They make clear that Jesus's friends had not been visited by his ghost; neither were they responding to anyone's hallucination or to vivid dreams about him. These people were convinced they had seen their Master alive in the flesh, displaying the wounds of the nails in his hands and the spear wound in his side. Moreover, they had conversed with him, touched him, and even shared food with him. The witnesses were *sure* of it, though Matthew and John also include references to some who doubted (Matt 28:17; John 20:24–25).

One of the best pieces of circumstantial evidence for the resurrection of Jesus is the utterly transformed demeanor of his disciples. Men who recently had abandoned their Master and gone into hiding for fear of sharing his fate (see 20:19) now suddenly decide to appear in the temple—the most public place in the land—preaching and healing in the name of Jesus, a man recently executed by the Romans at the direct

---

4. Keener, *Gospel of John*, 2:1177.

instigation of the temple authorities (see Acts 3:1–20). In the empire ruled by the increasingly paranoid Tiberius Caesar it is very dangerous to present oneself as a vocal advocate for someone recently crucified as a rebel against him. Even men of wealth and high status like Joseph of Arimathea and Nicodemus take a risk by visiting the governor and doing other things required in order to provide the executed man with a decent burial. Lower caste Galileans like Peter and John, however, court disaster for themselves and their families by proclaiming in the temple precincts that the executed traitor is not only still alive but also working wonders. Only those who have had a dramatically life-changing experience dare to do such things.[5] That sort of sudden change of character does not arise from the sharing of ghost stories or the re-telling of dreams. As N.T. Wright puts it,

> Early Christianity was, to its core, a 'resurrection' movement, with this hope standing at the centre, not the periphery of its vision. This is the reason why it was a messianic movement, even though its 'Messiah' had died on a cross; why it remained a kingdom-of-god movement, even though the 'kingdom' had not arrived in any of the senses a Second Temple Jew might have hoped for.[6]

We have observed that throughout the Fourth Gospel its author intentionally tells his story from a post-Easter perspective, inspired by the Spirit-Paraclete.[7] Obviously, in a strictly temporal sense, the entire New Testament is written subsequent to the resurrection. But John differs utterly from the Synoptics in that, from start to finish, the Fourth Gospel chooses to view Jesus through the lens of his resurrection. John portrays Jesus—whether teaching his disciples or debating his opponents—as acting in every situation during his ministry with the self-conscious authority and dignity of the exalted Lord. At the same time, however, Jesus remains for John fully and unquestionably human—a quality made especially visible in the Passion Narrative.

Unlike the Synoptic writers, John shares with Paul and the author of Hebrews an understanding of Christ which treats his significance both for Israel and the world as disclosed exclusively by the cross and resurrection, not by the substance of Jesus's preaching in the villages of Galilee and Judea. For that reason there exists no Fourth Gospel counterpart to Matthew's Sermon on the Mount or Luke's parable of the Prodigal Son. John writes in order to bring readers "to believe that Jesus is the Christ, the Son of God, and that believing [they] may have life in his name" (20:31).[8] He seeks to draw individuals to heartfelt, personal devotion to Christ and awareness of the new age that has dawned with his resurrection. The Fourth Gospel makes no effort to invite readers to repentance and amendment of life. Because John tells the entire story

5. Dunn, *Evidence*, 59–60. See also Keener, *Gospel of John*, 2:1185–86, who points out that even modern scholars who deny the empty tomb tradition affirm that the disciples sincerely believed they had seen Jesus alive.

6. Wright, *Resurrection*, 587–88.

7. Hurtado, "Remembering," 212.

8. Dunn, *Unity and Diversity*, 27–28, 216–23.

of Jesus with his rising from the dead in prospect, we do well to treat the Resurrection Narrative as the grand finale to which the Fourth Gospel inexorably builds.

Considering the two final chapters of John's Gospel in detail, we observe that while both chapters deal with the resurrection of Jesus, they form two distinct parts, two separate Resurrection Narratives. Narrative One (chapter 20) is the original conclusion to the gospel, which is evident from the final two verses of the chapter, a rhetorically well-designed ending summarizing the author's intent for his book. Narrative Two (chapter 21) is a supplement or epilogue, added most likely by a protégé of the Beloved Disciple who is also the final editor of his master's gospel.[9] If not for the order in which the stories appear in John, it would be logical for us to read 21:1–8 as an account of the *first* appearance of the risen Lord to his disciples and read 20:19–29 as a portrayal of his *final* appearance. It is logical to ask why John's final editor would append a second Resurrection Narrative to the finished—but not yet circulated—manuscript of the gospel.[10]

Several potential rationales are possible. I am persuaded the most likely impetus for John's final editor to compose the epilogue is to deal with his contemporaries' reaction to the recent (or perhaps impending) death of the Beloved Disciple. Such a response is called for because many members of the Johannine communities believe the risen Christ predicted their apostle and spiritual father would be alive to witness his Lord's return in glory (21:22–23). Since he needs to address the death of the Beloved Disciple, the author of chapter 21 seeks to accomplish some other objectives as well, the first of which is to preserve for his intended readers the Beloved Disciple's memories of certain events not included in the original manuscript of his gospel—notably the account of Jesus's initial post-resurrection appearance to Peter (and others) in Galilee upon the occasion of a miraculous catch of fish. A second objective is to comment briefly on the roles played by Peter and the Beloved Disciple in the spread of the gospel. The epilogue specifically addresses the ministry leadership of Simon Peter (21:15–17) and his death as a martyr (21:18–19), fulfilling Jesus's prediction given in 13:36; and then it recognizes the long life of the Beloved Disciple as a faithful and true witness (21:20–24).[11] We might consider this epilogue as a modest effort to

---

9. The same editor may also be responsible for the prologue (1:1–18); some commentators, in addition, think this editor is also author of 1 John; see Kysar, *John*, 311. Although the modern scholarly consensus treats ch. 21 as an epilogue appended to the gospel, there are notable arguments to the contrary. Gail R. O'Day makes a case for the second Resurrection Narrative being an essential element in the original plan of the book, *not* an addition; see O'Day, *Gospel of John*, 854–55. Bauckham, *Testimony*, 273, regards ch. 21 as an epilogue balancing the prologue, but he sees both prologue and epilogue as written by the author of chs. 1–20, not by an editor.

10. Since there is no extant manuscript of the Fourth Gospel which lacks ch. 21, we must assume that the epilogue is added soon after the gospel is completed and before many copies are produced. See Brown, *John XIII–XXI*, 1077–79.

11. Bauckham contends that John's Gospel presents "the Beloved Disciple as the 'ideal witness' to Jesus, who is therefore qualified to be the 'ideal author' of a gospel." Bauckham, *Testimony*, 283. See also Bauckham, *Jesus and the Eyewitnesses*, 127–29.

do something similar to what Luke does with much greater breadth in the Acts of the Apostles, the sequel to the Third Gospel.

We lack resources that might allow us to organize all the resurrection appearances described in the canonical gospels into a single, coherent, harmonious historical sequence. Furthermore, Paul's list of appearances (1 Cor 15:4–8), which antedates all of the canonical gospels, enumerates some appearances mentioned by none of them. Each gospel writer tells his story from a specific perspective, and each adapts his Resurrection Narrative to suit the literary structure and theological orientation of his gospel. John would seem more coherent to modern readers if its final editor had not decided to add an epilogue (chapter 21) containing a second Resurrection Narrative that does not mesh seamlessly with the Resurrection Narrative embodied in the main text (chapter 20), even though the editor asserts boldly that the Beloved Disciple himself "has written these things, and we know that his testimony is true" (21:24).

Jews in the time of Christ who believe in the resurrection of the dead—meaning nearly everyone except the Sadducees—anticipate that it will take place at the end of history, on the "last day." This is what Martha tells Jesus in 11:24, eliciting from him the rejoinder, "I am the resurrection and the life; he who believes in me, though he die, yet shall he live, and whoever lives and believes in me shall never die" (11:25–26). Most Jews expect the resurrection of all the dead to mark the occasion of God's final judgment and the beginning of a messianic age that will bring God's justice, peace, and healing to the whole world. Popular thinking anticipates this general resurrection as an event in the misty, distant future. Before the Sunday when Jesus's tomb is found empty, no one entertains the possibility that a solitary individual—even their dear Master—might rise from the dead.

John's Gospel is laced with anticipations of the resurrection, but it takes some time after their Master is raised for Jesus's disciples to ponder the Scriptures, discuss the things he told them, and figure out how to proclaim what his resurrection means—for them, for Israel, and for the world. In the context of John's theology, the resurrection of Jesus on the first day of the week signals the dawn of God's new creation, the messianic age. The former age, the old order, concludes at the moment on Friday when King Jesus from his cross/throne utters the words, "It is finished," and hands over his spirit (19:30). At his rising to life again on Sunday all creation is made new. For John, the new creation is the renewal of "all things" that were made by and through the divine *Logos* "in the beginning" (1:3). Easter is the time when the true light shines in the darkness and cannot be quenched (1:5), because "in him was life."[12]

---

12. Wright, *Resurrection*, 447. See 440–48 for Wright's summary of the theology of the resurrection in John.

Chapter Twenty

John 20:1–31. John's Resurrection Narrative 1. The empty tomb. The risen Lord comes to his disciples in Jerusalem and imparts the Spirit.

Vv. 1–10. Mary Magdalene discovers the empty tomb and reports to the disciples.

INTRODUCTION. John's first Resurrection Narrative is set in Jerusalem on the day of resurrection and the following Sunday. It is composed of four scenes, two occur at or near the empty tomb (20:1–10 and 11–18) and two behind locked doors where Jesus's disciples (presumably the twelve) are gathered (20:19–25 and 26–29). John's style is to illustrate his theological points by describing specimen events, e.g., a few particular signs rather than multiple miracle stories; and portraying Jesus's engagement with specimen characters, e.g., Nicodemus, the Samaritan woman, the paralytic at the Bethesda Pool, the man born blind, and Martha of Bethany. In this first narrative he draws our attention to four specimen events: (1) the discovery of the empty tomb by Mary Magdalene followed by its investigation by Peter and the Beloved Disciple; (2) the risen Lord's appearance to Mary Magdalene and her commissioning as the primary witness to the resurrection; (3) Jesus's appearance to his disciples, minus Thomas, when he imparts the Holy Spirit to them and sends them out to carry on his mission; and (4) the risen One's appearance to skeptical Thomas, surrounded by his fellow disciples, emphasizing Thomas' worshipful response. In these four scenes, we observe the reactions of three specimen characters to the news of the empty tomb and to Jesus's resurrection: (1) the Beloved Disciple, (2) Mary Magdalene, and (3) Thomas.[1]

The initial element in the Resurrection Narratives of all four gospels is an early Sunday morning visit by women to Jesus's tomb. Since the story of the empty tomb is so important, it is worthwhile to consider the likely layout and appearance of Jesus's burial place. There are many tombs from this era in the Jerusalem area, including

---

1. See Lindars, *Gospel of John*, 594–99.

some situated within the precincts of the Church of the Holy Sepulcher.[2] We picture the tomb as either a natural cave or a man-made chamber hollowed out of the rock of an ancient quarry—of which the hill called Golgotha is also a part. (See Figs. 12–16, pp. 255–56, above.) The entrance door is low—about three feet high—closed by a heavy boulder. In the case of an aristocrat's tomb like that of Joseph of Arimathea, the door might be a large, wheel-shaped stone instead of a boulder. Inside the tomb, the ceiling is higher than the entry door, perhaps more than six feet. On one or both sides of the burial chamber are wide semi-circular niches cut two or more feet into the rock above ledges or shallow troughs upon each of which the body of a deceased person could be laid. In the case of a rich man's tomb, there would probably be spaces for several bodies, perhaps even an additional chamber.[3]

In John's narrative, Mary Magdalene is the only woman named as coming to the tomb before dawn. However, when Mary discovers that the tomb is open and empty and runs to report the news to the disciples, her words to Simon Peter and "the other disciple, the one whom Jesus loved" are, "They have taken the Lord out of the tomb, and *we* do not know where they have laid him" (v. 2). John's preservation of the first person plural pronoun suggests that in an earlier form of the story, Mary has companions—probably the other women mentioned in the Synoptics. The Fourth Gospel chooses to focus readers' attention on Mary alone.

Upon hearing Mary Magdalene's message, Peter and his companion run to the tomb. Commentators propose various theories for why, in John's story, the Beloved Disciple arrives first and looks inside, but does not enter the tomb. Is he first to reach the scene because he is younger and fleeter of foot, but waits deferentially to allow his older colleague to go inside first? Or does John present the story this way in order to give pride of place to the acknowledged spokesman of the twelve? Or do we see Peter charging straight into the tomb without hesitation because that behavior fits what readers already know about Peter's impulsive character? There is no obvious answer.

Nevertheless, in this scene John wishes to focus readers' attention on the Beloved Disciple. He is the first to see the discarded linen grave cloths; he is the first to "see" and "believe" in the resurrection (v. 8). Peter also sees, but John says nothing about his believing. The Beloved Disciple's role as the first to believe in the resurrection is crucial to the theme of John's first Resurrection Narrative. The object of this narrative, and of the gospel as a whole, is spelled out in v. 31: "*that you may believe* that Jesus is the Christ, the Son of God, and that believing you may have life in his name." Jesus's

2. The Church of the Holy Sepulcher was originally a complex of three structures, built ca. 326–335 CE by Helena, mother of the emperor Constantine, to mark the site of Christ's death, burial, and resurrection. Constantine ordered all of the rock face around Jesus's tomb cut away, leaving the tomb a freestanding object of veneration in the center of the great rotunda-shrine of the *Anastasis* ("Resurrection"). Although the Shiite Fatimid Caliph Al-Hakim ordered the entire church destroyed in 1009, including the tomb-shrine, pilgrims to the site centuries earlier had left written descriptions, thus allowing us to reconstruct its appearance.

3. Brown, *John XIII–XXI*, 982–83; von Wahlde, "Archaeology," 581.

resurrection from the dead is the divine guarantee of his status as Son of God and Savior (see Rom 1:4). The Beloved Disciple's status as first to believe in Jesus's resurrection is important information for readers of John's Gospel, since the second Resurrection Narrative concludes by telling us it is the Beloved Disciple who "is bearing witness to these things, and who has written these things; and we know that his testimony is true" (21:24).

The reference to the grave cloths invites a comparison between the resurrection of Jesus and Jesus's raising of Lazarus (11:43–44). After being resuscitated, Lazarus comes forth from his tomb still wrapped in his burial cloths, from which he must be set free. Jesus's burial cloths are neatly folded and laid aside, including the rolled up "napkin" (v. 7), which was a strip of linen passed under the jaws of the deceased and tied over the cranium, to keep his mouth from gaping open. Describing the cloth as "rolled up" suggests that it is left in the tomb still tied in a loop, just as it had been on Jesus's head.[4] Unlike Lazarus, who needs someone to liberate him from his burial wrappings, the risen Christ is wonderfully set free, never to die again.

The two disciples—one believing their Master has been raised to life, the other perhaps wondering and worrying about what has happened—do not yet "know the Scripture, that he must rise from the dead" (v. 9). Surprised, puzzled, and unsure what else to do, the men return, not "to their homes" (as the English of the RSV puts it), but rather to their lodgings in the city.

> [20:1–10] *¹ Now on the first day of the week Mary Mag'dalene came to the tomb early, while it was still dark, and saw that the stone had been taken away from the tomb. ² So she ran, and went to Simon Peter and the other disciple, the one whom Jesus loved, and said to them, "They have taken the Lord out of the tomb, and we do not know where they have laid him." ³ Peter then came out with the other disciple, and they went toward the tomb. ⁴ They both ran, but the other disciple outran Peter and reached the tomb first; ⁵ and stooping to look in, he saw the linen cloths lying there, but he did not go in. ⁶ Then Simon Peter came, following him, and went into the tomb; he saw the linen cloths lying, ⁷ and the napkin, which had been on his head, not lying with the linen cloths but rolled up in a place by itself. ⁸ Then the other disciple, who reached the tomb first, also went in, and he saw and believed; ⁹ for as yet they did not know the Scripture, that he must rise from the dead. ¹⁰ Then the disciples went back to their homes.*

RESPONSE. It's difficult for Christians in our time to imagine how stunned Jesus's disciples feel on Sunday morning at dawn when Mary Magdalene comes running to them with the report that Jesus's tomb is now open and empty. Their first thought is not, "The Lord has risen from the dead," but rather "Someone stole his body." They have been grieving, and now—at this news—they're shocked and angry. How could

---

4. Brown, *John XIII–XXI*, 986.

this have happened? Did thieves watch while Nicodemus's servants brought a fortune in myrrh and aloes into the tomb on Friday afternoon, then come back later and steal Jesus's body in order to take the costly burial spices and re-sell them in the bazaar? (Some people have no respect for the dead!) Or did Jesus's enemies take his body away in order to dispose of it in a dishonorable, unmarked grave, so that his friends and family would never have a place to which they might come to mourn for him? (Those evil men not only plotted to have Jesus put to death, but now they want to erase his memory too!)

Arriving at the tomb and looking inside immediately dispels the idea that someone has taken away Jesus's body. Tomb robbers would not strip a body of its burial wrappings. Something different has happened—an event the Beloved Disciple is first to ascertain and believe: *the Lord has risen!* Why does the Beloved Disciple believe Jesus has risen, merely because he sees the empty tomb and the folded grave cloths? There are a number of possible reasons, the most obvious of which is that this is what he *wants* to believe, and he is willing to jump to that belief on the basis of this rather slim evidence.

Another, more spiritually mature reason for his believing Jesus has risen from the dead is that during all his time as Jesus's follower, this rather young disciple has accepted without question the trustworthiness of his Master's promises.[5] He knows in his heart that his Master has chosen him for a special task, and one of the most important tasks of a true disciple is to listen so closely to his Teacher's words that he can later repeat them flawlessly. The Beloved Disciple was in the temple two years ago when Jesus told the chief priests, "As the Father has life in himself, so he has granted the Son also to have life in himself" (5:26). He was with him in the synagogue at Capernaum after Jesus fed the multitude, when the Master asked the so-called disciples who were disturbed by what he had told them concerning their need to eat his flesh and drink his blood, "What if you were to see the Son of Man ascending where he was before?" (6:62). This year at Tabernacles the Beloved Disciple heard Jesus tell the Pharisees, "I shall be with you a little longer, and then I go to him who sent me" (7:33); and shortly afterwards he heard him tell the same people, "The Father loves me, because I lay down my life, that I may take it up again. No one takes it from me, but I lay it down of my own accord. I have power to lay it down, and I have power to take it up again. This charge I have received from my Father" (10:17–18, NRSV). *He has power to lay down his life and power to take it up again!*

The Beloved Disciple accompanied his Master to Bethany just a few weeks ago when they heard their dear friend Lazarus had died. He and the other disciples stood in the road with Jesus and clearly heard him say to Lazarus's sister, "I am the resurrection and the life" (11:25). *Then he called dead Lazarus out of the tomb, back into life!* Now the Beloved Disciple sees Jesus's empty tomb, sees his folded grave cloths, and remembers some words he heard from the Master just this past Thursday night—right

5. See O'Day, *Gospel of John*, 843–44.

before Judas betrayed him to the chief priests. This disciple now happily claims these words as a promise, "You have sorrow now, but *I will see you again and your hearts will rejoice*, and no one will take your joy from you" (16:22). For the Beloved Disciple the conclusion seems obvious. The tomb is empty and the grave clothes are left behind; this has to mean the Lord has done what he promised. He has taken up his life again, and it is only a matter of time until they will see him alive.

Seeing the empty tomb and the abandoned grave garments is all it takes to confirm for the Beloved Disciple what he already believes—that his Master cannot be defeated by death. He anticipates the resurrection before he sees the risen One, because he trusts the words he heard from the Lord. Like him, I believe Jesus was raised from death to life. And I believe for one of the same reasons the Beloved Disciple did. I heard the Lord speak, and I trust what he said.—This is my story.

I am not a professional New Testament scholar, but I *am* a historian. I had a first class professional education. In his wisdom and for his own purposes, after two years of graduate education, God called me to ordained ministry. I interrupted my doctoral work to attend seminary, with my university's promise to readmit me once I had finished my theological training. I was ordained on November 11, 1972. Six weeks later, I was home in Texas, visiting my family for Christmas. The pastor of my home parish had the flu, and he asked if I would fill in for him at services on the Sunday after Christmas. Naturally, as a 27 year old newly-ordained priest I jumped at the chance.

Preaching wasn't comfortable for me. In fact, I didn't like to preach. I planned to go back to graduate school and pursue a career as an academic historian. I intended to be a lecturer, not a preacher. Therefore, I worked extra hard on my sermon—which was only the second since my ordination. To tell the truth, that sermon from a young, newly ordained local boy—especially on the Sunday after Christmas (which was also New Year's Eve)—must have seemed to the sparsely-filled church as overly-long and tedious. My father, a man who always spoke his mind, told me after church, "Son, that sermon was awfully 'bookish.'"

What I remember most about that sermon I wrote so long ago is how deeply the gospel text I had chosen spoke to my heart as I was preparing it. The words connected intimately to what had been happening in my life during the preceding six weeks. You see, through three years of seminary my approach to study of the Bible had been firmly rooted in scholarly curiosity. I was a historian, and the Bible was a very interesting historical document. However, since my ordination, when the hands of the Bishop and presbyters had been laid on me, it seemed that everything I read from the Bible seemed alive—and personally directed at me.

In our church, the gospel reading for the first Sunday after Christmas is always the prologue to John (1:1–18), the Fourth Gospel's wonderful and mystical account of the incarnation of the Word. The portion I selected as the text for my sermon was vv. 10–13, which in those days was always the King James Version: "He was in the world, and the world was made by him, and the world knew him not. He came unto his own, and his own received him not. But as many as received him, to them gave he power to become the sons of God, even to them that believe on his name: Which were born, not of blood, nor of the will of the flesh, nor of the will of man, but of God."

My sermon on that First Sunday after Christmas in 1972 may not have inspired many members of the congregation, but the text I tried to expound deeply touched my heart. As I drove back to my parents' house after two services, I was still turning the words over in my mind. I mused on how much they resonated with all it seemed to me that Christ had done in my life recently, how I had truly "received him" and consequently come to know myself as God's own child.

I sat in the car at a stop light, feeling happy and peaceful, thinking about the gospel words, when suddenly I heard a Voice in my head, cutting through my reflections. (I was not the kind of person who heard "voices." I was a skeptical rationalist.) The voice sounded like a man talking while trying to suppress a laugh. I heard the voice of Jesus say, with a chuckle, "Yes, it's true. My gospel is true.—And behold, I am alive forever more!"

Tears began to run down my cheeks. And I sat there at the traffic light, crying, as the signal changed from red to green and back again and cars honked and drove around me. Finally, I collected myself and drove on to my parents' house. I'd gone no more than half a mile before I rationalized the whole thing. I told myself: "It's been a great day, and I've just had an emotional experience. That's all it was. The voice was a figment of my imagination, an echo of my own thoughts." I went to my parents' home and said nothing about this episode to anyone for four years.

Although I did not speak of the experience, its power became apparent right away. The experience at the stoplight changed me in two ways. The first was that I no longer doubted the reality of Jesus's resurrection. The scientific arguments against it now seemed beside the point to me.—And why? *Because I had an experience.* I heard the Lord speak to me. That told me, without a doubt, that he lives. The second change was that I suddenly *wanted* to preach. Though by then I was back at Princeton, working as a teaching assistant in the history department and trying to figure out a dissertation topic, the pulpit was now more attractive to me than the classroom—and I knew the reason why. For the first time, I had a story to tell: about my "Easter experience at Christmas."

A dear southern lady of my mother's generation, a member of my first parish, once told me, "A person with an *experience* is never at the mercy of somebody who just has an argument." If you have had an experience of the risen Lord, nothing can ever take it from you.

Vv. 11–18. Jesus appears to Mary Magdalene, commissioning her as first witness of the resurrection.

INTRODUCTION. John does not tell us Mary Magdalene accompanies Peter and the Beloved Disciple as they run to the tomb. Perhaps he intends for his readers to understand that Mary returns there later, after the men have departed. Some commentators assume that the gospel writer (or an editor) has inserted an originally separate story about the two disciples' visit into an earlier account of Mary's discovery of the empty tomb. If that theory is correct, then v. 11 originally followed v. 1.[6] Nevertheless, as the text of the gospel now stands, once Peter and the Beloved Disciple go "back to their homes" Mary comes once more and stands outside the tomb alone, weeping. When she stoops to look into the tomb again—which she must have done earlier, since she tells the disciples that the Lord's body is gone (v. 2)—"she sees two angels in white, sitting where the body of Jesus had lain, one at the head and one at the feet" (v. 12). Angels appear nowhere else in the Fourth Gospel, although at the beginning of his ministry Jesus tells Nathanael, "You will see heaven opened, and the angels of God ascending and descending upon the Son of Man" (1:51). John Marsh says angels "are the 'halo' around the event to mark it out as the action of God. . . . All that can be seen is emptiness and an abandoned shroud; but when angels attend, the eyes of the visitors are opened."[7]

Unlike the angels described in the Synoptic accounts of the empty tomb, John's angels make no announcement of Jesus's resurrection. Instead, in a fine example of Johannine literary artistry, the representatives of heaven simply ask, "Why are you weeping?" (v. 13). The Beloved Disciple remembered Jesus's promises, and when he looked into the tomb and saw the abandoned burial wrappings, he believed the Lord had risen. He did not weep, since he expected to see Jesus again soon, just as the Lord had promised. Therefore, John's angels simply ask Mary, "Why are you *weeping*?" She responds, "Because they have taken away my Lord, and I do not know where they have laid him" (v. 13), the Fourth Gospel's first use of the expression "*my* Lord."

Mary turns away from the tomb and sees Jesus, but like the disciples later (vv. 20–21 and 21:4; see also Luke 24:16, 31), she does not recognize him and apparently turns back to the tomb. Until Jesus calls her by name, she even imagines he is merely a humble workman, a gardener—another indication that the risen One in John's Gospel appears neither as a ghostly figure nor as a dazzling, glorified one. He is visibly quite ordinary, a man like other men. Note the questions the resurrected Jesus addresses to Mary (v. 15). First, he echoes the angels, "Why are you weeping," a subtle reminder that for those who truly believe Jesus's promises there is no cause for grief. Then he

---

6. Smith, *John*, 376. Wright, *Resurrection*, 664n6, describes as "quite unwarranted" the suggestion that the story about Peter and the Beloved Disciple has been inserted into an independent account concerning Mary.

7. Marsh, *Saint John*, 635–36.

reiterates the question he asked of his earliest followers, "What [*or who*] are you look-ing for?" (paraphrase of 1:38), the question the Fourth Gospel implicitly asks of its readers.

When the risen One calls Mary by name, she turns back to face him. Members of his flock recognize the good shepherd's voice (10:3, 5). Now she knows who he really is and cries out, in Aramaic, *"Rabboni!"* Although by the time John's Gospel begins to circulate "rabbi" is the ordinary title used for a respected teacher of Torah, *rabboni*, the elaborated form of the word here, does not literally mean "teacher." It is simply a more deeply respectful and personal form, meaning "My Master" or "My Great One." It is an Aramaic counterpart to the Greek expression Mary has already employed to describe Jesus, "My Lord" (v. 13).[8] Her behavior is not depicted, but from the language of Jesus's response we can imagine that Mary falls to the ground and clutches his feet, a gesture which is warm and profoundly respectful, even worshipful. When she does this, the risen One replies, "Do not hold me, for I have not yet ascended to the Father; but go to my brethren and say to them, I am ascending to my Father and your Father, to my God and your God" (v. 17). Scholars generally agree that a better translation is, "Do not cling to me" or "Stop holding on to me." It certainly is not a rejection of Mary's physical touch, since in v. 27 he will invite Thomas to touch him and recognize that he is not a ghost. Raymond E. Brown explains that when Mary sees Jesus, she concludes he has returned, just as he promised to do (16:22), and now he will remain with her and his other followers, resuming their former relationships. Brown writes,

> Mary is trying to hold on to the source of her joy, since she mistakes an ap-pearance of the risen Jesus for his permanent presence with his disciples. In telling her not to hold on to him, Jesus indicates that his permanent presence is not by way of appearance, but by way of the gift of the Spirit that can come only after he has ascended to the Father.[9]

He goes on to address a question sometimes raised by readers of the Fourth Gos-pel: "Does John (by v. 17) mean literally that Jesus's appearance to Mary Magdalene outside the tomb in the morning took place before the ascension, while the other appearances to the disciples in the evening took place after the ascension?" His answer is in the negative. John's story attempts to fit an essentially "timeless" theology of res-urrection and ascension into an ordinary sequential narrative. (We had a taste of this in the timeless quality of Jesus's High Priestly Prayer in chapter 17.) John wants his readers to contrast the transient nature of Jesus's presence in these post-resurrection appearances with the permanent nature of his presence that all his followers hereafter will experience through the Spirit-Paraclete.[10]

8. Lindars, *Gospel of John*, 606–7.

9. Brown, *John XIII–XXI*, 1012.

10. Ibid., 1014.

We tend reflexively to imagine Jesus's ascension as the event portrayed by Luke in Acts 1:6–9, just as we picture the coming of the Holy Spirit as the episode on Pentecost that Luke describes in Acts 2:1–4. However, John's Gospel telescopes Jesus's resurrection, ascension, and giving of the Spirit into a single, compressed sequence of events, the entire story of which is told in the Resurrection Narrative. By commanding Mary not to cling to him, but rather to go and tell his brothers that he is ascending to his Father and their Father, to his God and their God, Jesus does three things:

First, he warns her that although he is now briefly back among his brothers and sisters in the flesh, he is in the process of returning ("ascending") to the Father. Soon he will be at the Father's side. His relationship with them will always be deeply intimate, but it will be a communion in the spirit, different from the earthly affiliation they have known until now.

Second, because Jesus commissions Mary to bear his message to the male disciples, he designates her as his agent, the individual we may identify as the first "chosen witness" of the resurrection.[11] If we were using Pauline rather than Johannine categories, we would say Jesus formally designates Mary as the first apostle, even "the apostle to the apostles." Although extraordinary, this is almost certainly a historical datum. Given the existing broad antipathy of Mediterranean cultures towards acceptance of women's testimony, it is unlikely that any early Christians would have invented the story.[12]

Finally, by emphasizing their share with him in a personal relationship with his God and Father, Jesus calls attention to the unity that will forever bind him in union with his disciples after the coming of the Spirit-Paraclete. This is anticipated in his High Priestly Prayer on Thursday night, "The glory which thou hast given me I have given to them, that they may be one even as we are one, I in them and thou in me, that they may become perfectly one, so that the world may know that thou hast sent me and hast loved them even as thou hast loved me . . . I made known to them thy name, and I will make it known, that the love with which thou hast loved me may be in them, and I in them" (17:22–23, 26).

Mary Magdalene goes again to the disciples and tells them, "I have seen the Lord" (v. 18). Until this point, the word "Lord" has not been used in the Fourth Gospel except in personal address, where it roughly corresponds to the English word, "sir." Here, and again in vv. 20 and 28, it is a divine reference.

> **[20:11–18]** *11 But Mary stood weeping outside the tomb, and as she wept she stooped to look into the tomb; 12 and she saw two angels in white, sitting where the body of Jesus had lain, one at the head and one at the feet.*

11. Acts 1:21–24 describes the choice of Matthias as a "witness of the resurrection." In Acts 10:40, Peter says to the Gentiles gathered in the home of Cornelius the centurion, "God raised [Jesus] on the third day and made him manifest, not to all the people, but to us who were chosen by God as witnesses, who ate and drank with him after he rose from the dead."

12. Keener, *Gospel of John,* 2:1192.

¹³ They said to her, "Woman, why are you weeping?" She said to them, "Because they have taken away my Lord, and I do not know where they have laid him." ¹⁴ Saying this, she turned round and saw Jesus standing, but she did not know that it was Jesus. ¹⁵ Jesus said to her, "Woman, why are you weeping? Whom do you seek?" Supposing him to be the gardener, she said to him, "Sir, if you have carried him away, tell me where you have laid him, and I will take him away." ¹⁶ Jesus said to her, "Mary." She turned and said to him in Hebrew, "Rab-bo'ni!" (which means Teacher). ¹⁷ Jesus said to her, "Do not hold me, for I have not yet ascended to the Father; but go to my brethren and say to them, I am ascending to my Father and your Father, to my God and your God." ¹⁸ Mary Mag'dalene went and said to the disciples, "I have seen the Lord"; and she told them that he had said these things to her.

RESPONSE. Because our circumstances are always changing, the most important task for human beings, from childhood to old age, is the work of *letting go*. Letting go operates at a number of different levels. If we look at the composite New Testament portrayal of Jesus, we can regard his entire human sojourn—from his birth in Bethlehem to his death on Golgotha—as a process of letting go. The Bible says that the divine Son let go of his equality with God. He let go of his divine prerogatives and status and became a human being. (See Phil 2:5–11 and John 1:9–14.) At the beginning of his ministry, Jesus probably expected Israel would listen and respond to his teaching and his message. He expected they would recognize him as God's Son and servant. But the people who should have known better rejected both him and his message, so he had to let go of his expectations.

Jesus had to let go, and so do we. Following Jesus is about unclenching and emptying our hands, releasing our grip on one thing after another until finally we are no longer "full of ourselves" and are available to be filled with the fullness of God. This includes letting go of what is past, finished and dead, in order to reach out and take hold of the possibilities that are alive for us because *we're* alive in Christ.

Years ago I was invited to return and preach at the fiftieth anniversary of the founding of a church I had once served as pastor. In some ways I sincerely wanted to go, but I declined the invitation. An important reason for turning it down was that if I had accepted, I would have gone back full of memories of how things *used* to be there "in my time," only to discover things had changed. I probably would have found fault with many of the changes. As much as we wish it wouldn't, time always brings change. In truth, *life* brings change. Nothing stays the same if it's fully alive. We can't hold on to the past. We can't frame it and keep it like a favorite photograph. We're always in the process of letting go of what has been and reaching out for what is to be.

The story we read in vv. 11–13 about Mary Magdalene's encounter with the risen Christ on the day of resurrection tells us about the past and the future. When Jesus came to Mary there by the tomb as she lingered alone in her sorrow, she didn't recognize him at first. But when he spoke her name, she knew him at once. No doubt, she fell prostrate on the ground and gripped his feet with her hands. That's what a first century Jewish woman would do. Today she would have hugged him in her joy. But John's Gospel says that, as Mary clung to him, Jesus told her, "Don't hang on to me, because I have not yet ascended to the Father. But go tell the others . . ." (paraphrase of v. 17).

Jesus said, "Don't hang on to me." How might we best describe what Jesus was trying to communicate to this woman who was so glad to see him alive again? I think it was something like this: "Don't try to make our old relationship come back to life just the way it used to be. There will be more gladness for you in what is to be than in what you had before—no matter how wonderful you think your old life was. Your job right now is to let go of what used to be, and go tell the others about the possibilities that are dawning in the new world that is born today. Mary, this is the first day of God's new creation!"

Jesus who was crucified was raised to a new life by the power of God. It's vital for people in the twenty-first century to recognize that. He was raised to a *new* life, not restored to the old life he had lived first as a village carpenter and then as the wandering prophet and wonder-working Son of Man that Mary Magdalene and the disciples knew so well. He was the same Jesus, yes, but in an important sense he was also new. There was continuity, but there was *change*. I think that's one reason why his friends didn't recognize him right away.

In religious circles these days we hear a great deal about spiritual transformation. In the organizational world we hear about "transformational change." Transformation doesn't come through education, or positive thinking, or pious devotions. Listening to sermons doesn't bring transformation (unfortunately). Reading the right books does not bring transformation. Going on spiritual retreats doesn't bring transformation. Transformation only comes once our well-managed world falls apart and we've been broken, or after we've experienced a great loss and felt a great grief, or after we've been forced to let go of our hopes and accept the reality of our disappointments. Transformation doesn't come until we let go of everything except God, walk the way of the cross, and have a Good Friday experience of our own. After that, we are free to come to our own Easter morning—but not before. There is no "shortcut to resurrection."

The resurrection of the Lord tells you and me that we're not locked into "things as they are." Because Christ died and rose from the dead, transformed Christians can believe and tell the world that the future really does hold hope and possibility. Much awaits us in God's new creation, *if only we will not cling to the past.*

This means not holding on to old hurts and old resentments. Reconciliation between people is a sign of faith in the resurrection. Are not many families, communities, and churches wounded by broken relationships between people who have fallen out over something? There are parents who won't speak to their children. There are brothers and sisters who refuse to share a meal. There are people in churches who go to communion at the same altar, but refuse to smile at one another or exchange the peace of Christ. Nursing grudges, remembering past offenses, and rehearsing old quarrels denies the resurrection. We have to let go of feuds and resentments if we're to experience our own resurrection morning.

The resurrection of Jesus tells us the future is in God's hands. We can't hang on to "the good old days." (And when were those days, anyway? . . . Before 9/11? . . . When we were young and healthy? . . . When "everybody" went to church?) We can never return to the past, no matter how warmly we remember it. But because Jesus was raised from the dead we can proclaim that God has good things in store for us—now, in this New Creation. It's a sign of faith to let go of the past and reach out to take hold of the future God offers us, even in these frequently disturbing early decades of the third Christian millennium.

Jesus says to faithful Mary, *"Don't cling to me . . .* But go to my brethren and tell them" (paraphrase of v. 17). So she goes to the disciples, men still hiding behind locked doors in fear, and she tells them, *"I have seen the Lord!" (v. 18)*. I hope that as we believers reflect with faith on the Fourth Gospel's resurrection stories we ourselves will begin in a fresh, insightful way to "see the Lord." If that happens, then we can take for granted that we're sent, just as Mary Magdalene was, to tell the story of Jesus's resurrection and its connection with *our* own story. We're authorized to be witnesses to the transformation that happens when we finally quit clinging to anything but the promises of God. We become apostles of forgiveness and agents of reconciliation between enemies. Because the risen Lord has manifested himself to us, we can testify about the fresh possibilities that lie open to all who no longer are slaves to fear.

Vv. 19–29. The risen Lord commissions his disciples: "As the Father has sent me, even so I send you."

INTRODUCTION. In this section, John claims to describe the risen Lord's first appearance to his disciples, which the author describes as taking place on the evening of the day of resurrection. This is the grand climax of John's Gospel story.[13] It demonstrates the fulfillment of Jesus's promise to his friends that he will see them again (16:16, 22) and of his prediction regarding the Spirit-Paraclete (14:16–17, 25–26; 15:26–27; 16:7, 13–14). Early that morning, the risen One dispatches Mary Magdalene, the chosen first witness of the resurrection, to tell his "brothers" that he "is ascending" to their Father and his Father, their God and his God (v. 17). Now Jesus himself comes to these men who—except for the Beloved Disciple—last saw him on Thursday night in the garden, when Judas betrayed their Master into the hands of the chief priests' armed retainers. We need not attempt to harmonize this account with

---

13. This book treats ch. 21, the Fourth Gospel's second Resurrection Narrative, as an epilogue appended to an earlier version of the gospel which concluded with 20:31.

the resurrection appearances described in the Synoptics. Each gospel writer has his own agenda, his own points to make, and his own story to pass along.

The theme of a believing response to the revelation of God in Jesus runs straight through John, beginning with v. 7 of the prologue. Indeed, although the noun *faith* never occurs in the Fourth Gospel, the verb *believe* occurs more often in John than in the Synoptic gospels combined and more often than in all of Paul's letters put together. This pervasive theme achieves its fulfillment here.[14] The objective of the Fourth Gospel is (1) to establish firmly that the Jesus who was crucified is now the glorified, ever-present Lord of the church and (2) to make it possible for his readers to "have life in his name" (v. 31) through believing in Jesus as Messiah and Son of God.[15]

John tells us the inner circle of Jesus's friends are gathered behind closed—and probably locked—doors (v. 19), which can only be construed as an indication of their fear. Although Mary has presumably told them she has seen the Lord, they remain insecure and uneasy. They do not know what the chief priests might do next, now that they are no longer preoccupied with the weightiest priestly duties of the Passover celebration. Another reason for John's mention of the closed doors is to draw our attention to the nature of Jesus's resurrected body. It is tangible and corporeal, but can behave as if it were incorporeal. Locked doors are no obstacle. Jesus appears in the midst of their gathering and greets them with the ordinary Jewish salutation, "Peace be with you" (v. 19), a phrase that is both a blessing and an assurance that they need have no fear. John does not specify that the disciples are unsure of Jesus's identity, as Mary Magdalene had been earlier, but we may assume they have a similar degree of uncertainty until he shows them his hands and side. Since his resurrected body still bears the marks of his sacrificial death, his identity is beyond dispute, and they rejoice (v. 20).[16] His scars, indeed, are paradoxically the marks of Jesus's glory, just as the cross on which he was lifted up is his royal throne.

After repeating the blessing, "Peace be with you," Jesus tells them, "As the Father has sent me, even so I send you" (v. 21), and he breathes into them the gift of the Holy Spirit. They now have his own prophetic authority to carry the word of God to the rest of creation. Furthermore, this is the precise moment when the significance of v. 17 becomes clear, his declaration that his Father is also their Father. In becoming, children of God along with Jesus, those who receive his Spirit are given power to "beget children" of their own, which means to transmit the truth of their testimony from generation to generation.[17]

---

14. Wright, *Resurrection*, 669.

15. Marsh, *Saint John*, 639.

16. Keener, *Gospel of John*, 2:1202, notes that a strand of Jewish tradition held that at the general resurrection on the last day those who were resurrected would have the same form in which they had died. In this account, Jesus is visibly the "first fruits" of the resurrection, as Paul describes him in 1 Cor 15:23.

17. Lockwood, "Spiritual Fatherhood," 93.

The Fourth Gospel begins preparing us for this event in 1:33, where John the Baptist tells the crowd "'He on whom you see the Spirit descend and remain, this is he who baptizes with the Holy Spirit,'" and again in 7:39, when John tells his readers that Jesus's invitation for the multitudes to come to him and drink of living water is a reference to the Spirit, "which those who believed in him were to receive; for as yet the Spirit had not been given, because Jesus was not yet glorified." Jesus is now glorified, and he imparts the Spirit to those who believe.

In typical Johannine fashion, the episode has at least two layers of meaning. First, it is Jesus's commissioning of his disciples. He sends them out into the world as his agents to carry on his work, just as he was sent by God into the world to do the Father's work. Second, it is an act of creation by the divine *Logos* through whom all things came to be in the beginning (1:1–3). Use of the word "breathed," found nowhere else in the New Testament, is a deliberate reference both to Gen 2.7, where "the Lord God formed man of dust from the ground, and breathed into his nostrils the breath of life," and to Ezek 37:9, where the Spirit comes and breathes life into the dead who lie in the Valley of Dry Bones. Those who believe in Jesus are "new human beings" (see Eph 2:14–16), part of the new creation, the new age that has begun.[18] We keep in mind that in terms of John's theology this handing over of the Spirit is also a consequence of the death of Jesus—anticipated by him from the cross in 19:30. In Johannine thinking, Jesus's death, resurrection, ascension, and giving of the Spirit are connected parts of a *single* divine act.

As Jesus gives the Spirit, his words are, "If you forgive the sins of any, they are forgiven; if you retain the sins of any, they are retained" (v. 23). This verse ultimately will become a proof text, along with Matt 16:19, for the later Catholic doctrine regarding the authority of duly ordained presbyters to pronounce the forgiveness of sins. A great deal has been written regarding that connection, but it seems unlikely the author meant for his readers to arrive at that interpretation. John understands the Spirit as bestowed in v. 22 upon all who believe in Jesus, both in the present and in future generations. It is not a gift restricted to the group of disciples physically present at the moment when the risen One exhales upon them. Because the Spirit will continue to operate within them, all believers will carry forward the Spirit's work of convicting the world of sin, righteousness, and judgment (16:8–11).[19] The tense of the verbs, "forgive" and "retain," used in v. 23 indicate a timeless state of affairs (literally, "If you forgive the sins of any, they shall have been forgiven; if you retain the sins of any, they shall have been retained"). Those who believe in Jesus, who are his agents in the world, enact the truth which is God's eternal dispensation. Some commentators draw a connection between v. 23, Matt 16:19, and Luke 24:47, suggesting that all three refer to the message Jesus's disciples are to preach to the world: repentance and the forgiveness of sin in preparation for the rule of God. Those who respond and believe may be assured

18. Keener, *Gospel of John*, 2:1204; Lindars, *Gospel of John*, 611; Marsh, *Saint John*, 640.

19. Keener, *Gospel of John*, 2:1206.

of forgiveness, ratified by God himself; but those who refuse to respond must remain in their sin—that is, in their estrangement from God.[20]

Jesus's bestowal of the Spirit inaugurates the life of the new witnessing community of believers, but the purpose of John's first Resurrection Narrative cannot be fully achieved until he recounts what happens when the risen Lord returns to the same locked room one week later. Jesus's appearance to Thomas is the crowning moment of John's Easter story. The text does not tell us why Thomas is missing on the day of resurrection when Jesus appears in the room where the others are gathered. We only know that, despite his friends' glad testimony, "We have seen the Lord" (v. 25), Thomas refuses to believe that his Master is truly alive. Therefore, the risen One comes again, specifically to meet the needs of "unbelieving" Thomas.[21]

We recall two earlier references to Thomas which convey to John's readers this disciple's practical, no-nonsense temperament. In 11:16 Thomas is willing to accompany Jesus back to Judea from his refuge beyond the Jordan, even if doing so means dying with him. Later, in 14:4–6, when at the Supper Jesus tells his friends that he is going away, and that they know the way where he is going, Thomas' down-to-earth response, "Lord, we do not know where you are going, how can we know the way," prompts Jesus's grand rejoinder, "I am the way, and the truth, and the life; no one comes to the Father but by me." We can assume that devoted, sensible Thomas wants very much to believe that his Master has been raised to life, but he is innately unable to do so until he has a personal experience of the risen One. He wants to see and touch Jesus's wounded hands and side before he commits to believing in his resurrection.

When the Lord comes to Thomas and invites his touch, urging him to believe and not persist in disbelief, Thomas does not find actual physical contact essential. Instead, he responds not only by joining his brothers in believing that the Lord is risen, but goes a step further and *worships him as Lord and God* (v. 28). The risen One employs "disbelieving" and "believing" in his encounter with Thomas with exactly the same meaning Thomas uses when he refuses to accept the conclusion of his fellow disciples regarding the reality of their Master's physical resurrection. Jesus tells Thomas to reach out and touch his wounds and thus acquire tangible evidence that will lead him to *believe* that Jesus is truly risen in the flesh. Thomas replies to the command to touch his flesh, not with a logical admission of agreement, such as, "Lord, I believe that you have risen from the dead," but with the worshipful exclamation: "My Lord and my God!" Jesus then says, "Have you believed because you have seen me? Blessed are those who have not seen and yet believe." Here John gives a new meaning to the verb *believe*: adoring confession of Christ as Lord and God. Those who truly believe will *worship* Jesus.

---

20. Lindars, *Gospel of John*, 613.

21. The popular designation of this disciple as "doubting Thomas" is unwarranted. Thomas does not *doubt*. "Doubt" is a different Greek word—the meaning here, made explicit by vv. 25 and 27, is that Thomas does not (yet) *believe*.

The Beloved Disciple, perhaps the last surviving member of Jesus's original band of disciples, adds v. 29 as a divine message of assurance, a beatitude for the benefit of all who will read his testimony and choose to worship Jesus as the Son of God and Savior of the world. Jesus says to Thomas, "Have you believed because you have seen me? Blessed are those who have not seen and yet believe." The controlling theme of the Fourth Gospel is its invitation to believe in the Son of God. The essential prerequisite for believing, in future generations, will be *trust in the testimony of faithful witnesses*.

This is the meaning of vv. 30–31, the mission statement with which John's first Resurrection Narrative concludes. Thomas, the skeptic who wants to believe, is unable to trust that Jesus has really been raised to life until he meets the risen One. The truth to which John's Gospel bears witness is that the Lord himself abides in those who believe in him, they are one with him, as he says in his High Priestly prayer, "the glory which thou has given to me I have given to them, that they may be one even as we are one, I in them and thou in me, that they may become perfectly one, that the world may know that thou hast sent me" (17:22–23). To encounter a faithful witness is to meet the Lord himself.

> [**20:19–31**] *¹⁹ On the evening of that day, the first day of the week, the doors being shut where the disciples were, for fear of the Jews, Jesus came and stood among them and said to them, "Peace be with you." ²⁰ When he had said this, he showed them his hands and his side. Then the disciples were glad when they saw the Lord. ²¹ Jesus said to them again, "Peace be with you. As the Father has sent me, even so I send you." ²² And when he had said this, he breathed on them, and said to them, "Receive the Holy Spirit. ²³ If you forgive the sins of any, they are forgiven; if you retain the sins of any, they are retained."*
>
> *²⁴ Now Thomas, one of the twelve, called the Twin, was not with them when Jesus came. ²⁵ So the other disciples told him, "We have seen the Lord." But he said to them, "Unless I see in his hands the print of the nails, and place my finger in the mark of the nails, and place my hand in his side, I will not believe."*
>
> *²⁶ Eight days later, his disciples were again in the house, and Thomas was with them. The doors were shut, but Jesus came and stood among them, and said, "Peace be with you." ²⁷ Then he said to Thomas, "Put your finger here, and see my hands; and put out your hand, and place it in my side; do not be faithless, but believing." ²⁸ Thomas answered him, "My Lord and my God!" ²⁹ Jesus said to him, "Have you believed because you have seen me? Blessed are those who have not seen and yet believe."*
>
> *³⁰ Now Jesus did many other signs in the presence of the disciples, which are not written in this book; ³¹ but these are written that you may*

believe that Jesus is the Christ, the Son of God, and that believing you may have life in his name.

RESPONSE. I'm a pretty skeptical person. I started out to be a professional historian, and historians should be skeptics. Skepticism is essential if we're to answer two fundamental questions about an event in the past. The first demands details about who, what, when, where, and how—*"What really happened?"* And the second asks about its essential meaning or significance—*"What difference does it make?"* We frequently have to piece together fragmentary information, or make educated guesses about what's missing when the evidence is incomplete.

Historians love to get their hands on eyewitness reports, but any lawyer can tell you that eyewitnesses frequently disagree. The more evidence we find, the easier it is to come up with answers to our two big questions. But those answers always remain open to further questions. There's rarely sufficient evidence to eliminate all questions and erase every doubt. The best historians can do in complex cases is propose reasonable answers—not airtight ones—to "What really happened?" and "What difference does it make?"

This brings me to the current portion of John's Resurrection Narrative, his story of skeptical Thomas—the disciple often called "doubting Thomas." I like Thomas. He's curious, skeptical, serious-minded, and stubborn. We will never know why he's missing on the evening of the first Easter, when Jesus appears to the other disciples, but from the story John tells, we can recognize Thomas as an independent thinker, not a person who just goes along with the crowd. Mary Magdalene claims to have met the risen Lord on Easter morning, and she probably tells Thomas her story. Ten other disciples say they saw him that same evening, and they tell Thomas their story. Does the skeptic simply accept his friends' word for what they saw? No. Thomas wants to see Jesus for himself. No number of eyewitness reports—even from his best friends—will convince him. He wants to see for himself, and not only see, but touch. Thomas knows about visions, ghosts, and tricks, and he refuses to be persuaded by anything that might turn out to be one of those. His friends might possibly be deceived, but Thomas will not allow that to happen to him. Thomas is serious. If he is going to believe—truly *believe*—and commit himself to a resurrected Jesus with the same degree of intensity with which he committed himself to the pre-crucifixion Jesus, then Thomas needs persuasive evidence. For him, that means nothing less than a first-person, eye-witness experience of his very own.

We live in a skeptical, scientific century. What can contemporary century skeptics learn from the Fourth Gospel's story about Thomas refusing to believe until he sees the resurrected Christ with his own eyes? I think Thomas' story teaches us this: that the Lord, in his love for us, will provide whatever it takes to overcome the doubts of a serious seeker who truly *wants* to believe—no matter how skeptical the seeker might be.

Note that the key element is whether a person *wants* to believe or not. Believing is always a decision, a choice. Does the choice to believe seem reasonable to us, or *un*reasonable? Believing is never inevitable. It always involves more than arriving at a professional historian's answer to the question, "What really happened?" Our decision to believe almost always arises from how we handle the second question: "What difference does it make?"

We have to assume Thomas truly loves Jesus and grieves deeply at his death. After all, he'd once been willing to go to Judea and die with Jesus (see 11:16). Because he loves Jesus, Thomas *wants* to believe that his Master has risen from the dead. He really wants to believe that the tomb could not hold him. But before Thomas can permit himself to believe that Jesus is truly alive again, he needs a personal experience on which to ground his belief. He loves Jesus too much and has been committed to Jesus as his disciple for too long to accept anything less than an authentic encounter with the risen Lord. The Fourth Gospel tells us Jesus honors Thomas' honest doubt and gives him what he needs in order to move from disbelieving to believing, from skepticism to confidence.

Doubt is not a bad thing. Asking hard questions is not a bad thing. But skeptical or questioning spiritual seekers—if they truly love the Lord and aren't simply playing philosophical games—are willing to be persuaded. They're willing to believe, if they're given reasonable grounds for believing. There's a way of distinguishing between serious seekers and people who only want to play games. Serious seekers are ready to let believing change their lives—*if* they have the personal experience they need. Believing is always relational, always rooted in God's relationship with us as individuals and as a community.

Jesus once healed the son of a man who said to him, "Lord, I believe. Help my unbelief" (Mark 9:23–25). Many people in our own day find themselves in that position, including people who read the Bible and go to church. (Maybe even some who are reading this book.) They are saying, in effect, "Lord, I do believe—at least a little. Anyway, I *want* to believe. Please do something to help my *un*belief."

Here's a promise I can make. If you want to believe in Jesus, but need to have a personal experience to sustain your faith, God will give you the kind of experience you need. Just ask him for it.—But keep this in mind: the belief-building experience you ultimately have may turn out to be quite different from the one you originally thought you needed.

It's important for modern spiritual seekers to understand that when Jesus shows himself to serious, no-nonsense, disbelieving Thomas on that first Sunday after Easter, he doesn't do it on a lonely road where Thomas is all alone. Jesus comes to Thomas when Thomas is surrounded by people who have already seen the risen One and believe in him. *Thomas meets the Lord in the company of believers.* This is where the serious, but skeptical seeker is most likely to meet the living Christ today: in the midst of believers. That raises a serious, perhaps awkward question for all of us: does our church possess, as a community, the kind of faith that provides a setting where unbe-lievers can truly meet the living Lord?

In the account of the risen Lord's appearance to the ten disciples and then to the ten plus Thomas, we notice one key factor: all of them recognize Jesus by the physical scars of his sacrificial death—the nail wounds in his hands and the spear wound in his side. Although they've spent three years as his disciples, they don't identify him by his facial features or his hair color, or his height and weight. Only the marks of his self-offering love, earned on the cross, give them assurance of his identity. This is the message of Christ for every church and for every believer who wants to help skeptic-schoose to believe: "He who has seen me has seen the Father. He who sees *you* must see *me*. And I am identified only by the costly marks of sacrificial love." The world is filled with skeptical seekers who demand to meet Jesus before they're willing to trust him. They need a personal experience with the living Christ before they can believe he's for real, and they instinctively know how to identify him. By his wounds.

Doing Your Own Theology

Questions for reflection after reading John 20.

- The Beloved Disciple sees Jesus's empty tomb, sees his folded grave cloths, and remembers his Master's numerous words of promise, especially those he spoke on Thursday night before Judas betrayed him to his enemies: "You have sorrow now, but *I will see you again and your hearts will rejoice,* and no one will take your joy from you" (16:22). For the Beloved Disciple the conclusion seems obvious. The tomb is empty and the grave clothes are left behind; this has to mean that the Lord has done what he promised. He has taken up his life again, and it is only a matter of time until they will see him alive. Seeing the empty tomb and the abandoned grave cloths is all it takes to confirm for the Beloved Disciple what he already believes—death cannot defeat his Master. He believes in Jesus's resurrec-tion before he lays eyes on the risen One, because he trusts the words he heard from the Lord.—*What role does belief in Jesus's resurrection play in your personal life? Does your faith organize your experience and inform your perception? Does it make you willing to see what you believe? Have you had a personal experience of the risen Lord? What were the circumstances of that experience?*

- When Mary Magdalene sees Jesus outside the empty tomb, she concludes that he has returned to life and will now remain with her and the others, resuming their old relationship. In telling her not to hold on to him, Jesus indicates that now the mode of his presence with those who love him will be different from what they knew before his death and resurrection. Jesus who was crucified is raised to a *new* life by the power of God, not restored to his former life as the wandering prophet and wonder-working Son of Man that his disciples knew so well. He is the same Jesus, but in an important sense he is also new. There is continuity, but there is also *change*. As we consider our understanding of "resurrection life," we recognize that resurrection implies *transformational change*; it is not mere resuscitation. But that which is truly alive is always changing.—*Did you experience a change in your life after you came to believe in Jesus's resurrection? What did that signify to you? Mary Magdalene had to let go of her former relationship with Jesus in order to have a new one. Was it necessary for you to let go of an old way of thinking about God in order to claim a new way? Of what else have you successfully let go? What did God give you to take the place of what you let go?*

- Despite having heard Mary Magdalene's report of meeting the risen Lord, the inner circle of Jesus's friends remain afraid, and they hide behind locked doors (v. 19). Suddenly Jesus appears in their midst and greets them with the ordinary Jewish salutation, "Peace be with you." Then he shows them his hands and his side. Although they have spent three years as his disciples, they do not identify him by his facial features or his hair color, or his height and weight. Only the marks of his self-offering love, earned on the cross, give them assurance of his identity. The response to vv. 19–21 says, "This is the message of Christ . . . 'He who has seen me has seen the Father. He who sees *you* must see *me*. And I am identified only by the costly marks of sacrificial love.'"—*Do you agree with the point made in that response? If so, how may ordinary believers and ordinary churches practice Christlike, self-offering love? If Christ is only to be identified in us by his wounds, what will the "wounds" we bear as his disciples look like to those who see us? How does your church bring Christ to the seeker, rather than the other way around?*

Chapter Twenty-one

John 21:1–31. The Epilogue: Resurrection Narrative 2.
The risen Lord comes to his disciples in Galilee. Peter's commissioning.

Vv. 1–14. Jesus reveals himself to his disciples on the lake shore.

INTRODUCTION. If we had known nothing at all about John's Gospel in advance, but were reading it now for the first time and discovered the book concluded with chapter 20, we would be content. John 1–20 conveys the whole story of Jesus. It tells how the Son of God is sent by his Father into the world to save it, how the eternal Word—God's agent in the creation of all things—enters human history as one of us, a man called Jesus of Nazareth. These twenty chapters tell about the signs by which Jesus reveals his divine identity and redemptive mission and describe the bitter hostility he faces from precisely the people who should best understand him. They tell about the little group who do believe in him—his best friends, his disciples—and about the much larger number who misunderstand the meaning of his presence among them, even though they are impressed by his miracles and what he says. These twenty chapters conclude with a long, poignant account of Jesus's last days—how he tries to explain to his disciples why it is necessary for him to go away and leave them behind, then how he is betrayed into the hands of his enemies, brutally treated, and put to death on a Roman cross. They communicate the sorrow and confusion Jesus's friends feel at his death and their surprise and happiness at his resurrection three days later. The first twenty chapters of John reach a fitting climax with accounts of the risen Lord appearing, first to Mary Magdalene outside the tomb and then to his inner circle, assuring his followers that he is indeed alive and demonstrating that God's New Age has dawned. He breathes the new life of the Spirit into the disciples and sends them into the world, just as his Father has sent him.

To put it simply, we do not need chapter 21. Everything the gospel writer needs to tell us is told in chapters 1–20. Yet the gospel has an epilogue, a second Resurrection Narrative—a second, anticlimactic conclusion. It probably was added by an editor, perhaps a disciple of John who is preparing his teacher's gospel for distribution.[1] It's logical for us to ask, "Why add an epilogue to John's Gospel? What purpose does it serve?" At best we can only make educated guesses regarding the purpose of the epilogue. Furthermore, we recognize that a few respected modern experts dispute that chapter 21 is an epilogue.[2] Instead, these scholars contend that this anticlimactic chapter actually fits into a broader comprehensive scheme. Puzzling out such details is an intriguing exercise for specialists, but it goes beyond the purposes of *Believing is Seeing*. What we want is a concise answer to an obvious question: *If* chapter 21 is indeed an addition to John's Gospel as originally written, what is the best guess for why the epilogue is added?

My theory is that chapter 21 is appended to John's Gospel by one of his own disciples, probably between 90 and 95 CE, after the original manuscript is written, but before more than a few copies are circulated. This friend and student of the Beloved Disciple may have helped the elderly apostle organize his thoughts and assemble such written materials as he accumulated over the many decades since Jesus was raised from the dead. Perhaps he even served as John's secretary and did the actual writing, though there is no way to know about that. In any case, this apprentice to the Beloved Disciple feels competent to add a new conclusion to his teacher's gospel because he feels the same kind of inspiration from the Spirit-Paraclete. Still, what motivates John's protégé to write an epilogue for his master's work of genius?

I believe the most plausible impetus for the addition of an epilogue is the death or impending death of the Beloved Disciple. The last living link between the Christian community and the Lord himself is gone, the last eyewitness to the earthly life of the Lamb of God. Early Christians believe the Son of Man will return in glory and judgment during their lifetime. Vv. 20–23 of the epilogue lead us to think that the community which formed around the Beloved Disciple expects their spiritual father, their teacher and mentor, will live to witness his Lord's return. These believers feel sure Jesus made such a promise to his friend. As time passes and all the others who had known Jesus personally die, collective disappointment among Christians begins to grow. Still, many in John's own community cling to the conviction that their apostle will survive to see the Son of Man "coming with the clouds of heaven."[3] Not long after his gospel is finished, the aged Beloved Disciple dies. The man we might label

---

1. Bauckham, *Testimony*, 271–74, makes a strong case for ch. 21 as an epilogue, added as an appendix to a gospel originally meant to conclude with 20:31, but written by the author responsible for chs. 1–21 rather than by a later editor. Anderson, "Johannine Riddles," proposes a two-edition theory of the gospel's composition, with the Johannine epistles being composed between them.

2. See O'Day, *Gospel of John*, 854–55.

3. See, e.g., Mark's description of Jesus's hearing before the Sanhedrin, at which the high priest demands that Jesus tell them whether he is "the Christ, the Son of the Blessed"; Jesus responds, "I am; and you will see the Son of man sitting at the right hand of Power and coming with the clouds of heaven" (Mark 14:61–62). See also Mark 8:38; 13:26; Matt 24:3, 36, 44; Acts 1:7, 10; 1 Thess 4:14–17; 5:2; 2 Thess 1:7–10; 2:1–4.

as John's "literary executor"—his editor, disciple, and friend—is moved to offer the community a theological manifesto to comfort them and inspire them to continue trusting in Jesus as they fulfill their own unique vocation as disciples. Recognizing that the Lord's return in glory could be long delayed, the author of the epilogue wants to help his community think about the future. He decides to attach an epilogue to his master's gospel before allowing it to be published. He works carefully, relying on various sources—including both stories from outside his own circle and stories told by the Beloved Disciple. Because he is devoted to John, the editor can speak and write with the voice of his master. I believe the epilogue to John's Gospel is the product of his efforts.

The Resurrection Narrative in the epilogue is set on the shore of the "Sea of Tiberias" (the Roman name for the Sea of Galilee) rather than in Jerusalem, supposedly at a later date than the appearances in chapter 20. Describing only appearances of the risen Lord that occur in Jerusalem would fit neatly into the story world of chapters 1–20, since John situates the most important events of Jesus's life in the Holy City. However, the author of the epilogue knows an additional resurrection story, one the Beloved Disciple sometimes told but did not include in his gospel, the description of an event that took place on the shore of the Sea of Galilee, near the spot where Jesus once fed the multitude.

The author of the epilogue may want to add this story because it clearly links John's Resurrection Narrative to other gospels known in his community.[4] He tailors this additional story to fit with those in 20:19–29 by labeling Jesus's appearance on the lakeside as a *third* appearance to the disciples after his resurrection (21:14). Most modern commentators, however, think this story was originally told as a description of Jesus's *first* resurrection appearance, one anticipated by both Matthew and Mark.[5] Except for the reverse order in which the Fourth Gospel presents its resurrection stories, it is easy to read 21:1–8 as a misplaced account of Jesus's *first* appearance to his disciples and 20:19–29 as a credible portrayal of his *final* appearance.[6] We know the Fourth Gospel sometimes re-orders the chronology of events, and for theological reasons it gives priority to resurrection appearances in Jerusalem for the same reason it situates most of Jesus's active ministry there.

The story of Jesus appearing to his disciples after they return to their trade as fishermen in Galilee has greater dramatic power than the story told in 20:19–29, *only* if we make the following two preliminary assumptions:

4. I believe the epilogue to John (ch. 21) was composed around the year 90 CE. Scholars typically date Mark to ca. 70 and Matthew to ca. 80–85 CE. It seems very likely to me that the author of John and his editor had access to Mark and might possibly have also seen Matthew. Bauckham asserts his conviction that "the author of the Gospel of John knew Mark's Gospel and expected many of his readers to know it." Bauckham, *Jesus and the Eyewitnesses*, 127.

5. Lindars, *Gospel of John*, 619; Brown, *John XIII–XXI*, 1070.

6. Wright, *Resurrection*, 675n35, disagrees with this hypothesis and asserts that such a supposition is "purely imaginary." If so, it is imagined by a large number of his peers.

First, Peter and his comrades are aware only that Jesus died and was buried on Friday, that the women found his tomb empty on Sunday morning, and that Mary Magdalene claims she—and perhaps the other women—saw him and spoke with him on Easter morning. This assumption fits well with Mark 16:6–7 and Matt 28:5–10, in which the explicit Sunday morning message for Jesus's disciples is that they should go to Galilee. There they will see the risen Lord.

Second, the disciples remain in Jerusalem until the end of the eight-day Passover feast, after which they return to their homes near "the Sea of Tiberias," which is the Roman name for the Galilean lake.[7] Since it would require people on foot about a week to travel from Jerusalem to Capernaum, we may guess that two weeks (or more) elapse between the day of resurrection described in 20:1–18 and events portrayed in 21:1–23.

These assumptions give dramatic intensity and symbolic power to Jesus's interaction with Simon Peter in the epilogue, and they are plausible conjectures on the basis of the Resurrection Narratives in Mark and Matthew. Nevertheless, they are only speculation, not data we can treat as historically certain.[8] The fishing story in the epilogue closely resembles an episode that Luke situates at the beginning of Jesus's ministry, when he calls Peter and Andrew and the sons of Zebedee to follow him and begin "catching men" instead of fish (Luke 5:1–11).[9] As in Luke's story, the disciples fish all night but catch nothing (v. 3). At dawn, the risen Jesus stands on the beach, watching his friends in their boat. He calls out to them, but they do not immediately recognize him. Jesus ascertains they have caught no fish and tells them to cast their net on the right side of the boat where "you will find some" (v. 6).[10] They comply, and their net is filled with so many fish the men can scarcely haul it in (v. 6). The Beloved Disciple, already recognized as first among the twelve to believe in the resurrection, is now the first to perceive that the man standing on the beach is Jesus.

Among Jews the sharing of a meal is a sacred act. Jesus himself has provided bread for his friends and fish, which he now cooks over a charcoal fire (v. 9). John emphasizes that just as Jesus provides food and acts as host at meals before his passion, he remains his disciples' host and provider after the resurrection. In chapter 2, Jesus first reveals his glory at a family wedding banquet where he changes water into wine, a

---

7. According to the apocryphal *Gospel of Peter*, XIV, 93, the disciples remained in Jerusalem until the end of the Passover, after which they returned to their homes; "while I, Simon Peter, and Andrew my brother, took our nets and returned to the sea."

8. Wright, *Resurrection*, 625.

9. Some ask: "Does Luke take material which originally came to him as an account of the Lord's first appearance to his disciples and transpose it to an earlier time in Jesus's ministry—making it into a call story—because he wishes for some reason to confine his gospel's resurrection appearances to the Jerusalem area?" There is no way to answer this question.

10. Bauckham, *Testimony*, 271–84, addresses the symbolic significance of the 153 fish caught in the disciples' net as well as a number of other numerological questions related to ch. 21. He points out, for example, that the prologue (1:1–18) contains 496 syllables and the epilogue (21:1–25) contains 496 words.

sign which leads his disciples to see his glory and believe in him (2:1–11). Here in the epilogue, the risen Lord provides a miraculous meal for the same disciples, who now behold him in the full glory of his resurrection.[11]

In an apparent allusion to the feeding of the five thousand (6:1–14) as well as a connection to the many prior occasions when Jesus acted as the host at their common table, the Lord gives his friends food to sustain them in their weariness (vv. 12–13). Jesus's personal provision of the bread for the breakfast is symbolically significant, reminding readers that he is the bread of life (6:25–59), the Word made flesh, mediator of God's living presence.

The disciples feel certain they are sharing a meal with their Master, now raised from the dead. However, the author of the epilogue knows these friends of Jesus discerned a subtle difference in the appearance of the risen Lord. This is hinted at by the words, "Now none of the disciples dared ask him, 'Who are you?' They knew it was the Lord" (v. 12). It seems they had a sense both of continuity and discontinuity about him.[12]

> [21:1–14] *¹ After this Jesus revealed himself again to the disciples by the Sea of Tibe'ri-as; and he revealed himself in this way. ² Simon Peter, Thomas called the Twin, Nathan'a-el of Cana in Galilee, the sons of Zeb'edee, and two others of his disciples were together. ³ Simon Peter said to them, "I am going fishing." They said to him, "We will go with you." They went out and got into the boat; but that night they caught nothing.*
>
> *⁴ Just as day was breaking, Jesus stood on the beach; yet the disciples did not know that it was Jesus. ⁵ Jesus said to them, "Children, have you any fish?" They answered him, "No." ⁶ He said to them, "Cast the net on the right side of the boat, and you will find some." So they cast it, and now they were not able to haul it in, for the quantity of fish. ⁷ That disciple whom Jesus loved said to Peter, "It is the Lord!" When Simon Peter heard that it was the Lord, he put on his clothes, for he was stripped for work, and sprang into the sea. ⁸ But the other disciples came in the boat, dragging the net full of fish, for they were not far from the land, but about a hundred yards off.*
>
> *⁹ When they got out on land, they saw a charcoal fire there, with fish lying on it, and bread. ¹⁰ Jesus said to them, "Bring some of the fish that you have just caught." ¹¹ So Simon Peter went aboard and hauled the net ashore, full of large fish, a hundred and fifty-three of them; and although there were so many, the net was not torn. ¹² Jesus said to them, "Come and have breakfast." Now none of the disciples dared ask him, "Who are you?" They knew it was the Lord. ¹³ Jesus came and took the bread and gave it to*

11. Keener, *Gospel of John*, 2:1231.

12. Wright, *Resurrection*, 679.

them, and so with the fish. ¹⁴ *This was now the third time that Jesus was revealed to the disciples after he was raised from the dead.*

RESPONSE. It's hard to imagine an emotional roller coaster with higher highs and lower lows than the one Jesus's disciples rode from the day he entered Jerusalem to shouts of "Hosanna," to the night he was seized in Gethsemane, the next day abused and crucified by his enemies, laid in a borrowed tomb—and then, a couple of days later, amazingly raised by God from death to life.

There is not enough evidence to place this episode of John's second Resurrection Narrative accurately on a defined, post-Easter historical timeline. Experts have their theories, but—as I wrote above—what works best for me is to conceive of this as a story based on the risen Christ's first appearance to his disciples, rather than an event which takes place several weeks after Jesus appeared a second time to the disciples and showed his wounded hands and side to the skeptical Thomas. I imagine this as the sequence of events:

- Jesus arrives in Jerusalem on the Sunday before Passover and meets with great fervor from the holiday crowds. His enthusiastic disciples are sure their Master is about to be acclaimed as the Messiah.

- However, four days later Jesus is betrayed by Judas, arrested by the temple police, and handed over to Pilate, who treats him brutally and crucifies him. Jesus's battered body is buried in a rich man's tomb.

- Three days after his burial, some of the women disciples find the tomb empty except for an angel who tells them Jesus has risen from the dead and is going to meet all of them soon in Galilee. Mary Magdalene says she saw Jesus himself not long afterwards, right outside the tomb, and talked to him.

- However, after that amazing Sunday morning, there's *nothing*. Nothing more happens. Days pass. There are no more visions of angels and no more visits from Jesus to anyone. The excitement is over.

- The Passover feast ends, and the Galilean disciples return home from Jerusalem.

Jesus's disciples have a wild emotional ride between Palm Sunday and the week after Easter. When we've been up and down and then up and down again, don't we feel wrung out and exhausted? At such times most of us settle down and comfort ourselves by going to a familiar place and performing a familiar activity—doing what we know how to do best, something that feels useful, something fulfilling. We want to exert control over our lives instead of being at the mercy of ever-changing circumstances. If we're avid readers, we lose ourselves in a good book. If we're gardeners, we pull the weeds in the flowerbed or plant new shrubs. If we're hikers, we take a familiar trail and walk for miles. If we're fishermen, we go fishing.

John never mentions the fact, but the Synoptics identify at least four of Jesus's disciples as fishermen. After all the excitement passes, these men return to doing what comes naturally to them, what they understand best. They go back to the lake, back to their boats and fishing gear. As is typical for this crew, Peter takes the lead.

I picture Peter sitting in the courtyard of his simple home in Capernaum late on an April afternoon with some of his fellow disciples, two weeks after Mary Magdalene told them she had just seen the risen Lord. We must remember that Jesus's disciples are young men, and most of them are probably accustomed to hard physical work. They're not grey-bearded senior citizens, content to sit placidly in the sunshine and reminisce about days gone by. I imagine Peter rising from his seat and pacing with frustration around his little courtyard. Suddenly he tells the others, "I'm finished sitting around waiting for something to happen. I can't keep doing this day after day! I've got to *do* something. I'm going fishing.—Do you men want to come along, or not?"

His comrades answer right away, "You bet. Count us in!"

In a couple of hours the men are on the lake in Peter's boat, prepared for a night of fishing. They have torches to lure the fish and clean nets that were carefully packed away when they'd left the lake to follow Jesus. Now they're back in the same place, doing the same work they were doing when the Master called them to follow him and learn how to "fish for people."

And in that very spot, *Jesus comes to them again.*

They fish all night but don't have even a minnow to show for their toil. Now the sun is rising over the hills of Bashan and the fishermen are tired and hungry. It's time to beach the boat and go home—get some breakfast and then take a nap, if their children cooperate and keep quiet.

Suddenly a voice from the shore calls across the water, "You haven't caught anything, have you, boys?" (paraphrase of v. 5).

"*No,*" they answer.

Then the voice—and doesn't it seem a *familiar* voice?—replies with words that send a shiver up Peter's spine, "Cast your net to the right of the boat, and you'll catch some" (paraphrase of v. 6). They do as directed, and immediately they have more fish in their net than they can manage. The one who calls himself "the Beloved Disciple" is first to give voice to what all of them are thinking, *"It's the Lord!"* (v. 7).

John's second Resurrection Narrative points out two things that were true for Jesus's disciples and are true for us: (1) a human reality, and (2) a spiritual truth.

First, the *human reality*. No matter how excited and energized we get about a surprising spiritual experience, it's impossible to stay permanently at a high emotional pitch. Every form of excitement inevitably fades, even the kind that's heaven-sent. No matter how much our spirits soar in mountaintop moments—like the overwhelming gladness the disciples feel when they hear Mary tell them Jesus's tomb is empty and she has seen him alive—we're ultimately going to fall back into our old routines, return to our conventional, manageable, familiar life.

Recall the Synoptic gospels' story of the transfiguration. Peter, James and John can't stay on the mountain forever with Jesus, Moses, and Elijah, even though Peter thinks it would be a great idea to build three little huts and prolong the experience as long as possible (cf. Mark 9:5–6). They have to go back down from the mountain peak to the valley floor, where there is work to do, where there are challenges and frustrations to deal with and ordinary life to live, with its everyday tasks—a family to feed, a business to manage, and fish to catch. Life must go on . . . Right?

Now, the *spiritual truth*. "Business as usual" can never be the same once we know—once we truly *believe*—that Jesus lives. Oh, we may go back to working at our job, tending our flowers, looking after our children, or even fishing. We may settle back into our old rut. But once we know the Lord is risen, once we're aware that we could possibly meet him right around the next corner, our life is permanently changed. We see things differently. The risen One comes to us and surprises us in our ordinary surroundings, in the workaday environment we know so well. In a world where we presume that we're in charge, Jesus comes and reminds us that now we're his and he is ours. And he will not allow us to forget we have his work to do.

Encounters with the risen Lord do not occur according to a timetable. They can't be scheduled or precisely predicted. But they happen. Afterwards, however, we inevitably come down from the spiritual "high" they induce and slip slowly again into our ordinary, humdrum routines. Later—maybe after two months, or three years, or even longer—the living Christ surprises us. He returns to us and warms our hearts once more for the mission to which he originally called us.

In my experience, that's what church life is like. A pastor and congregation may have an astonishing, vivid experience of the presence of Christ—a communal mountaintop moment. This moment may happen on a parish retreat, or during an especially inspiring sermon by a visiting preacher, or at a particularly moving Easter celebration. On these occasions there's enthusiasm among the faithful, a high level of expectation, and an exalted vision of what God is going to accomplish with us and through us.

Then, a month or two passes after the wonderful retreat weekend or the dynamic sermon or the amazing Easter. The spiritual buzz gradually subsides to a golden memory, and soon we discover ourselves merely "doing church business" again. Back to totally predictable Sunday worship, back to worrying about the budget deficit and whether we can afford to pave the parking lot, back to trying to build up the youth ministry, and back to bantering about mundane affairs during the post-service Sunday social time instead of sharing spiritual excitement. It's easy to drift away from a dramatic, visionary encounter with Jesus and slide back into purely institutional religion. We're most comfortable with old habits and time-tested routines. That's simply human behavior. It's quite normal.

But the Living Lord won't allow us to slip permanently into our old ruts and get comfortable there. He won't permit us to settle for business as usual. The Lord comes to us again—sometimes in the very place where we first encountered him. He comes to rekindle our enthusiasm and redirect our energy away from stale routines and towards the life-giving work of the kingdom. Jesus will never let the vision he has shown us fade away. He surprises us when we least expect to see him and calls out, *"Hey there, you people in the church boat. Cast your net on the other side!"*

In this story at the end of John's Gospel, the risen Christ provides breakfast on the lakeshore for his weary friends after a night of fruitless toil that ended with fifteen minutes of panic as they tried to manage a miraculously filled net. Jesus comes to them after they've forsaken their dreams and worked themselves to exhaustion doing their Galilean version of business as usual. He arrives on the scene and supplies the inspiration, energy, and vision required for them to fulfill their calling. By the same token, you and I can rely on the living Lord to provide the direction, motivation, and strength we pray for—as well as the proper nourishment for those who go fishing for people.

Vv. 15–25. The risen Lord identifies the future ministries of Peter and the Beloved Disciple.

INTRODUCTION. In this closing section of the epilogue, its author draws his readers' attention to Simon Peter and the Beloved Disciple, specifically to forecast how each in his own way will follow Jesus faithfully as a disciple, each implicitly providing the wider church with an example worthy of imitation. In Acts, Luke focuses attention on the singular roles played in the young church by Peter, Paul, and James the brother of Jesus. Along with these three, however, Acts also singles out some others for special attention, notably John the son of Zebedee—the man tradition regards as the Beloved Disciple, author of the Fourth Gospel. Chapters 1, 3, 4, and 8 of Acts pair Peter with John in particular ways, while Paul in Gal 2:9 names *only* Peter and John along with James, the brother of Jesus, as the "pillars" of the church in Jerusalem.[13] The fact that Luke and Paul both link Peter closely with John while the Fourth Gospel frequently pairs Peter with the Beloved Disciple provides a circumstantial reason for the traditional identification of the Beloved Disciple as John, the son of Zebedee.[14]

Jesus's commission of Peter as a shepherd for his flock (with a prediction of his martyrdom) and his explanation of the Beloved Disciple's long survival are combined

13. The list of disciples given in Acts 1:14 names Peter first and John second; Acts 3:1–11 and 4:1–22 describe a healing miracle performed by Peter and John and their subsequent arrest and interrogation by the temple authorities; Acts 8:14–17 describes Peter and John being sent from "the apostles at Jerusalem" to minister to people in Samaria "who had received the word of God"; in Gal 2:9 Paul names James [Jesus's brother], Cephas [Peter], and John as those "who were reputed to be pillars" among the apostles in Jerusalem.

14. Anderson, "Aspects," 598, finds a first-century clue to the authorship of the Fourth Gospel in Acts 4:19–20, which portrays the examination of Peter and John before the high priest and his colleagues, the only occasion where John is represented as speaking in Acts. Some of the words Luke quotes have a Johannine ring to them: "We cannot but speak of what we have seen and heard" (cf. John 3:32; 1 John 1:3).

in the scene which comprises vv. 15–23. Jesus takes a walk with Peter and engages the spokesman of the twelve in a dialogue that appears to be a formal reconciliation of this once-bold disciple following his triple denial of the Master on the night Jesus was arrested in the garden (see 18:15–17, 25–27). If Jesus's talk with Peter (whom he solemnly addresses three times by his formal name, "Simon, son of John") is understood as the occasion when he forgives the disciple upon whom he long before bestowed the nickname, "Rock," that is a reason for us to treat both scenes in the epilogue as transposed stories of the risen One's initial appearance to his friends. In their conversation, Jesus probes the question of Simon's love for him three times and three times admonishes this chastened disciple to feed and care for his sheep (vv. 15–17). He also tells Simon Peter that when he is an old man he will experience martyrdom by crucifixion (vv. 18–19). The dialogue between Jesus and Peter as they walk on the lakeshore has a direct connection with the exchange between the two of them at the Last Supper (13:36–38), when Peter professes his willingness to lay down his life for his Master and Jesus replies, "Will you lay down your life for me? Truly, truly, I say to you, the cock will not crow, till you have denied me three times" (v. 38).

When Jesus asks Simon, "Do you love me more than *these*" (v. 15) the reader is required to discern whether Jesus is asking if Peter loves him more than the other disciples do or asking whether Peter loves Jesus more than he loves the boat and fishing gear to which he has so readily returned. The comparison is probably between Peter's love for Jesus and the love of the other disciples, but the author employs typical Johannine ambiguity here, making either option possible.[15] When Jesus asks a third time whether Peter loves him, the man's feelings are hurt and he replies, "Lord, you know everything. You know that I love you" (v. 16). The good shepherd knows his own, and his own know him (10:14). In this dialogue with Simon Peter, the risen Lord makes the point that his disciples' love for their Master must entail loving and providing for one another, replicating his own life of self-offering love. Such love is to be the identifying mark of a true disciple (13:34–35).

The Beloved Disciple appears to be walking closely behind Jesus and Peter. Peter looks back and sees his friend, which prompts him to inquire about the other disciple's future. Perhaps Peter would like to know whether the Beloved Disciple will also meet death as a martyr. This inquiry about his comrade's destiny earns Peter a rebuke from Jesus, who cautions him to concentrate on staying faithful to his own vocation and not concern himself with what the Lord calls his fellow disciple to do. Jesus tells Peter, "If it is my will that he remain until I come, what is that to you? Follow me!" (v. 22)

Unlike most other modern commentators, Gail R. O'Day treats chapter 21 as a concluding message to the church concerning the nature of true discipleship, an intentional element in the design of the Fourth Gospel rather than an epilogue added as an afterthought. O'Day remarks that Peter is one whose love for Jesus is to lead him

15. In Matthew's account of the supper, Peter makes a bold comparison of himself with the others, when he tells Jesus, "Though they all fall away because of you, I will never fall away" (Matt 26:33).

on a path of discipleship in which he imitates the life of his Master, even to the laying down of his own life, a reminder of 15:13, "Greater love has no man than this, that a man lay down his life for his friends." The Beloved Disciple is one whose love for Jesus and commitment to following him is equally faithful and true, but whose path of discipleship is to be quieter and less overtly heroic than Peter's. In 21:1–23 the risen Lord manifests himself to both of these quite different disciples, and their companions. He blesses the entire company with the divine abundance and sustenance that are symbolized by the miraculous catch of fish and the providential meal on the lakeshore, a sign anticipated in the prologue, "From his fullness have we all received, grace upon grace" (1:16). Those who are not martyrs for their Lord are not excluded either from his love or his gifts.[16] Each disciple is to follow Jesus in the unique way the Spirit leads (16:13) and to bear witness to the Lord in a way that inspires others to believe, so that the whole world might ultimately share with them in the unity of the Father and the Son (17:20–23). O'Day's interpretation is certainly plausible.[17]

John's epilogue in vv. 21–23 makes clear that at the time of its composition many of those for whom the gospel was first written believed that the Beloved Disciple, their own apostolic witness, would be alive to welcome the Lord at his Second Coming (cf. Mark 9:1). Now it appears that this man who is so important to their community has either died or is on the verge of death. Johannine Christians are distracted by concern for what the Beloved Disciple's death might mean for their own future. Are they, too, going to die before the Lord returns in glory as he has promised? I think these issues most likely compelled the composition of vv. 20–23.

The rebuke Jesus addresses to Peter in v. 22 applies not only to Peter but to the community whose needs inspire the author of the epilogue. He warns readers to refrain from speculation, either about the Beloved Disciple or about one another. One should, instead, focus on one's own discipleship, one's own mission as a follower of the risen Lord. In this closing scene of the gospel's epilogue, its final chapter, the editor who was most likely not only responsible for the epilogue but also for the prologue and the final structure of the entire book, brings to his readers a reprise of the gospel's opening scenes, when Jesus—accompanied by his first three followers, Andrew, the Beloved Disciple, and Peter—goes to Galilee, where he finds Philip and tells him, "Follow me" (1:37–45). Each reader of the epilogue hears the command of Jesus as addressed not only to Peter and the others, but to himself or herself. Regardless of each disciple's life path, each one is sent by the Master and directed by the Spirit. As Jesus says to the disciples at the supper table after he washes their feet. "Truly, truly, I say to you, he who receives any one whom I send receives me; and he who receives

16. O'Day, *Gospel of John*, 864.

17. Bauckham, *Jesus and the Eyewitnesses*, 128–29, describes the relationship between Peter and the Beloved Disciple as a "friendly rivalry." Peter is to be "the chief shepherd of Jesus's sheep," but the Beloved Disciple is to be "the ideal witness."

me receives him who sent me" (13:20). Every disciple in every age is sent by Jesus. To receive Jesus's disciples—now or in the future—is to welcome God himself.

> **[21:15–25]** ¹⁵ *When they had finished breakfast, Jesus said to Simon Peter, "Simon, son of John, do you love me more than these?" He said to him, "Yes, Lord; you know that I love you." He said to him, "Feed my lambs."* ¹⁶ *A second time he said to him, "Simon, son of John, do you love me?" He said to him, "Yes, Lord; you know that I love you." He said to him, "Tend my sheep."* ¹⁷ *He said to him the third time, "Simon, son of John, do you love me?" Peter was grieved because he said to him the third time, "Do you love me?" And he said to him, "Lord, you know everything; you know that I love you." Jesus said to him, "Feed my sheep.* ¹⁸ *Truly, truly, I say to you, when you were young, you girded yourself and walked where you would; but when you are old, you will stretch out your hands, and another will gird you and carry you where you do not wish to go."*
>
> ¹⁹ *(This he said to show by what death he was to glorify God.) And after this he said to him, "Follow me."*
>
> ²⁰ *Peter turned and saw following them the disciple whom Jesus loved, who had lain close to his breast at the supper and had said, "Lord, who is it that is going to betray you?"* ²¹ *When Peter saw him, he said to Jesus, "Lord, what about this man?"* ²² *Jesus said to him, "If it is my will that he remain until I come, what is that to you? Follow me!"* ²³ *The saying spread abroad among the brethren that this disciple was not to die; yet Jesus did not say to him that he was not to die, but, "If it is my will that he remain until I come, what is that to you?"*
>
> ²⁴ *This is the disciple who is bearing witness to these things, and who has written these things; and we know that his testimony is true.* ²⁵ *But there are also many other things which Jesus did; were every one of them to be written, I suppose that the world itself could not contain the books that would be written.*

RESPONSE. John records that at the supper table on his last night with his friends Jesus tells them, "A new commandment I give to you, that you love one another; even as I have loved you, that you also love one another. By this all men will know that you are my disciples, if you have love for one another" (13:34–35). Then he tells them a bit later, "If you love me, you will keep my commandments" (14:15). *Love is the defining mark of a disciple.* Jesus sets the standard, "I have given you an example, that you also should do as I have done to you" (13:15). The task of the disciple is to reproduce the life of his Master—in this case a Master who stoops to take the role of a slave and washes his disciples' feet, a Master who humbles himself to die on the cross for them. As we come to the end of our reading of the Fourth Gospel, we contemplate two of those who take important roles on the night when Jesus washes his disciples' feet and whom this gospel links together subsequently in many ways, particularly here in its concluding scene: Simon Peter and the Beloved Disciple.

On the night after Jesus washes his feet and gives him and his comrades the new commandment, Simon Peter does two clearly opposite things. First, he fights to defend his Master, even to the extent of inflicting a physical injury on one of Jesus's enemies. Then, later, he publicly denies three times whether he even knows who Jesus is. Peter exhibits both great physical courage and abject cowardice in the space of perhaps two hours on a single night. What kind of "Rock" is Simon? Did Jesus give him his nickname as a joke? The man seems more like sand than rock. He's shifty.—Does Peter love Jesus, or does he not?

I'm convinced the closing scene of the epilogue makes logical sense only if we read it as the *first* occasion for the risen Lord to have a conversation with Simon Peter after that fateful Thursday night in the garden. John doesn't tell us explicitly that Peter is sorry for his three-fold act of cowardice that night, but we may be confident he is. Jesus understands his friend wants to redeem himself, so he takes a walk with him along the lakeshore and the two have a heart-to-heart talk. Peter once heard Jesus say, "If you love me, you will keep my commandments" (14:15), now his Master looks into Peter's eyes and asks him three times, "Simon, son of John, *do you love me?*" When the Galilean fisherman hears his love questioned a third time, he's cut to the heart, and all he can say in reply is, "Lord, you know everything; you know that I love you" (v. 17). The love of which Jesus speaks is not merely a feeling; it's a choice, a decision. To love another is to *choose* that person intentionally. To love is to favor that person, to care about him or her, to devote oneself to that person in ways that may ultimately prove costly. Jesus chooses Simon when he calls him to be a disciple. He washes Simon's feet, despite his objection to being served in such a fashion. When Jesus goes to the cross, he lays down his life for Simon. Now Jesus asks him, "Simon, do *you* choose *me*?"

Jesus knows Simon Peter loves him. He knows the answer before the other man replies. He knows the answer before he even asks the question, because he *knows* Simon. He knows Simon's heart. He knows Simon's character, his bright, endearing qualities—strength, boldness, and readiness to serve—as well as his dark, unattractive attributes—presumptuousness, cockiness, and cowardice. Simon has personal defects, but there is no doubt that he loves his Lord. When Jesus commands him to feed and care for his sheep, this fisherman hears himself called to become a shepherd. Peter will answer this new call, and the church will come to remember him as a brave pastor and bold leader—truly a rock and an example for others.

Seated at Jesus's right hand at the table on the night Judas betrays him and Peter denies him is another member of Jesus's inner circle of disciples, one whose real name is kept secret in the Fourth Gospel. Every time the gospel mentions this man, he's identified simply as "that disciple whom Jesus loved" (vv. 7, 20). We suspect that occasionally he may only be labeled as "another disciple" (or not named at all as in 1:35–40). Christians have given this individual the nickname, "the Beloved Disciple."

That isn't what Jesus calls him or what his fellow disciples call him. They know him well, and there are good reasons to believe they call him John—though exactly *which* of a number of possible men named "John," we can never know for certain, though we can be sure the first readers of this gospel knew.

How did this man named John come to be known as "the disciple Jesus loved"? This gospel shows that Jesus loves all his disciples—not only the twelve who form his inner circle but also the larger community that includes Mary, Martha, and Lazarus, and the faithful women who stand with Jesus's mother and the Beloved Disciple at the cross and come to his tomb on Easter morning. John tells us Jesus's new commandment is for his disciples to love one another in the same way Jesus loves them. Jesus is certain his disciples all perceive the reality of his love for them. But it's possible not all of Jesus's closest disciples are equally adept at describing his love, putting it into words—telling how it affects them, or how it makes a difference in their relationship with God and each other.

Could it be that "the disciple whom Jesus loved" acquires his nickname because he is the member of the inner circle who most clearly has a gift for describing Jesus's love and communicating its meaning to others? Possibly John is the one who shows himself best at expressing the many ways he personally experiences the love of the Father and the Son. I suspect John *feels* his Lord's love so strongly and speaks of it so readily that others ultimately come to identify him with his gift. It's also possible he is the youngest of the twelve. If John is the most decidedly junior of the company in that age-deferential society, he will spend a great deal of his time not talking but watching, listening to Jesus and the others talk, learning from all of them, and *remembering*. Young John will linger behind, as youngsters often do, and ask Jesus questions after the Master has finished speaking and the more mature disciples have been dismissed to do other things.

John is empathetic, and he is a communicator. As years go by and the youthful disciple grows into an elder, he will meditate on his experiences with Jesus, recalling particularly how his Master spoke to them about himself, about his intimacy with the Father, and about the bond he felt with them—his friends, his brothers. This disciple, who even in old age still feels the Spirit of his risen Lord so intensely, ultimately commits his memories and reflections to writing, perhaps with the help of someone more accustomed to wielding a pen. The church will remember him as the ideal eyewitness, an evangelist and mystic—the disciple who knew how much he was loved.

The word of the risen Lord to Peter that morning by the Galilean lake is *"Follow me!"* If we trust the call stories of the Synoptic gospels, Jesus once made the same request of both Peter and John three years earlier, near this same stretch of shoreline. His Master wants Peter to recognize and fulfill his personal calling and not be preoccupied with what God may have in store for his companions, especially the brother who's walking on the rocky beach behind them. Peter has unique gifts, and the Spirit will guide him to use those gifts in ways that will encourage the community of believers and equip the church to face adversities which are soon to come.

By the same token, the most junior member of their apostolic band, the little brother now trailing along in their footsteps listening to what the two of them are saying, has his own set of gifts, his own special vocation from God: to be an exemplary and faithful eyewitness. The same Spirit-Paraclete who will direct Peter will also inspire young John. This disciple who feels his Lord's love so deeply and listens so intently will one day immerse himself in the task of interpreting for others—even for people in distant lands—the truth revealed in Jesus's life, death, and resurrection.

The Beloved Disciple will do his work so effectively that through his eyewitness testimony countless people are inspired to believe that Jesus is the Christ, the Son of God. Believing what John says, generations yet to come will have life in Jesus's name. Believing, these future saints will see beyond what their mortal eyes can discern. They will see the glory of God.

Doing Your Own Theology

Questions for reflection after reading John 21.

- This book invites readers to think of chapter 21, John's second Resurrection Narrative, as an epilogue to the gospel, written by a protégé of John, a "beloved disciple of the Beloved Disciple," someone whose relationship with Christ is rooted in the eyewitness testimony of his teacher. It tells a story about some of the disciples returning to Galilee after Easter and resuming their trade as fishermen, then being encountered on the lakeshore by the risen Lord after a long night of fruitless toil in a boat with their net. Although the writer presents his story as the *third* occasion the disciples see Jesus after the resurrection, both logic and the Resurrection Narratives of the Synoptic gospels (as well as the details of the story itself) give us reason to think that this story is actually an account of the *first* time the risen One appears to any of the twelve. Until this point, their awareness of Jesus's rising from the dead derives exclusively from discovery of the empty tomb and Mary Magdalene's story of seeing him in the garden outside the tomb. Now, after they return to "the real world" of their old home and their old job, the risen Lord comes to them.—*Imagine yourself as Peter or one of the other fishermen. What would you do after a week or more passed since the day you learned of the empty tomb, would you go home to Galilee and back to your old job? Why or why not? What significance do you see in Jesus not coming to his friends until* after *they returned to their old life? Often, so much time passes between our spiritual "mountain top moments" that we lose touch with what happened. What would help you stay connected to those moments of feeling the closeness of God?*

- Jesus understands Peter wants to redeem himself after his denial in the high priest's courtyard, so he takes a walk with him and the two have a heart-to-heart talk. Peter once heard Jesus say, "If you love me, you will keep my commandments" (14:15), now his Master looks into Peter's eyes and asks him three times, "Simon, son of John, do you *love* me?" When the Galilean fisherman hears his love questioned a third time, he's cut to the heart, and all he can say in reply is, "Lord, you know everything; you know that I love you" (v. 17). The love of which Jesus speaks is not merely a feeling, an emotional attachment; this kind of love is a *choice*, a decision. Truly to love another is to choose that person intentionally, regardless of the circumstances. To love is to favor that person, to care about him or her, to devote oneself to that person in ways that may ultimately prove costly. Now Jesus asks him, "Simon, do *you* choose *me*?"—*What intentional choices have you made that express your love for Christ? Are there ways that show you love Christ more than you love yourself? Have you ever had to pay a price for choosing Jesus?*

- The word of the risen Lord to Peter that morning by the Galilean lake was *"Follow me!"* His Master wants Peter to recognize and fulfill his personal calling and not be preoccupied with what God may have in store for others, especially the Beloved Disciple who is walking behind them. Peter has unique gifts, and the Spirit will guide him to use those gifts in ways that will encourage and equip the church to face adversities that are sure to come. By the same token, the most junior member of their group, the little brother now trailing along in their footsteps, has his own set of gifts, his own special calling from God: to be an exemplary and faithful eyewitness. The Spirit who will direct Peter will also inspire young John.—*Jesus' universal call is "Follow me!" However, the Spirit supplies each disciple with a specific assortment of gifts. Do you believe the work of every disciple is equally significant? Do you honor every task the Lord may call you to do, or do you respond selectively, based on whether you feel sufficiently gifted for the task?*

A question for reflection after reading Believing is Seeing.

- This question is for those who read through the entirety of John's Gospel using *Believing is Seeing* as a guide. The Beloved Disciple states this as the purpose of his gospel, "that you may believe that Jesus is the Christ, the Son of God, and that believing you may have life in His name" (20:31).—*If "believing is seeing," what do you see now that you did not see before this reading of John's Gospel?*

Appendix One

Who was "the Beloved Disciple"?
When and for whom did he write?

How much confidence can we place in the story he tells?

Though *Believing is Seeing* is an extended personal reflection on the message of John's Gospel rather than a traditional commentary, I want to present in this appendix my personal conclusions about the identity of the gospel's writer, when and why it was written, and its relative historical accuracy. Scholars have debated these matters since the early nineteenth century, and discussion will not stop as long as people continue to study the Bible. Inquiry about "what really happened" in the life of Jesus and "who really wrote" the Gospels keeps biblical researchers happily employed, and no evidence is likely to turn up that will end the debate. Besides, the pendulum moving the academic consensus swings back and forth. Opinions regarded as conventional wisdom when I was a seminarian have fallen out of favor because of new research, while it seems that some ideas deemed passé forty-odd years ago are now being rehabilitated. Reputable commentators inevitably disagree on various points; biblical experts can be as diverse in their thinking as political pundits (though usually more cordial in their published observations). Many would argue strenuously with some of my conclusions while others would warmly agree. Since I am a historian by training, not a New Testament specialist, I possess the amateur's license to indulge in speculation and imaginative reconstruction—practices that might be risky for a professional biblical scholar hoping to maintain academic credibility.

Readers of this book should be clear about one thing, however. Neither the historical identity of the author of John nor the circumstances of its writing, nor the relative accuracy of its incidental narrative details has any final bearing on this gospel's incalculable value. It is inspired. Whether or not John the son of Zebedee authored every word of it has little bearing on whether the text, as used by the church today, is itself a product of divine revelation.[1] It discloses the truth of God and points readers to the Word that became flesh and lived among us, Jesus, the Son of God, our Savior. Countless Christian souls have found the bread of life in John since it began to circulate, perhaps in Asia Minor, in the closing decade of the first century. They attest to the power of the Spirit who works in and through it.

Regarding the true identity of the Beloved Disciple and the date and purpose of his gospel.

I believe it is certain that the testimony of an eyewitness lies behind the Gospel according to John. New Testament scholars call this person the Beloved Disciple. His precise personal identity is much debated, and there exists no obvious and indisputable device by which to resolve the uncertainty and end the debate. The traditional understanding, dating back to the second century, is that the Beloved Disciple is John, the brother of James, one of the two sons of Zebedee, men the Synoptic gospels describe as commercial fishermen on the Sea of Galilee. This view was out of favor in the last century but it is gaining renewed interest today. There is much to support the traditional view but also good reason to question it—not the least of which is that, with few exceptions, Jerusalem is the center of action for the Fourth Gospel, not Galilee. John the son of Zebedee is portrayed in the Synoptics as a fisherman who lived in or near Capernaum—a Galilean town mentioned only in passing in the Fourth Gospel outside chapter 6. Critics ask a logical question: if the son of Zebedee wrote the gospel, why does he not describe many of the Galilean episodes to which the Synoptics tell us he was a witness?

Joseph Ratzinger (Pope Benedict XVI) discusses various theories about the authorship of the Fourth Gospel in his 2007 book, *Jesus of Nazareth*. Predictably, the Pope *emeritus* endorses the traditional view, although he offers an intriguing rationale. Quoting 2002 research by French exegete Henri Cazelles, Benedict XVI proposes that John, the son of Zebedee, was indeed a fisherman, but from a priestly family. Ordinary Jewish hereditary priests—of whom there were about 7,200—served in the temple at each of the three pilgrim festivals and for two other weeks out of each year. For the rest of the time they pursued ordinary livelihoods, including agriculture, manual labor, commerce, and scholarship.[2] Cazelles proposes that Zebedee and his sons were prosperous commercial fishermen who maintained at least a small residence in Jerusalem as well as a home in Capernaum. Well-off priestly families from the hinterland are known to have kept dwellings in Jerusalem. He suggests John might even have been

---

1. Lockwood, "Spiritual Fatherhood," 121n21.

2. Jeremias, *Jerusalem*, 206–7. Since only priests could enter certain areas of the temple, priests were trained as stonemasons and in other crafts that would be called upon to make repairs. Some ordinary priests were also learned scribes; some priests were "unlearned."

the host at the Last Supper, since according to prevailing Jewish protocol of the time a guest of honor would sit at the host's left.[3] "The disciple whom Jesus loved" does not make an appearance under that designation until 13:23 at the Supper, although he may also be understood as one of the two disciples of John who leave their teacher and follow Jesus in 1:35–42. In addition, some surmise that the Beloved Disciple is intended in the reference to "another disciple known to the high priest" who accompanied Peter to the residence of high priest after Jesus had been arrested in the garden (18:15–16). This is only a guess, of course, but if John and James, the sons of Zebedee, were from a prosperous priestly family, perhaps one with roots in Jerusalem, it is at least a conceivable suggestion. It also provides an explanation for why the Beloved Disciple might be literate, concerned with the Jewish festivals, and interested in situating much of Jesus's ministry in or near the temple.

It is possible the Beloved Disciple was not one of the twelve. Cazelles' theory, endorsed by the Pope *emeritus*, overlaps somewhat with a theory advanced by Brian D. Capper, an expert on the Essenes. He suggests that the Beloved Disciple was a priest with a home in the priestly quarter of Jerusalem, southwest of the temple, where he hosted the Last Supper—although it does not identify him with John, the son of Zebedee. (In this scenario, Jesus's position at the host's left would put him in the place of honor.) Capper believes this affluent, ascetic, and aristocratic priest was part of a quasi-Essene group that owed its origins to the political maneuverings of Herod the Great and friendliness of the Herodians to the Essenes from the time of Herod to the death of his son Archelaus in 10 CE. This group was no longer connected with the Qumran Essene community by the time of Jesus's interactions with the Beloved Disciple. According to his theory, the connection of this Beloved Disciple with the preaching and activity of John the Baptist, also an ascetic priest and prophet, might be the link between the Baptizer, Jesus, and the community of aristocratic Jerusalem ascetics.[4]

After the description of the Supper, the Beloved Disciple is mentioned five more times: with Jesus's mother at Golgotha (19:26–27); running with Peter to investigate the empty tomb on Sunday morning (20:2–10); and three times in chapter 21—as being the first fisherman to identify the stranger on the shore as "the Lord" (21:7), as following Jesus and Peter when they walk together and discuss Peter's destiny (21:20), and as the witness "who has written these things; and we know his testimony is true" (21:24). We should take note that, just as John never states the proper name of "the disciple Jesus loved," neither does he ever identify the mother of Jesus by her name—although there is no doubt about whether her name was known to the earliest Christians. It is plausible, therefore, to assume the proper name of the Beloved Disciple was equally familiar, in which case the name's omission would create no confusion among the gospel's original readers.

3. Ratzinger, *Jesus*, 218–38. For his discussion of Cazelles's theories, see 224–25.

4. See Capper, "With the Oldest Monks."

Even though "the twelve" are mentioned specifically as a group at two places in John (6:67–71 and 20:24), their names are never listed, which suggests the author of John wants to portray Jesus as having a diverse assortment of disciples—including others who were part of his inner circle along with the twelve. The only person given the name John in the Fourth Gospel is the baptizing prophet, the son of Zechariah. One of my New Testament professors tried to convince us that John Mark wrote the Fourth Gospel rather than the Second.[5] Acts 12:12 tells us the mother of "John whose other name was Mark" had a house in Jerusalem, which would make this John at least a candidate for consideration as the Beloved Disciple (including also the fact of his being named John). Others propose that the Beloved Disciple must be Lazarus, since in the Fourth Gospel Lazarus and his sisters are the only people specifically named as ones whom Jesus loves, and Bethany is located just outside Jerusalem, on the slopes of the Mount of Olives.[6] In a substantial, carefully-researched book published in 2004, James H. Charlesworth contends that Thomas, one of the twelve "called the Twin," was also the Beloved Disciple.[7] Richard J. Bauckham asserts that the Beloved Disciple was indeed an eyewitness whose name was John, but a *third* John, neither the son of Zebedee nor the John whose other name was Mark. He maintains the Beloved Disciple was a "disciple of the Lord" identified as "John the Elder" in a quotation from Papias of Hierapolis, ca. 100 CE.[8] Other suggestions about the identity of the Beloved disciple include Jesus's brother James and Mary Magdalene. Some assert that the Beloved Disciple is not meant to be treated as a historical person at all, but rather as a poetic figure, created by the gospel writer to represent the ideal believer—about whom Jesus says in 20:29*b*, "Blessed are those who have not seen and yet believe."

The foregoing discussion demonstrates the variety of theories put forward concerning the true identity of "the disciple Jesus loved." Nevertheless, until definitive contrary evidence is put forward, I will regard John the son of Zebedee as the Beloved Disciple, relying on the tradition of the church and the conclusions of numerous scholars working today—at the same time conceding that this conservative point of view is open to dispute.[9] However, the fact that since earliest times this gospel has invariably been ascribed to "John" strikes me as sufficient reason to trust that its author

5. For references to John Mark, see Acts 12:12, 25; 13:5, 13–14; and 15:37–40.

6. In 11:3 the reader is told that Lazarus's sisters sent Jesus a message, saying, "Lord, he whom you love is ill." See Culpepper, *Anatomy*, 141n84.

7. Charlesworth, *Beloved Disciple*, 29–121, 225–87.

8. Bauckham, *Testimony*, 14–16, 33–72; Bauckham, *Jesus and the Eyewitnesses*, 412–71. Using the techniques of word counting and gematria, Bauckham finds the name "John" encoded in the epilogue as the proper name of the Beloved Disciple; see *Testimony*, 282–83. If Bauckham's numerological analysis is correct, the name "John" still leaves us with three candidates bearing that name: John the son of Zebedee, John Mark, and John the Elder (the latter being Bauckham's candidate for authorship of the gospel).

9. Keener, *Gospel of John*, 1:81–138, offers an excellent survey of all the arguments about authorship and concludes that the traditional view of John the son of Zebedee as the Beloved Disciple should continue to stand.

was probably *not* named James, Thomas, Lazarus, Mary Magdalene, or something else.

The claim in 21:24 that the gospel is a document produced by the Beloved Disciple's own hand does not preclude his use of a secretary who might have smoothed out some (but certainly not all) of the awkwardness in his Greek. Some New Testament experts choose to identify the Beloved Disciple as the authority *behind* the gospel, regarding it as based on teachings he gave and stories he told his own followers in the first Christian generation, ultimately compiled into this book, probably in several stages. This may be so. According to this hypothesis, the picture of Jesus portrayed by the Fourth Gospel and the voice and theological perspective of the narrator of events in it should be understood as dependent on the recollections of John, the Beloved Disciple, an intimate companion of Jesus throughout his ministry, articulated by one of the Beloved Disciple's own most trusted personal followers. This is a reasonable argument. However, if John the son of Zebedee is conceived as coming from a well-to-do, literate family—either priestly or secular—it is also plausible to eliminate the hypothetical middle-man and assume the gospel is the work of Jesus's own dear friend and follower. However, the prologue and epilogue—as well as the arrangement of the material and various parenthetic remarks in the text—appear to be the work of at least one or more editors.

The idea that John and the other disciples were illiterate peasants is a once-common assumption, now outdated. These men may not have been scribally-trained, formal students of the Torah of a sort that would cause the chief priests to acknowledge them as "educated men" (Acts 4:13), but most of them were probably not only literate, but also functionally bilingual in Aramaic and Greek.[10] Galilee and Samaria together constituted a populous and fertile region of small villages and cities like Sepphoris, Tiberias, and Sebaste, crisscrossed by major overland trade routes that extended from Central Asia to the Mediterranean. Lush, warm Galilee was much more prosperous than the rugged hill country of Judea, which boasted neither major caravan routes nor fertile farmland. The temple with its constant pilgrim traffic from distant places was the sole engine of prosperity for the city of Jerusalem and the surrounding area. Much of Judea proper, except for the oasis of Jericho, was a bleak wilderness stretching from the Mount of Olives to the Jordan River and the Dead Sea.[11] The tetrarchy

10. Ong, "Multilingualism," makes a plausible argument for Jesus being functionally bilingual in Aramaic and Greek, and the same argument might be applied to at least some of his disciples.

11. Until the time of Herod the Great, the population of rural Judea and Galilee is mostly composed of small-scale farmers cultivating their own land. Herod dispossesses many of these minor landowners in order to create estates for his family and a new ruling class composed of his supporters and Roman friends. Therefore, during the lifetime of Jesus, a large number of impoverished, landless laborers come on the scene—many of whom either resort to brigandage or, at least in Judea, turn to the charity of the Essenes. See Hirschfeld, "Ramat Hanadiv," 384–85, 389; see also Capper, "Holy Community," 114–15. Some of these dispossessed smallholders, particularly in Galilee, become "social bandits," insurrectionists of the sort possibly represented by Barabbas. (See 18:40; see also Malina and Rohrbaugh, *Social Science Commentary*, 262–63.)

of Galilee was in no way a rustic hinterland. It was also half-Gentile, which means that most Galilean Jews needed to speak at least some Greek, even if people in their own village spoke Aramaic among themselves. Fishermen and carpenters were part of what we would regard as the economic middle class of that society, although they had lower social status. The sons of Zebedee were apparently partners with their father (and perhaps Simon and Andrew) in a commercial fishing business that was prosperous enough to employ other workers and make use of several boats. (See Mark 1:20; Luke 5:1–11.) In this regard, contemporary readers need to know that, according to custom, scribes—the learned class in Jewish society at the time—always had a trade by which they could earn a living. Saul of Tarsus, clearly a wealthy man and a Roman citizen as well as a disciple of the great rabbi Gamaliel, was himself both a scribe and a tent-maker.[12] Being a carpenter by trade defines Jesus as neither poor nor illiterate.

Though most scholars assign the Gospel of John a publication date between 90 and 100 CE, I believe the book could have evolved slowly over its author's lifetime, being finished only in his last years.[13] In the time of Jesus, disciples were almost invariably younger than their teachers. In an age-deferential culture it would be awkward for a man to submit himself as the disciple of someone obviously younger than he. There is also evidence that some disciples of traditional rabbis began their apprenticeship in adolescence. Since he appears to have lived the longest of them all, it's reasonable to conjecture that John started out as the youngest member of Jesus's band of disciples. He could have been still in his teens when he began to accompany Jesus, and it took years of spiritual reflection after Jesus's death and resurrection for his personal theology to mature. I imagine, as time passed and he shared his eyewitness testimony with many people—including, quite possibly, the apostle Paul—John never stopped meditating on and extracting new significance from the things he remembered his Master saying and doing. Some of these memories grew in their importance to him as the years went by, especially after the Palestinian disciples of Jesus endured the trauma of the 66–73 CE war with Rome, a war that resulted in the destruction of the temple and the dispersion of countless thousands of their countrymen to distant provinces as slaves. If John the son of Zebedee were the youngest of Jesus's disciples, perhaps in his late teens, and—according to Cazelles' theory—belonged to a priestly family, he would be below the age (usually 20 or 25) at which priests were first summoned to serve in the temple. His father Zebedee would serve his turn, of course, and so would John's brother James, if James were older. John would have begun his priestly service some time after Jesus's resurrection.

---

12. Jeremias, *Jerusalem*, 234.

13. Robinson, *Redating*, 256–84, who represents a minority opinion on the subject among modern biblical scholars, makes a case for dating John very early, suggesting a date no later than the '60s of the first century. He points out that the earliest known papyrus fragment of a gospel (P52) is from a manuscript of John, dated to ca. 125. He agrees with the early tradition that John lived to a great age and was the last of the apostles to write, but disputes that he produced his gospel as an old man.

A currently popular school of New Testament thought proposes there were a series of editors (concluding with a final major editor or redactor) who shaped the Gospel of John over an extended period of time, through several stages of composition, drawing on a variety of documentary sources as well as the recollections of the Beloved Disciple. However, I regard it as equally possible that young Beloved Disciple, John the son of Zebedee, wrote slowly and revised his material personally more than one time before it took final shape—with the help of a secretary—around the year 90 or so, when the author was about eighty years old. When it began to seem obvious he might not survive to greet the Lord on his return in glory, John—perhaps aided by a trusted protégé—brought together for publication the materials he had accumulated over his lifetime.

Acts implies that John the son of Zebedee knew Paul.[14] In addition, the great missionary apostle himself describes a meeting at which John and the other "pillars" of the Jerusalem leadership give approval to the "gospel" Paul preaches among the Gentiles (Gal 2:1–10). John later may have had access to copies of some of Paul's letters, since they were written long before the year 90, the earliest date usually assigned to the publication of the Fourth Gospel. In addition, Paul was connected intimately with the church in Ephesus where John reputedly lived and put together his gospel in old age. It does not surprise me that John's Gospel displays evidence suggesting its author is acquainted with Pauline ideas. A few scholars urge the view that, even though there is no obvious literary dependency of John on any of Paul's letters, there is clear influence of Pauline theology, or at least the same theology that influenced Paul.[15]

The Beloved Disciple recognizes the churches have all been taught the basic outline of Jesus's life and ministry and already possess a written gospel, perhaps more than one, but he portrays himself as an eyewitness—which none of the Synoptic writers claim to be. John is writing, not so much to present fresh information about Jesus's life in a general sense as to preserve for future generations his own memories, insights, and perspective.[16]

By the year 90, no others from among Jesus's disciples and almost no other eyewitnesses to the events his life remain alive. John is able to describe deeds and report sayings of Jesus about which readers cannot learn from the other gospels known to John. He carefully selects the events he describes, choosing to offer—for example—only seven or eight works of Jesus as "signs," even though there are many more he could describe if he chose to do so. In this respect, the Beloved Disciple displays a skill

14. Acts 9:27; 15:2; 21:17 describe Paul meeting with the "apostles and elders" of the church in Jerusalem.

15. For a thorough discussion of this question, see, e.g., Bird and Willitts, eds., *Paul and the Gospels* (2011).

16. New Testament scholars propose a number of different, more complex theories to explain why the Fourth Gospel was written (and by whom). Among the most influential theories is that of Louis J. Martyn, who understands the Fourth Gospel as initially written to address a local conflict about Jesus within a Jewish synagogue community situated somewhere outside Palestine. See Martyn, *History.*

expected of historians in the first century, "judicious selectivity about the events he chooses to narrate."[17]

For episodes to which the Beloved Disciple was not a witness—and his gospel shows there were times when Jesus was alone, with few or sometimes none of his disciples nearby—John has to depend on others for information. Various plural forms of the verb *remember* occur often in the Fourth Gospel, and the remembering subject is always the "we" of the community gathered around Jesus.[18] After the resurrection, Jesus's disciples meditated together on the events to which they were witnesses and the sayings of Jesus which they remembered. The events and sayings would call to mind portions of Scripture. Combining their memories with scriptural connections provided a way for them to understand the deeper meaning of their Master's words and deeds. They regarded this as a work of the Spirit, as Jesus had promised.[19] Even for occasions when John was in the presence of Jesus, he probably depended largely on memory in creating his gospel, not a shorthand transcript.[20] However, we err if we presume that memories were only transmitted orally in the earliest Christian community. We know the rabbis used what we would call notebooks, written memoranda collected as aids to memory, and there is no reason to assume that Jesus's disciples dispensed with such written resources.[21] (The "books and parchments" mentioned in 2 Tim 4:13 could refer to documents of this kind, which would have been utilized by apostles such as Paul or John.)

John, moved—as he would say—by the Spirit-Paraclete (see 14:25–26), uses his inspired imagination to compose Jesus's dialogues and theological teachings, elements that make the Fourth Gospel quite different from the others. However, we assume that John, like Hellenistic historians of his era, makes an effort to reproduce the speaking style of his subject and to include memorable quotations, when he has them available either in memory or in his notes. For example, the so-called *"Amen* pronouncements," which are always introduced in the Revised Standard Version with the words, "Truly, truly, I say to you," are quite possibly marked in that way in order to indicate they are direct quotations of Jesus.[22] John also creates his gospel's narrative commentary— which conveys the Beloved Disciple's singular theological perspective. And he organizes his gospel in the way which he feels will make it most effective in leading those who read or hear it to believe in Jesus as Messiah and Son of God. We need not assume all of the episodes described in the Fourth Gospel occurred in the chronological sequence John describes. Nevertheless, the author's employment of descriptive details,

17. Bauckham, *Testimony*, 103, 104.

18. Ratzinger, *Jesus*, 232–34.

19. Ibid., 230.

20. Shorthand was used in this period. It was invented in Greece before the second century BCE precisely for the purpose of transcribing the speeches of famous orators.

21. Bauckham, *Jesus and the Eyewitnesses*, 287–88.

22. The Hebrew words, *"Amen, amen,"* are rendered, "Truly, truly" in the RSV.

indication of precise geographic locations, and frequent use of (otherwise unknown) personal names leaves readers with the impression that in the Fourth Gospel we are reading the words of an eyewitness.[23]

Comparing the historical reliability of John with that of the Synoptics.

The four gospels are indeed historical biographies, but biographies written according to Greco-Roman rather than modern norms. The work of a historian, as we understand it today, is two-fold—first, to describe an event in the past as precisely as possible (i.e., to answer the questions of "who, what, when, where, and how" the event transpired) and, second, to explain the significance and ultimate meaning of the event (i.e., to answer the questions "why did it happen," and "what difference does it make"). Pre-modern historians tried to be as accurate as possible, but they often lacked both adequate data and an academic, objective approach to their subject matter. The initial audience for all four gospels would have thought of them as falling within the literary genre the ancients called "lives" (biographies), similar to the various lives of philosophers produced in that age.[24] Justin Martyr in the second century called the Gospels "the memoirs of the apostles."[25] Each gospel writer intends to communicate a theologically nuanced understanding of the person and work of Christ, applicable to the audience he has in view. In some cases, the prospective audience changed between the original and later versions, and this necessitated some editorial alterations.

Ancient authors knew of no such categories as "fact" and "fiction." Those are modern, not antique literary distinctions. The intent to communicate *truth*, in a metaphysically profound sense, did not entail for the gospel writers a demand that they use only data which our contemporary sensibilities would esteem as historically verifiable. It was not until modern times that some Protestants became fixated on the idea that the Bible is "literally inerrant." No ancient writers, biblical or otherwise, describe any such phenomenon as literal inerrancy. Biblical authors intended to *tell stories that communicate God's truth*—truth understood as metaphysical, not historical. Therefore, they were comfortable with rearranging the sequence of some events to make their story-telling more effective in communicating that truth, except in circumstances where specific empirical details were so widely known that a rearrangement would be confusing to their audience. This seems to characterize John's Gospel, for example, where Jesus's expulsion of the money changers and sellers of sacrificial animals is placed very early in his ministry, at his first Passover visit to Jerusalem, whereas the Synoptics place the episode at the time of his last Passover in Jerusalem.

23. Anderson, "Aspects of Historicity," 597–99.

24. Keener, *John*, 1:3–52, provides a helpful discussion of the various historical literary genres of the Greco-Roman era and the process by which the ancient writers produced their books.

25. Justin Martyr, "Dialogue with Trypho," CVI, 3.

The prevailing theory concerning the origin of the Gospels is that Mark wrote first, perhaps prior to the destruction of Jerusalem by the Romans in 70 CE, constructing his gospel around the memories of Peter. Matthew and Luke wrote between 70 and 85, both making use of the basic outline and even reproducing a great deal of the text of Mark, supplementing it with their own unique source materials. The three Synoptics are sufficiently similar that they can be printed in parallel columns for purposes of comparison, but each is still distinctive. Each has its own theological perspective, and each tells about the ministry of Jesus in a way the author assumes will be most effective for his target audience. Quaker biblical scholar, Paul N. Anderson, proposes what he calls a "bi-optic" hypothesis regarding the gospel tradition, asserting there are really only two distinctive memories of Jesus's ministry, two "views," represented by Mark and John. Matthew and Luke are basically built on Mark. John writes to augment and sometimes correct Mark, intentionally offering an alternative view.[26] Anderson's hypothesis is intriguing. He suggests that John 20:30, "Now, Jesus did many other signs in the presence of the disciples which are not written in this book," acknowledges the gospel writer's familiarity with Mark and explicitly states that (in the original edition of his gospel) he chooses to describe signs performed by Jesus other than those already recorded by Mark.[27]

John is substantially different from the Synoptics in the events that are depicted, the over-all chronology, and the way Jesus's behavior is described. In John, Jesus is portrayed as always conscious of his status as Son of God. The Johannine Christ, with few exceptions, seems to speak and act with more calm self-assurance and emotional coolness than he displays in the Synoptics.[28] The Johannine Jesus says more about love than the Synoptic Jesus, yet his personal manner is portrayed as more aloof than affectionate.[29] John presents Jesus—even during the early events of his ministry—with the respect that derives from a post-Easter point of view.

Each of the four gospels is a work of art. To use a metaphor from the world of visual art, I would say that John paints a picture of the same subject as Mark, but from a radically different perspective, using his own unique palette and his own style. He does not aim to disagree with Mark's depiction of the person and work of Jesus, but seeks to *augment* it in a distinct way. Is the Markan picture of Jesus right and the Johannine picture wrong, or vice versa? No. Nor is the Johannine perspective simply late and the Markan early. We might say John is a like a Byzantine icon of Christ the

---

26. See Anderson, "John and Mark," 175–88; and "Jesus of History," 4–5.

27. Anderson, "On Wading with Children," 9–10. Anderson sets aside ch. 6 (which contains the description of the feeding of the five thousand and Jesus walking on the sea) and ch. 21, considering those two chapters to be part of a second edition of the Fourth Gospel, the work of an editor.

28. Exceptions are in 12:27–28, where Jesus says, "Now is my soul troubled. And what shall I say, 'Father, save me from this hour'? No, for this purpose I have come to this hour. Father, glorify thy name"; and 13:21 in the Upper Room, where the narrator says, "When Jesus had thus spoken, he was troubled in spirit, and testified, "Truly, truly, I say to you, one of you will betray me."

29. Culpepper, *Anatomy*, 110–11.

Almighty, while Mark resembles a page of daVinci sketches for his fresco of the Last Supper.

It is likely that in many instances the specific sequence of events in Jesus's ministry, as well as many other details, were forgotten even before the earliest versions of the Gospels were written, despite living eyewitnesses who claimed to remember particular episodes. In reality, eyewitnesses to an event frequently disagree with one another. One need only ask a trial lawyer, or read an assortment of Civil War memoirs written by soldiers—both Union and Confederate—who survived Bull Run or Gettysburg. With the best of intentions, witnesses relying on their eyes and ears and memories make mistakes. In addition, the more frequently one tells a familiar "true story," a description of his or her own experience from long ago, the more one reinforces one's memory of that oft-repeated version of the story. The most a person can ever say is that the story one tells is precisely *what he or she remembers*. Others on the scene at the same time might tell a different story about it because they noticed other aspects of the event than those which impressed the story teller. Our version of a story is only our *version*, not necessarily "the whole truth and nothing but the truth," even though it is an honest effort to convey all we saw and heard. Our story cannot report all that happened, particularly in a complex situation.

Unless one subscribes to the view that the Holy Spirit guided the gospel writers to have supernaturally inerrant, photographic memories of all the episodes they recount and the words of Jesus they presume to repeat, then we have to acknowledge that none of the Gospels is historically inerrant. Neither is any of them a complete fabrication, disconnected from events that actually happened. To be charitable to the four gospel writers and their later editors, each one is trying to communicate the truth of Christ. All four of the canonical gospels are primarily faith statements, but they are also "historically based interpretations of the significance of Jesus within people's lives."[30] Regarding the details they choose to report, the four gospels are probably as historically reliable as any other ancient documents on which we rely for accounts of events that happened long ago.

Unless they took notes—which some may have done—those who listened to Jesus teach were unlikely to remember every detail of what he said. I am sure Jesus often expressed himself in memorable language, and it is probable that—like other rabbis of his time and all good teachers today—he repeated the same lessons many times in a variety of settings. His faithful disciples had opportunities to hear some of his teachings often. Nevertheless, Bible-reading realists of our time must concede that Jesus's extended theological discourses in John are constructed by the Beloved Disciple (and his editor)—inspired by the Spirit-Paraclete (14:25–26)—while attempting to be faithful to his Master's customary manner of speaking. John reports that in his Farewell Discourse Jesus tells the disciples, "I have yet many things to say to you, but you cannot bear them now. When the Spirit of truth comes, he will guide you into all

---

30. Just, epilogue to *John, Jesus, and History*, 293.

the truth; for he will not speak on his own authority, but whatever he hears he will speak, and he will declare to you the things that are to come. He will glorify me, for he will take what is mine and declare it to you" (16:12–14). It is this truth that the Fourth Gospel aims to share.

Appendix Two

Who are "the Jews" in John's Gospel?

Is the Fourth Gospel "anti-Semitic"?

Contemporary readers of the Fourth Gospel are often taken aback by the way its author refers to "the Jews." Although John clearly presents Jesus and his disciples as devout Jews, the people in his narrative that demonstrate the greatest hostility to Jesus, including those who seek his death, are frequently labeled simply as "the Jews." To describe this feature of John's vocabulary as "anti-Semitic"—which readers in our time sometimes do—is a mischaracterization. Not only does the adjective anti-Semitic apply a contemporary category of ethnic-religious-social bigotry not suited to an ancient context, it is also illogical, since the author of the gospel and the central figure of its story are both Jews. In addition, John's original target audience is composed mostly of Jews. However, despite various plausible explanations proposed for John's use of "the Jews" in reference to Jesus's enemies among his own people, no perfect rationalization is in view. Modern readers need to know that the Greek word *Ioudaioi*, rendered "Jews" in the RSV and other English-language versions of the Bible, is technically a geographic descriptor meaning "people of Judea." The traditional religious descriptor for one who worshiped the God of Abraham, Isaac, and Jacob according the Law of Moses was not "Jew," but "Israelite."[1] To call Israelites "Jews" was common in the New Testament era—even within the religious community of Israel itself—but it was always an informal designation not unlike the common practice of referring to the federal government of the United States as "Washington."

---

1. Danker offers this warning: "Incalculable harm has been caused by simply glossing *Ioudaios* with 'Jew,' for many readers or auditors of Bible translations do not practice the historical judgment necessary to distinguish between circumstances and events of an ancient time and contemporary ethnic-religious-social realities, with the result that anti-Judaism in the modern sense of the term is needlessly fostered through biblical texts." Danker, *Greek-English Lexicon*, 478.

At certain points in his narrative, it seems obvious John wishes to emphasize a distinct division between Jesus and his followers and many others of their co-religionists. This division was not based on what the Nazis and other twentieth century anti-Semites called "race." I believe it was rooted in two phenomena: (1) a competing theological vision and divergence in religious practice between followers of Jesus and their fellow Israelites, and (2) a localizing of hostility to Jesus geographically in the Jerusalemite-Judean ruling class, particularly the chief priests and Sanhedrin. The chief priests and Sanhedrin not only constituted the highest religious and civil authority in the city and province, they also represented the families whose social status and wealth depended on the economic prosperity of Jerusalem—prosperity deriving in various ways from the temple.

Relatively soon after his resurrection, followers of Jesus begin to *worship* him as Lord.[2] They identify Jesus as Son of God and Savior. They pray to him. They anticipate his return in glory, at which time they believe the Messianic kingdom of God foretold by the prophets will be established on earth. Worship of Jesus and identification of Jesus as "Lord," a title Jews apply only to God, quickly becomes troublesome for some of the friends and neighbors of Jesus's followers. It is perhaps most upsetting to scribes and Pharisees, particularly in Jerusalem and the surrounding area of Judea, where strict Pharisaical attitudes are generally-speaking more influential at that time than in Galilee or the diaspora. Scribes and elders most deeply offended by this practice probably take steps to shun Jesus-worshipers. Sometimes this entails merely expelling these "Jesus people" from the local synagogue, but at other times hostility to Jesus's followers and their worship and preaching leads to floggings or worse. The obvious implication is that followers of Jesus are not behaving as proper Jews should behave—meaning they are not worshiping as Jews should worship. They are treating Jesus—a man—as "a second God."[3]

Doctrinal diversity characterizes Judaism in the time of Jesus; the concern of Pharisees is more with correct practice than with doctrinal conformity. We see from Paul's self-description in Gal 1:13–14 and Luke's narration of Paul's story in Acts 9:1–2, 13–14, 20–25 that official hostility against those who worship Jesus as Lord and Son of God arises early. However, followers of Jesus continue to think of themselves as Jews and continue to be identified as Jews—albeit sectarians—both by their co-religionists and by Gentiles.

Even though the Fourth Gospel is not anti-Semitic, Christians in Europe for many centuries assumed its adversarial portrayal of "the Jews" provided divine justification

---

2. Thomas's acclamation of Jesus, "My Lord, and my God" (20:28), is the archetypal instance wherein *worship* of Jesus becomes a definitive sign that one *believes* in Jesus.

3. Boyarin, *Border Lines*, 128–47. Boyarin asserts that the idea of "two powers in heaven" (i.e., the Creator and the Word/Wisdom), sometimes spoken of as "two Gods," was ancient Jewish teaching, antedating the time of Christ and an option for Jewish belief at the time of Jesus. He asserts, "The very category of heresy did not exist in Judaism before the rabbinic formation," which dates from the compilation of the *Mishnah*, ca. 200 CE. (*Border Lines*, 131.)

for labeling their Jewish neighbors as "Christ killers." In particular, they pointed to John's report that "the Jews" shouted to Pilate "Away with him, away with him, crucify him!" (19:15), linking their cry to the one recorded by Matthew, "His blood be upon us and upon our children" (27:25). Official practice of violent and murderous anti-Semitism based on these out-of-context gospel proof-texts is a shameful fact of church history.

The balance of power between Christians and Jews is now and has been for at least sixteen centuries the categorical opposite of what John's little church experienced. We who read the Fourth Gospel in the twenty-first Christian century must never forget that when John's Gospel was first written and circulated, the community to whom it was addressed was a small, powerless, oppressed Jewish sect, scorned and rejected by the Jewish establishment. The bitter invective we read in John is "the language of the minority group spoken in protest to the majority culture."[4]

Nevertheless, in the period with which we are concerned, Johannine followers of Jesus regard themselves as members of Israel. They almost certainly keep the Sabbath and the Jewish festival seasons, observe the dietary laws, circumcise their male infants, and worship at the temple in Jerusalem until it is destroyed by the Romans. Unlike what is suggested by the letters of Paul and Acts, neither the gospel nor the three letters of John imply the presence of Gentiles within the Johannine churches. Christian assemblies composed of the Beloved Disciple's spiritual offspring, as well as their counterparts among Paul's followers, probably were known among other Jews as "*synagogues* of the Christians," while their Gentile neighbors surely regarded all of them as Jews. The Johannine churches—at least at the time the Fourth Gospel begins to circulate—are probably composed almost entirely of Greek-speaking, diaspora Jews, perhaps especially Jews whose families come from Galilee and other areas outside Judea proper. If there are Gentile believers among them, the non-Jews probably constitute a small minority.

What moved John to describe Jesus's adversaries as "the Jews"?

Gail R. O'Day suggests the author (or editor) of the Fourth Gospel writes about "the Jews" in a vindictive, reactive rhetorical style adopted by Christians during the period when the small Jewish sect of Jesus-worshipers (self-identified as "the church") was feeling under condemnation by the elders of the post-73 CE, Pharisee-controlled Yavneh Sanhedrin.[5] The author of the Fourth Gospel puts this angry, defensive rhetoric in the mouth of Jesus himself in his confrontation with "the Jews," especially in

---

4. O'Day, *Gospel of John*, 648.

5. After the Romans destroyed the temple in 70 CE and the priestly Sadducees ceased to exist as the dominating power within Judaism, the Sanhedrin was reconstituted with reduced authority in the coastal city of Yavneh (Jamnia). This new Sanhedrin was controlled by Pharisaic rabbis and it ultimately generated rabbinic Judaism.

chapter 8, the events of which occur roughly six months prior to the crucifixion and about forty years before the destruction of the temple. In chapter 8, John describes Jesus as calling his adversaries "children of the devil" (vs 44) and "liars" (vs 45) during a face-to-face confrontation in the temple. O'Day claims it unlikely the historical Jesus ever spoke to his opponents with such aggressive vehemence, a style which characterizes John, writing about sixty years later. She regards this angry Johannine language as the vocabulary of a Jewish minority feeling marginalized and forbidden from claiming its Jewish identity, "speaking against those who have denied them their heritage."[6] Although the historical Jesus may have been quick to point out the errors of his enemies, he is not likely to have thought of them in the same resentful way John's community had come to think of the rabbis of the Yavneh Sanhedrin by the 80s and 90s.

R. Alan Culpepper understands use of "the Jews" in the Fourth Gospel as, in general, describing the category of those who refuse to believe, who cannot see beyond the literal, and who are "of the world" while Jesus is "not of this world" (8:23). Although they are religious people, they are the antitype of Jesus's disciples. Despite the obstinate category of worldly people for whom John makes them the representatives, some of "the Jews" *do* believe (8:31; 11:45), even some of the Pharisees (7:43; 9:16; 10:19). In John's Gospel Jesus demonstrates a critical attitude towards his own people, the Jews, but in this respect he is like Isaiah, Ezekiel and other Hebrew prophets who judge the majority of Israel unfaithful while only a "remnant" is faithful. Culpepper writes, "The Jews carry the burden of the 'unbelief of the world' in John. In that respect at least they are not unlike 'the Lamb of God that takes away the sin of the world' (1:29; cf. 16:9)."[7]

John sometimes may choose to use the expression "the Jews" sarcastically, thinking of the leaders of the people—the elders of the Great Sanhedrin, chief priests and prominent Pharisees—as a group whose standards of "Jewishness" are so strict they deny the name "Jew" to other descendants of Abraham whose piety is less rigorous than their own. The Beloved Disciple writes as spokesman and patriarch of a small sect of Jewish followers of Jesus who are stung by the rejection they suffer from the rabbinical puritans of the Yavneh Sanhedrin. John calls his enemies "the Jews" with bitter and sarcastic irony, since he regards his own small community rather than the followers of the rabbis as the *authentic* Jews, the true Israel of God. For John, "becoming a true Jew and becoming a Christian was one and the same thing."[8] This is similar to what Paul asserted in Rom 2:28–29 long before John wrote his gospel.[9] In 1 Thess 2:14–16 Paul writes of "the Jews, who killed both the Lord Jesus and the prophets, and drove us out, and displease God and oppose all men by hindering us from speaking to the Gentiles that they may be saved—so as always to fill up the measure of their sins."

6. O'Day, *Gospel of John*, 649.

7. Culpepper, *Anatomy*, 130.

8. Keener, *John*, 2:993, quoting J. A. T. Robinson.

9. See Keener, *John*, 1:218–19.

1 Thess (usually dated ca. 53) generally is regarded as Paul's earliest extant letter, and in it we see the apostle using "the Jews" as an ironic title, in much the same way the Fourth Gospel does forty years later.[10] Therefore, John is clearly not unique in using "the Jews" as a reference to Jewish leaders who act with hostility toward their countrymen who worship Jesus.

Use of "the Jews" as a geographic as well as a political descriptor.

I think it is distinctly possible that by using "the Jews" as a common reference for Jesus's enemies, John along with Paul and Luke may intentionally emphasize the obvious connection between Jesus's enemies and Jerusalem/Judea. It is no surprise that, as best we can guess, only a single member of Jesus's inner circle of twelve disciples is clearly from Judea—the traitor, Judas Iscariot. As already indicated, a "Jew" means literally an inhabitant of Judea in comparison with an inhabitant of Galilee or another region. The Great Sanhedrin is composed of dignitaries—chief priests, elders, and scribes—from Judea. Its members are virtually all residents of Jerusalem, regardless of the village where they were born, such as Joseph "of Arimathea." In addition to being the highest court and administrative authority for its native people (collaborating closely with the Roman prefect, whose authority is supreme) the Sanhedrin is also more or less what Americans might call "the Greater Jerusalem Chamber of Commerce"—an assembly of the commercial and professional leaders of the area.

The temple is the economic heart of Judea; the region has little beyond the temple to make it prosperous. The temple is not only the center of Israel's worship, the place where Yahweh "has made his name to dwell;" it is also an industry. At the annual pilgrim feasts of Passover, Pentecost, and Tabernacles multitudes stream to Jerusalem from the surrounding territories and the Jewish diaspora. Like a modern city whose economy is based on tourism, Jerusalem's wealth derives from pilgrims who come to the temple to worship. In addition, the temple is also a kind of bank, the most secure repository for the gold and silver of Judea's richest families. Finally, the temple is the source of livelihood and status for the most politically and religiously powerful people in the nation, the chief priests—members of the families from which the high priest is typically chosen. If the high priest and his allies suspect Jesus wants to "destroy the Temple" (see 2:19 and Mark 14:56–58) or somehow change the temple's role (see 2:16, "Take these things away; you shall not make my Father's house a house of trade"), they must take action to stop him. What will happen if people stop coming to Jerusalem on pilgrimage three times a year? The high priest and his wealthy, aristocratic secular peers perceive Jesus as a threat to their wealth and influence. The Jerusalem scribes and Pharisees of the Sanhedrin care more about theology than about business

---

10. See Smith, *John*, 291–92.

or politics, but if they see Jesus as a dangerous blasphemer, then many of them are sure to unite with the priestly Sadducees in opposition to Jesus and his followers.

For the Galilean author of the Fourth Gospel and his constituency of mostly non-Judean followers of Jesus, it is but a small step from recognizing the Sanhedrin's hostility to seeing how intimately its members are identified with the city and the temple. The Sanhedrin are archetypal (i.e., *Judean*) Jews. The sarcastic way John refers to "the Jews" might remind American readers of the way the political party out of power in the US government typically refers to "Washington." Leaders of that party pride themselves on being "outsiders." Nevertheless, they plan to get the upper hand if possible and "change how things are done in Washington." A similar attitude may characterize the powerless followers of the Beloved Disciple, for whom "the Jews" means primarily "the Judeans who are in charge of things right now."

Final separation of Christians from Jews took centuries.

Recent research demonstrates that identification of Christianity as a religion separate from Judaism was a very long time in coming. Indeed, our contemporary definition of "religion" had its origin in the new, post-Constantinian explanation—by Christian bishops—of religion as a category distinct from national identity, kinship, and language. *Religio* in Roman law had always been identified simply as the customary rites and sacrifices required by the tutelary deities of various cultures, kinship groups, nations, or cities—a set of practices rather than an institution. (Traditional Romans did not offer sacrifice to "foreign divinities" unless these Romans were residing in or passing through domains where the alien deities were presumed to have power.) Constantine's adoption of Christianity and the subsequent influx of large numbers of Gentiles into the church led bishops and theologians by the late fourth century to begin identifying Christianity as a religion. They were beginning to understand religion in a new way; no longer simply the practice of rituals embedded in the traditional complex of ethnicity, language, and culture and intended to honor the god(s) of a culture, but as an institution. For the fifth century bishops, Christianity was the only religion entitled to be identified with the Empire.[11] The rabbinical authorities of Judaism did not protest such a shift in the categorical understanding of religion, but apparently embraced it. They seemed as eager to mark Judaism as distinct from its offshoot, Christianity, as the bishops were to erect a wall of separation between church and synagogue.

The boundary between Judaism and what the fifth century saw as a different religion, Christianity, had in earlier centuries been far less distinct in the minds of ordinary worshipers than later, polemically-minded Christian apologists implied. Heresiologists on the Christian side and rigorous rabbinical authorities on the Jewish side labored more than two centuries to identify and police the boundary between

---

11. Boyarin, *Border Lines*, 202–5, 214–20.